HANDBOOK OF CRM:

Achieving Excellence in Customer Management

Adrian Payne

ELSEVIER

AMSTERDAM • BOSTON • HEIDELBERG • LONDON • NEW YORK • OXFORD
PARIS • SAN DIEGO • SAN FRANCISCO • SINGAPORE • SYDNEY • TOKYO
Butterworth-Heinemann is an imprint of Elsevier

Butterworth-Heinemann is an imprint of Elsevier
Linacre House, Jordan Hill, Oxford OX2 8DP
30 Corporate Drive, Suite 400 Burlington, MA 01803

First published 2006

British Library Cataloguing in Publication Data
A catalogue record for this book is available from the British Library

Library of Congress Control Number: 2005922524
A catalogue record for this book is available from the Library of Congress

ISBN-13: 978-07506-6437-0
ISBN-10: 07506-6437-1

For information on all Butterworth-Heinemann publications
visit our website at http://books.elsevier.com

Typeset by Newgen Imaging Systems (P) Ltd, Chennai, India
Printed and bound in Great Britain

Working together to grow
libraries in developing countries

www.elsevier.com | www.bookaid.org | www.sabre.org

ELSEVIER   BOOK AID
            International   Sabre Foundation

HANDBOOK OF CRM:

Achieving Excellence in Customer Management

To

Penelope and Christopher

Contents

342880

Preface

RE-INVENTING CRM

Like the dotcom organizations that went bust at the end of the last century, CRM (Customer Relationship Management) is making a powerful and dramatic comeback. Today, the most exciting growth areas of the commerce are being found in the electronic arena. The same is true of CRM.

In the late 1990s and early years of the 21st century, CRM was offered up as the next wave of marketing. The tools and techniques that would make traditional marketing obsolete. The automated approaches that would make customer relationships automatic and would enable the marketing organization to sell anything to anyone they chose. CRM was the single solution that would solve every marketing problem. Simply install the software, plug in the customer data and sit back and watch the profits roll in.

But, it wasn't that simple. It wasn't that easy. And, it simply didn't work that way. Millions of dollars and pounds and yen and Euros were spent on CRM systems, software and structures but, not enough seemed to come back.

So, why a Handbook of CRM? If CRM doesn't live up to expectations, why would a distinguished academic such as Adrian Payne develop such a text. Surely Professor Payne has better things to do!

The truth is, Adrian Payne is one of the few people, either academic or professional, who truly understands CRM ... what it can do, what it can't do, why the first CRM efforts failed and why, today, CRM may well be able to deliver the expected benefits that were promised half-a-decade or so ago.

As Payne explains in this comprehensive text (handbook is a truly apt title, for you will want to keep it close at hand), the first versions of CRM over-promised and under-delivered ... in too many cases, badly. It is only now, once the angst and roar has subsided that clear-sighted business strategies such as Payne can illustrate and demonstrate what CRM truly is and what it can and cannot do for an organization.

That's what you will find on the following pages ... a clear, concise, proven, business-orientated approach to CRM. The one that was either missed, overlooked or never developed in the heydays of the recent CRM past.

This book is a roadmap, if you will, of how CRM truly can revolutionize the way marketing programs are developed and delivered. It is based on a strategic, process-driven, business-oriented, results-focused view that was missing from the sales-type that accompanied earlier descriptions, discussions and approaches to CRM.

In reviewing this text, five things struck me about Payne's approach to CRM. As you use this text, and it is likely that you will be using it at least on a regular basis, look for the following differences between what you may think, know or may have heard about CRM and the way Professor Payne approaches it.

1. **Strategy, not more tactics.** Early descriptions of CRM focused on the tactics of CRM ... add-on selling, up-selling, development of mailing lists, direct marketing applications, customer classifications and the like. In short, the tools of CRM, but, not the management reasoning or rationale. In this text, you'll find the why of CRM that justifies its existence and its success. In Payne's approach, CRM is a business decision, made by business managers to achieve business goals. So, most of all, this approach to CRM is strategic; the often missing element in earlier views of the subject.

2. **Customers, not companies.** In too many instances, previous views of CRM were based on the benefits the marketing organization would receive from a CRM approach, with little or no thought to any benefits or value to the customer. All the focus was on what the firm could do, nor what the customer would get. Payne's approach puts the company and the customer in perspective. If there is no benefit to the customer, there can be no benefit to the company. If there is no value created for the customer, there can be no on-going value created for the marketing organization. CRM is a reciprocal process. There must be benefits to both parties for CRM to be successful. The story is clearly and forcefully told on the following pages.

3. **Process, not software.** Too much of the earlier versions of CRM focused on the software: Install our software and all your marketing

problems are over was the common promise. But, the software couldn't deliver because there was no on-going, organization-wide, repeatable process in place. Nor were there supportive, enthusiastic employees to implement the approaches. CRM was supposed to be automated but without process and people, no automation will occur. Payne presents a clearly articulated process of how to use a CRM approach found in this text is something the organization does, not something the IT group or the marketing department does or the customer service group does. Process is the key to CRM and Payne takes the reader through the entire process of CRM use in a clearly articulated way. Where to start. What to add. What the result should be.

4. **Outcomes, not outputs.** The earlier approaches to CRM primarily focused on outputs. What the CRM system did. Create customer lists. Organize customers into classifications. Aggregations. Activities. Things the organization could identify and push out toward the customer or prospects. In Payne's approach, the focus is on outcomes. What is supposed to happen as a result of the implementation of a CRM approach. What will the outcome be … not just descriptions of what the outputs will be. By focusing on outcomes, that is, business results, Payne has avoided much of the technical jargon that permeates the CRM landscape. You'll find business discussions and descriptions, not technological hijinks on the following pages

5. **Long-term, not short-term, views.** Payne describes CRM through a long-term, brand-building and shareholder value view, not a short-term approach to reaching organizational quarterly goals. Thus, this view of CRM really looks at the **R** in CRM, that is, the relationship to be created and maintained over time, not the short-term, sales burst that has too often been set as the CRM goal. It is this long-term view that ties all the concepts and methodologies and approaches together. Thus, it allows the organization to focus on customers, not just activities or immediate actions. Customers are, hopefully, continuous while marketing programs, add-on and cross-selling are short-term outputs. It is here that Payne makes the greatest contribution to the new CRM thinking. And, it is here that CRM programs should be evaluated. If the organization can adopt Payne's long-term, strategic approach to CRM, most of the previous challenges and restrictions will simply fall away.

So, this is my roadmap to the CRM Handbook you have before you. As you read through it, see if you don't agree. I suspect, after reading you too will have a totally different view of CRM. And, after all, that is what books are supposed to do … give us a new view of what may be a familiar subject or give us a new subject with a view that can become familiar. No matter what your background in CRM, it is my expectation that you will take one or the other view. So, read on. Decide for yourself.

Don E. Schultz
Professor Emeritus-in-Service
Northwestern University

About the Author

Professor Adrian Payne is Director of the Centre for Customer Relationship Management, Academic Leader of the Marketing Group and Professor of Services & Relationship Marketing at the Cranfield School of Management, Cranfield University in the UK. He is an authority on CRM, relationship marketing, services marketing and marketing strategy.

He has practical experience in marketing, market research, corporate planning and general management. His previous appointments include positions as a chief executive, senior management positions in strategic planning and marketing, and a number of non-executive directorships.

He is an author of numerous articles and twelve books. His books have been translated into many languages and include: *Relationship Marketing: Creating Stakeholder Value, CRM: Perspectives from the Market Place, Marketing Plans for Service Businesses, Relationship Marketing: Strategy and Implementation,* and *Creating a Company for Customers.*

He has acted as an advisor, consultant and educator to numerous leading organisations. His professional experience covers many industries including financial services, professional services, telecommunications, IT, pharmaceuticals, automotive and utilities. He has also worked widely within the manufacturing sector and with a number of government departments.

He is a frequent keynote speaker at industry conferences, company seminars and executive education programmes around the world. He has a special interest in using executive education to help top management implement their business strategy.

He can be contacted at Cranfield School of Management, Cranfield University, Cranfield, Bedford, MK43 0AL, UK or emailed at a.payne@cranfield.ac.uk

Acknowledgements

The development and publication of this book would not have been possible without help from a considerable number of people. I wish to acknowledge the assistance and support of not only the people and organisations listed below, but also numerous executives who have generously given up their time to discuss issues relating to CRM in their businesses.

First, I would like to thank the organisations, listed in alphabetical order below, who provided special assistance and support including development of the case studies in this book. Support from the following organisations is gratefully acknowledged: BT, Broadvision, Chordiant, E.piphany, Royal Mail, SAS, Teradata – a division of NCR, Unisys and Vectia Ltd.

Second, a very special thanks to Pennie Frow and Margrit Bass who both made a major contribution to this book, their input and support were outstanding. Also, thanks are due to Anna Newman-Brown who provided patient support during the writing process and to Bob Barker, Chris Bebbington, John Chidley, Andrew Dickson, Dave Fagan, Christopher Hemingway, Lee O'Bryan, Alistair Sim and Ian McDonald Wood who made a significant contribution in the technology areas of this book. I wish to thank partners at Vectia Ltd, formerly the CRM Group, who generously provided insights and contributed towards some of the concepts developed in this book. In particular, thanks to Kaj Storbacka, Reinhold Rapp, Markus Westerlund, Kari Kaario, Stephan Schusser and Reg Price.

Third, many researchers and scholars at other institutions and practitioners have contributed to my thinking in this area. In particular, I would like to thank Christian Grönroos at the Helsinki School of Economics, Philip Kotler and Don Shultz at Northwestern University, Evert Gummesson at Stockholm School of Business, Jagdish Sheth of Emory University, George Day of Wharton School and Flemming Poulfelt of Copenhagen Business School. Also to Don Peppers, Martha Rogers and Ron Swift – pioneers who have made great advances in the area of CRM.

Fourth, many companies have been a great inspiration to this book. I wish to highlight several companies who are exemplars in managing customer relationships – Amazon, Tesco, TNT, Rolls-Royce, Southwest Airlines, and Virgin Atlantic.

Finally, thanks are due to my colleagues involved in CRM and relationship marketing at the Cranfield School of Management at Cranfield University. My work in this area started with a rewarding and ongoing collaboration more than fourteen years ago with Martin Christopher and David Ballantyne who worked with me on our first book on relationship marketing. I also acknowledge the contribution of them and my other colleagues at Cranfield including: Susan Baker, Moira Clark, Hugh Davidson, Sue Holt, Simon Knox, Ralph Levene, Malcolm McDonald, Andy Neely, Stan Maklan, Roger Palmer, Helen Peck, Joe Peppard, Lynette Ryals and Hugh Wilson. I acknowledge their great contribution. Parts of our co-authored work are drawn on within the book. Other sections of the book and figures are drawn from five academic articles and working papers that have been published or are in the review process.

Introduction

In less than a decade Customer Relationship Management, or CRM, has escalated into a topic of major importance. Although the term CRM, more recently relabelled Customer Management, only came into use in the latter part of the 1990s, the principles on which it has been based have existed for much longer. CRM builds especially on the principles of relationship marketing, the formal study of which goes back 20 years but the origins of it, involving building relationships of mutual value between suppliers and customers, have existed since the start of commerce. However, what has changed over the past decade is a series of significant trends that collectively shape the opportunity better to serve customers through *information-enabled relationship marketing*, or CRM.

There are a number of factors that have impacted organizations' ability to build more sustained relationships, especially for those businesses with a large customer base. The main ones include:

- the increasing power of computers
- the decreasing cost of computers, in real terms
- the increased storage capacity of computers
- the significant reduction in the cost of storage of a megabyte of data
- the availability of increasingly sophisticated tools to undertake data analysis, data mining and data visualization
- the rise of e-commerce and the ability to be able to target customers via the Internet at a much lower cost
- an increased recognition of the importance of customer retention and customer lifetime value, and
- an increased sophistication in marketing approaches and the development of better ways of targeting customers, including:
  - one-to-one marketing
  - permission marketing
  - mass customization.

As we explain in the first chapter of the book, there are many perspectives and definitions of CRM. At its most simple, CRM could be thought of at three levels:

- CRM is about the implementation of a specific technology solution project
- CRM is the implementation of an integrated series of customer-oriented technology solutions
- CRM is a holistic strategic approach to managing customer relationships in order to create shareholder value.

We believe that the full potential of CRM will only be realized by addressing CRM from this latter strategic perspective. This book, therefore, focuses on developing a *strategic approach* to customer relationship management.

The book develops this strategic approach to customer relationship management through a *process* approach. Through our research work we have concluded that there are five key cross-functional CRM processes that need to be considered by most organizations. These are:

- the strategy development process
- the value creation process
- the multi-channel integration process
- the information management process, and
- the performance assessment process.

After an initial discussion on the nature of CRM in the first chapter, the next five chapters address each of these processes. Within these chapters, brief case study vignettes on aspects of CRM best practice are discussed and a more detailed discussion of each case appears at the end of the chapter. The final chapter focuses on organizing for CRM implementation.

By disaggregating these CRM processes into their component parts it is hoped readers will be able to view CRM as a set of strategic processes concerned with the creation of shareholder value and start to develop their own implementation plans based on an understanding of what key elements they need to address in their own individual context.

Several comments should be made about the content and scope of this book. First, its focus is on understanding CRM from a strategic perspective; it is not a detailed manual on implementation. The territory covered by CRM is considerable and, as a result, the implementation of CRM within organizations is so varied that a detailed exposition of the full scope of CRM implementation activities is not addressed here.

Second, a distinction is not made between CRM and e-CRM. If managers wish to make a distinction, e-CRM is an emphasis on using e-commerce tools or electronic channels in CRM. It is fine to make this distinction, but to us it is all part of CRM.

Third, this book does not examine CRM to provide a detailed examination of specific technology solutions such as data warehousing or data mining and specific approaches such as one-to-one marketing or permission marketing, or to examine the products of the considerable number of CRM vendors in detail. These topics are dealt with amply by excellent books such as that by Ron Swift, Don Peppers and Martha Rogers and by reports produced by leading analyst firms such as Gartner, Data Monitor and Forrester.

To help the reader explore the component parts of CRM in greater detail, further reading appears in the references relating to each chapter. Also, a reading list of books relating to CRM appears at the end of the book. This detailed list follows the structure of the book and outlines the significant books written around each of these topics. This will enable the interested reader to delve more deeply into the topics of interest to them. In the text we have kept referencing to a minimum to improve readability.

With a contemporary history of only a decade or so, CRM is still in its infancy. Much work remains to be done in understanding its dynamics and realizing its potential. With both many success stories and numerous failures, CRM clearly needs to be positioned or re-positioned as a strategic approach focused on achieving shareholder results. This book's purpose is to help firmly anchor CRM in this strategic perspective and to provide guidelines for making progress on the journey towards achieving customer excellence.

Chapter 1

A strategic framework for CRM

Customer Relationship Management, or CRM, is increasingly found at the top of corporate agendas. Companies large and small across a variety of sectors are embracing CRM as a major element of corporate strategy for two important reasons: new technologies now enable companies to target chosen market segments, micro-segments or individual customers more precisely and new marketing thinking has recognized the limitations of traditional marketing and the potential of more customer-focused, process-based strategies.

CRM, also more recently called 'customer management', is a business approach that seeks to create, develop and enhance relationships with carefully targeted customers in order to improve customer value and corporate profitability and thereby maximize shareholder value. CRM is often associated with utilizing information technology to implement relationship marketing strategies. As such, CRM unites the potential of new technologies and new marketing thinking to deliver profitable, long-term relationships.

Although the term CRM is relatively new, the principles behind it are not unfamiliar. Organizations have for a long time practised some form of customer relationship management. What sets present day CRM apart is that organizations can manage one-to-one relationships with their customers – all one thousand or one million of them. In effect, CRM represents a *renewed* perspective of managing customer relationships based on relationship marketing principles;

the key difference being that today these principles are applied in context of unprecedented technological innovation and market transformation.

The marketplace of the twenty-first century bears little resemblance to bygone eras characterized by relatively stable customer bases and solid market niches. Nowadays, customers represent a moving target and even the most established market leaders can be ousted quickly from their dominant positions. The urgent need to find alternative routes to competitive advantage has been driven by profound changes in the business environment, including: the growth and diversity of competition; the development and availability of new technology; the escalating expectations and empowerment of the individual; the advent of a global operating environment; and the erosion of conventional timeframes in this electronic-enabled era. These changes have reinforced the adoption of wider business horizons and more customer-oriented perspectives.

Companies have realized that it is no longer simply enough to offer excellent products: ease of duplication and market saturation can quickly dispel initial indications of a winning formula. Today's key differentiator is exceptional service provided on a consistent and distinctive basis. Service is more difficult to imitate than a product because service requires customer input and involvement. Competitive advantage can therefore be gained by leveraging knowledge of customers' expectations, preferences and behaviour. This involves creating an ongoing dialogue with customers and exploiting the information and insights obtained at every customer touch point.

CRM is aimed at increasing the acquisition and retention of *profitable* customers by, respectively, initiating and improving relationships with them. The development of strategically targeted relationships is enabled through the opportunities afforded by advances in information technology (IT). Companies today can seek to improve their customer management by utilizing a range of database, data mart and data warehouse technologies, as well as a growing number of CRM applications. Such developments make it possible to gather vast amounts of customer data and increase customer feedback, as well as to analyse, interpret and utilize them constructively. Furthermore, the advantages presented by increasingly powerful computer hardware, software and e-services are augmented by the decreasing costs of running them. This plethora of available and more affordable tools of CRM is enabling companies to target the most promising opportunities more effectively. Credit Suisse, for example, made a rewarding investment in learning more about the source of customer satisfaction and profitability within its own operations.

Credit Suisse Group is one of the world's leading financial services companies. It operates in fiercely competitive banking and insurance markets where customer acquisition is very expensive and the retention of profitable customers is critical. In the late 1990s Credit Suisse launched a Loyalty Based Management programme to retain its most profitable customers. Using sophisticated data mining techniques, the company analysed its data warehouse of 2.5 million customers and identified the most profitable customers and their common characteristics. Targeted marketing programmes were then established for each market segment. The data analysis also revealed potential leads which could be followed up by sales consultants, providing a cost-effective basis for developing cross-selling and customer acquisition strategies.

Over the past decade there has been an increased interest in CRM among executives, academics and the media. Success stories such as that of Credit Suisse have heightened this interest. However, despite the many books, articles, conferences and web sites devoted to the topic of CRM, there remains a singular lack of agreement about what exactly CRM is, who the main beneficiary is and how it should be addressed to give a better return. This book sets out to provide a *strategic* framework for understanding and defining CRM as an effective means of ensuring that overall business strategy delivers improved shareholder results.

Before entering into a detailed discussion of the key processes involved in strategic CRM, it is important to explore some background to CRM. This chapter starts by examining the development of CRM and the issues underpinning its increased business significance.

The origins of CRM

CRM is based on the principles of relationship marketing, so a brief review of the development of marketing is helpful to understanding the evolution of CRM. As industries have matured, there have been changes in market demand and competitive intensity that have led to a shift from transaction marketing to relationship marketing.

In the 1950s, frameworks such as 'the marketing mix' were developed to exploit market demand. The shorthand of the '4Ps' of product, price, promotion and place were used to describe the levers that, if pulled appropriately, would lead to increased demand for the company's offer. The objective of this 'transactional' approach to marketing was to develop strategies that would optimize expenditure on the marketing mix in order to maximize sales.

During the latter years of the twentieth century some of these basic tenets of marketing were increasingly being questioned. The marketplace was vastly different from that of the 1950s. Numerous markets had matured in the sense that growth was low or non-existent, resulting in increased pressure on corporate profitability. In many instances consumers and customers were more sophisticated and less responsive to the traditional marketing pressures, particularly advertising. Greater customer choice and convenience existed as a result of the globalization of markets and new sources of competition and the emergence of new media and channels. Innovative business thinking and action was required to meet the challenges of this new competitive environment.

In the early 1990s Philip Kotler, a professor at Northwestern University, proposed a new view of organizational performance and success based on relationships, whereby the traditional marketing approach – based on the marketing mix – is not replaced, but is instead 'repositioned' as the toolbox for understanding and responding to all the significant players in a company's environment. He outlines the importance of the relationship approach to stakeholders:

> The consensus in ... business is growing: if ... companies are to compete successfully in domestic and global markets, they must engineer stronger bonds with their stakeholders, including customers, distributors, suppliers, employees, unions, governments and other critical players in the environment. Common practices such as whipsawing suppliers for better prices, dictating terms to distributors and treating employees as a cost rather than an asset, must end. Companies must move from a short-term *transaction-orientated* goal to a long-term *relationship-building* goal.[1]

Kotler's comments underscore the need for an integrated approach for understanding the different stakeholder relationships. In many large industrial organizations, marketing is still viewed as a set of related but compartmentalized activities that are separate from the rest of the company. Relationship marketing seeks to change this perspective by managing the competing interests of customers, staff, shareholders and other stakeholders. It redefines the concept of 'a market' as one in which the competing interests are made visible and therefore more likely to be managed effectively.

The development of this broader wave of marketing thinking by marketing academics and practitioners has influenced the perceived role of marketing in business. In effect, marketing is given lead (but not sole) responsibility for strengthening the firm's market performance. In an earlier book, we have described relationship marketing as:[2]

- a move from functionally based marketing to cross-functionally based marketing
- an approach which addresses multiple 'market domains', or stakeholder groups – not just the traditional customer market
- a shift from marketing activities which emphasize customer acquisition to marketing activities which emphasize customer retention as well as acquisition.

The transition from traditional, 'transactional' marketing to relationship marketing is depicted in Figure 1.1.

Relationship marketing emphasizes two important issues. First, you can only optimize relationships with customers if you understand and manage relationships with other relevant stakeholders. Most businesses appreciate the critical role their employees play in delivering superior customer value, but other stakeholders may also play an important part. Second, the tools and techniques used in

Figure 1.1   The transition to relationship marketing

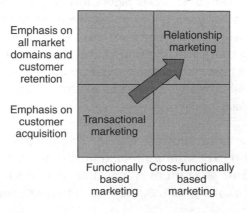

marketing to customers, such as marketing planning segmentation, can also be used equally as effectively i non-customer relationships.

The key principles of relationship marketing

Figure 1.1 suggests three distinguishing characteristics of relationship marketing. The first is an emphasis on customer retention and extending the 'lifetime value' of customers through strategies that focus on retaining targeted customers. The second is a recognition that companies need to develop relationships with a number of stakeholders, or 'market domains', if they are to achieve long-term success in the final marketplace. The third feature of relationship marketing is that marketing is seen as a pan-company or cross-functional responsibility and not solely the concern of the marketing department.

An emphasis on retention of profitable customers

Maximizing the lifetime value of a customer is a fundamental goal of relationship marketing. In this context we define the lifetime value of a customer as the future flow of net profit, discounted back to the present, that can be attributed to a specific customer. Adopting the principle of maximizing customer lifetime value forces the organization to recognize that not all customers are equally profitable and that it must devise strategies to enhance the profitability of those customers it seeks to target.

Loyal customers are an intangible asset that adds value to the balance sheet. They represent the goodwill earned by the brand. Domino's Pizza chain in the USA, for example, estimates that a customer who purchases one pizza for $5 may represent a net worth of approximately $5000 over the 10-year life of a Domino franchise. Similarly, the Ford Motor Company has calculated that a loyal Ford customer is worth $142 000 over their lifetime. Loyal and repeat customers not only contribute revenue by returning again and again to purchase from the same company or brand, but act as advocates, referring new customers and reducing acquisition costs.

An emphasis on multiple markets

Relationship marketing focuses marketing action on multiple stakeholder markets. The six markets stakeholder model[3] provides a useful framework for reviewing the role of an extended set of stakeholders. The model identifies six key groups, or market domains, that contribute to an organization's effectiveness in the marketplace. They are customer markets, influencer (including shareholder) markets, recruitment markets, referral markets, internal markets, and supplier/alliance markets.

Each market domain is made up of a number of key participants. Customer markets, for example, may include wholesalers, intermediaries and consumers, while influencer markets may comprise financial and investor groups, unions, industry and regulatory bodies, business press and media, user and evaluator groups, environmental groups, political and government agencies and competitors. Relationship marketing recognizes that multiple market domains can directly or indirectly affect a business's ability to win and keep profitable customers.

An emphasis on a cross-functional approach to marketing

For a long time marketing strategies have been developed within functionally based marketing departments. As a result, the marketing strategies developed often do not take into account their organization-wide implications. The problem is that they are functionally focused not market focused. They typically seek to optimize the use of inputs and hence are budget driven, rather than seek to optimize around outputs and hence be market driven. Rarely do they consider the interrelationship of different shareholders.

To succeed in managing the multiple stakeholders effectively, marketing must be cross-functional. David Packard, co-founder of Hewlett-Packard, is reported to have said that 'marketing is too important to be left to the marketing department'. His comment could be interpreted in a number of ways, but we understand it as a call to bring marketing out of its functional silo and extend the concept and the philosophy of marketing across the business enterprise. In practice, a cross-functional approach to marketing requires an organizational culture and climate that encourages collaboration and cooperation. Everyone within the business must understand that they perform a role in serving customers, be they internal or external customers.

CRM builds on these principles of relationship marketing. However, with new market demands and new technologies, the management of customer relationships has been taken to a new and more complex level. CRM is a response to this new and more challenging environment. Put simply, CRM is 'information-enabled relationship marketing'.

The rise of CRM

The emergence of CRM as a management approach is a consequence of a number of important trends. These include:

- the shift in business focus from transactional marketing to relationship marketing
- the realization that customers are a business asset and not simply a commercial audience
- the transition in structuring organizations, on a strategic basis, from functions to processes
- the recognition of the benefits of using information proactively rather than solely reactively
- the greater utilization of technology in managing and maximizing the value of information
- the acceptance of the need for trade-off between delivering and extracting customer value
- the development of one-to-one marketing approaches.

Marketing on the basis of relationships

The shift in marketing focus from increasing the number and value of transactions (transactional marketing) to growing more effective and profitable relationships with multiple stakeholders (relationship marketing) has profound benefits. Marketing on the basis of relationships concentrates attention on building customer value in order to retain customers. By building on existing investment, in terms of product development and customer acquisition costs, firms can generate potentially higher revenue and profit at lower cost. Marketing on the basis of transactions, by contrast, involves greater financial outlay and risk. Focusing on single sales involves winning the customer over at every sales encounter, a less efficient and effective use of investment.

Relationship marketing also produces significant intangible benefits. The prominence given to customer service encourages customer contact and customer involvement. As a result, firms can learn more about customers' needs and build this knowledge into future product and service delivery. Clearly, customer encounters that end once the transaction is completed and with only a record of purchase details for reference, do not offer the same wealth of opportunities for service and relationship enhancement that enduring customer relationships do.

Viewing customers as business assets

This focus on the 'relationship' rather than the 'transaction' is evident in the emergent view that customer relationships represent key business assets. The implication is that relationships with customers can be selectively managed and further developed to improve customer retention and profitability. This represents a significant departure from the more traditional view that customers are simply a commercial audience that need to be broadcast to by a range of advertising and other promotional activities.

One aspect of a company's market value is future profit stream generated over a customer's lifetime. If customers are viewed as business assets then the company will focus on growing these business assets and its market value. CRM stresses identifying the most profitable customers and building relationships with them that increase the value of this business asset over time.

Organizing in terms of processes

In the present highly competitive marketplace it is imperative that customers are viewed as individual and complete entities that comprise a relationship, rather than be viewed as a series of individual transactions. To obtain and present a unified view of customers requires internal coordination and collaboration that is oblivious to functional boundaries. Traditionally, sales, marketing and customer service and support have operated from disparate functional silos with little or limited interaction. Figure 1.2 depicts the traditional 'command and control' organizational structure. Such a functionally oriented approach tends to focus too heavily on the operations of the

Figure 1.2 Marketing as a functional activity – the 'command and control' organizational structure

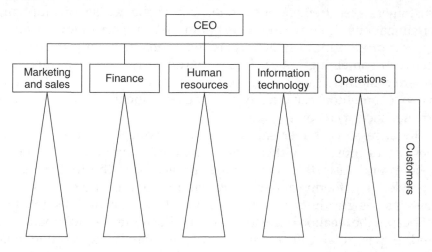

company and too little on customers. The danger is that customers may be undervalued by the firm and effectively put to one side – as shown in this figure. As a result opportunities for maximizing customer value and corporate profitability are often lost.

In recent years, companies have started to realize the advantages of organizing in terms of processes rather than functions. Process-oriented firms retain their functional excellence in marketing, manufacturing and so on, but recognize that processes are what deliver value to the customer as well as to the supplier. A process is essentially any discrete activity, or set of activities, that adds value to an input. In the modern marketplace, customers rarely seek an 'isolated' product; they also want immediate delivery, guaranteed warranty and ongoing service support. The product or service offer has therefore become multifaceted; the culmination of cross-functional expertise. Process integration and cross-functional collaboration are defining strengths of CRM.

From reactive to proactive use of information

CRM is also about achieving, maintaining and improving competitive strength by anticipating customers' future needs as well as satisfying their current requirements. With an ever-expanding wealth of options on offer, customers are faced with increasingly personalized choices.

The move from 'mass market' to 'mass customization' in marketing has created a buyer's market. Empowered to choose (and to refuse), customers exert tremendous influence over the actions of supplying organizations. Their weapons are a diminished sense of loyalty and a greater propensity to switch to organizations that can promise (and deliver!) something better. This is particularly true in e-commerce where customers can change their minds at the click of a button and savvy competitors can quickly redefine or refine their offers to gain a greater slice of customer share.

To increase customer satisfaction and reduce customer attrition, businesses must know their customers (and competitors) like never before and use this knowledge proactively. Improvements in knowledge-gathering and -sharing activities within and across organizations has greatly enhanced access to information and insights that underpin the creation of customer value. Customer service operations and, in particular, call centres, often focus mainly on 'reactive' relationships with customers. Experience has shown, however, that carefully designed 'proactive' customer care initiatives can be much more effective and rewarding. Proactive customer support operations do not wait for complaints to be registered but actively seek to uncover and remedy customer dissatisfaction. They recognize that customers often never lodge a complaint and simply take their business elsewhere. Similarly, proactive call centres research prospective, current and lapsed customers, feeding valuable information to cross-functional customer information and customer management teams.

Deploying IT to maximize the value of information

The development of customer relationships is enabled by the deliberate exploitation of customer information. The investment that CRM requires in terms of IT infrastructure is often substantial and has to be justified in terms of both cost savings and profit generation. Many organizations that have already adopted enterprise resource planning (ERP) to improve internal efficiencies are now turning to CRM better to respond to individual customer's needs. Whereas ERP employs customer and other information to reduce costs by improving internal efficiencies in back office processes related to manufacturing and finance, CRM emphasizes the use of customer information to enhance revenue by increasing external effectiveness in front office activities including sales, marketing and customer service and support. However, a firm's ability to exploit the value of information relies heavily on the existence of a supportive IT environment.

A CRM system has two major IT components: a *data repository* that enables the organization to collect a complete set of information on customers (used with a set of analytical tools to develop a better understanding of customers in terms of past and likely future behaviour); and a set of *applications* that enable value-adding interactions with customers, often across different channels, in order to meet their needs. Technological innovations such as clever screen prompts, which advise customer service representatives of a customer's profile and appropriate call centre tactics can be used to increase cross-selling and upselling, provided that staff are suitably trained, equipped and motivated. By using IT to listen to and learn from customers, companies can create opportunities for securing a greater share of wallet as well as market share.

Balancing the value trade-off

Crucially, CRM highlights the trade-off between delivering and extracting customer value. The overall value creation process can be considered in terms of three key components. These are: determining what value the company can deliver to its customers (the value the customer receives); determining what value the organization can extract from its customers (the value the organization receives); and, by managing this value exchange, maximizing the lifetime value of desirable customers and customer segments. Relationships are built on the creation and delivery of superior customer value on a sustained basis. This is why the identification of what constitutes customer value in specific markets and segments is so important.

Creating an appropriate balance between the value delivered to customers and the value received in return and recognizing how this may need to change for different customer segments, is an essential element of CRM. Giving the customer too much by way of value, at realizable market prices, may cost the organization too much and satisfactory profit margins may not be sustained. Conversely, taking too much value from the customer through reductions in product quality or customer service levels is likely to result in customer defections. Furthermore, the economic value of different customer segments will vary and this needs to be taken into account.

In a sense, optimizing the value trade-off means marrying the aforementioned principles of relationship marketing with current marketing trends. For example, grocery shoppers are increasingly turning to the convenience of the Internet for their weekly shopping. More sophisticated e-shoppers are demanding online options that will allow them to compare prices among similar products, select items based on the nutritional information provided by manufacturers and check out new products. The experience of Danish food retailer, ISO, is testament to the value of exploring changes in the food shopping habits of customers.

The ISO supermarket chain in Denmark operates in a country where e-commerce is strong. Exploiting this trend, ISO offers customers the option of shopping using the Palm Computing platform. Customers can create their electronic grocery lists by scanning the bar codes on products in their larder, refrigerator and medicine chest using their PalmPilot handheld device. Bar codes can also be accessed by printing them from the ISO web site. The electronically generated order can then be transmitted to ISO directly from the PalmPilot or via uploading the order to a PC for transmission. Picking, packing and home delivery within four hours can be arranged at a small additional charge. Alternatively, customers can collect their orders, all ready and waiting, from their local ISO store at a designated time and date.

ISO has benefited from this innovative practice in two ways. Their research suggests that ISO's e-shoppers are a highly profitable customer segment, buying larger orders more frequently and with less price sensitivity than the average purchaser. In addition, ISO has captured detailed information on this highly lucrative market segment that can be used to manage customer relationships and future profitability more effectively.

Developing 'one-to-one' marketing

A key foundation of marketing strategy is the identification of appropriate target markets or segments. In consumer markets these segments may be determined by factors such as age, sex or lifestyle, while in business-to-business (B2B) markets segmentation criteria include industrial sector, size of company and so on. As markets become increasingly competitive and consumers and organizations seek increasingly specific solutions to their needs, markets fragment into ever smaller segments. Don Peppers and Martha Rogers point out, however, that when segmentation reaches the level of individual customers, the very nature of marketing changes. 'Segments' have no memories, do not interact, complain, or refer other segments – but individual customers do all those things, and a one-to-one marketer will try to harness those activities in order to develop continuing relationships with customers.[4]

One-to-one marketing is a form of marketing in which dialogue occurs directly between a company and individual customers or groups of customers with similar needs. Many B2B organizations with large customers practise one-to-one marketing through key account management strategies. Smaller customers may be dealt with in a more impersonal way through call centre or mail order strategies. In business-to-consumer (B2C) markets the cost of dealing with customers on a one-to-one basis is frequently prohibitive and other means of facilitating dialogue must be found.

The Internet has proven to be a powerful tool for involving both B2C and B2B customers in the marketing process, enabling a one-to-one dialogue rather than relying on mass communications. The unique capabilities of the Internet allow marketers to capture the anonymous behaviour necessary to be able to answer the question, 'What does each customer want?'

CRM systems and processes enable a company to commit to memory each relevant customer encounter and to recall all past encounters with that customer at every future association. In effect, the capture of customer data, the interpretation of data analyses and the dissemination of resultant customer knowledge becomes a natural and automatic function of the organization. How well CRM fulfils this role depends very much on how CRM is defined and adopted within the organization concerned.

The role of CRM

The trends outlined here help explain why CRM has become a critical business issue. However, the problem faced by many organizations, both in deciding whether to adopt CRM and in proceeding to implement it, stems from the fact that there is still a great deal of confusion about what constitutes CRM. To some it means direct mail, a loyalty card scheme or a database, while others envisage a help desk or a call centre. Still others see CRM as an e-commerce solution such as a personalization engine on the Internet or a relational database for sales management. As a result, organizations often view CRM from a limited perspective or adopt CRM on a fragmented basis.

This confusion surrounding CRM may be explained by:

- the lack of a widely accepted and clear definition of its role and operation within the organization
- an emphasis on information technology aspects rather than its benefits in terms of building relationships with customers
- the wide variety of tools and services being offered by information technology vendors, which are often sold as 'CRM'.

Varying definitions of CRM

The lack of clarity about CRM is evident in CRM terminology. Customer relationship management is often used interchangeably with the terms 'relationship marketing', 'customer relationship marketing', 'enterprise relationship marketing' (ERM), 'technology enabled relationship marketing' (TERM), 'customer managed relationships' (CMR) or 'customer management' (CM). It is also used to refer to a specific IT solution such as a data warehouse or a specific application such as campaign management or sales force automation. Moreover, the definitions and descriptions of CRM used by different authors and authorities vary greatly, as illustrated in the representative sample shown in Figure 1.3.[5–15] In our experience of dealing with many companies we have found that the term 'CRM' is used very differently across different industries and within specific vertical markets. In one large technology company, we found that the use of the term CRM even varied greatly within that organization.

The CRM continuum – three perspectives of CRM

A review of these definitions of CRM and how organizations use them indicates that a range of approaches is used to define CRM. These are portrayed as a continuum in Figure 1.4.[16] At one extreme, CRM is defined as a particular technology solution. For example, in one organization that had spent over $20 million on IT solutions and systems integration, CRM was described solely in terms of its large sales force automation project. In another organization CRM was

Figure 1.3 Some definitions and descriptions of CRM

CRM is a business strategy combined with technology to effectively manage the complete customer life-cycle[5]

A term for methodologies, technologies and e-commerce capabilities used by companies to manage customer relationships[6]

CRM is an e-commerce application[7]

A comprehensive strategy and process of acquiring, retaining and partnering with selective customers to create superior value for the company and the customer[8]

CRM is about the development and maintenance of long-term mutually beneficial relationships with strategically significant customers[9]

Numerous aspects, but the basic theme is for the company to become more customer-centric ... methods are primarily Web-based tools and Internet presence ...[10]

CRM can be viewed as an application of one-to-one marketing and relationship marketing, responding to an individual customer based on what the customer tells you and what else you know about that customer[11]

A management approach that enables organizations to identify, attract and increase retention of profitable customers by managing relationships with them[12]

It involves using existing customer information to improve company profitability and customer service[13]

Seeks to provide a strategic bridge between information technology and marketing strategies aimed at building long-term relationships and profitability. This requires 'information-intensive strategies'[14]

Data-driven marketing[15]

used to refer to a wide range of customer-oriented IT and Internet solutions, reflecting some of the descriptions given in Figure 1.3. A further company used CRM to describe its initiatives for becoming more customer-centric, which had more to do with creating value

Figure 1.4 The CRM continuum

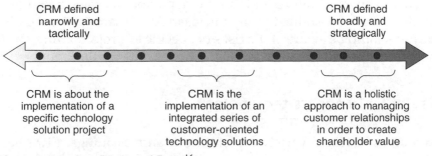

Source: based on Payne and Frow[16]

propositions and training staff to deliver them and relatively little to do with IT.

The importance of how CRM is defined is not merely semantics. Its definition has a significant impact on how CRM is accepted and practised by the entire organization. CRM is not simply an IT solution to the problem of getting the right customer base and growing it. CRM is much more. It involves a profound synthesis of strategic vision, a corporate understanding of the nature of customer value within a multi-channel environment, the utilization of the appropriate information management and CRM applications and high quality operations, fulfilment and service. CRM emphasizes that managing customer relationships is a complex and ongoing process and a response to and reflection of a rapidly changing marketing environment. Thus we advocate positioning CRM in any organization in a broad strategic context, or to the far right in Figure 1.4.

The dangers of not adopting this strategic perspective of CRM are made all too apparent by media coverage of CRM failures. Widespread concern regarding the performance of CRM initiatives is represented in the following quotations from Insight Technology Group, The CRM Institute, Giga and Gartner:

- '69 per cent of CRM projects have little impact on sales performance'.
- 'Companies think that their CRM projects are significantly less successful than their consultants or suppliers'.
- '70 per cent of CRM initiatives will fail over the next 18 months'.
- '60 per cent of CRM projects end in failure'.

CRM, viewed from a strategic perspective, is concerned with how the organization can create increased shareholder value through developing superior customer relationships. Rejecting CRM and the potential benefits that it can deliver in terms of shareholder value because of specific failures of IT implementation in other companies would seem short-sighted to say the least! At the same time, organizations should be aware of the risks of specific IT project failures and their associated cost, a point we will return to later in this book.

Use of CRM and its terminology

As well as having a variety of definitions and meanings, CRM has attracted the interest of a wide range of company types and industry sectors. For example, one UK study focused on identifying the top ten organizations using CRM effectively.[17] The study found that the leading practitioners of CRM are an interesting mix of more traditional businesses (e.g. RAC, Boots and Kwik-Fit), companies which have historically used call centres for their customer interactions, but are also now utilizing e-commerce (e.g. First Direct and Direct Line Insurance), 'pure play' internet companies (e.g. Amazon.com and Egg) and 'hybrid' or 'bricks and clicks' businesses (e.g. Citibank, Tesco and Barnes & Noble). This emphasizes the point that CRM strategies are by no means confined solely to companies that have a high dependence on Internet and technological innovation.

Given the widespread use of CRM across different industries we were interested to find out what terminology companies used to describe the management of their relationships with customers. We were especially interested in how the three most common terms, i.e. relationship marketing, CRM and customer management were actually being used by organizations. To gain an understanding of how the terms were used, we undertook a study of the most advanced sector in terms of adoption of CRM – the financial services sector.

Research by Datamonitor had confirmed that the financial services vertical market was by far the most developed with approximately 36 per cent of global revenues being spent within it.[18] (The closest vertical sector, telecommunications, accounted for only half this amount.) Our study[19] confirmed that while there were no firm distinctions made between CRM, relationship marketing and customer management, certain common patterns did exist in the way the terms were used.

It was clear from the interviews with senior executives in this sector that *relationship marketing* was, for the most part, associated with high-level strategic thinking about relationships with all key stakeholders (a view echoed in the description of relationship marketing above).[20] Respondents described relationship marketing using phrases such as bespoke development, partnerships, joint planning and alliances. The terms CRM and customer management were used more in connection with the management of relationships with customers. When describing *customer relationship management*, managers used phrases reflecting the development of marketing strategies over the customer lifetime, such as understanding the customer base in total, understanding needs, attitudes, lifestage, profitability and lifetime value. By contrast, *customer management* was seen by the majority of respondents as being more concerned with the tactical implementation of CRM, in particular using specific tools such as campaign management or call centre activities. Based on our discussions with respondents in our study we developed a hierarchy which helps explain the terms relationship marketing, customer relationship management and customer management (Figure 1.5).

Figure 1.5   Relationship marketing, CRM and customer management – a hierarchy

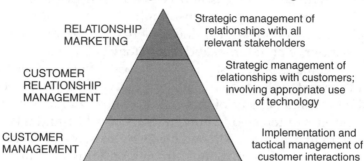

A definition of CRM

Atul Parvatiyar and Jagdish Sheth have pointed out that for an emerging management discipline it is important to develop an acceptable definition that encompasses all facets so as to allow focused understanding and growth of knowledge in the discipline.[21] The description of CRM given in Figure 1.5 represents only one approach to explaining the differences among the terms used in managing customer relationships. Hopefully, over time clear definitions of CRM and associated terms will develop into common usage. Until that time organizations need to be clear about what they mean when they discuss CRM or related terminology.

Any organization will benefit from adopting a definition of what CRM means in strategic terms for their business and ensuring that this definition is used in a consistent manner throughout their organization. For the purposes of this book we define CRM as follows:

CRM is a strategic approach concerned with creating improved shareholder value through the development of appropriate relationships with key customers and customer segments. CRM unites the potential of IT and relationship marketing strategies to deliver profitable, long-term relationships. Importantly, CRM provides enhanced opportunities to use data and information both to understand customers and implement relationship marketing strategies better. This requires a cross-functional integration of people, operations, processes and marketing capabilities that is enabled through information, technology and applications.

As to where CRM sits in relation to relationship marketing and customer management, we adopt the representation given in Figure 1.5. The main point is that firms must describe their management of customer relationships using a terminology that is appropriate to them and ensure it is used in a consistent manner throughout the organization. As a veteran CRM expert, Ron Swift has observed: 'Ultimately, each company must decide what CRM means to the organization and to the future of its success in the marketplace'.[22]

Types of CRM

Analyst firms, including Meta Group, classify CRM into several types:

- *Operational CRM* – This is the area that is concerned with the automation of business processes involving front-office customer contact points. These areas include sales automation, marketing automation and customer service automation. Historically, operational CRM has been a major area of enterprise expenditure as companies develop call centres or adopt sales force automation systems. CRM vendors focus on offering an increasingly wide range of operational CRM solutions.
- *Analytical CRM* – This involves the capture, storage, organization, analysis, interpretation and use of data created from the operational side of the business. Integration of analytical CRM solutions with operational CRM solutions is an important consideration.
- *Collaborative CRM* – This involves the use of collaborative services and infrastructure to make interaction between a company and its multiple channels possible. This enables interaction between customers, the enterprise and its employees.

Together, these three components of CRM support and feed into each other. Successful CRM, which results in a superior customer experience, requires integration of all three of these component parts. Collaborative CRM enables customers to contact the enterprise through a range of different channels and undergo a common experience across these channels. Operational CRM facilitates the customer contacts with the organization and subsequent processing and fulfilment of their requirements. Analytical CRM enables the right customers to be targeted with appropriate offers and permits personalization and one-to one-marketing to be undertaken through superior customer knowledge. While historically operational and collaborative CRM had the greatest emphasis, enterprises are now more cognisant of the need for analytical CRM to enable better optimization of their customer-facing activities and creation of value for the customer and the enterprise.

Other terminology used in the CRM market includes:

- *Strategic CRM* – This involves the development of an approach to CRM that starts with the business strategy of the enterprise and is concerned with development of customer relationships that result in long-term shareholder value creation. This is the approach emphasized throughout the book. It should be noted some authors use the term strategic CRM in a more restrictive sense to refer to analytical CRM.
- *e-CRM* – The term e-CRM refers to the use of e-commerce tools or electronic channels in CRM. As noted in the introduction to this book, we do not make a distinction between CRM and e-CRM. (Confusingly, e-CRM is sometimes used to refer to 'enterprise CRM' – that is having an enterprise-wide view of the customer across different channels.)
- *Partner relationship marketing or PRM* – This term is used to refer to CRM activities that involve the enterprise's activities with its alliance partners or value added resellers (VARs). The majority of IT business is done through indirect channels, so PRM activities with intermediaries are an essential element of a vendor's CRM programme. For example, Siebel has five types of partner: consulting partners, platform partners, technical partners, content partners and software partners. Within each of these are three levels of programme: technical, marketing and sales.[23]

The size and nature of the CRM market

The CRM market has experienced dramatic growth over the last decade despite the effects of an economic downturn in the early 2000s. However, the exact size and rate of growth of the CRM market depends very much on how it is defined.

Sector growth within the CRM market

Leading market analysts such as Gartner adopt a broad definition of the CRM market. Their estimates of annual CRM growth in terms of market size, shown in Figures 1.6 and 1.7, include hardware and software maintenance and support, consulting integration services, education, management services and business process and transaction management.

Figure 1.6 shows the worldwide global market for CRM is estimated to grow in size from around $US 20 billion in 2000 to $US 47 billion in 2006. Of the sectors analysed by Gartner, two of them are dominant. 'Development and integration' and 'business process and transaction management' represent around 65 per cent of the total.

Gartner also predict a strong year-on-year growth rate from 2000 to 2006. Overall, they expect the CRM market to grow at a compound annual growth rate (CAGR) of 16.4 per cent over this period. As shown in Figure 1.7, all sectors are expected to have double-digit growth with the exception of hardware maintenance and support.

CRM and software vendors

The need for increasingly sophisticated and scalable options means almost infinite scope for providers of CRM products and services. However, despite the popular claim to be 'complete CRM solution providers', relatively few individual software vendors can claim to provide the full range of functionality that a complete CRM business strategy requires. The IT challenge is that the requirements for sales, marketing, and customer service and support are complex. Software vendors are now offering 'front-office suites', integrated applications for enabling customer-facing activity. The increasing number, variety, and combination of applications and services to choose from stresses the highly customized nature of CRM, as well as the burgeoning sector of CRM providers.

Analysts have pointed out that companies seeking to adopt or improve their CRM and customer-facing activities need to appreciate that when they are being offered a CRM solution by a particular vendor, its nature will vary according to the category of vendor. The Gartner Group, for instance, identifies the key vendor groups as marketing, selling, servicing and e-commerce. This variation derives not only from the differences in the products and services sold, but

Figure 1.6 Estimate of CRM market size 2000–2006

CRM category	2000	2001	2002	2003	2004	2005	2006	CAGR 2001–2006
Hardware maintenance and support	1027	1102	1203	1306	1410	1522	1629	8.1%
Software maintenance and support	945	1095	1224	1454	1719	1982	2257	15.6%
Consulting	2026	2188	2433	2737	3157	3636	4113	13.5%
Development and integration	7470	8126	9175	10 528	12 179	14 201	16 208	14.8%
Education and training	333	358	401	441	516	607	669	13.4%
Management services	2870	3258	3820	4500	5258	6154	7163	17.1%
Business process and transaction Management	5228	5895	7070	8502	10 371	12 711	15 057	20.6%
Total	**19 900**	**22 022**	**25 325**	**29 469**	**34 610**	**40 813**	**47 096**	**16.4%**

Note: Columns may not add up to totals shown because of rounding. All figures in $USbn.

Source: Gartner Dataquest (March 2002), used with permission.

Figure 1.7 Estimate of CRM market growth 2000–2006

CRM category	2000(%)	2001(%)	2002(%)	2003(%)	2004(%)	2005(%)	2006(%)
Hardware maintenance and support (%)	12	7	9	9	8	8	7
Software maintenance and support (%)	32	16	12	19	18	15	14
Consulting (%)	30	8	11	13	15	15	13
Development and integration (%)	31	9	13	15	16	17	14
Education and training (%)	29	7	12	10	17	18	10
Management services (%)	21	14	17	18	17	17	16
Business process and transaction (%)	29	13	20	20	22	23	18
Management (%)							
Total (%)	**28**	**11**	**15**	**16**	**17**	**18**	**15**

Source: Gartner Dataquest (March 2002), used with permission.

from the differences in the way the vendors define CRM. Gartner have segmented vendors of CRM applications and CRM service providers into the categories outlined below.[24]

The key segments for CRM applications include:

- Integrated CRM and ERP Suite (e.g. Intentia, Oracle, PeopleSoft, SAP)
- CRM Suite (e.g. E.piphany, Siebel)
- CRM Framework (e.g. Chordiant)
- CRM Best of Breed (e.g. Avaya, NCR Teradata, Broadvision)
- Build it Yourself (e.g. IBM, Oracle, Sun).

The wide variety of CRM service providers and consultants that offer implementation support include:

- Corporate strategy (e.g. McKinsey, Bain)
- CRM strategy (e.g. Peppers & Rogers, Vectia, Detica, Sophron)
- Change management, organization design, training, HR, etc. (e.g. Accenture)
- Business transformation (e.g. IBM, PwC)
- Infrastructure build, systems integrators (e.g. Logica, Siemens, Unisys)
- Infrastructure outsourcing (e.g. EDS, CSC)
- Business insight, analytics, research, etc. (e.g. SAS, dunnhumby)
- Business process outsourcing (e.g. Acxiom).

A number of these companies operate in more than one of these sectors.

It is important for those supplying CRM solutions to position CRM in its strategic context so that their propositions and business benefits to potential customers are represented strongly. CRM sales conducted in the absence of such a perspective should be a source of concern to both companies and their vendors. Establishing this strategic context involves more than simply understanding the overall business strategy of an organization and where a CRM solution fits in. It also entails getting closer to customers and gaining an in-depth understanding of their situations, motivations and behaviours. While sophisticated technological tools and techniques have made this task easier, the secret of success in using them lies in their specification, integration and careful implementation. In essence, this means determining the key CRM processes relevant to that organization and asking the right questions about them. This task should guide the actions of both providers and users of CRM.

Five key cross-functional CRM processes

Earlier in the chapter we pointed out the dangers of the traditional 'command and control' organizational structure, shown in Figure 1.2, commonly adopted by marketing departments and its 'functional' orientation to the customer. We also emphasized that successful CRM requires a cross-functional approach, involving not only marketing but the entire enterprise. Developing a cross-functional approach to CRM requires first determining the key processes that need to be addressed and second identifying the key issues or questions that need to be addressed by the organization for each of these processes.

We have concluded that there are five key cross-functional CRM processes that need to be considered by most organizations.[25] These are:

- the strategy development process
- the value creation process
- the multi-channel integration process
- the information management process
- the performance assessment process.

These five cross-functional processes are shown in Figure 1.8. Unlike the functional approach portrayed in Figure 1.2, they are fully oriented towards customers.

The identification of these key CRM processes is the result of considerable research, which included discussions with business executives from a wide range of industries. In hindsight, these processes are predictable, given our definition of CRM.

CRM should be viewed as a strategic set of processes or activities that commences with a detailed review of an organization's strategy (*the strategy development process*) and concludes with an improvement in business results and increased shareholder value (*the performance assessment process*). The notion that competitive advantage stems from the creation of value for the customer *and* for the company (*the value creation process*) is key to the success of any relationship. CRM activities for all substantial companies will involve collecting and intelligently utilizing customer and other relevant data (*the information management process*) to build a superior customer experience, at each touch-point where the customer and supplier interact (*the multi-channel integration process*).

Figure 1.8 CRM as a cross-functional activity

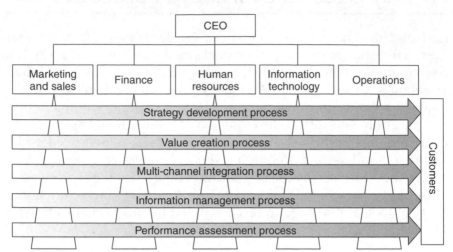

While these CRM processes appear to have universal application, the extent to which they are adopted will need to vary according to the unique situation of the organization concerned. Some organizations may wish to add to the key CRM processes identified here. For example, one telecommunications company we interviewed pointed out that its billing process (involving every telephone interaction that customers had with the company) was so pervasive, complicated and pivotal that the billing process itself needed to be considered as a key CRM process.

The need for a CRM strategic framework

Because CRM is a cross-functional activity and one that, in large companies, seeks to focus on potentially millions of individual customer relationships simultaneously, it can be unwieldy to implement and impossible to get right without a purposeful and systematic framework. The specific purpose of this book is to present a conceptual framework which positions CRM as a strategic set of processes that can be creatively managed to achieve an improvement in shareholder value.

The *Strategic Framework for CRM* shown in Figure 1.9 is based on the interaction of five cross-functional business processes that deal with strategy formulation, value creation, information management, multi-channel integration and performance assessment. These processes make a greater contribution to organizational prosperity collectively than they can individually and they should therefore be treated as an integrated and iterative set of activities. It is also important to point out that the framework is not intended to include all the aspects of implementation; for CRM implementation issues will vary greatly from one organization to another. However, CRM implementation should begin with strategic planning and end, ultimately, with performance improvement. We address these issues in the last chapter on organizing for CRM implementation.

The arrows in Figure 1.9 represent interaction and feedback loops between the different processes, emphasizing the iterative nature of CRM. For example, likely shifts in disintermediation within a given industry, considered within the strategy development process, will have an impact on channel choices within the multi-channel integration process. Likewise, changes within the multi-channel integration process will have a direct impact on decisions taken within the value creation process. Further, decisions on choice of customer segments taken as part of the strategy development process may be changed as a result of economic modelling undertaken as part of the value creation process.

The framework is the result of extensive research and the synthesis of experience. It was developed using a number of sources, including: an extensive review of the CRM and relationship marketing literature; in-depth interviews with senior executives working in

Figure 1.9   The strategic framework for CRM

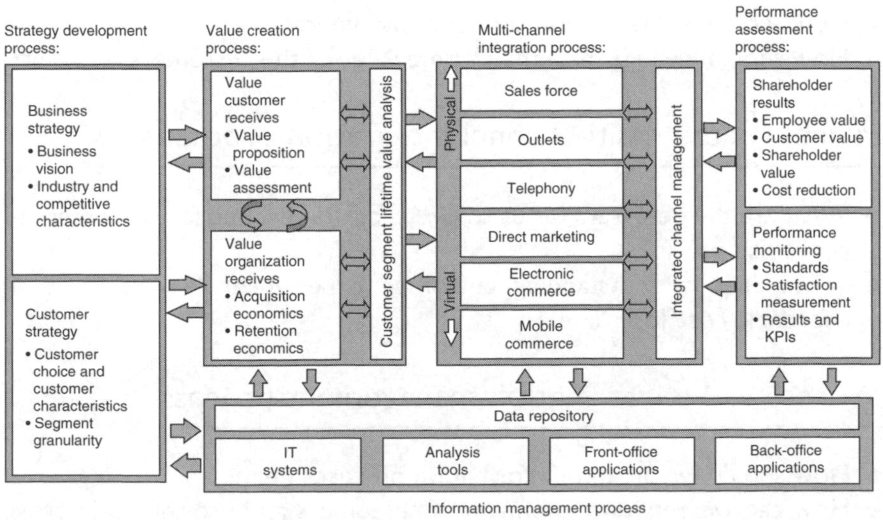

Source: based on Payne and Frow[26]

CRM, marketing and IT; interviews with a variety of CRM vendors; discussions with a number of leading CRM and strategy consultancies; and many individual and group discussions with corporate representatives at CRM seminars and workshops. The framework has been used and validated by several companies. Two companies in particular provided a valuable testing ground through use of the framework with over 400 managers. Its development also benefited from the input of a leading strategy consulting firm, which used the framework as the basis for a major benchmarking study in a large global financial services company.

The main attraction of the Strategic Framework for CRM is that it can enable organizations to identify and address those CRM issues which are preventing them from achieving better performance. In considering each of the five CRM processes, working essentially from left to right in Figure 1.9, organizations need to ask themselves some fundamental questions.

Process 1: the strategy development process

- Where are we and what do we want to achieve?
- Who are the customers that we want and how should we segment them?

Process 2: the value creation process

- How should we deliver value to our customers?
- How should we maximize the lifetime value of the customers we want?

Process 3: the multi-channel integration process

- What are the best ways for us to get to customers and for customers to get to us?
- What does an outstanding customer experience, deliverable at an affordable cost, look like?

Process 4: the information management process

- How should we organize information on customers?
- How can we 'replicate' the mind of customers and use this to improve our CRM activities?

Process 5: the performance assessment process

- How can we create increased profits and shareholder value?
- How should we set standards, develop metrics, measure our results and improve our performance?

While these five CRM processes have universal application, the extent to which they are emphasized will vary according to each organization's unique situation. Large customer-facing businesses will certainly need to review these CRM processes and the key questions underpinning them. However, small and medium-sized enterprises (SMEs) and other organizations such as those in the public sector may need to modify some of the questions to ensure they are of utmost relevance.

The structure of the book

The book adopts a process-by-process approach to assist readers in working through the Strategic Framework for CRM. Having introduced the topic of CRM and the five key processes comprising the framework in Chapter 1, Chapters 2 through 6 then examine each of the five CRM processes in detail. Chapter 7 finally pulls the five processes together by highlighting crucial organizational issues that are so often overlooked in efforts to implement CRM. Real-life case studies are included at the end of chapters to illustrate some of the main issues discussed. The following overview of chapter content should provide a useful summary for first-time readers as well as a reference for those returning to the book.

Chapter 1: Developing a strategic framework for CRM

Chapter 1 lends historical perspective to the topic of CRM by tracing the origins of CRM to the evolution of relationship marketing. A look at the terminology currently used to describe and deliver CRM reveals a management discipline still in the formative stages of development. Meanwhile the increasing demand for CRM solutions suggests the continuation of strong market growth.

The key to effective CRM lies not so much in what technology is used, but how well the organization is able to manage five cross-functional business processes, namely, strategy development, value creation, information management, multi-channel integration and performance assessment. The development of a Strategic Framework for CRM, based on these five processes, is an attempt to help resolve the often problematic nature of adopting a customer relationship management approach in individual organizations.

Chapter 2: The strategy development process

Chapter 2 highlights the importance of grounding any CRM initiative in a well thought-out strategy. Most companies today recognize that their future depends on the strength of their business relationships and, most crucially, their relationships with customers. The strategy development process demands a dual focus on the organization's business strategy and its customer strategy: how well the two interrelate will fundamentally affect the success of its CRM strategy.

A comprehensive review of the business strategy will provide a realistic platform on which to construct the CRM strategy and also generate recommendations for general improvement. The organization must fully understand its own strengths and limitations as well as those of its competitors if it is to exploit the marketing environment. Deciding which customers to attract and to keep and which customers to be without, is also a crucial activity if organizational resources are to be optimized; this is the role of customer strategy. The management of customer relationships is best accomplished by determining and applying the appropriate degree of segmentation, or *segment granularity*.

Chapter 3: The value creation process

Chapter 3 is concerned with transforming the outputs of the strategy development process into programmes that both *extract and deliver* value. The three key elements of the value creation process are: determining what value the company can provide for its customers (the 'value the customer receives'); determining what value the company can extract from its customers (the 'value the organization receives'); and, by successfully managing this value exchange, maximizing the lifetime value of desirable customer segments.

The value the customer receives is the total package of benefits he or she derives from the core product or service. The aim is to create a value proposition which is superior to and more profitable than those of competitors and which delivers a seamless customer experience. This requires some form of value assessment. Moreover, the proven link between customer retention and profitability means that customer relationships must be managed on the basis of acquisition and retention economics at segment, or better yet, at micro-segment or individual level. In many instances the acquisition and retention of customers can be improved through insights drawn from the value proposition and the value assessment.

Chapter 4: The multi-channel integration process

Chapter 4 focuses on decisions about what is the most appropriate combination of channels to use; how to ensure the customer experiences highly positive interactions within those channels; and, where customers interact with more than one channel, how to create and present a 'single unified view' of the customer. This chapter initially addresses the nature of industry structure and channel participants.

To determine the best customer interface, it is necessary to consider the key issues underlying channel selection; the purpose of multi-channel integration; the channel options available; and the importance of integrated channel management for maintaining the same high standards *across* multiple, different channels. An effective multi-channel service must match the individual (and changing) needs of customers who may belong to a number of different customer segments simultaneously. CRM success will depend heavily on the organization's ability to gather and deploy customer knowledge from the channels used as well as from other sources.

Chapter 5: The information management process

Chapter 5 concentrates on the collection, collation and usage of customer data and information from all customer contact points. This is the process that enables the organization to construct complete and current customer profiles that can be used to enhance the quality of the customer experience.

The key material elements of the information management process are: the data repository, consisting of databases and a data warehouse, which provides a powerful corporate memory of customers that is capable of analysis; IT systems comprising the organization's computer hardware and related software and middle-ware; analytical tools to undertake tasks such as data mining; and front office and back office applications which support the many activities involved in interfacing directly with customers and managing internal administration and supplier relationships. These front office and back office applications cover a wide range of organizational tasks such as sales force automation, call centre management, human resources, procurement, warehouse management, logistics software and some financial processes.

With regard to the organization's CRM technologies, the capacity to scale existing systems or plan for the migration to larger systems without disrupting business operations is critical. The overriding concern about front- and back-office systems is that they are sufficiently connected and coordinated to optimize customer relations and workflow.

Chapter 6: The performance assessment process

Chapter 6 covers the essential task of ensuring the organization's strategic aims in terms of CRM are being delivered to an appropriate and acceptable standard and that a basis for future improvement is established. Discussion centres on the two main components of this process: *shareholder results* which provide a 'macro' view of the overall relationships that drive performance; and *performance monitoring* which gives a more detailed 'micro' view of metrics and key performance indicators (KPIs).

As traditional performance measurement and monitoring systems, which tend to be functionally driven, are inappropriate for the cross-functional approach of CRM, care must be taken in defining the drivers and indicators of good performance across the five key CRM processes. The key drivers of shareholder results are highlighted: building employee value; building customer value; building shareholder value; and reducing end-to-end supply chain costs. Recent studies, such as the 'service profit chain' research conducted at Harvard, emphasize the relationship between employees, customers and shareholders and the need to adopt a more informed and integrated approach to exploiting the linkages between them. More detailed standards, measures and key performance indicators are needed to ensure CRM activities are planned and practised effectively and that a feedback loop exists to maximize performance improvement and organizational learning.

Chapter 7: Organizing for CRM Implementation

Having outlined the status of CRM as a maturing management discipline and a growth market and examined each of the five key CRM processes of the strategic framework in detail, this final chapter considers the all-important task of organizing for CRM implementation. Numerous reports of CRM disappointments have caused many to question the value and implications of investing in customer relationship management activities and technologies. While some CRM failures are inevitable, most of them can be prevented by paying more attention to the organizational issues involved in: assessing the organization's readiness for CRM; fully addressing the project management and change management requirements; understanding the role of employee engagement and planning; and carefully executing and evaluating the CRM programme. Experience has shown that successful CRM implementation is preceded by the development of a clear, relevant and well-communicated CRM strategy. Short-term wins have more chance of securing enterprise-wide commitment than do drawn out CRM projects with over-ambitious goals. Moreover, a CRM strategy designed to deliver incremental returns provides the flexibility and scope for progressive improvement. The adoption of best practice, underscored by strong leadership, is key to a positive outcome. No amount of IT can compensate for the requirement of human investment. This is evident in the aim of CRM: to create a seamless personalized customer experience that is consistently and continually enhanced. For attracting existing and potential customers, anything less is inappropriate.

Checklist for CRM leaders

CRM leaders should ask the following questions in considering the role of CRM in their organization:

1. How important are the following relationship issues for my organization?
   (a) the retention of profitable customers
   (b) developing a cross-functional approach to marketing
   (c) managing multiple markets in a more integrated manner
2. How important are the following trends in my organization?
   (a) the shift in focus from transactional to relationship marketing
   (b) the realization that customers are a business asset rather than a commercial audience
   (c) the transition from functions to processes
   (d) the use of information proactively rather than reactively
   (e) the greater utilization of technology in managing and maximizing the value of information
   (f) the need to balance delivery and extraction of customer value
   (g) the utilization of one-to-one marketing approaches
3. How is CRM considered in my organization?
   (a) do we view CRM from a strategic perspective where it is concerned with how the organization can create increased shareholder value through developing superior customer relationships?
   (b) is CRM viewed in a consistent and uniform manner throughout the organization?
   (c) are we clear on the distinction between operational CRM, analytical CRM and collaborative CRM?
4. Are we familiar with the CRM marketplace:
   (a) in terms of the key segments for CRM applications?
   (b) in terms of the CRM service providers and consultants?
5. Do we understand the rationale behind addressing CRM from the perspective of the following five processes?
   (a) the strategy development process
   (b) the value creation process
   (c) the multi-channel integration process
   (d) the information management process
   (e) the performance assessment process.

Chapter 2

The strategy development process

The strategic framework for CRM

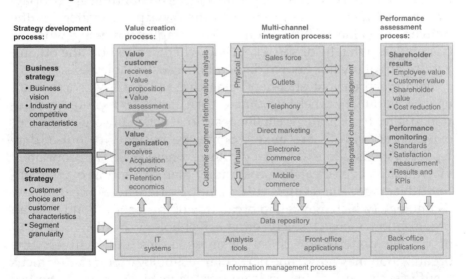

Information management process

The strategy development process is deservedly the first process to be considered in the CRM Strategic Framework. It not only shapes the nature of the other four key CRM processes but, more importantly, it defines the overall objectives and parameters for the organization's CRM activities. As highlighted in the figure above, the strategy development process involves determining the business strategy and the customer strategy and ensuring that they are integrated.

There are numerous definitions of strategy, but the one by management consultants Richard Norman and Rafael Ramirez best captures the concept of strategy in the context of CRM. It is one that highlights the criticality of customer relationships.

> Strategy is the art of creating value. It provides the intellectual frameworks, conceptual models and governing ideas that allow a company's managers to identify opportunities for bringing value to customers and for delivering that value at a profit. In this respect, strategy is the way a company defines its business and links together the only two resources that really matter in today's economy: knowledge and relationships or an organization's competencies and customers.[1]

While most companies recognize the importance of having clearly defined business and customer strategies, relatively few actively develop a formal CRM strategy with a focus on building appropriate *customer relationships*. Yet, central to the concept of strategy is the delivery of value to the customer. This implies knowing who the customer is, what he or she wants and whether and how the organization can satisfy this known demand on a sustainable basis.

With much current attention being directed at CRM, some managers advocate the quick introduction of a particular technology solution to solve their strategic challenges. However, many organizations' experiences with IT are mixed. Some are hostages of out-of-date legacy systems, some of a legacy culture where IT is inappropriately viewed as an ever-escalating cost rather than as a source of competitive advantage. The result is either inappropriate investment in new technology (which may fail to break free of the legacy 'bonds') or an organization focused solely on the technology challenge instead of on the underlying critical business issues. Alternatively, the organization may adopt one particular technology too rapidly; focus insufficiently on building customer relationships; or resist the use of new technologies for improved CRM. Rather than concentrate immediately on a technology solution, managers should first consider CRM in the context of their organization's overall strategy development. In other words, what are the goals of the organization given the opportunities and constraints within which it operates?

The strategy development process focuses on addressing the following key issues:

- Where are we and what do we want to achieve in our business?
- Who are the customers that we want and how should we segment them?

In this chapter, we address these issues under the following headings:

- Business strategy
  - The role of business strategy
  - Business vision
  - Industry and competitor characteristics
  - Analysing the industry and competitive environment
  - Determining business strategy
- Customer strategy
  - The role of customer strategy
  - Customer choice and customer characteristics
  - Segment granularity
- CRM strategy development
  - CRM strategies
  - Transition paths for CRM.

Business strategy

The first part of the CRM strategy development process is to review the organization's *business* strategy. A detailed understanding of the business strategy is essential if an appropriate *customer* strategy is to be implemented. We should emphasize from the outset that CRM is *not* about developing a business strategy. Rather it is about fully understanding the business strategy in order to determine how the appropriate customer strategy should be developed and how it should evolve over time. CRM should not seek responsibility for business strategy development. However, it should intervene and ensure top management's attention is directed at business strategy where a thorough review of it clearly shows that it is wrongly directed or it is not taking account of changing competitive landscape. This is because it is crucial for the CRM activities to be aligned with and supportive of an appropriate business strategy.

We do not attempt a fully comprehensive coverage of all aspects of business strategy here. Rather we examine the key issues that need to be considered and some frameworks that can be used to make an assessment of the organization's business strategy in order that the CRM strategy is appropriately focused.

The role of business strategy

Business strategy is a top management responsibility that involves identifying the future direction of the enterprise as well as managing the creative interaction of the functional disciplines of operations, marketing, finance and human resource management. It is both a process and a way of thinking which leads to the development of a set of strategies that assist the business in achieving its corporate objectives.

Virtually all companies have a business strategy; however, this may be implicit or explicit. While some companies are successful with only an implicit strategy guiding the chief executive and the management team, it is our experience that companies developing an explicit strategy through a planned approach have a greater chance of long-term success. Almost all large companies who have introduced CRM will have developed an explicit strategy. However, our newspapers and business journals are a constant reminder that such strategies are often not well-formulated or well-implemented, or both and do not automatically result in success.

Corporate success can be the result of an implicit strategy being evolved based on creative entrepreneurial insights on the part of a company; or it may be the result of opportunistic effectiveness. That is, effective intuitive responses to short-term opportunities in the marketplace. A further factor that can influence corporate success is luck, which often plays an important role in success. However, these factors cannot be relied upon to produce long-term results. While they may result in initial success for a company, a further factor, developing a formal business strategy, provides an opportunity to influence sustained success over the longer term. Companies wishing to adopt such an approach need clearly to define their business vision and formulate a business strategy that takes full account of the competitive characteristics within the areas in which they have chosen to operate.

Business vision

The process of business strategy formulation should commence with a review or articulation of a company's vision. The business vision should explicitly reflect the basic beliefs, values and aspirations of the organization. It should be noted, however, that many companies' statements of their vision display a great deal of similarity and read like public relations promotions rather than reflect the commitment to values that they are intended to be. A business vision should be an enduring statement of purpose that distinguishes the organization from its competitors and it should act as an important device for coordinating activity in an organization. A company's business vision should reflect the shared value systems which are held within the organization. It can provide a framework to enable the diverse staff of an organization to work together in a coordinated manner towards the achievement of the overall objectives and philosophy of the enterprise. Unfortunately, many companies' vision statements do not conform to these requirements.

Vision statements need not be long and platitudinous. Tom Watson, the founder of IBM, articulated his company's philosophy in the phrase 'IBM means service'. The business vision described by Watson was simple: not just to be a *good* service company, but to be the *best* service company. Tom Watson argued the vision of the organization had a great deal more to do with its performance on this dimension than did technological or economic resources, organizational structure, innovation or timing. Over most of the company's history it has maintained this strong customer service focus.

The most recent and authoritative work on business vision and identifying and communicating values is that undertaken by Hugh Davidson, a consultant and visiting professor at the Cranfield School of Management. His research was prompted by the fact that most of the written material on vision and values discusses how important they are and provides guidance on how to design statements, but there is little published about how to make vision and values work in practice. He undertook a two-year research study on how to make vision and values really work in organizations. His research involved interviewing top management (chairmen and chief executives) in 125 well-run companies and non-profit organizations in the USA and UK – companies which included BP, FedEx, DuPont, Tesco, Nestlé, Johnson & Johnson and IBM, as well as many non-profit organizations.[2]

Organizations use a variety of terms to describe their business vision. These include mission statements or 'missions', business definition, statement of business philosophy, belief statement, credo, vision statement, statement of purpose and so on. Davidson found the term 'mission', which has been widely used over the last 25 years, has become less popular in recent years as managers feel the use of the term has been abused. He concluded that it did not matter which words were used to describe the business vision; what was important were three fundamental questions. The questions and terms he uses to describe them are:

- What are we here for? – Purpose
- What is our long-term destination? – Vision
- What beliefs and behaviours will guide us on the journey? – Values.

A good example of a company putting this into practice is Goldman Sachs. They are a market leader in their sector and one the best companies in the investment-banking industry. The box below shows how they define their purpose, vision and values.

Goldman Sachs

Purpose/mission: To provide excellent investment and development advice for major companies

Vision: To be the world's premier investment bank in every sector
Values: • Client first
          • Teamwork

But just having a statement of vision and values is not enough. Companies such as Goldman Sachs live these on a day-to-day basis. Goldman Sachs are no longer a partnership but they still maintain a partnership ethos. Their vision is to be the world's premier investment bank in every sector in which they operate. As Davidson points out, *values* are where they differ radically from most of the other investment banks. They put their client before profit. Everybody at Goldman Sachs understands the importance of always putting their client first. They also place teamwork very high on their agenda.

The business vision and its associated values form an important element of a company's strategy. Put simply, without a clear, concise and well-communicated vision the company is unlikely to be highly successful in achieving its goals. Organizations are now realizing that developing a vision and a set of values associated with it may be difficult but is a very worthwhile activity. A business vision is typically developed as part of an enterprise-wide consultative process, which involves input from different functional areas and management levels.

Competitive advantage is difficult to create and sustain. As the service economy continues to grow, few purely product-based businesses now exist. Where they do, their products can be reverse-engineered and imitated. Companies providing services have no patent protection and are open to ever greater and faster copying of their service range. Those businesses that are highly successful tend to have a strong culture and compete on the basis of their people and process skills. A strong and appropriate vision and values enable companies to develop a distinctive culture and a focus for their employees. This can result in a 'people advantage' that is difficult, if not impossible, to imitate. Davidson concluded that a strong vision and values can create differentiation and build motivation, trust and customer focus among employees.

Experience has shown that vision and values are often developed the wrong way. Inventing slogans like: 'the customer is king' or 'let's be customer focused' are exactly the wrong way to develop vision and values. You have got to start off by identifying what are the key future factors for success in your marketplace and then build the values around achieving those key factors for success. In that way if you make your values work, they build competitive advantage. Otherwise they are quite irrelevant.[3]

To assist in the development of business vision and values Davidson identified seven best practices for making vision and values work (Figure 2.1). He applied these best practices to the 125 organizations he studied, defining 'excellence' as the achievement of all seven of them. Only 6 per cent of the organizations, including Johnson & Johnson and the Mayo Clinic, attained an excellence rating. The average company only addressed four of the seven practices. Davidson concluded that 'the seven best practices are synergistic and work together: Four out of seven is not 55 per cent, it's about 33 per cent in terms of performance'. His research findings show most organizations still had a long way to go in making their vision and values deliver demonstrable returns.

Figure 2.2 gives some examples of strong visions, which Davidson identifies as meeting his seven best practice criteria. Sun Microsystems'

Figure 2.1   Seven best practices in making vision and values work

Seven best practices in making vision and values work

1. *Building foundations*: Needs of key stakeholders understood and linked through vision and values
2. *Strong vision*: Vision is memorable, clear, motivating, ambitious, customer related and translated into measurable strategies
3. *Strong values*: Values support the vision, are based on key factors for success and turned into measurable practices
4. *Communication*: Consistent communication by action, signals, words
5. *Embedding*: Recruitment, training, appraisal, rewards, promotion and succession, all reflect values
6. *Branding*: Organization's branding expresses vision and values
7. *Measurement*: Rigorous measurement of how effectively vision and values are implemented

Source: Based on Davidson[4]

vision is a particularly good example of how a strong vision can act as a compass for employees. As Robert Youngjohns, the company's Vice President, explains: 'Sun Microsystems' vision of open systems and computers as easy to operate as a mobile phone was developed in 1987. Our consistently followed vision has been the key to our success in the past 10 years. Without it, we would have become diverted and lost direction, like some of our competitors'.[5]

Developing a strong business vision represents an important first stage in establishing a successful business strategy. We will revisit this subject when CRM change management is discussed in the final chapter.

Figure 2.2   Examples of strong business visions

Examples of strong visions

'To connect anyone, anywhere anytime – using almost anything – to the resources they need'
Sun Microsystems

'A computer on every desk and in every home'
Microsoft, original vision

'The best care to every patient every day'
Mayo Clinic

'Making communication with pictures as easy as using a pencil'
George Eastman, Kodak, c.1920

Source: Based on Davidson[6]

Industry and competitive characteristics

Having developed the business vision, the next step in business strategy formulation is to undertake a review of the industry and competitive environment including an assessment of both existing and potential competition. This addresses the issue raised above of 'where are we?'

The new competitive landscape

The last decade or so has seen a new competitive landscape emerge which has profound competitive and technological implications for most businesses. All companies need to understand this new environment impacts on their ability to create value and attract and retain customers, at present and in the future.

The means of value creation they use and in what combination will depend on each company's specific circumstances. However, what is imperative to all is the need to be continually learning about their customers and innovating new ways in which to provide them with ever-greater value. C K Prahalad, a professor at the University of Michigan, has pointed to a new fiercely competitive environment where customers have so much choice and so much power. In this environment the capacity to learn and act fast is increasingly a major source of competitive advantage.[7]

We are still at the beginning of a revolution in the competitive environment in which companies find themselves operating. Ian McDonald Wood, a leading digital business observer, has developed a detailed exposition of the nature and implications of changes taking place in the new competitive environment. Of particular note are a number of technological issues he has identified.[8]

Digitization and information processing power
With the rise in digital technology has come the ability to capture, store and utilize information in ways unthinkable even ten years ago. Moreover, as processing power has continued to double every eighteen months at no extra cost to the user, the volume and detail of information that can be so exploited has similarly increased, enabling companies and individuals to make decisions on an ever more information-rich basis.

Interconnectivity
In parallel with this, open software platforms enable these information-processing devices to be connected together into networks

across which information can readily flow. Thus the user of any one device can access information on any other user's device on the network regardless of distance and as the network gets larger, the information available to any user (and thus the usefulness to them of the network) increases. Although one tends to think of personal computers in this regard, the falling cost of processing power is increasingly also seeing a whole array of domestic appliances from phones to videocassette recorders with embedded processors and thus information processing capability.

Information transmission speed

Moreover as bandwidth (i.e. the speed and volume of information that can be transmitted electronically) continues to increase soon it will pose little limitation on the amount and richness of the information that can be exchanged instantaneously between devices on a network. In short, there has been a rise of networks of devices providing a huge information resource for users and which also allows them to interact with each other in real time regardless of distance.

Real time activity

The volume and speed with which information can be passed between companies and customers enables an individualized dialogue, where the company can adapt to the particular needs and profiles of its customers. However, to achieve such interactivity, the company needs to be able to respond to information provided by customers. A company needs to take advantage of the speed with which volumes of market intelligence data can be collected from customer interactions to guide a continual review and adaptation of the services it offers, to ensure the firm continues to meet its chosen customers' needs better than any alternative organization open to them. If a company can capture, learn from and adapt to information so gained quicker than its competitors, it stands a greater chance of achieving and maintaining superiority over them with respect to its ability to meet its chosen customers' needs.

Putting the new economy in context

An early review should be undertaken of the opportunities and threats posited by this new competitive landscape. An awareness of these significant changes and their implications will assist the development of the enterprise's business and customer strategies. However, while the growth of the digital economy has strong implications for strategy, it is essential that the on-line world is seen in context. As Harvard Business School's Michael Porter comments:

> We need to move away from the rhetoric about 'Internet Industries', 'e-business strategies', and a 'new economy' and see the Internet for what it is: an enabling technology – a powerful set of tools that can be used, wisely or unwisely in almost any industry, and as part of almost any strategy. ... In our quest to see how the Internet is different, we failed to see how the Internet is the same.[9]

Thus companies need to understand the implications of the new digital world, but ensure the integration of strategies developed for the new economy with their existing business activities. DnB NOR Bank, is a good example of an organization that has built a new business strategy that fuses new digital opportunities with its existing business.

Case 2.1: DnB NOR Bank – Case study overview

DnB NOR Bank is the largest financial institution in Norway after the recent merger between DnB and Union Bank of Norway (UBN). It combines the use of traditional methods of service delivery with new technologies to serve both B2C and B2B markets. With increasing customer sophistication and competitive intensity in the Norwegian market, the bank recognized that it needed to move away from a product orientation and towards a customer and event focus in order to improve margins and grow profitability.

With a decline in the frequency of branch visits by customers there was less opportunity for it to develop improved customer relationships. Their biggest challenge was to find complete information on customers and making it actionable. The bank needed a means of identifying and exploiting the drivers of customer satisfaction and loyalty in a real-time operating environment. It needed a radical, customer-led solution. If it could track customer trends and understand individual profitability, it could improve revenue and margins through cross-selling and increasing customer use of its most profitable products and services.

In 1996, the bank needed to build an enterprise data warehouse to consolidate its disparate data sources and thus capitalize on its key business assets: a substantial customer base; the country's best financial distribution system; and a strong financial brand image. They selected Teradata, a division of NCR for this solution. Using Teradata's data warehousing, they are now better able to analyse each customer's use of different services, as well as an individual's total net worth to the bank. They now understand the profit and costs associated with *each* customer which means better, more customized services for customers and increased profitability for the bank. Company-wide use of this powerful data warehouse has enabled more cost-effective interaction between distribution channels as well as the delivery of more integrated customer strategies. This initiative has helped support the vision and values which emphasize 'being actively helpful and accessible'. As CRM Manager Kari Opdal observes, delivering on these values nurtures a trusting and caring relationship that results in them being willing to pay a bit more and staying with the bank a lot longer.

The full case study is at the end of this chapter (see p. 92)

Changes in industry structure and evolution

The characteristics of the industry need to be assessed not only in terms of the existing structure, but also in terms of future possible structural changes. Recent developments in electronic channels as well as new strategic insights have led to greater competitive activity on the part of both new entrants and existing competitors. This has created increasing challenges to traditional business models. In many industries, ranging from bookselling to automotive suppliers, the fundamental industry structure and dynamics are being reconfigured

Over the last decade, the traditional channel structures of many industries have been dismantled and reconfigured in response to new technologies that have opened new paths to market. Managers responsible for business strategy need to understand both the nature of their industry structure now and how it is likely to alter in the future. Valuable insights into emerging trends within industry structures can be gained from examining the experiences of other sectors or other industries on a global basis.

Two types of structural behaviour are important: *disintermediation* – where a company ceases to need to use one or more intermediaries or channel members; and *reintermediation* – where changes in the current business model result in the emergence of additional new intermediaries. In particular, the Internet has had a role in both these forms of structural change. These changes in industry structure need to be considered first at a macro-level as part of the strategy development process. Once macro-level decisions have been made regarding the most appropriate paths to market, the extent to which intermediaries are to be used and how these may change over time, the organization then needs to consider multi-channel options and their combination in greater detail at a micro-level. We will address this in greater detail when we consider the multi-channel integration process in Chapter 4.

Analysing the industry and competitive environment

A number of frameworks and conceptual models are especially helpful in both developing business strategy and assessing if it has been formulated with sufficient clarity and detail in the context of the competition. We now review three of the more important frameworks for assessing the industry and competitive environment in order to develop an improved business strategy, including:

- the industry analysis model
- the generic strategies framework
- the market leaders framework.

Industry analysis model

The industry dynamics in which the firm operates are commonly analysed using a framework such as Michael Porter's five forces model, so that all known forces and not so well understood contingencies are brought into consideration. A consideration of these 'forces' should be augmented by a more contemporary analysis.

Porter's model of industry analysis is an important aid to understanding the competitive characteristics, identifying the key factors for success and determining the profit potential in an industry. In undertaking an analysis of any industry, he proposed that its characteristics and long-term prospects should be analysed in terms of five dimensions: the nature and degree of competition, the barriers to entry to that business, the competitive power of substitute products, the degree of buyer power, and the degree of supplier power.[10]

However, as US professors Stanley Slater and Eric Olson have observed, industry dynamics have changed in subtle and not so subtle ways over the past two decades: 'We have moved closer to a global marketplace in many industries; technology has advanced rapidly and in unforeseen ways; deregulation has opened the door for aggressive forms of entrepreneurship; and the Internet has created an entirely new way to do business'.[11] They suggest augmenting Porter's five forces model to reflect these and related developments. Newer thinking suggests we should supplement Porter's analysis with a consideration of: co-opetition and networks; deeper environmental analysis; and the impact of disruptive technologies.

A framework for undertaking industry analysis, based on the forces, is shown in Figure 2.3.

Through analysis of these eight dimensions, which include Porter's five forces, insights can be gained into both opportunities and threats as well as the key factors for competitive success in the industry under consideration.

Potential entrants

Two factors determine how strong this force will be: the existing barriers to entry and the likelihood of a strong competitive reaction from established competitors. The threat of entry tends to be low if barriers to entry are high and/or aspiring new entrants can expect extremely hostile retaliation from the established firms within the industry. If the threat of entry is low, profitability of the industry tends to be high.

Buyer power

The bargaining power of buyers is high if a number of factors are present. These include: if the products that a company purchases form a large proportion, in terms of cost, of its own product; if the buyer group is operating in an industry of low profitability; if the products supplied are undifferentiated and it is easy for the buyer to switch between

Figure 2.3   A framework for industry analysis

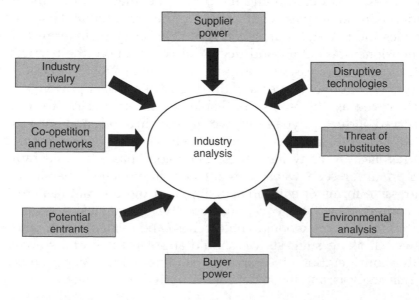

suppliers at little cost; if the products are purchased in large volumes; or if the buyers have the potential to integrate backwards. Such conditions of high buyer power will result in lower industry profitability.

Supplier power
Similarly, the bargaining power of suppliers can be high if there are relatively few suppliers; if the industry is not an important customer of the supplier group; if the supplier has the potential to integrate forward into the customer's business; if there are few or no direct substitutes for the product; if the industry is dominated by only a few suppliers; or if the suppliers products are sufficiently differentiated so that the firm being supplied the goods cannot easily switch to another supplier. Conditions of high supplier power lead to reduced industry profitability.

Threat of substitutes
In many product areas it is possible to identify products which can serve as substitutes. In industries ranging from telecommunications to car making, the threat of substitution is present. The higher the threat of substitution, the lower the profitability is likely to be within the industry because threat of substitution generally sets a limit on the prices that can be charged. The factors which influence the threat of substitution include the substitute product price-performance trade-off and the extent of switching costs associated with changing from one supplier to the supplier of the substitute. If the threat of substitution is low, industry profitability will tend to be high.

Industry rivalry and competition
The degree of industry competition is characterized by the amount of rivalry between existing firms. This can vary considerably and is not related necessarily to whether or not the industry is highly profitable. Intense rivalry can exist if there is slow growth within the industry; if competitors are evenly balanced in size and capability; where switching costs are low; where there is a high fixed cost structure and companies need to keep volumes high; where exit barriers are high such that unprofitable companies may still remain within the industry; and where competitors have different strategies, the result of which is that some firms may be willing to pursue a strategy that results in considerable conflict within the industry. A common outcome of this is price wars. A high degree of rivalry depresses industry profitability.

Environmental analysis

This analysis, known as a PESTE analysis, involves a review of political, economic, social, technological and environmental issues. Managers should develop a detailed list of major factors under each of these headings. PESTE analysis encourages managers to review broad environmental influences on the enterprise. A PESTE analysis helps understanding of the competitive dynamics of your industry and should lead to the identification of opportunities and threats facing your business.

Disruptive technologies

The environmental analysis should help consideration of evolutionary technological factors impacting on your business. Successful companies are usually good at responding to such evolutionary changes in their markets but have problems initiating revolutionary changes in their markets, or dealing with disruptive innovation. As Harvard academics Clayton Christensen and Michael Overdorf point out, such innovations are disruptive in that they did not address the next-generation needs of leading customers in existing markets.[12] Rather they had attributes that enable new market applications to emerge – and the disruptive innovations improved so rapidly that they ultimately could address the needs of customers in the mainstream of the market as well. Such disruptive technologies or innovations should be closely studied as they can create an entirely new market.

Co-opetition and networks

Increasingly networks of companies are being developed that combine simultaneously cooperation and competition. Such 'co-opetition' is widely present in the information technology and CRM industries. Although competition has been increasing among these firms, so too has the nature of their collaborative activities. The concept of co-opetition, developed by professors Adam Brandenburger and Barry Nalebuff, illustrates how in an increasingly networked economy, companies cooperate and compete at the same time to maximize customer and firm value creation within their markets.[13] As Julie Bowser, of IBM's Strategy & Change consulting group, has pointed out, changing business dynamics make the collaborative value inherent in co-opetition more necessary. Companies need to challenge themselves to develop their business by initiating, leveraging and redefining relationships with other players to create and capture value.

The aim of this analysis is for managers to identify a position in their industry where their company can best take advantage of, or defend itself against, these forces. This analysis can be performed by different groups of managers within the organization to help gain additional insights regarding competitive characteristics. As the strategy evolves, it can also be undertaken at a more specific level by applying it to particular customer segments. A complete and balanced analysis of the competitive environment in which a firm is operating should lead to a good understanding of the key factors for success within that industry and the key tasks to be addressed in the firm.

The generic strategies framework

Once the industry structure has been analysed, an enterprise can consider the appropriate strategy to compete within it. A number of natural or generic strategies that can be adopted by an enterprise have been proposed by various writers. One approach, also developed by Porter, suggests that a choice of one of three generic strategies is appropriate for a given business. These include a cost leadership strategy, a differentiation strategy, or a focus strategy.[14] These three strategies include:

Cost leadership strategy

A cost leadership strategy requires a company to set out with the objective of being the lowest cost producer in the industry. Companies must seek economies of scale, proprietary technology not available to other firms, preferential access to raw materials and cost minimization over a wide range of areas.

Differentiation

With a differentiation strategy a firm seeks to be different within the industry it is operating in by being unique on some dimension or set of dimensions of value to buyers. The company seeks one or more dimensions to differentiate itself on and, as a result, hopes to earn a premium price for its products or services.

Focus strategy

A focus strategy involves concentrating on a particular buyer group, geographic area or product/market segment. By selecting a particular segment or group of segments the company attempts to tailor its strategy to serving the needs of its segment better than the competition.

It is essentially a strategy of gaining competitive advantage in the target segment because the company is not likely to enjoy competitive advantage across the market as a whole. A focus strategy may emphasize differentiation or cost advantage.

Cost leadership is often pursued by businesses with a low cost position that wish to create shareholder value by gaining market share through very competitive pricing. Texas Instruments historically adopted a cost leadership strategy by seeking high market share through low pricing and thus benefiting from the cost effects of the experience curve.

An industry-wide differentiation strategy seeks to create differentiation that is perceived as different and unique across that industry. The appropriate means of differentiation vary considerably across different industries. Differentiation could be in terms of technology, features, customer service, dealer network used, styling and product positioning. Mercedes-Benz has, for example, differentiated itself from its competition by adopting a strategy on the basis of design, image, styling and engineering.

The approach adopted for a focus strategy can take many forms. The focus strategy is concerned with a specific market segment and is more concentrated than the differentiation approach which appeals to a wider market. While Japanese motor car manufacturers adopt a cost leadership approach and manufacturers such as Mercedes a differentiation approach, other manufacturers such as Ferrari and Lamborghini (now owned by larger automotive groups) focus on a very tightly defined market segment. The focus strategy is concerned with servicing a particular target market better than any of the other competitors within the industry who are adopting either focus strategies aimed at other segments or broader strategies of differentiation and cost leadership.

The dilemma facing managers is to choose the best strategy. In particular, how should they choose between cost leadership and differentiation? Conventional strategists have suggested that attempting to follow more than one generic strategy at the same time is inappropriate as firms which attempt to do this become 'stuck in the middle', a situation where they fail to achieve a strong competitive position on any dimension. More recently, examples of companies which have successfully adopted more than one of Porter's generic strategies have been used to illustrate how hybrid strategies can be adopted. Figure 2.4 illustrates a revised view of the generic strategies based on differentiation and cost.

Figure 2.4 Alternative strategies based on differentiation and cost

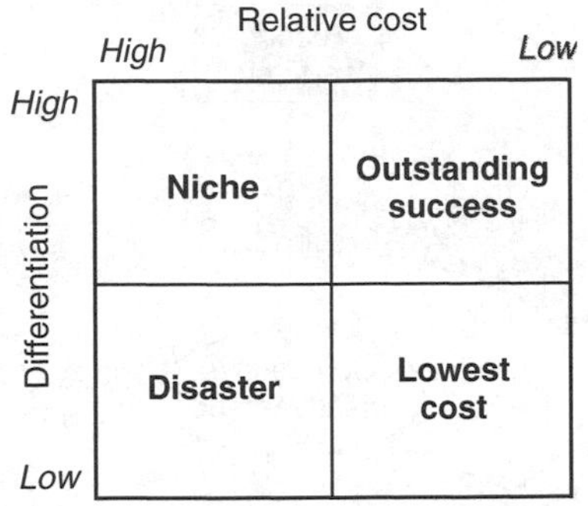

The alternative strategies in this figure illustrate that companies must avoid having a high cost structure and low differentiation – a recipe for disaster. They should adopt a strategy of low cost or differentiation. However, the greatest success comes if both can be done together. For example, Ikea has been successful by creatively combining both a differentiation strategy and cost leadership strategy that results in prices lower than those of its major competitors.

The market leaders framework
A further framework of generic strategies has been developed by US consultants Michael Treacy and Fred Wiersema. Their 'disciplines of market leaders' framework suggest three broad business strategies:

● operational excellence
● product leadership
● customer intimacy.

Treacy and Wiersema called these three routes to success 'value disciplines' (Figure 2.5). Based upon their research they suggest that marketplace success is usually based upon what kind of value proposition the companies pursued – best total cost, best product, or best total solution.[15] Their work is especially useful as it is supported by many examples.

They state 'by operational excellence, we mean providing customers with reliable products or services at competitive prices, delivered with minimal difficulty or inconvenience. By product leadership, we mean providing products that continually redefine the state of

Figure 2.5   Value disciplines for market leaders

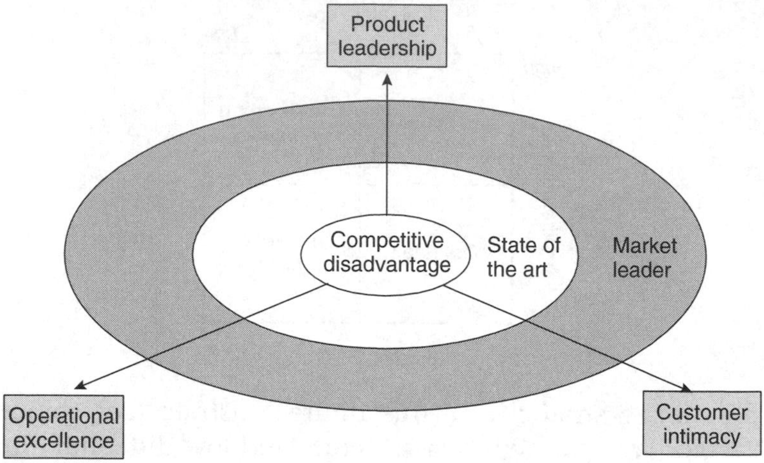

the art. And by customer intimacy, we mean selling the customer a total solution not just a product or service'.

While these three 'disciplines' or 'generic' strategies should not be assumed to be mutually exclusive, it will more often be the case that companies have different strengths – or weaknesses – in each of the three. While a strong position in each of these markets should be the aim of any business it is suggested that the activities within the business should reflect the chosen underlying generic strategy. Thus choosing one discipline to emphasize does not imply ignoring the others; as suggested by Figure 2.5 the business chooses one dimension of value upon which to base its market reputation.

Organizations seeking to follow the discipline of operational excellence need to have an internal culture that is based on 'lean thinking'. This involves focusing on continuing improvement, multi-skilling and all those CRM activities that lead to greater internal efficiency. Equally, significant emphasis must be placed upon developing superior supplier relationships since, for many organizations, the cost of materials and supplies is a major proportion of total cost. By working more closely with suppliers many opportunities for cost reduction and quality improvements can usually be identified. In the same way, it can be argued, the interface with downstream intermediaries such as distributors and retailers will need to be managed closely. For example, through the use of Electronic Data Interchange (EDI) and other forms of electronic commerce, it will often be possible significantly to enhance the responsiveness and cost-effectiveness of the supply chain.

Companies that seek to place the emphasis in their strategic focus upon product leadership will need to invest in creating an internal culture that encourages innovation, risk-taking and entrepreneurship. Here recruitment practices need to focus on attracting and retaining people who will be able to contribute to the innovation process – perhaps with a skills profile and experience that indicate their creativity or their in-depth knowledge of technologies or markets. It is interesting to reflect that Microsoft, an acknowledged world leader in its field, has declared that its sole criterion in recruitment is 'intelligence'. Businesses that seek product leadership also need to concentrate on supplier relationships as today a significant proportion of innovation is supplier driven. Closely related to the focus on suppliers for those companies seeking product leadership is the leverage that can be gained through developing alliances with other organizations' specific skills, knowledge bases and market understanding that they can impact. This is especially true of the relationships that CRM vendors have with their alliance partners.

The third 'discipline' is customer intimacy. This requires a continuing focus on the means whereby the relationship with customers can be made more personalized and customized. As such it is the 'internal' market that becomes of critical importance. A vast amount of research confirms the impact of employee motivation and commitment on customer satisfaction. Customer intimacy emphasizes building relationships with existing customers with the greatest potential for growth and profitability.

In terms of CRM, customer intimacy strategies are especially appropriate. Here emphasis is placed on understanding customer segments, micro-segments and determining where one-to-one strategies are appropriate – a topic which we consider shortly. Some companies are rethinking their strategy and are developing more intimate direct relationships with the consumer. For example, Procter and Gamble are now focusing their attention on developing direct relationships with the consumer through direct response promotion with their Pampers brand of nappies. Consumers are offered the opportunity of obtaining discounts by completing a coupon which provides valuable data including name, address, telephone number, and number of children and their ages. This allows them to track consumer needs more closely and make appropriate and timely offers to them.

Focusing on business strategy

Business strategy is a process which leads to the development of an effective strategy or set of strategies that help the business achieve its corporate objectives. It involves undertaking an in-depth analysis of the external environment of the company and undertaking an analysis of the internal competencies of the company. The external analysis should review issues in the political, social and technological environments as well as provide an in-depth examination of markets, customers and competitors. The internal analysis consists of a review of a wide range of factors that can ultimately affect the company's success or failure. The output of these analyses should enable a thorough assessment to be made of the overall attractiveness of the business and the firm's competitive position within that business. The fundamental objective of this analysis is to identify those trends, forces and conditions that have a potential impact on the formulation and implementation of the company's strategies.

A variety of techniques can be used to help determine the business strategy. The industry analysis framework described above enables a complete and balanced analysis of the competitive environment in which a firm is operating and should lead to a good understanding of the key factors for success within that industry. Such an analysis can make a major impact on managers' understanding of their strengths and weaknesses and the opportunities and threats within their industry. Other analytical techniques can also be used to support the review of business strategy. The reader wishing to explore them should consult the strategy section of the bibliography at the end of the book.

One of the most important aspects of this analysis is the identification of the key factors of success in that business. If these key factors are not correctly identified this could have a disastrous effect on the business because it could result in an inappropriate strategy being adopted. Consequently, the identification of the key factors for success should be a high priority area when using the analytical frameworks discussed above. It should be noted that these key factors can change over time. For example, in the motor car industry the key factors for success have changed considerably in recent years. Demand has changed to smaller cars, SUVs (sports utility vehicles) and four wheel drive vehicles. Factors such as quality of styling, reliability, fuel efficiency, safety and after-sales service have become more important.

The objective of addressing business strategy, as part of the strategy development process in CRM, is to determine how the enterprise's customer strategy should be developed or extended and how it will evolve in the future. For companies with a clear and appropriate business strategy, a review of it will help ensure the resulting customer strategy is properly focused. For those companies where an examination of the business strategy shows it is unclear, inappropriate or has inconsistencies, a more detailed review, using appropriate analytical techniques, needs to be carried out. The resulting analysis should lead to a carefully chosen and well-argued case for pursuing a particular business strategy.

The business strategy should be developed into specific actions that will lead to its implementation and the achievement of its objectives. If this does not occur all the effort expended in developing the business strategy will have been wasted. The successful strategy will be one in which the company differentiates itself from its competitors in a positive sense using its strengths and distinctive competencies to satisfy customer needs better than the competition. While a company can pursue any of the strategies we have outlined in this section, we consider a business strategy based on customer intimacy is particularly appropriate to the underlying principles and ethos of CRM.

Customer strategy

The other half of the strategic equation is deciding which customers the business wants most to attract and to keep and which customers it would prefer to be without. The significance of being clear on who is the target customer base (and who is not) is that every organization possesses weaknesses as well as strengths. In an environment of increasing competition, few firms can successfully be 'all things to all people'. Thus determining a distinctive customer strategy and directing all efforts to maintain and develop it is the only way for a business to survive and indeed thrive.

The role of customer strategy

While business strategy is usually the responsibility of the CEO, board and strategy director, customer strategy is typically the responsibility of the marketing department. However, as we have pointed out in Chapter 1, both marketing and CRM require a cross-functional or pan-company approach if they are to be fully effective.

In reality, in most organizations marketing is still represented by a functionally based marketing department. Responsibility for CRM, as we discuss in Chapter 7, is also often vested in functionally based roles including IT and marketing, although an increasing number of enterprises are now starting to adopt a pan-company approach. While alignment and integration of business strategy and customer strategy is a high priority for all organizations, special attention should be placed on alignment where different departments are involved in the two areas of strategy development. The prior review of business strategy will be instrumental in reaching a view on broad customer focus. However, organizations need to determine more specifically their choice of customers and their characteristics. This is the role of customer strategy.

Customer strategy involves examining your existing and potential customers and identifying which forms of segmentation are most appropriate. The organization needs to identify the characteristics of their customers and customer segments. This may require analysis of a considerable number of customer data, which has significant implications regarding the collection and organization of these data in appropriate data repositories, such as a data warehouse. We examine this topic in Chapter 5. As part of this process the organization also needs to consider the appropriate level of subdivision of broad customer segments, or segment granularity. This involves making decisions about whether a macro-, micro- or one-to-one segmentation approach is appropriate.

Customer choice and characteristics: the role of market segmentation

It is important to recognize that customers differ and thus relationships with customers will have to be managed differently if they are to be successful. This is a key principle of CRM. The aim of CRM is to build relationship strategies that refine and redefine relationships and in this way increase their value. Creating competitive advantage through the skilful management of customer relationships will normally require a reappraisal of the way in which customers are approached and segmented and the way in which resources are allocated and used. To achieve this level of refinement requires a careful choice of the levels at which segmentation is undertaken. However, first we need to consider the nature of the 'customer'.

Who is the customer?

For businesses that sell directly to final consumers, the answer to the question 'who is the customer?' may seem straightforward. However, many companies, in at least parts of their business, sell their products and services through some form of intermediary. In such case the issue 'who is the customer?' becomes more complicated. The 'customer' may include three broad groups: direct buyers, intermediaries and final consumers such as those shown in Figure 2.6.

Figure 2.6   Determining balance of marketing efforts to the 'customer'

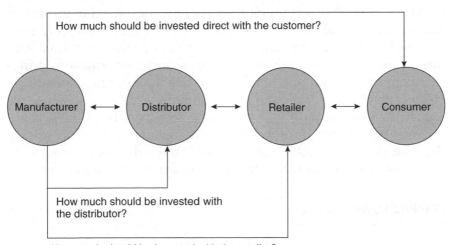

To illustrate these groups, consider a manufacturer of microwave ovens. This manufacturer sells to a number of approved distributors or wholesalers, who in turn sell the products to retail outlets, which then sell the microwaves to individual consumers. In this example the distributor is the direct buyer, the retailer the intermediary and the individual who purchases the appliance from the retailer, the final consumer. We can use the term 'customer' generally to apply to all these groups. In some industries there may be further intermediaries, which create additional steps within the channel chain.

Where companies operate in an intermediated market such as this they need carefully to consider 'who is the customer?' The answer is, of course, *all of them* are customers and the company needs to balance the amount of time, money and effort that should be directed at each group.

We have found many businesses where this is poorly balanced. Examples include:

- an FMCG company which placed most of its emphasis on an advertising programme aimed at final consumers; in doing so it failed to build strong enough relationships with its retailers
- a consumer durables company that placed most of its emphasis on trade marketing to the retailer; as a result it failed to invest enough resources to build the brand franchise with their final consumers
- a 'captive' finance company of a major car manufacturer that historically had placed virtually all of its effort on the motor dealers; more recently it has recognized the importance of the retention of final customers and has readdressed this balance.

Further, advances in information technology are changing the nature and importance of different groups. Many organizations are now finding that in order to build stronger relationships with final consumers they need to change the emphasis and expenditure at different channel levels or, alternatively, refocus the existing expenditure in ways that build deeper and more sustained relationships. In some industries, intermediaries are becoming increasingly valuable channel members, while in others the value of intermediaries is being challenged. We will examine the role of intermediaries in more detail in Chapter 4 in the context of the multi-channel integration process.

Market segmentation

In both business-to-business and business-to-consumer markets, market segmentation is essential for the successful development of a customer strategy. (Once companies understand the distinctive characteristics of their segments they can adopt a much more targeted approach to their customers.) As the previous section suggests, in intermediated businesses segmentation often needs to be undertaken at the distributor, intermediary and final consumer levels.

Market segmentation involves dividing a total market up into a series of sub-markets (or market segments) based on customer characteristics. A market segmentation exercise involves the following steps:

- defining the relevant market to be addressed
- determining the criteria for market segment viability

- considering the alternative bases for segmentation
- choosing specific segments to focus on.

As part of this process, the degree of disaggregation of segments, or segment granularity, needs to be determined.

Definition of the relevant market

The definition of the relevant market to be addressed involves specifying the broad customer group at which the company is seeking to market its products or services. In undertaking this task, the organization needs to consider its strengths and weaknesses and review the resources which are available to it. The choice of the market to be addressed or 'served market' will be based around decisions relating to:

- the breadth of the service line
- the types of customers
- the geographic scope
- the areas of 'value added' in which the service firm decides to operate.

Successful market segmentation means satisfying the needs of existing and potential customers in a clearly defined market. This involves understanding customer attitudes and customer preferences, as well as the benefits which are sought. Definition of the target market and its requirements is the first essential step in the segmentation process.[16]

Criteria for market segment viability

The identification and selection of particular market segments for targeting with a distinctive offering may depend on many factors, but particularly on the size of the segment, its special needs, the extent to which these needs are already being met by the company or by competitors and whether the company has the resources available to meet the service requirements.

There are various widely accepted criteria for determining if a market segment is viable:

- the segment must be measurable in size and characteristics
- the segment must be meaningful. It must be capable of generating sufficient long-run profit to merit separate marketing attention
- the segment must be reachable within budget confines

- the segment must be durable over time; if the distinction between segments is likely to diminish as the service matures, then it is not suitable for a segmented marketing approach.

Companies may wish to develop their own criteria according to their specific circumstances.

Considering the alternative bases for segmentation

Markets may be segmented in many ways, but the following categories are the most important in B2B and B2C segmentation. These categories include both traditional forms of segmentation such as demographics and more contemporary value, or needs-based, segmentation.

Business-to-business market segmentation
Segmentation by industry type

The segmentation of markets on the basis of Standard Industrial Classification (SIC) is quite widespread, but only partially useful. Sometimes these segments are thought of as 'vertical' markets and defined around business sectors such as the construction industry or the telecoms industry. The problem with this type of segmentation is that it provides no guide as to how the behaviour of buyers might differ simply because they happen to be in different industries.

Segmentation by service

This approach is concerned with how customers respond to service offerings. Companies can offer a range of different service options and provide different service levels within those options, giving them considerable scope to design service packages appropriate to different market segments. If a supplier measures the perceived importance of different customer service elements across market segments, they can respond to that segment's identified needs and allocate an appropriate service offering to it.

Segmentation by value sought

Different customers may respond differently to the seller's 'value offering'. Knowing what customers value and what weight they put on the difference elements of a value proposition can help a company develop more targeted solutions. It is critical to have a deep understanding of the motivations behind the purchase decision.

Business-to-consumer market segmentation
Geographic segmentation
This approach differentiates customers on the basis of where they are located. So customers may be segmented into urban, suburban or rural groups, for example. Customers are commonly segmented by postcodes, which might also represent different groups in terms of relative wealth, and socioeconomic and other factors.

Demographic and socioeconomic segmentation
Demographic and socioeconomic segmentation is based on a wide range of factors including age, sex, family size, income, education, social class and ethnic origins. So it is helpful in indicating the profile of people who buy a company's products or services.

Psychographic segmentation
Psychographic segmentation involves analysing lifestyle characteristics, attitudes and personality. Recent research in several countries suggests that the population can be divided into between ten and fifteen groups, each of which has an identifiable set of lifestyle, attitude and personality characteristics.

Benefit segmentation
Benefit segmentation groups customers together on the basis of the benefits they are seeking from a product. For example, car buyers seek widely varying benefits, from fuel economy, size and boot space, to performance, reliability or prestige.

Usage segmentation
Usage segmentation is a very important variable for many products. It usually divides consumers into heavy users, medium users, occasional users and non-users of the product or service in question. Marketers are often concerned with the heavy user segment.

Loyalty segmentation
Loyalty segmentation involves identifying customers' loyalty to a brand or product. Customers tend to be very loyal, moderately loyal or disloyal. These groups are then examined to try to identify any common characteristics so the product can be targeted at prospectively loyal customers.

Occasion segmentation

Occasion segmentation recognizes that customers may use a product or brand in different ways depending on the situation. For example, a beer drinker may drink light beer with his colleagues after work, a conventional beer in his home and a premium or imported beer at a special dinner in a licensed restaurant.

We would advise both B2C and B2B companies to categorize markets according to value preferences or benefits sought, at least initially, when undertaking market segmentation. If organizations understand what different customers value and how this influences their purchase decisions, then they can subsequently see if those value preferences correlate with other segmentation criteria.

Choosing specific segments

Organizations are now taking a more rigorous approach to segment choice. For example, one bank examined the number and percentage of heads of households in each lifestyle category in terms of:

- demographic profile: including age of household head, occupation, education, home ownership, number of full time wage earners in household, annual household income and net worth and average balances
- service penetration: by transaction accounts, regular savings accounts and time deposits. Details of credit services, credit cards used, trust-related services and electronic funds transfer services were included
- average dollars balances: by transactions accounts, savings accounts, time deposits, instalment credit and revolving lines of credit.

The bank then measured the dollars profit produced after each dollar of delivery cost required to service that segment before deciding on which segments it wished to concentrate on.

Choice of the resulting target markets segments should be based on detailed review of existing and potential value and profitability of the segments. Identification of the economic value of customer segments to the enterprise is critical. This is where there is a high degree of interactivity between the strategy development process and the value creation process. The strategy development process leads to an initial view being taken on the economic desirability of different segments. The value creation process refines this view by identifying segment variables such as expected acquisition costs, profit per customer, retention rates and customer acquisition targets. These variables can then be used to identify economic value of different segments including estimates of annual contribution and profitability and lifetime value expressed in terms of net present value. We examine the economics that determine both segment focus and segment granularity in the next chapter.

We have now reviewed the four steps involved in the market segmentation process. However, choice of customer segments has an additional layer of complexity – segment granularity. Added to this is the possibility that some customers may fit into more than one segment. This can result in the need for a more detailed analysis of economic value at a more stratified level before final choice of segments can be made.

Segment granularity: from mass marketing to 'one-to-one' marketing

In addition to considering the relevant segmentation base for its business, the company also needs to consider the *level* of segmentation. Segment granularity refers to the decision of whether a macro-segmentation, micro-segmentation or a 'one-to-one' approach to segmentation should be adopted. We can also call this one-to-one approach 'individualization' or 'personalization'.

Decisions regarding level of segmentation need to be taken in the context of a number of considerations including: the existing and potential profitability of different customer types; the available information on customers; the opportunity to 'reach' customers in terms of both communication and physical delivery; and the cost of doing it. Figure 2.7 provides an overview of the options in terms of levels of segmentation, together with the tailoring of the product or service offer; the style of communication needed and suggested means of measuring success.[17]

'One-to-one' markets and permission marketing

We are now seeing markets fragment into ever smaller segments. There are a number of possible explanations for this trend towards greater fragmentation, but it seems that customers – consumers and organizations – are increasingly seeking specific solutions to their buying 'problems'. Organizations cannot just offer a choice these days; they have to be able to meet their customers' precise requirements. Relationships will increasingly need to be built on the platform of individualized marketing, where the customer and the supplier in

Figure 2.7   Levels of segmentation emphasis

	Mass marketing	Traditional segmentation	Needs-based segmentation	Micro-segmentation	One-to-one marketing
Vendor		**Relationship with customer**			**Partner**
Key focus:	Product	Segment	Segment	Micro-segment	Customer
Market segment:	One segment-homogeneous market	Segments based on demographics, etc.	Segments based on psychographics, lifestyles, etc.	Narrowly defined, high value segments	Segment of one
Product/service offering:	One standard offering	Offerings modified to segment	Integrated offerings to segment needs	Integrated offerings to micro-segment needs	Mass-customization
Communication:	Broadcast marketing	Tailored messages	Tailored messages	Highly tailored messages	Dialogue marketing
Measure of success:	Market share	Segment share	Segment share	Segment share	Share of customer

Source: Adapted from Arthur D. Little[17]

effect create a unique and mutually satisfactory exchange process. The Internet now provides a powerful means of involving customers much more closely in the marketing process through enabling dialogue rather than one-way communication.

Over the last decade, much attention has been directed at the leading edge work by consultants Don Peppers and Martha Rogers.[18] Their work has excited many managers with respect to the potential for shifting from a mass market to an individualized or 'one-to-one' marketing environment. Exploiting e-commerce opportunities and the fundamental economic characteristics of the Internet can enable a much deeper level of segmentation granularity than is affordable in most other channels.

However, segment granularity needs to be examined in the company and industry context in which it is being considered. In some cases, especially in an e-commerce environment, a migration to a 'one to one' or a 'one to few' may be undertaken relatively easily. However, in more traditional businesses, more 'macro' forms of segmentation may be relevant. It is worth making the point that many companies in the B2B arena have for a long time adopted one-to-one marketing through a key account management system, although it has not been referred to as such.

An obvious but important point is that 'one-to-one' marketing does not imply adopting a 'one-to-one' approach with every single customer. Rather, it suggests understanding customers in terms of their economic importance and then adjusting the marketing approach to reflect the importance of different customer groups according to their existing and potential profitability. Peppers and Rogers emphasize this in their work, however, it is sometimes disregarded when a discussion of one-to-one marketing is underway.

Permission marketing is especially relevant in the context of one-to-one relationships. Seth Godin of Yoyodyne Entertainment introduced the concept of permission marketing. This involves consumers giving marketers permission to send them certain types of promotional messages. Proponents of permission marketing argue that the biggest problem with mass marketing is that it fights for people's attention by interrupting them. Potential customers are often annoyed when their most coveted commodity – time – is interrupted. Permission marketing involves offering consumers incentives to accept information and promotional activity voluntarily. By reaching out only to those individuals who have signalled an interest in learning more about a product, permission marketing enables companies to develop long-term relationships with customers, create trust, build brand awareness and greatly improve the chances of making a sale.[19] However, most individuals are unlikely to join a permission marketing programme just to make some monetary benefit. The main attraction is to receive promotional offers consistent with one's needs.[20]

Interactive technology means that marketers can now inexpensively engage consumers in one-to-one relationships fuelled by two-way 'conversations' played out with mouse clicks on a computer, or touch-tone buttons pushed to signal an interactive voice response unit, or surveys completed by mail or at a kiosk. Although permission marketing can be implemented in any direct medium, it has emerged as a serious idea only with the advent of the Internet due to the low cost of marketer-to-consumer communication and the rapid feedback mechanisms due to instantaneous two-way interactions.[21] Permission marketing will have an increasingly important role to play in personalizing communications in a one-to-one context.

Mass customization

Closely related to one-to-one marketing is the concept of mass customization. One-to-one marketing requires individual solutions for individual buying problems. Customers may not want the physical product to be differentiated, although many do, but require the accompanying service package to be tailored. Today, efforts are being directed at developing cost-effective strategies to achieve what is now termed 'mass customization'.[22] Mass customization is the ability to take standard components, elements or modules and, through customer-specific combinations or configurations, produce a tailored solution.

In a manufacturing sector the aim would be to produce generic semi-finished products in volume to achieve economies of scale and then finish the product later to meet individual customers' requirements. An oft-quoted example of mass customization is the Japanese National Bicycle Company, which offers customers the opportunity to configure their own bicycle from different style, colour, size and components options. Within two weeks the company delivers the tailored bike to the customer. The company has become the market leader in Japan as a result of this marketing and logistics innovation.

In an on-line environment, mass customization is made possible because it enables information about an individual's particular interests and needs to be captured each time they interact with the company, stored and processed to guide the specific offers made to them in the future. With each successive interaction, the company can learn more about that specific customer and adapt their offer to be even more suited to their particular needs and circumstances. In a sense, the customer is progressively teaching the company about themselves in order to receive a service that is ever more tailored to their needs and that is thus of greater value. The understanding the firm gains of its customers can then be used not only to drive the offers made to them in the immediate term but also to drive the longer term strategic development of the organization, the alliances it forms with other organizations and the products and services it offers in the future.

Peppers and Rogers, working with consultant Joseph Pine, distinguish between the production process of mass customization and the parallel marketing approach of 'one-to-one' strategy:

A company that aspires to give customers exactly what they want must ... use technology to become two things: a mass customizer that efficiently provides individually customized goods and services, and a one-to-one marketer that elicits information from each customer about his or her specific needs and preferences. The twin logic of mass customization and one-to-one marketing binds producer and consumer

together in what we call a learning relationship – an ongoing connection
that becomes smarter as the two interact with each other, collaborating
to meet the consumer's needs over time.[23]

As well as ensuring that the organization develops in line with the
needs of its most valuable customers, mass customization helps
retain customers. The tailored service the customer receives is a result
of their 'teaching' the company about themselves over the lifetime of
their relationship. To receive the same service from a competitor
would involve that organization having to learn about them from
'scratch', which will of course take time. Thus, if a company practices
mass customization effectively, its customers are presented with a
significant switching cost if they defect to a competitor organization.

Under mass customization, the value proposition the organization
offers its customers ceases to simply reside in the individual products
it offers them. Rather it lies in the company becoming a trusted partner who can be relied upon to meet their ongoing individual needs
over time, helping them to live their lives. Thus it also becomes more
difficult for customers to make simple direct comparisons between
one company and another on a product-by-product basis, helping to
alleviate downward price pressure and commoditization.

Achieving mass customization involves attending to three areas.
First, the company needs to set up the technological infrastructure
to enable it to set up a dialogue with its individual customers
and capture their responses. Second, it needs to have the means of
processing that data if this dialogue is to enable the firm to gain an
ever better understanding of its customers as individuals. Finally, it
needs to be able to structure its processes such that the organization's manufacturing of products or services is customized to the
needs of individual customers. These present fundamental changes
to most organizations but, in the emerging network economy, their
implementation not only offers high rewards, in many cases it will
also be imperative for survival.

Communities or segments?

One of the inherent problems in segmentation is that customers may
not conform to the neat market segments that companies allocate
them to. Consider the dilemma faced by an airline in allocating a
specific individual customer to a market segment and understanding their purchasing behaviour.

The airline has only a limited amount of information on this
particular customer's travel with that airline based on details of

frequent flyer or executive club activity. If the airline has records of three business class and three economy tickets for this customer – what are they to make of this?

The airline may then develop a data warehouse that captures all that passenger's travel with the airline, including travel not registered on the frequent flyer card database (by, for example, requesting details of the passport number each time the customer takes a flight). As a result, they identify the passenger has made five business class trips and three economy trips – what are they to make of this?

If they incentivize the customer to keep a complete diary of all airline travel or can collect the information through market research, the picture for this frequently travelling executive may be different. Suppose the full diary for all airlines shows the following return trips: 2 First Class, 8 Business Class and 12 Economy.

Making sense of this is difficult until you understand that the customer is a member of a number of different communities. His travel type may depend on whether he is acting as a business executive, a member of a sports club or a family member. Even within a given community he may purchase different types of travel. A brief interview with this executive elicited the following 'rules' for his travel purchase behaviour within each community (see box).

The airline, armed with this knowledge as well as 'share of wallet' information on the relative use of their airline and competitive airlines can then mould their CRM programme on an individual basis to such clients. The challenge is to identify if this information can be

---

Business executive community member: always travels business class (exceptions: his director sent him first class when he had to travel on his birthday and he had just sold a huge project to a client; when he is on overseas business trip he may be accompanied by family member and travel economy class provided the costs to the company of both tickets do not exceed one business class fare).

Family community member: always travels on cheapest economy fare on vacations as prefers to spend money on quality accommodation on arrival; but only on flights up to 12 hours (exceptions: for trips of over 12 hours to Asia and Australasia the family travel on the cheapest business class tickets available; for his 10th wedding anniversary he travelled on first class with his wife to the USA).

Sports club community member: always travels on cheapest economy fare with his football club (exceptions: none. The club never chooses a location where cheap tickets cannot be purchased for travel to it).

collected and acted upon in a cost-effective manner. Acquiring such customer knowledge on *all* customers, even the highest value ones, is not likely to be cost-effective in most businesses. However, the insights gained from selective market research can be used to identify customers who are members of such communities.

Focusing on customer strategy

Customer strategy involves taking the business strategy and identifying which customer the enterprise needs to focus on. It starts with a definition of the target market to be served and how it plans to serve this market. In an intermediated market, the enterprise recognizes that it may have a number of customer groups and each of these needs to be fully considered. Regardless of whether the customer group comprises distributors, intermediaries or final consumers, an effective customer strategy requires each group to be segmented in an appropriate manner.

The market segmentation process involves consideration of the alternative bases for segmenting the market and determining the appropriate level of segmentation – macro-, micro- or one-to-one. In the next chapter we provide an example of a UK electricity supplier that historically had treated all residential customers in the same way. About six mailings per annum were sent to every customer and no attempt had been made at segmentation. The review of customer economics outlined in Chapter 3 illustrates how macro-, micro- and one-to-one segmentation approaches were all applicable depending on the segment or sub-segment economics.

The identification of segmentation bases and the appropriate level of segment granularity should involve a high degree of creativity. Companies should constantly be considering alternative ways of segmenting the market and seeking ways in which they can create differential advantage over their competitors. Readers needing a more detailed discussion on market segmentation should consult a standard text on market segmentation such as McDonald and Dunbar's work[24] or one of the references in the reading list at the end of this book. Once the organization has identified and chosen the appropriate customer segments to target and the level of segment granularity, the enterprise needs to focus on the customer relationships within them. Here permission marketing, mass customization and whether a customer fits into more than one segment or community need to be considered.

Customer strategy is not only concerned with which customer segments to serve but also what products and services to sell to them. Although the latter is primarily a concern of product policy and marketing planning some brief discussion should be made here.

Product and service options for a company can be conveniently divided into existing products and services and new products and services. When these options are placed in a matrix with present and new products on one axis and present and new markets or customer segments on the other this gives rise to the following four broad product/market options:

- concentrating on marketing existing products or services to existing markets
- developing new products or services for existing markets
- developing new markets or customer segments for existing products or services
- diversifying into new products for new markets or customer segments.

Each of these broad customer strategies represents a number of specific opportunities. These are shown in Figure 2.8.

A final issue to consider under the heading of customer strategy is the need for creativity and innovation. In an era of unparalleled change

Figure 2.8 Review of product/service and market/customer segment options

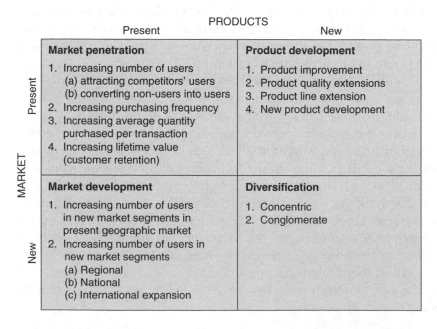

and 'hyper-competition' managers need to pay special attention to this, as the traditional approach of identifying and responding to new customer needs is not enough. Figure 2.9 illustrates the dangers of an approach that is highly dependent on traditional market research as a source of new initiatives. Here the value opportunities are greatly restricted. Companies such as 3M and Sony rely just as heavily on their own creativity and intuition with respect to new market developments as they do on customer research. Customers often cannot clearly articulate their future needs. Companies who do not think outside their traditional mindset will find their customers going to those who do.

Figure 2.9   The danger of 'current focus'

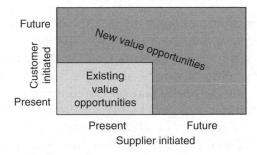

A good example of such creativity is the initiative launched by Starbucks when they introduced their mobile wireless service that enabled customers to have wireless Internet connection in Starbucks retail coffee outlets (see box).

- Launched in August 2002, Starbucks' 'T-Mobile Hot Spot service' offers wireless Internet connectivity in about 2,000 locations in the US and Europe.
- Uses technology to enhance its core offer – the Starbucks experience.
- $5 for a cup of coffee and $49.99 per month for a wireless access connection.
- The average network customer is in the store 45 minutes, which exceeds average, 90% outside peak times; they buy more products and create revenue from the wireless network subscriptions
- Starbucks is becoming the 'other place' in people's lives where they want to be connected to the Internet.

This initiative resulted in a significantly enhanced revenue stream through a subscription service as well as increased revenue in its core business. Further, many customers using this service did so outside peak times. The challenge in the years ahead will be for Starbucks to retain this advantage as wireless LANs (local area networks) become more common.

Aligning business strategy and customer strategy

As noted earlier, alignment and integration of business strategy and customer strategy should be a high priority, especially where they are developed within different functions of the business. This lack of alignment between business strategies may be more common than expected. The author was recently running a CRM workshop as part of a ten-day senior management development programme for a group of country heads and senior executives for a well-known consumer durables brand. One of the country heads reported that the contents of a workshop on business strategy held on the previous day, given by the Group Strategic Planning Director, 'had absolutely no connection to the real-life customer strategy issues and problems in his country'. His colleagues from other countries unanimously agreed with him. Subsequent discussion showed major gaps in alignment between the business strategy and customer strategy and the specific needs of the customers in many of their markets.

Experienced observers of industry, be they managers, consultants or academics will have their own examples of instances where business strategy and customer strategy are not clearly aligned or where they come into conflict (see box for an example).

CRM strategy development

Business and customer strategy represent the major components of CRM strategy. From this earlier discussion it is clear that a given

The Leisure Group

The Leisure Group was formed by two young MBAs who had recently left a leading firm of US strategy consultants. Over a number of years they purchased some thirteen companies operating in the leisure industry. These were organized into three divisions – lawn and garden, youth recreation and sporting goods. A further acquisition, Himalayan Industries – a manufacturer of backpacks based in Monterey, California – was considered for purchase. Despite a clear business strategy and a set of acquisition criteria at group level, which indicated that the candidate was a poor strategic fit and far too small in terms of turnover, this business was acquired.

Prior to the acquisition, Himalayan's progress had been restricted by a poor choice of distribution partner, inadequate marketing and restrictions in capacity in the company's operations. Following the acquisition of Himalayan, an extremely expensive marketing campaign was introduced. A completely new range of backpacking equipment was designed. The marketing programme was complex in terms of different quality levels being introduced and a significant number of new product lines being developed.

Expensive design and marketing consultants were involved and a considerable amount of time was spent on the programme by the parent company's top management. Although the company's existing sales were very small in relationship to other companies within the group, a disproportionate amount of resources and effort was placed on the customer strategy and marketing activity.

However, from a group perspective, the company should not have been acquired in the first place as it was not a good fit with the existing product lines and placed additional stress on the already heavily extended group sales force. In terms of the company's business strategy, the amount of resources and money spent on the customer strategy was not justified by the future business prospects of the new subsidiary.

This lack of fit between business strategy and customer strategy resulted in the subsidiary's subsequent sale 'because it resulted in the diversion of working capital that would be better placed in more profitable businesses'. Not long afterwards the parent company experienced huge losses and collapsed. The clear conclusion was that business strategy and customer strategy were not aligned and that the business leaders were better at acquiring companies than effectively running them.

organization needs to consider its current position within its industry and the future role it realistically can play within it. Central to this will be making decisions about customer choice, customer characteristics and segment granularity. This includes determining the extent to which an individualized customer, or one-to-one, approach is appropriate and affordable for the enterprise and determining the completeness of customer information that exists and is potentially available. Such decisions should be based on both the present situation and the possible situation in the future. In this section we discuss how a consideration of business and customer strategies leads to CRM strategy development.

The evolving nature of the competitive situation and the likely costs inherent in creating change need to be carefully assessed as part of the CRM strategy development process. The CRM strategy matrix, shown in Figure 2.10, provides a tool for considering a company's present and future circumstances.[25] The vertical axis of the matrix in this figures shows *completeness of customer information*, a combination of (a) how much information is held on customers and (b) how sophisticated is the analysis of that information. The horizontal axis shows the *degree of customer individualization*, the extent to which the organization uses whatever information it has on customers to give

Figure 2.10   The CRM strategy matrix

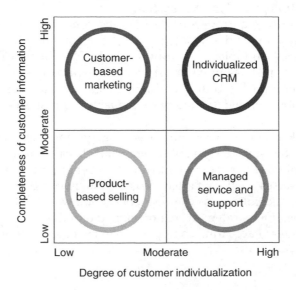

them individualized or customized service. The matrix shows four broad strategic positions which may be appropriate for a particular organization depending on the business issues outlined above and its specific circumstances.

Over time there is a general trend for organizations to want to migrate towards the top right-hand corner of the matrix. A shift from the lower left to upper right position reflects a movement away from a transactional approach, a very unsophisticated form of CRM (some would say it is not really CRM at all) to individualized CRM, a much more sophisticated form. We would argue that there may be a strategic advantage in your company being the first to reach this individualized or one-to-one position within a given industry as competitors will have to offer significant inducements to get your customers to switch.

The rate at which different industries are maturing to this position of course varies: supermarkets and telecommunications suppliers are fairly advanced. However, it is may be some time before we see a used car dealer develop a loyalty card programme! The most advanced Internet booksellers and electrical component distributors are examples of where top right-hand corner positions have been achieved. Each business will need to consider where it should be now and where it should migrate to in the future. These four strategy options in the matrix are now outlined in more detail.

Product-based selling

At the bottom left-hand position of the CRM strategy matrix is 'product-based selling'. Here the organization has information about transactions and wishes to do simple analysis of variables such as product sales over time and channel productivity. There may be a customer mailing list, but there is probably little or no detailed information on individual customers.

For product-based selling a number of simple things can be done to improve marketing using a relatively unsophisticated database. For example, simple query and analysis tools can be used directly on one or more of the existing operational systems of the organization or, for more sophisticated analysis, operational data can be combined with additional data (often taken from external sources) using specialist tools. These may be used to undertake analyses such as:

- simple mailing list analysis
- elementary segmentation based on product or channels
- simple query and reporting for sales productivity and channel productivity.

With product-based selling, the emphasis is on product and channels, not on the customer. It is highly unlikely that any segmentation undertaken would be based on the customer except in single product organizations or those with a very simple set of related products. The level of sophistication in terms of CRM is fairly low. Nevertheless, this approach may represent a perfectly appropriate strategy for some organizations.

A retailer that has not yet adopted a loyalty card programme is an example of a business having a product-based selling strategy. Although it may have a significant amount of information about activity right down to the individual transaction level which will allow it to predict sales revenues and optimize stock levels, it cannot connect these sales back to the customer.

It is interesting to note that some high street retailers who have outsourced the management of their store payment or credit cards do not have control of the information and as a result cannot make this customer connection easily or affordably. Organizations are increasingly finding that power in the supply chain is held by the organization that has the ownership of customer information.

Managed service and support

On the bottom right-hand corner of the matrix is 'managed service and support'. In practice, most companies tend to move from product-based selling to managed service and support as their first extension of CRM by setting up a call centre or help desk. Here the business is seeking both to identify which specific customers it wishes to retain and to place greater emphasis on its most important customers.

Essentially this approach is about applying customer service to selling. The business is seeking to build improved relationships with customers through enhanced levels of service and support, e.g. through call centres or telemarketing. This form of CRM does not need comprehensive information on customers, but the communication is person to person or individualized.

This usually involves using more sophisticated applications on relatively unsophisticated customer data. Examples of such applications include:

- contact centres/help desks
- telemarketing
- contact management
- sales force automation.

Utility companies represent examples of this approach. Here the customer service staff of, for example, a telco have basic customer data – such as name, address, phone number and most frequently called numbers. They deal with individuals by phone and they can tailor individual service to customers on a person-to-person basis. A further example is direct banking or insurance companies who know quite a lot about their customers, but do not make this information available to their sales force (to enable them to change pricing to take account of customers' risk profile or to make marketing decisions based on customers' expected lifetime value).

Customer-based marketing

In the top left-hand corner of the matrix is 'customer-based marketing'. Organizations undertaking customer-based marketing now shift their emphasis from individual product sales to a focus on the customer. Here the organization seeks to develop a more detailed understanding of its customers. It may also wish to undertake a range of analyses including:

- customer profitability
- competitor responses
- loyalty and churn management
- credit scoring
- customer loyalty
- fraud detection and management
- risk management
- delinquency detection.

Not all of these analyses will be relevant for every company. Their relevance will depend on the industry sector, the company's position in the market and other factors.

To move from product management to customer management, an organization will want to undertake detailed segmentation and analysis of customers in order to calculate customer profitability, churn or retention, etc. so it can:

- make different offers to different customers – the essence of CRM
- monitor the organization's progress towards this goal
- identify individual cross-selling and upselling opportunities to maximize customer profitability.

While customer-based marketing is a more advanced form of CRM, those businesses that adopt this approach will not be offering the highly individualized customer service and support found on the right-hand side of the matrix.

Supermarkets are a good example of companies that have been able to exploit customer-based marketing. Using the information about customer behaviour collected at the checkout via loyalty cards and also video recordings of customers' movements within stores, they can draw conclusions about store layout, position of products on the shelves, presentation and packaging and so on. They can then alter layout and placement and also mail out tailored offers to individual customers. This information enables them to:

- alter the mix of products on a shelf on a store-by-store basis to take account of varying socio-demographics
- identify and develop additional 'own-label' products that exactly match the needs and aspirations of customers with high net lifetime value
- develop and promote new products more effectively.

The detailed information that is now being held by supermarkets is shifting the balance of power from the manufacturers of branded products to the supermarket, as they are increasingly able to sell this information to manufacturers. Having reached this position, the most advanced supermarkets such as Tesco have now identified ways to move towards the upper right-hand side of the matrix through more individualized interactions with their customers.

Individualized CRM

In the top right-hand corner of the matrix is 'individualized CRM'. This usually requires both sophisticated data platforms and sophisticated applications running on them. Such applications include:

- advanced one-to-one marketing (both business-to-business and business-to-consumer)
- advanced computer telephony integration (CTI) (which enables the business to use the computer interactively during telephone contact with a customer creating individualized service to the customer)
- multi-channel integration
- advanced web services and Internet (perhaps using tools such as collaborative browsing which enable the customer and the company to browse web pages together from different locations).

In particular, this strategic position is relevant for organizations that are seeking to adopt a wide range of channel options. These may include direct selling, selling through indirect channels such as distributors or brokers and sales over the Internet using electronic commerce. This latter channel option represents considerable opportunities for building one-to-one marketing systems which can learn from electronic interactions with customers and which develop a differentiated service, look and feel for every individual customer that comes onto the system. At the most advanced level of individualized CRM, the business is able to respond instantaneously to customer enquiries and as the communication or transaction with the customer takes place, information feeds back into the operational systems. The whole process becomes a dynamic form of CRM rather than a static one.

Organizations adopting the individualized CRM will seek to offer a complete, individualized and customized service. This could be via telephone, mail or face-to-face, or it may take the form of electronic commerce via the Internet where customers can use a web browser to make enquiries or purchases. An illustration of a company adopting this approach is RS Components (see box below).

Case 2.2:   RS Components: Case study overview

RS Components, an international distribution company, is an example of an organization that has shifted its focus to individualized CRM. Its electrical component catalogue weighed 4 kilos, was nearly 20 cm (8 inches) thick and contained over 100 000 products. Upgraded quarterly and despatched to over 150 000 account customers, the cost of the printed catalogue was a good reason to embrace first a CD ROM version and then an Internet site. With a direct presence in 13 countries, the company's ability to find and service customers was constrained economically by the costs associated with catalogue-based business. Today, the Internet gives it global reach, with close to zero engagement costs.

The drive to create a new channel to market, not just an ordering channel, led RS Components to choose BroadVision as its technology solution. Working with BroadVision and its other technology partners, RS developed an Internet trading channel capable of migrating, acquiring, developing and retaining online customers. The sophisticated web site took just five months to implement and contained a personalized e-purchasing solution for RS's range of business customers.

A key differentiator for the Internet site is the customer personalization, which is driven by profile questions such as job type, industry type and product interests. On entering the site, each customer has his or her own dynamically generated welcome page showing tailored editorial, advertising and new product alerts relevant to that particular customer.

The Internet site has been designed to provide individualized relationship marketing including direct customer access to more than 10 000 documents in the RS technical data library. With its customer service, personalized operation, downloadable technical information and tools for navigation (to make finding the required products easier), there is clearly an improved value proposition for customers. RS confirms that the site has exceeded its performance expectations.

The full case study is at the end of this chapter (see p. 97)

This form of CRM does not have to be personalized (i.e. have direct person-to-person contact with the customer) but it must be individualized. For CRM to be individualized the business needs to develop IT systems that 'know' the customer. Here the business develops a corporate memory of the customers it is dealing with. The customers may not be personally known to the business but whenever they contact it (and whomever they contact) they feel that the business knows all about them. Relationships between customer and supplier are continually strengthened through on-going interactions. In addition, customers are likely to build an emotional bond with the organization because they have invested time in the relationship and they may be unwilling to invest that time again with competitors.

Migration paths for CRM

Using the CRM strategy matrix we have explained that most organizations will need to shift towards more sophisticated forms of CRM. Some organizations have already successfully implemented 'managed service and support' or 'customer-based' marketing. A few, such as the most developed Internet booksellers, have already adopted advanced forms of individualized relationship marketing. However, many companies still need to develop from the position of product-based selling.

Organizations starting with product-based selling should initially be concerned with integrating their key existing customer-facing activities. They need to look forward in time to see what business benefits would be realizable through a more advanced form of CRM. A range of possible transitions is shown in Figure 2.11.

The choice of migration paths from product-based selling will depend heavily upon the specific industry and business issues outlined earlier. Two paths are common. In some cases the transition will emphasize building increased customer intimacy through elements such as call centres and computer telephony integration – Path 1. In other cases, it will involve developing greater database

Figure 2.11 Transition paths for CRM

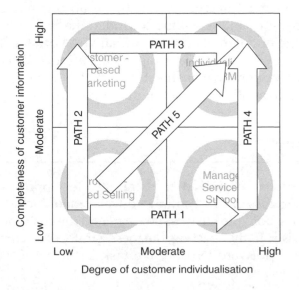

completeness and exploiting clearly targeted but relatively simple marketing approaches – Path 2. This latter path focuses on improving quality, management and utilization of data.

In many industries there will ultimately be opportunities to shift towards one-to-one applications through individualized CRM. As yet, relatively few organizations have adopted this position. There are two reasons why some organizations might not want, or not be able, to do so:

- Some lack the necessary direct interaction with customers: for example, a manufacturer who sells through wholesalers and/or retailers, or through a dealer network may not have direct contact with final customers.
- Others are not culturally ready: even if they had comprehensive information about customers, they would not make real use of it. This may be because they are more focused on selling an existing product than understanding customers' needs; or because they are organized around individual product lines with little sharing of information between product managers.

Those organizations wishing to adopt one-to-one marketing applications may do so by migrating from customer-based marketing – Path 3, or from managed service and support – Path 4. RS Components is an example of the latter transition. A few organizations may undertake a more radical transformation directly from transaction-based selling to individualized relationship marketing – Path 5. This radical shift will be easier for a start-up or smaller company without existing investment in legacy systems, or an organization that has strong leadership and is willing to undertake heavy investment to make a range of different and new initiatives work together concurrently. Whichever path is taken, the organization will need to choose technology solutions that enable it to grow from one position on the CRM matrix to another without undue difficulty.

Summary

This chapter has examined the strategy development process in CRM. The process of CRM strategy development includes a detailed exploration of both the business strategy and the customer strategy of the enterprise. If the existing business strategy is comprehensive, thorough and forward-looking, the task is to then ensure that the subsequent customer strategy is clearly aligned and integrated with it. If the existing business strategy is incomplete, unclear or fails to consider the future business environment, then the role of CRM is to ensure that top management's attention is directed at addressing this.

Once an appropriate business strategy is determined and agreed, the customer strategy needs to be addressed. The customer strategy involves examining the existing and potential customer base and making choices about which customers it wishes to serve. This involves undertaking a detailed analysis of their characteristics and determining the most appropriate customer segments to serve. It also involves decisions about segment granularity and whether a macro-, micro- or one-to-one approach to segmentation is needed. Additionally, decisions need to be made about the products and services to be offered to these segments.

CRM strategy development involves considering the present and potential future position that the enterprise has within its industry and determining how it needs to address its customer base. Depending on the industry and competitive issues each organization needs to consider the CRM strategy that is appropriate to it now and in the future. We have described four broad strategic options: product-based selling, customer-based marketing, managed service and support and individualized CRM. The choice of strategy will depend on a number of factors including the completeness of customer information and the extent to which the company can and wishes to use this information to provide customized service. Of these options, individualized CRM is the most sophisticated – it requires collection and analysis of extensive information about customers, the ability and desire to give customers individualized service and it needs to be economically viable. However, the CRM strategy option adopted should not be a static one; most companies should consider a suitable migration path over time from one option to a more advanced one in terms of CRM sophistication.

Once an appropriate business strategy has been agreed, market segmentation is probably the most important element of the CRM strategy development process. A review of all the successful business strategy assignments undertaken by one of the world's leading strategy consulting firms concluded that over 50 per cent of them were based on creative segmentation strategies. Segmentation is also vital to the value creation process, which we consider in the next chapter.

Checklist for CRM leaders

CRM leaders need to review the following issues about the *Strategy Development Process.*

Business strategy (including leadership and sponsorship)

1. Senior management in my organization has demonstrated strong leadership in introducing and supporting CRM initiatives
2. There is a strong and well-supported board level executive who is a committed sponsor of the organization's CRM initiatives
3. Senior management works together in a united manner and resolves cross-functional conflicts
4. My organization has a vision, mission, purpose, or statement of direction that clarifies its commitment to quality and customer focus and that is clearly understood by staff. My organization has a clear set of values that support the vision and these are shared by most of our staff
5. My organization develops and reviews strategic and annual business plans that incorporate an analysis of market trends, customer characteristics, industry evolution, the competitive landscape and technology impacts
6. My organization has a clear view on the value discipline on which it competes: customer intimacy, operational excellence or product leadership
7. The future impacts of electronic commerce and shifts in role of channels and intermediaries are considered on a regular basis by senior management
8. The overall strategic plan serves as the basis for the annual business plans of the organization and its functional departments
9. Managers and supervisors understand their specific responsibilities in carrying out the actions in the strategic plan
10. My organization comprehensively reviews and improves its management systems at least annually to an international, industry-specific or internally developed standard.

Customer strategy

1. My organization has a clear view on which customers it wishes to serve and which ones it does not wish to serve
2. My organization considers not only its immediate customers but also its customer's customer in making its marketing decisions
3. My organization has done a thorough and recent segmentation of its customer base

4. My organization has selected the appropriate level of segmentation of its customer base, i.e. macro- segments, micro-segments or one-to-one
5. We consider customer segments in terms of value preferences of benefits sought, in addition to more general customer characteristics
6. My organization customizes its product or service offer to different segments where appropriate
7. At least annually my organization seeks new customer opportunities beyond its existing offer to customers
8. Our business strategy and customer strategy are closely aligned
9. We have considered the appropriate degree of customer individualization given our position in the market and the nature of our competition
10. My organization has plans for future customer individualization and customer information requirements.

Each issue should be considered in terms of:
Rating for our organization   (5 = applies fully; 0 = does not apply at all)
Importance to our organization (5 = very important; 0 = no importance)

Case 2.1   DnB Nor Bank pursues an enterprising strategy with Teradata

The company

With about NOK 1200 billion in assets, DnB Nor Bank is the largest financial institution in Norway, after the recent merger between DnB and Union Bank of Norway (UBN). It currently serves almost two million customers and commercial businesses through a highly acclaimed financial distribution system. Customers have a choice of channels through which to interact with the bank, including a branch network, ATMs, call centres, investment centres, business centres and an Internet bank. The combined use of traditional methods of service delivery and new technologies reinforces the company's longstanding reputation for local knowledge and expertise.

DnB offers a conventional mix of banking, mortgage and other credit services, with a growing emphasis on savings and investment. Mutual funds, stocks and bonds are also offered to retail customers. The company's aim is to become the automatic first choice for retail customers and local industry throughout the country.

In pursuit of its business goals, DnB has set upon a decisive customer strategy: to create, retain and expand customer relations in order to increase the bank's and the group's profitability. Product and service development is based on the company's regional bank concept and driven by a desire to meet the total needs of customers.

The challenge

In 1995, as a major player in the highly competitive and fast changing financial services sector, UBN faced unprecedented challenges. An escalation in the types of channels and services available was fuelling trends of diminished customer margins and customer loyalty. The take-up of Internet banking by personal and business customers, for example, was to be matched by an incursion of rivals into the Norwegian market. The bank recognized that to improve margins and grow profitability, it needed to move away from a product orientation and towards a customer and event focus.

Customers were becoming increasingly sophisticated and heterogeneous in their banking requirements and behaviours. They wanted more control over the management of their money and easy access to new financial products and services. The provision of greater individualization, however, necessitated greater customer intelligence and customer responsiveness.

A substantial decline in the frequency of branch visits by customers (at minimum, weekly in 1984 but less than monthly by 2001) meant less opportunity for UBN to elicit 'soft' data and to present a human face on what are often perceived as impersonal business interactions. The strategic importance of retaining and growing existing customer relationships was evident by a significant bias in the bank's customer portfolio: 20 per cent of customers were generating 80 per cent of profits.

'Our biggest challenge was finding complete information on our customers and making it actionable', says Torbjorn Gjelsrik, Head of Datawarehousing at DnB Nor. 'Most of our information was derived from various production systems that contained insufficient customer information. It was an information labyrinth and we didn't know how to get the right data out or even how to ask the right questions'.

The local branch network that rendered the advantage of close customer contact operated on multiple computer platforms and systems, with disparate data scattered throughout the decentralized branches. The bank could not easily gather, store and analyse customer-specific information, which limited its ability to understand individual profitability by customer, product and service.

The bank wanted a means of identifying and exploiting the drivers of customer satisfaction and loyalty in a real-time operating environment. It needed a radical, customer-led solution. By tracking customer trends and understanding individual profitability, UBN reasoned it could improve revenue and margins through cross-selling and increasing customer use of its most profitable products and services.

The solution

In 1996, UBN obtained a licence to build an enterprise data warehouse to consolidate its disparate data sources and thus capitalize on its key business assets: a substantial customer base; the country's best financial distribution system; and a strong financial brand image. Teradata, a division of NCR, was chosen as the principal technology partner. The data warehouse runs on a Teradata database and a massively parallel processing system also developed by Teradata.

The data warehouse captures and retains all available information about customers from the bank's core data and accounting systems, including relationships in other companies in the group and various subsidiaries (unit trusts, insurance and financing), transactions over the last six years, marketing communications history, selected demographics and details from customer survey responses. Strict compliance with data protection legislation ensures that data collection and usage conforms to current codes of privacy, security and ethical practice.

More than 1.5 terabytes of data are held in a responsive, easy-to-use format. Remote users are connected to the central database via TCP/IP. Teradata replicates information and copies it to the decentralized databases. Similarly, updated information from the branches is fed into the central database in real time by front-end staff and systematically through data-specific daily and weekly updates and a monthly main refresh. To ensure UBN has a scalable and flexible solution, Teradata's service provision also encompasses business and information discovery, technology design and integration, database design and data transformation.

With this profound emphasis on data usage, data quality is crucial to the bank's success. Staff are trained in data discipline and data management to avoid what it's CRM Manager, Kari Opdal refers to as the 'boomerang effect': 'If we gather poor data, or misinterpret or misuse data, it will rebound on us'. She adds that this is particularly true in event-based marketing, where even the strongest brands walk a fine line between enlightening and annoying customers.

According to Opdal, customer segmentation used to be 'mass market' and 'key customers'. 'With Teradata's data warehousing solution, we are now better able to analyse each customer's use of different services, as well as an individual's total net worth to the bank. We can understand the profit and costs associated with each customer, which means better, more customized services for customers and increased profitability for the bank.'

The bank's approach to gaining share of wallet and share of mind is based on lifestage analyses. At any point in time, the customer relationship is seen to reside at a typical life phase. A student, for instance, might be predominantly concerned with utilizing the bank's loan and cash facilities, whereas a senior business executive may need to manage multiple accounts, mortgage repayments and insurance covers. Customer relationship development occurs along a spectrum defined by 'age' at one end and 'situation' at the other. The point of greatest potential for launching a lifetime relationship with a customer is when their financial service needs become a 'mixed bag' involving, for example, credit, savings and daily banking activity.

Importantly, the Teradata warehouse supports the proactive use of data to drive customer value, customer care and customer service. Using information from the data warehouse, the bank can identify changes in a customer's behaviour or circumstances that may indicate a change in their financial service needs. The customer is then contacted via the relevant media or distribution channel in order that the bank can find out about the apparent changes, rather than make a specific product offer.

Viewing the customer as a person with individual needs and circumstances and not solely as an account with costs and risks, is integral to DnB's philosophy. The bank's dialogue programmes, loyalty programmes and product packages reflect customers' banking habits and status. The first-home loan product, for example, targets the first-time buyer segment by offering superior rates of interest normally reserved for experienced mortgage holders. 'Rather than penalize young customers for lack of a credit history, we prefer to look ahead at their value potential', explains Opdal. This insightful price benefit secured first year-end total loans disbursed of NOK 3200 million.

The results

Managing customer relationships and company resources on the basis of complete and dynamic customer profiles, as opposed to piecemeal 'snap-shots', has enhanced the bank's market relevance and performance. UBN can supply relationship markets with customized servicing and a mass market with the main focus on standardized servicing. For example, the launch of a customer loyalty programme targeted at the bank's most prof-itable customers saw approximately 70 per cent take up membership, far exceeding the typical 2 to 4 per cent response rate of traditional direct mail campaigns. Replacing a batch-driven approach with a real-time approach has delivered comparable improvement across other campaigns. Up to 60 per cent sales conversion rates have been achieved on event-based market-ing activities. 'Knowing which customers to target saves us time and money', says Opdal.

Company-wide use of the powerful data warehouse has enabled more cost-effective interaction between distribution channels as well as the deliv-ery of more integrated customer strategies. Within the first full year of its operation, investment costs were recouped and margins were up. The development of in-house skills and knowledge sharing has had a positive impact on employee motivation, satisfaction and productivity, which contin-ues to reverberate throughout the customer experience.

Multiple usage of the data warehouse (user communities now extend beyond Marketing and IT to include Technology, Finance, Accounting and various Business Units) has greatly enhanced the bank's ability to increase its market share by reacting better and faster to opportunities in the marketplace. With a single, up-to-the-minute view of customer activity and decision support applications at their fingertips, UBN staff across the enterprise can make highly informed judgements with just-in-time precision. For example, teller performance has dramatically improved with the introduction of an inbuilt contact management tool that advises which customers are the most important to contact each day.

The data warehouse has also been instrumental in increasing usage of the bank's automated payment services, saving the bank – and ultimately its customers – unnecessary expense. Bill payment at a teller window costs the bank 25 kroner, whereas that made through a national payment clearing house (which directs funds, as instructed by the customer, from the bank to the appropriate body, such as a utilities provider) costs the bank 4 kroner. A payment made by telephone costs the bank only 2 kroner. UBN uses the data warehouse to monitor what option customers are using to pay their bills and then designs a promotion to encourage those paying at teller windows, for instance, to pay through the clearing house or by phone. By pinpointing which customers are not using the payment service best suited to their needs, calculating the amount of money they lose as a result and persuading them to exploit a better alterative, the bank is able to provide mutual benefit through actual added value.

'Our customers feel they have a relationship with the bank because we live our core values of being actively helpful and accessible', concludes Opdal. 'For this trusting and caring relationship, they are willing to pay a bit more and stay a lot longer.'

This case study was made with Union Bank of Norway prior to its recent merger with DnB. The focus, customer oriented strategy and CRM philosophy is further emphasized in the new bank.

Case 2.2   RS Components: towards individualized CRM with BroadVision

The Company

RS Components, part of Electrocomponents plc, is Europe's leading distributor of electronic and mechanical products. It supports engineers in 160 countries worldwide and has an annual turnover of £760 million (2004). From its humble origins in 1937, supplying spare parts to radio repair shops under the name 'Radiospares', RS has grown to a leadership position that encompasses both traditional trading environments and e-commerce.

RS UK provides an unrivalled choice of 130 000 products held in stock for same-day dispatch. In 1998, with the launch of its award-winning, transactional web site (http://rswww.com), the company gave its customers immediate online access to this extensive product portfolio. The advantages of joining search, order and fulfilment capabilities with the ease, convenience and ubiquity of the Internet have led to demonstrable returns. RS's use of technology to support customer's purchasing policies and processes is a tactical way of exploiting the e-commerce selling model (one supplier to many customers) to secure cost efficiencies and enhance service provision. At a broader strategic level, it is a means of getting closer to customers by converting customer transactions into longer-term, mutually beneficial relationships.

The challenge

RS Components specializes in the provision of office consumables, tools and equipment at short notice. Research has shown that the cost of purchasing low value, high frequency items – such as the maintenance, repair and operations (MRO) items offered by RS – often outweighs the actual cost of the goods themselves. For example, RS's average order value is £100. The average cost to the customer, in terms of internal processing, is between £30 and £150 per paper order. The reason for the disproportionate outlay is that much of the inherent workflow is paper based and manual, or only partially automated. Searching through voluminous catalogues for current product information and keeping track of hundreds of paper requisitions is time- consuming and labour-intensive.

The time taken by management to approve Low Value Orders (LVOs) and by Finance to respond to queries as well as to record and reconcile invoices prolongs LVO processing and adds to administration costs. Understandably, staff often turn to 'maverick', or unauthorized, buying to shortcut the system and obtain the items they need to proceed in performing their tasks. Consequently, such purchases can go undetected by the purchasing function and can even stray outside contracts negotiated with preferred suppliers, costing the company the full retail price.

For many organizations, increasing pressure to improve profit margins and shareholder value has meant a greater focus internally on containing costs and applying controls. The challenge for RS as a competing supplier of LVO items was to exploit this trend by offering a more cost-effective proposition that would also satisfy the unmet customer need for more stringent purchasing control.

In 1997, RS Components saw the opportunity to operate an electronic channel alongside its traditional routes to market. Historically, RS customers have selected required products from a six-volume printed catalogue and placed orders via the call centre or fax for next-day delivery. They have also enjoyed the option of going to one of the UK's 13 RS Trade Counters (branch outlets) personally to inspect items and take immediate delivery. The addition of a web-enabled channel offered scope for expediting the order process and integrating the multiple channels.

The provision of online ordering would allow customers to undertake their own 'self-service' product selection and purchase, regardless of purchasing office hours. Empowered to purchase direct, users could be encouraged to expand their breadth of purchase and to make RS their exclusive supplier. Moreover, Internet technology could be employed creatively to join the different channels into a single, cross-communicating delivery system. This would permit customers to choose the channel most relevant to them at any point in time and RS to manage customer relationships more effectively. In short, RS would be able to serve existing customers better and to gain market entry to new customer segments.

RS was particularly keen to use e-commerce to develop relationships with larger organizations. However, serving numerous users within a core customer account would mean addressing complex administrative procedures and financial and reporting controls. Because Internet trading can take place at contact level, the web site would have to manage both RS-Customer Organization relationships (T&Cs) and RS-Individual contact level preferences (product interest, job function, etc). Furthermore, until now all RS customers had received the same printed catalogue listing 130 000 plus products in very much a 'one size fits all' approach. RS wanted to personalize the offer so each individual user received offers of fewer items but offers of ones that were more relevant to them. An initial e-commerce goal was, in effect, 'to motivate a change in customer behaviour through relevance'.

In order to achieve rapid profitable growth, RS needed to establish an e-channel that was flexible, scaleable and responsive – it needed an Internet technology solution with a 'personalization engine'.

The solution

The drive to create a new channel to market, not just an ordering channel, led RS Components to choose BroadVision as its technology solution. Working with BroadVision and its other technology partners, RS developed an Internet trading channel capable of migrating, acquiring, developing and retaining online customers. The sophisticated web site took just five months to implement and contained a personalized e-purchasing solution for RS's range of business customers.

The launch of http://rswww.com in February 1998 was an historic event, marking the first business-to-business implementation of BroadVision in the UK and the first UK plc in the industrial distributor market to have a transactional web site integrated with its backend systems. Integration not only meant that the full range of RS products was available online, but that any purchasing controls already set up between RS and a client company were acknowledged and observed. It also meant that customers wishing to move to ordering RS products online were spared any integration costs and were able to bypass the need for investment in e-procurement software or in integrating e-commerce within their own ERP systems. They could also elect to receive a consolidated monthly summary of invoices generated, complete with a breakdown of individual users' spend for management information purposes.

The web site's design catered to the different needs of the two communities of potential site users: purchasing departments and 'user choosers'. Purchasing departments, which are primarily concerned with supplier selection, commercial terms and service level agreements (SLAs), are principally focused on reducing costs. 'User choosers', on the hand, are technical staff such as R&D personnel, production technicians and maintenance engineers whose main interest is speed and efficiency.

The e-channel enabled user choosers to make direct purchases under the control of the business rules set by the purchasing department. They could initiate purchases and receive goods within 24 hours whereas, if they were to raise purchase orders in the traditional way through the purchasing department, it would often be several weeks before they received the item ordered. Moreover, ordering the goods directly increased the level of accuracy and efficiency in the purchasing process, in terms of communicating correct stock numbers and pack sizes and current stock availability. (Inventory information on the site is updated every fifteen minutes.)

The subsequent launch of the PurchasingManager™ functionality in February 2002 replaced basic e-purchasing with total online purchasing control. This powerful procurement tool provided the controls, workflow and reports necessary to ensure organization compliance while empowering end users. A no-cost, no-risk option, it can be implemented immediately as the preferred platform or a stepping-stone to e-procurement.

PurchasingManager™ evolved from an RS analysis of customer needs which identified workflow approval and visibility in reporting as major concerns. Taking account of increasing trade across national boundaries, the programme was designed to work in multiple languages and currencies, including the Euro. As Julian Wright, Group Ecommerce Marketing Manager at RS Components, observes: 'PurchasingManager allows us to talk to groups of customers we couldn't reach before'.

The results

Customer feedback to the new delivery channel has been overwhelmingly positive. Wright highlights the demonstrable link between managing customer perception and managing customer behaviour: 'Customers perceived they were getting faster deliveries, where in fact it was just getting faster at the customer end in placing orders.'

The psychological benefit has delivered measurable returns. Since the introduction of the web site, RS has seen customer retention and campaign efficiency improve. Customer churn levels now firmly reside below the industry average, while marketing response rates of 6–10 per cent excel the 2 per cent rate considered good for direct mail. RS's two metrics of average order frequency and average order value maintain an upward trajectory. RS has gained a significant increase in volume from new customers who are inherently more responsive to a self-service Internet channel. In particular, the Internet enables a level of empowerment not easily replicated through traditional channels. In the last 12 months, over £60 million of revenue has been received via the RS UK web site, http://rswww.com.

The company has completed an International roll out programme of the common BroadVision platform. Localized online trading sites are now live in 66 countries in 16 languages, which include solving technical challenges using Japanese and Chinese characters. A full list of international RS websites can be found at http://www.rs-components.com. E-commerce revenues continue to grow strongly – 43 per cent last year to over £110 million with adoption levels across markets ranging from 15 to ~50 per cent in Japan. Furthermore, the company won the prestigious E-commerce Strategy of the Year Award at the National Business Awards 2003.

Internet-based purchasing reduces the cost of processing LVO purchases by cutting the price of materials and services and lowering inventory costs. The purchase and fulfilment cycle is shortened, giving quicker supply and increased satisfaction. Error reduction via an error detection and correction facility on the web site minimizes the cost of processing returned goods. The web site also places rich information and a search capability at the user's fingertips, while providing the controls and audit trails that Purchasing needs but often lacks in paper systems.

RS's integrated channel offer has improved customer service levels through greater coordination and customer choice. For example, customers can place their orders online and collect from a nominated local RS Trade Counter. Such flexibility is invaluable where jobs are subcontracted or components are used out in the field. Multichannel integration has also enabled RS to build more complete pictures of customers and to apply this understanding proactively. RS now targets customers on the basis of customer behaviour instead of customer profile. User preferences are categorized in terms of product interest rather than region or function. As a result, customer strategies are more pertinent to the user's individual requirements and relationship with RS.

Importantly, RS is making gains right across its client mix. The company is augmenting the value of existing customers through cross-selling and upselling, attracting new contacts among existing customers through enhanced relationships and acquiring new customers in new markets, such as Japan's high-growth community of online purchasers, without incurring heavy expenditure. RS's successful expansion into international markets is attributed to the multilingual nature of the BroadVision engine, which enables RS to supply local language products with local pricing and manage local customer details via a transferable web site format. (RS's competitors rely on more crude systems and are not able to create and operate country-specific sites so readily.) The development of Purchasing-Manager™ has helped strengthen client confidence and supplier credibility, especially with all-important purchasing departments.

By removing non-value added activity and expediting the purchase process, RS has reinforced its own competitiveness and that of its customers. The insightful introduction of an e-channel and integration of multiple channels has served the company twofold: RS is able to provide a more superior service for its customers and a more profitable return for its shareholders.

Chapter 3

The value creation process

The strategy framework for CRM

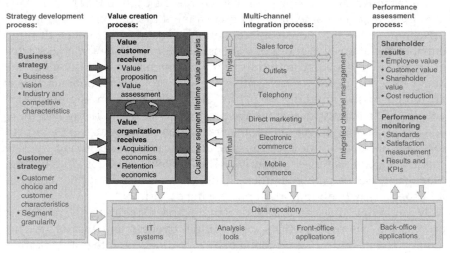

Information management process

Creating customer value is increasingly seen as a key source of competitive advantage. Yet, despite growing attention to this aspect of strategic development, there is remarkably little by way of agreement among managers and commentators on what constitutes 'customer value'. Further, companies typically do not specify in sufficient detail *what* value they seek to deliver to clearly identified customer segments and micro-segments and *how* they propose to deliver this value.

The value creation process consists of three key elements: determining what value the company can provide its customers with (the 'value customer receives'); determining the value the organization receives from its customers (the 'value organization receives'); and, by successfully managing this value exchange, maximizing the lifetime value of desirable customer segments. In summary, the process addresses two key questions:

1. How can we create and deliver value to our customers?
2. How should we maximize the lifetime value of the customers that we want?

However, the emphasis in many companies is on this latter element of value. To these companies, customer value means:

- how much money can we extract from the customer?
- how can we sell them more of the existing products and services they are buying?
- how can we cross-sell them new products and services?

Yet in today's competitive arena where a growing number of businesses vie for a greater share of a finite customer pool, it has become imperative to consider customer value also in terms of customer benefit and how we can ensure the customer proposition is relevant and attractive and that the customer experience is consistently positive.

This chapter examines *the value creation process*. The value creation process is a critical component of CRM as it translates business and customer strategies into specific statements of what value is to be delivered to customers and, consequently, what value is to be delivered to the supplier organization.[1]

The value the customer receives

The value the customer receives from the supplier organization is the total package of benefits, or added values that enhance the core product. As pointed out by Harvard Business School's Theodore Levitt, competition exists not between what companies produce in their factories but between 'what they add to their factory output in the form of packaging, services, advertising, customer advice, financing, delivery arrangements, warehousing, and other things that people value'.[2] The value the customer attributes to these benefits is in proportion to the perceived ability of the offer to solve whatever customer problem prompted the purchase.

In this section we first review the nature of what the customer buys by explaining how the core and augmented product, relationships and brands all contribute to an enterprise's value proposition. We then examine the nature of the value proposition and the value assessment.

The nature of value – what the customer buys

Customers do not really buy products or services – when they buy they expect benefits and value from the *total offer* the company provides. This is not just a semantic point, it is an important distinction which can be strategically vital for the long-term survival of a firm. There are many examples of companies who have taken a narrow view and considered their business purely in terms of the traditional products or services. As a result they were forced out of business when a competitor or competitors effectively reshaped the market by not only getting customers, but by keeping them!

How the core and augmented offer add value

For an effective CRM strategy to be realized an understanding of exactly what the customer is buying is critical. Customers derive benefits from the purchase of either goods or services. This is called 'the offer'. An offer can be visualized as a central core surrounded by a series of tangible and intangible attributes, features and benefits. If you think of the core as offering the customer essential solutions, then the surrounding elements are about services and support of various kinds. These may include packaging, information, finance, delivery, warehousing, advice, quality of the web site, warranty, reliability, styling and so on.

The offer can be viewed at several levels. These include:[3]

- *Core or generic.* For consumer or industrial products this consists of the basic physical product. The core elements for a camera, for example, consist of the camera body, the viewer, the winding mechanism, the lens and the other core basic physical components which make up the camera. For a banking service, the core elements might be safety and transactional utility in the form of deposits and withdrawals.

- *Expected.* This consists of the generic product together with the minimal purchase conditions which need to be met. When a customer buys a videocassette recorder they expect an instruction book which explains how to programme it, a warranty for a reasonable period should it break down and a service network so that it can be repaired.
- *Augmented.* This is the area that enables one offer to be differentiated from another. For example, IBM's hardware has a reputation for excellent after sales service. Because of this high quality service it may be preferred by customers even though the core product – the hardware – may not be the most technologically advanced. They differentiate by 'adding value' to the core, in terms of service, reliability and responsiveness.
- *Potential.* This consists of all potential added features and benefits that are or may be of utility to some buyers. The potential for redefinition of the product gives advantages in attracting new users or enhancing relationships with existing customers. This could make it difficult or expensive for customers to switch to another supplier.

Thus a firm's offer is a complex set of value-based promises and the offer that is developed by the enterprise often needs to be varied according to the target market being considered. People buy to solve problems and they attach value to any offer in proportion to this perception of its ability to achieve their particular ends. In other words, value is assigned by buyers in relationship to the perceived benefits they receive matched against their expectations.

This approach reconciles the company's traditional view of the *product*, seen in the terms of various inputs and processes needed to produce it and the consumer's view of the offer, as being a set of solutions and supporting benefits. Together these elements comprise the total value offer. An example of this is shown in Figure 3.1 based on the personal computer.

The core product for a computer is a machine that permits input, processing, storage and retrieval of data. This is the minimum requirement. The expected product consists of not just the above but also service support, warranty, a recognizable brand name and attractive packaging. The augmented product may include the supply of free diagnostic software, a generous trade-in allowance, user clubs and other augmentations which are valuable to personal computer buyers.

The potential product may consist of future applications including a systems controller, facsimile machine or a music composer.

This concept has had a significant impact on thinking of managers. Its special contribution lies in a recognition that additional elements, beyond that of the product itself, have a profound impact on the value that can be added for customers. Its limitation has been that there has been no structured approach available for managers to use to identify which elements could be added to the core product. Thus the 'total value offer' highlights the importance of extending the core offer but does not provide much guidance on how to do it.

Figure 3.1   The total value offer

Product level	Customer's view	Marketer's view	Personal computer example
Core product	Customer's generic need which must be met	Basic benefits which make product of interest	Data storage, processing, speed of processing, retrieval
Expected product	Customer's minimal set of expectations	Marketer's product decisions on tangible and intangible components	Brand name, warranty, service support, the computer itself
Augmented product	Seller's offering over and above what customer expects or is accustomed to	Marketer's product decisions on tangible and intangible components	Diagnostic software, trade-in allowance, base price plus options, dealer network, user clubs, personal selling
Potential product	Everything that potentially can be done with the product that is of utility to the customer	Marketer's actions to attract and hold customers regarding changed conditions or new applications	Use as a system controller, facsimile machine, music composer, and other areas of application

Potential
Augmented
Expected
Core

Total product is the sum of all four levels

Source: Adapted from Collins[4]

The supplementary services model

The 'supplementary services' model, developed by consultant and former Harvard professor Christopher Lovelock, operationalizes the total value offer by providing specific guidelines on where to seek value enhancement for customers. His model identifies eight key elements of supplementary services that can be used to add value to the core product or service. This provides a far more structured approach for considering the expected, augmented and potential elements of a product or service. He suggests there are potentially dozens of different supplementary services, but most can be classified into the following eight clusters:

- information
- consultation
- order taking
- hospitality services
- safe keeping
- exceptions
- billing
- payment.

Lovelock views these eight supplementary service elements as 'a flower of service' as shown at the top of Figure 3.2. A brief description of these eight clusters and the elements within them, based on his pioneering work,[5] now follows.

1. *Information*: To obtain full value from any service or good, customers need relevant information about it especially if they are first time users. Information elements include directions to the site, hours of opening, pricing and instructions for use. The enterprise may be able to attract and keep many more customers if everybody knows about your product, its capabilities, where to get it and how to obtain maximum value from it.
2. *Consultation*: Providing information suggests a simple response to customers' questions. Consultation, by contrast, involves a dialogue to probe customer requirements and then develop a tailored solution. In B2B markets, 'solution selling', used with expensive industrial equipment and services, is a good example of consultation. Here the sales engineer researches the customer's situation and offers objective advice about the particular package of equipment and systems and service which will yield the best results for the customer.

Figure 3.2   Using the 'Lovelock supplementary services' checklist – a personal lines insurance example

1. Information element
- Easy recognizible phone number
- 24-hour service
- Clear pricing policy
- 'Plain English' wording
- Simple claims handling
- Brochure with full details of product range and features
- Clear details of who we are and where we are
- Easy methods of contact (phone, reply paid form, letter, internet)
- Contact name(s)/team
- Train staff and have systems (e.g. CTI) to deliver
- Mambers' magazine
- Service guarantee

2. Consultation element
- Information dafabase & CTI
- Quick response
- Technically competent
- 'Customer-freindly' help desk and call centre
- Inventory pro-forma
- Exploit cross-selling oppurtunities
- Internet advice (detailed)
- Add on benefits (for specifc segments or customers)
- Security calculations of sum assured
- Legal advice services

3. Order taking element
- Make it easy for different customer segments
  - mail
  - phone
  - fax
  - Internet
  - partially pre-completed forms
- Offer alternative payment mechanism
  - credit card
  - instalment
  - payment timings
- Cooling down period
- Add on benefits
- Use of clubs and special programmes
- Generate additional customer information for event-driven marketing

4. Hospitality element
- Toll free claims number
- Telephone number
- Empathy
- Fast replacement system
- Immediate assisstance
- Empowered claims staff
- Dedicated client team
- Free gifts (on 2nd anniversary)
- Add on benefits (car hire, towing)

5. Safe-keeping element
- Data security/protection
- Security advice
- Photocopying items
- Anti-theft devices at free or heavily discounted prices
- Help line for emergencies
- Personal alarms

6. Exceptions element
- Specialist help desks for
  - high sums assured
  - high risk items
  - high risk areas
- Bad claims record
- Antiques special cover
- Complaints hot line
- Unconditional service guarantee
- Quality control on repairers
- Customer feedback surveys
- Publicize advocacy

7. Billing element
- No claims discount structure
- Offer of other insurance at discounted rates
- Bonus on second anniversary of policy
- Tips of value/other product offers
- Offers at highly attractive terms for customer e.g. AMEX

8. Payment element
- Loyalty discount
- Continuous collection
- Monthly payments
- Credit card only
- Use as cross-sale opportunity
- No renewals

3. *Order taking*: Once customers are ready to buy, a key supplementary service element – order taking – comes into play, which involves accepting applications, orders and reservations. Clear and accurate order taking is essential. Some companies like banks and insurance companies and utilities establish a formal relationship with customers and screen out those who do not need basic enrolment criteria. However, is this policing function excessively bureaucratic involving lengthy forms and delays? There is a risk that the effort to get rid of poor prospects will turn off good ones.

4. *Hospitality services*: Hospitality involves taking care of the customer. It finds its full expression in face-to-face encounters with the customer. The enterprise should show pleasure at meeting new customers and recognizing existing ones when they return. It may include elements such as offer of transport to and from the service site, availability of drinks and other amenities, customer recognition systems, etc. Here there is a need to adopt the Disney philosophy and treat all customers as guests.

5. *Safe keeping*: The list of potential safe-keeping supplementary services is a long one, but many of these will only be relevant to a given enterprise. For example, customers who purchase computers, motor cars or cameras will be greatly interested in supplementary services such as repair and maintenance services and if they can purchase contracts as a form of insurance against breakdown or damage. Some safe-keeping services add value to physical products and may include packaging, pick up and delivery, assembly, installation, cleaning and inspection.

6. *Exceptions*: Exceptions involve a group of supplementary services that fall outside the routine of normal service delivery. Exceptions include special requests for customized treatment that require a departure from normal operating procedures, problem solving when normal service delivery fails to run smoothly as a result of accidents or delays, equipment failures or customers experiencing a difficulty using the product. Complaints, suggestions or compliments should be developed through well-defined procedures that make it easy for employees to respond. Restitution in compensating customers for performance failures may involve refunds; compensation or free repair should also be addressed.

7. *Billing*: Billing is common to most transactions. Inaccurate, illegible or incomplete bills are very likely to disappoint customers who, up to that point, may have been quite satisfied with the service. Billing should be timely because it will probably result in faster payment. Customers value well presented billing information. American Express is excellent at doing this. Some companies help customers view their bills at their convenience at an earlier stage than normal. For example, by having billing information on an Internet or Extranet site.

8. *Payment*: In most cases billing and payment are still separate activities. A bill usually requires the customer to take action on payment which may take a lot of time. A challenge is to balance the needs of the organization for security and efficiency with the customer's own preference for convenience and credit. One element within payment is verification and control. Here organizations need to ensure appropriate controls are in place to ensure correct payment is made without alienating customers through unduly intrusive processes.

The eight supplementary services act as a checklist in a search for new ways to augment existing core products as well as to help to design new offerings. Companies wishing to use this framework should start with a workshop with relevant managers to undertake the following tasks:

1. Review generic elements for each of the eight areas of supplementary service and determine which elements are relevant to your business. Service blueprints or flowcharts are useful here to identify the current service activities which will consist of a combination of elements of the core product and supplementary services.
2. Determine if all eight areas are important for your team/business. (Not all products have eight clusters and the nature of the product helps determine which of the supplementary services must be offered and which might be used to enhance customer value.) Identify any new areas and delete those which are not relevant.
3. For each of the important areas selected, identify the key elements that:
   (a) exist at present
   (b) should be improved or enhanced
   (c) should be added to enhance customer value
4. Design an improved offer, subgrouping elements where appropriate.

The text under each heading in Figure 3.2 from an example of an exercise undertaken for a major general insurance company for their 'personal lines' business. This is a disguised summary of the output of several workshops held to identify a new enhanced insurance product.

Lovelock points out that over time core products become commoditized, so competition shifts to the supplementary services. It is these supplementary services that differentiate successful firms from the less than successful ones. Major new product/service development often takes years to implement and is very costly. Improvement to supplementary services can be more modest in cost and scope but can have a dramatic impact on the customer.

However, creating a superior offer is not enough. It needs to be leveraged by building lasting relationships with those customer groups the enterprise has chosen to do business with plus brand leveraging to develop greater value for customers.

How relationships add value

Once a superior offer has been developed, the enterprise needs to focus on building enduring relationships with customers. Customers value relationships with trusted suppliers who make a superior offer. As relationships are an important dimension of value, considerable efforts need to be expended on building and enhancing these relationships over time.

However, experience suggests that most companies direct the greater part of their marketing activity at winning new customers. But while businesses need new customers, they must also ensure that they are directing enough of their effort at existing customers. Those companies that focus too much on marketing to new customers often experience the 'leaking bucket' effect, where they lose customers because they are directing insufficient marketing activity generally, and customer service specifically, at them.

Author William Davidow has highlighted this problem: 'It has always been incredible to me how insensitive companies can be to their customers. Most of them don't seem to understand that their future business depends on having the same customer come back again and again'.[6] Too many companies, having secured a customer's order, then turn their attention to seeking new customers without understanding the importance of maintaining and enhancing the relationships with their existing customers.

Customer ladder of loyalty

The customer ladder of loyalty, illustrated in Figure 3.3, identifies the different stages of relationship development. Sales management and charity marketing have used such ladders for many years. We have shown the ladder steps but have depicted the ladder as a rock-face in this figure. This suggests that the transition of customers from one level to another is not necessarily an effortless one but may require considerable energy on the company's part to effect the change. The ladder is relevant for all groups within a channel chain referred to above – direct buyers, intermediaries as well as final consumers.

The first task is to move a new 'Prospect' up to the first rung to a 'Buyer'. The next objective is to turn the new purchaser into a

Figure 3.3   The customer ladder of loyalty

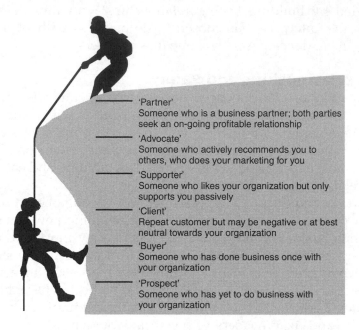

'Partner'
Someone who is a business partner; both parties seek an on-going profitable relationship

'Advocate'
Someone who actively recommends you to others, who does your marketing for you

'Supporter'
Someone who likes your organization but only supports you passively

'Client'
Repeat customer but may be negative or at best neutral towards your organization

'Buyer'
Someone who has done business once with your organization

'Prospect'
Someone who has yet to do business with your organization

'Client' who purchases regularly and then a 'Supporter' of the company and its products. The next step is to create 'Advocates' who provide powerful word-of-mouth endorsement for a company. In a business-to-business context an advocate may ultimately develop into a 'Partner' who is closely linked in a trusting and strategic relationship with the supplier.

General Electric's (GE) Appliance Division in the USA is a good example of an organization which has created value by building a closer relationship with its final consumers through an innovative call centre and moving customers from a 'buyer' or 'client' level to a 'supporter' or 'advocate' level on the ladder (see box).

Positions on the ladder, once reached, are not necessarily stable over time. Different patterns occur in different industries. Research in industries such as retailing suggests that advocacy may reach a peak at the time of purchase but may drop off after that. Thus relationship-based efforts may need to be put in place to build on earlier transactions. On the other hand, the position on the ladder may build slowly over time as a result of continued product use or experience with a company. The author only became an advocate of Hewlett Packard printers after many years of faultless printer operation, during

The GE Answer Centre

GE's Answer Centre is widely regarded as one of the best in the world. In setting up of this call centre in the 1980s GE sought to 'personalize GE to consumers and to personalize the consumer to GE'. Unlike most manufacturers, who avoided any contact with the final consumer, GE did an unusual thing and gave its phone number to customers. The Answer Centre has now evolved over two decades into an increasingly important CRM capability where the current network of five call centres receives millions of calls each year. Management consultants Robert Wayland and Paul Cole have outlined how GE's Answer Centre has contributed to increased customer relationship value in three key areas:

'First, resolving immediate problems results in a probability-of-repurchase rate of 80 per cent for the previously dissatisfied customer, as compared to 10 per cent for the dissatisfied but uncomplaining customer and 27 per cent for an average customer. In other words, by making it easier to reach the company and by responding effectively, GE gets more opportunities to convert dissatisfied customers and to strengthen relationships. Second, contact with the centre significantly increases customers' awareness of the GE appliance line and their consideration level. Finally, the knowledge that is generated through customer interactions provides valuable input to the sales, marketing and new product development processes.'[7]

which time all his other pieces of office equipment developed faults or broke down.

It is not always desirable to progress a relationship with every customer. Some customers or customer segments may not justify the investment needed to develop a 'Supporter' or 'Advocate' relationship, as it may prove too costly to do so. Some customers at the 'Client' level may be 'mercenaries' who exhibit little loyalty and are often expensive to acquire and quick to defect; others may be 'hostages' who are dissatisfied but are locked in by switching costs or monopolistic supplier behaviour. Managers therefore need to consider the existing and potential lifetime value of customers and determine whether it is appropriate to make this commitment. We address this later in the chapter.

The role of advocates

The 'Advocate' level on the customer ladder of loyalty is worthy of special emphasis. Referrals from customers are among the most relevant, effective and believable sources of information for other customers. A number of researchers have argued that word-of-mouth is the most effective source of information for consumers. While commercial sources normally inform the buyer, personal sources legitimize or evaluate products for them. Legitimization makes the step of converting prospects into customers on the ladder of loyalty that much easier.

Research by Tom Jones and Earl Sasser of Harvard Business School has found that, except in rare cases, total or complete customer satisfaction is key to securing customer loyalty and that there is a tremendous difference between the loyalty of merely satisfied and completely satisfied customers. They cite Xerox research that found totally satisfied customers were six times more likely than satisfied customers to repurchase Xerox products and services over the next 18 months. (See box for their view on loyalty.)

The Harvard Business School view on loyalty

Customer referrals, endorsements and spreading the word are extremely important forms of consumer behaviour for a company. In many product and service categories, word of mouth is one of the most important factors in acquiring new customers. Frequently, it is easier for a customer to respond honestly to a question about whether he or she would recommend the product or service to others than to a question about whether he or she intended to repurchase the product or service. Such indications of loyalty, obtained through customer surveys, are frequently ignored because they are soft measures of behaviour that are difficult to link to eventual purchasing behaviour.[8]

Which companies have a high proportion of customers who make such referrals and endorsement and exhibit advocacy? Discussions with consumers and executives suggest the following as examples:

● Airlines: Singapore Airlines, Virgin Atlantic, Southwest Airlines
● Banking: First Direct
● Computers: Dell Computers
● Healthcare: Shouldice – a Canadian hospital
● Industrial services: Service Master – a US cleaning services company
● Motor cars: Mercedes-Benz, Lexus

- Retailing: Nordstroms, Marks & Spencer
- Trucks: Scania, Volvo
- Watches: Rolex.

But neither company practice nor academic research pay sufficient attention to the important area of advocacy and referral marketing. Few organizations have any formal processes that utilize referrals from existing customers. Though many organizations recognize that customers can be the most legitimate source of referrals to their prospective customers, most tend to simply let referrals happen rather than proactively developing marketing activities to leverage the power of advocacy.

The role of terrorists

The Jones and Sasser research identifies a similar set of customer types to those in the ladder above. They point out that customers behave in one of four basic ways: as loyalists, as defectors, as mercenaries, or as hostages. 'Turning as many customers as possible into the most valuable type of loyalist, the apostle, and eliminating the most dangerous type of defector or hostage, the terrorist, should be every company's ultimate objective'.[9] In particular, this latter category 'the terrorist', not mentioned earlier, is of special interest.

Terrorists represent the most dangerous group of defectors. These are customers who have had a bad experience and make it a crusade to tell others about their anger and frustration. Unfortunately, terrorists are typically far more committed and effective at creating negative word of mouth than advocates are at demonstrating positive word of mouth.

Consumer 'terrorism' and militancy is on the increase and as customer expectations appear to increase at a faster rate than organizations' capacity to improve customer service, we can expect increased activity in this arena in the years ahead. Television programmes such as Watchdog in the UK (www.bbc.co.uk/watchdog), consumer advocate columns in Sunday newspapers and many sites on the Internet provide enormous opportunities for 'terrorist' activity. Websites such as www.Grumbletext.com shown in Figure 3.4 provide a structured environment for individuals to vent their displeasure.

The low cost and pervasive nature of the Internet make it an ideal channel for aggrieved customers to communicate their dissatisfaction, frustration or anger to a wide range of existing or prospective customers. The following selection represents a very small number

Figure 3.4   Grumbletext.com website home page

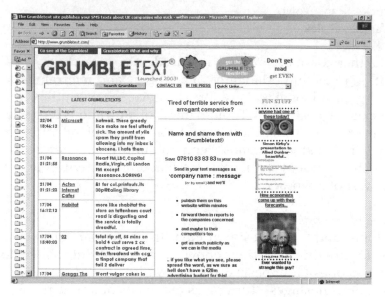

of the many web sites aimed at such communications:

www.insurancejustice.com
www.financevictims.com
www.screwedbyinsurance.com
www.outofthedark.com
www.allstateinsurancesucks.com
www.equitablelife.org.uk
www.financevictims.co.uk

As part of their value creation activities, organizations should consider not just the task of building customer satisfaction and advocacy but also how to deal with negative reactions to their products or services. A content review of the web sites listed above suggests that in many cases it was not so much the issue that there was a problem experienced by customers, but rather little or nothing was done to address it.

Leading CRM companies take the view 'the customer who complains is your friend'. They create customer value by building mechanisms to surface problems and to react accordingly. For example:

● Procter and Gamble publish 0800 telephone numbers and Internet addresses on all their products to encourage customer feedback

- Johnson and Johnson responded immediately and with total integrity to the Tylenol incident
- Marriott Hotels put enormous emphasis on encouraging all guests to complete customer satisfaction forms on completion of a visit to their hotels
- Many companies are now offering unconditional service guarantees that signal a customer promise to both external customers and internal employees.

Such initiatives may not represent a high level of sophistication in terms of CRM but are as important to building customer value as advanced technology solutions.

How brands add value

The brand is also an important element in contributing to the value proposition. Originally the role of a brand was to enable a customer to identify the manufacturer of a product. Over time the concept of a brand broadened to include further meaning: symbols, images, feelings and relationships. Brands add value to the company because they add value to the customer. Thus a product is something that is made by a company; a brand is something that is bought by a customer. A product can be imitated by competitors, while a brand is different from that of its competitors. A strong brand is unique.

David Aaker, a professor of Marketing Strategy at the University of California at Berkeley has neatly summed up the role of the brand in value creation for the customer:

> Brand-equity assets generally add or subtract value for customers. They can help them interpret, process and store huge quantities of information about products and brands. They also can affect customer confidence in the purchase decision (due to either past-use experience, familiarity with the brand and its characteristics). Potentially more important is the fact that both perceived quality and brand associations can enhance customers' satisfaction with the use experience. Knowing that a piece of jewellery came from Tiffany can affect the experience of wearing it: the user can actually feel different.[10]

We discussed above how the core and augmented product offer adds value. A brand adds to this offer in ways that differentiate it from other similar products, ways that are important and of *value* to the customer. What distinguishes a brand from an unbranded product and gives it value to the customer is the sum total of customers' perceptions about both product performance and their complete experience with the brand. Brands have become a major determining factor in repeat purchase and an important way of adding differentiation. Branding also has an important role in helping customers be assured of high and consistent quality.

Perceived quality is as dependent on factors such as reliability, responsiveness, assurance and empathy, as it is on tangibles. This means that managers should give increased attention to these factors, which increase customer value as a means of brand building. The American Express green card is a good example of a strong brand that is valued highly by customers as a result of association with these factors. Historically, in strict product terms, it has compared unfavourably with Visa or Mastercard:

- Until relatively recently American Express offered no convenient option to pay off its bill monthly. The entire balance had to be paid upon receipt of the statement
- Only a quarter of the number of merchants worldwide that take Visa/Mastercard accept American Express
- Emergency cash is available to American Express holders at only 20 per cent of locations at which it is available to the Visa or Mastercard holder
- The American Express yearly fee is typically more than any Visa or Mastercard, some of which do not charge any annual fees.

Despite these shortcomings, American Express green card is a highly successful brand. Many consumers are willing to pay more for a less useful, less convenient credit card. By positioning their card as a 'travel and entertainment card' and themselves as a customer-focused organization, American Express have created a distinctive set of perceived benefits that no other card has achieved. Among these is a high degree of responsiveness when the cardholder has a real problem such as a lost card. The author recently reflected on how, over 15 years ago, the American Express office in New York could replace a stolen card within two hours, while in the 2000s it took a major British bank over 15 days to accomplish the same task. As a result of such experiences, the brand image is further enhanced or diminished in the eyes of the customer.

The importance of brand image
Examples of the value of brand image is apparent in all industries. One of the best illustrations of this is the taste test for Coke and Pepsi,

shown in Figure 3.5. The column titled 'open' shows the results of a survey of an open taste where the two products were placed in front of the respondents. Apparently using their most discriminating taste sensitivities, 65 per cent of those surveyed preferred Coke, while 23 per cent preferred Pepsi and 12 per cent of them ranked them equally.

Figure 3.5 Brand image

	Open	Blind
Prefer Pepsi	23%	51%
Prefer Coke	65%	44%
Equal/Can't Say	12%	5%

When a matched sample was subjected to a blind taste test (where the identity of the two colas was concealed – see column titled 'blind'), there was a very different result. The blind taste test showed 44 per cent preferred Coke and 51 per cent preferred Pepsi, an increase in preference for Pepsi of over 120 per cent. Significantly different results were obtained from the consumers in the two different controlled tests.

How can this great difference and resulting brand loyalty be explained? The answer is that customers 'taste' both the drink and its brand image. This brand image adds value to the consumer when they see the familiar Coke package and logo. While these 'added values' may relate to an emotional level they are, nevertheless, real for the customer perceiving them. The subsequent New Coke debacle when Coca-Cola introduced a new product that tasted better in blind taste tests, but was not acceptable to customers, taught them a painful lesson about their brand. Coke is not only seen as a drink by its consumers, but also in the light of what it represents in terms of Americana and its heritage and past relationship with them.

In the business-to-business sector, a similar form of trust and loyalty can be built with the brand. Many executives who have purchased from companies such as IBM and McKinsey & Company have heard such quotes as: 'No purchasing manager in recorded history has ever been fired for buying IBM'; and 'McKinsey is the safe option'. Brands such as these have historically been able to create customer value by positioning themselves as highly trusted partners.

Value for the customer is added through the creation of brand image. As a result, the owners of strong brand names can command higher prices for their offerings as they are valued more by customers. The value embedded in brands can be profound, as Kevin Lane Keller, a professor at Amos Tuck School, has pointed out: 'the relationship between brand and the consumer can be seen as a type of bond or pact. Consumers offer their trust and loyalty with the implicit understanding that the brand will behave in certain ways and provide them utility through consistent product performance and appropriate pricing, promotion and distribution programs and actions.'[11]

Building brand value through relationships
Don Peppers and Martha Rogers have noted that CRM is about persuading consumers to participate in a dialogue by establishing a relationship that helps bond the consumer to the brand. By building a relationship with customers, the organization can create real and tangible value for them. A good example of this value creation can be seen in motorcycle manufacturer Harley-Davidson's successful turnaround. Harley's success is closely tied to needs, aspirations and relationships with its customer base and they have played to that strength (see box).

Harley-Davidson: Building a relationship brand

The Harley-Davidson story is one that shows how a world-famous brand has used customer relationships to emerge from near extinction and reclaim its pre-eminent position in the market. It has delivered double digit growth in both turnover and profits over the last decade. In 1903, Harley-Davidson produced a total of three motorcycles. In 2003, they built more than 250 000 and shipped them with extensive lines of branded clothing, parts and accessories and collectibles, to more than 60 countries worldwide. Sales were over $4 billion. Gross profit over $1 billion and net income more than $0.5 billion.

A well-established Harley Owners Group (HOG) holds regular rallies around the world. These are often attended by company executives so that they can meet customers and talk about the company's vision and values. Anyone who buys a Harley-Davidson motorcycle becomes a member of the Harley-Davidson Club. The clubs meet at the dealerships, where they can ride together and also buy the company's branded clothing.

HOG is a sub-brand that represents a relationship to a community of people, an affinity group of motorcycle owners. With HOG clubhouses strategically located in the dealerships, owners consume their product as part of a Harley-Davidson community. They have not only bought a Harley motorcycle, they have formed a relationship with other members of the owners club and identify with the group through wearing branded merchandise. Harley-Davidson owners place great value on the brand and are extremely loyal with a 95 per cent repurchase rate.[12] A good number of them demonstrate their relationship to the brand by having a Harley-Davidson tattoo on their arms – a unique and permanent symbol of loyalty to the brand!

The behaviour of employees also contributes greatly to the brand. Singapore Airlines is known as one of the most successful airlines in the world and one of the best for customer service. It is a good example of an enterprise putting considerable emphasis on building a brand relationship through moments of truth. The brand, through its 'Singapore Girl' campaign, is closely associated with high quality service. It delivers this outstanding service by having a ratio of one flight attendant for every twenty-two passengers, the highest in the world and well above the industry average. Singapore Airlines' branding places great emphasis on its staff. In a very real sense its staff are the brand.

Branding and the Internet
Two brand experts, Martin Lindstrom and Tim Andersen, use Procter & Gamble as an illustration of the increasing importance of branding on the Internet. In 1930 Procter & Gamble did not spend any media dollars on radio. All money was dedicated to the print media. By 1935, some 50 per cent of the total Procter & Gamble media budget was devoted to radio. In 1950, three per cent of Procter's media spending went to television. By 1955, 80 per cent of their total media budget was devoted to television. In 1998 Procter & Gamble established their first worldwide online centre. The purpose: to ensure that Procter & Gamble would be ready to move their television budget onto the Internet at the right time.[13]

By 1999 P&G Interactive were named Marketer of the Year by Advertising Age. They have led the way in gaining online consumer acceptance, standardizing measurement and defining advertising models and making online media easier to buy. They have also demonstrated considerable ingenuity in their Internet branding campaigns. For example, in an online campaign for Bounty paper towels, P&G created a new advertising format called 'sequential messaging' in which it broke down the message into four units and delivered them to the user at different areas of the site, based on their level of involvement with the company. P&G found that sequential messaging significantly increased purchase intent.[14]

At the time of writing, US consumers spend some $93 billion annually on shopping directly online. A further $138 billion is spent by them on goods and services purchased offline after first seeking information online. This research, carried out by the Dieringer Research Group for the American Interactive Consumer Survey, underlines the importance of the Internet as a channel for the brand. Overall, some 23 million Americans spend $500 or more, both online and offline, after first gathering product information online. When asked about the impact of the Internet on brand images, 45 per cent of all online adults, which equates to 25 per cent of all US consumers, said that their brand opinions had changed in one or more of the ten common product categories covered by the survey.[15]

However, despite this great shift to Internet activity, Lindstrom and Andersen point out that the future Internet generation does not trust the Internet as an information source. They cite a Time-CNN survey on young people that shows trust of information on the Internet is only one third the level that it is in other media such as newspapers and television. They conclude that brands will need to act as a trusted 'consumer guide' on the Internet, a development which will make much greater future demands on the online brand to create customer value.

Goodwill and trust cannot be bought; they are earned over time. Considering no online brand can represent more than a five-year history, there have been only a few online brands that have earned consumer trust, for example, Yahoo!, Amazon, AOL and Excite. It could be said that 'real world' trusted brands such as Disney have 'free tickets' to consumer web trust while the online brand market is still immature. However, established brands like Disney have realized they have to employ the same brand management respect for the customer that they would have in the real world to maintain and extend that 'Disneyesque' trust from real world to online world. Disney takes all that is good about their company (family values, safe community and trust) and transfers it online.[16]

Value and branding in context

Three decades ago branding was mainly the domain of consumer goods. Now we see efforts to establish and sustain distinctive brands in every sector. In the past, many companies have emphasized the brand name rather than brand equity. Brand equity represents the set of brand assets and liabilities that collectively add to or subtract from customer value and this has recently become a key area of focus for all enterprises. With a widespread acceptance of the importance of brands, there has been increasing recognition that the consumer's choice depends less on evaluation of the functional benefits of a product or service and more on their assessment of the company and the people behind it.

In an offline environment, the relationship that customers have with a brand is frequently the result of their interactions with the staff of that organization and their perceptions of service quality. The brand relationship is the outcome of a series of brand contacts that the customer has with the organization. Over time these customer contacts or 'moments of truth' result in increased or decreased customer value.

In an online environment, the Internet creates major opportunities and threats for brands. The greatest opportunities relate to speed and cost. The great advantage the Internet has over more traditional media is its ability to manage customer relationships from awareness to buying action. It also potentially enables customer contact 24 hours per day at much lower cost. However, as noted above it is a much less trusted medium.

Overall, there are more similarities than differences when building a traditional versus an online brand. The key issue is to ensure that where customers use offline and online channels there is brand consistency and they have superior customer experiences. We will return to this issue in Chapter 4.

The value proposition

Having examined how product and service offers, relationships and brands can be utilized in order to create customer value, we now turn our attention to how these components of customer value can be utilized in a formal statement of value, or *value proposition*.

In recent years managers have started to use the term value proposition increasingly frequently. This term is employed in two ways by organizations. First, in general terms it is used to describe the notion of creating value in a very broad sense. Second, in more specific terms, it is used to describe a detailed analytical approach to value creation. However, the term is most frequently used in the general sense without any analytical underpinnings. Discussions with many organizations suggest that relatively few attempts have been made by them to develop a structured approach to formulating value propositions. Where they do have a formal statement of their value proposition, this is often not based on any analysis.

A value proposition defines the relationship between what a supplier offers and what a customer purchases by identifying how the supplier satisfies the customers' needs across different customer activities (e.g. acquiring, using and disposing of a product). Specifically, it defines the relationship between the performance attributes of a product or service, the fulfilment of needs and the total cost. The aim of all businesses is to create a value proposition for customers, be it implicit or explicit, which is superior to and more profitable than those of their competitors.

Value propositions explain the relationship between the performance of the product, the fulfilment of the customer's needs and the total cost to the customer over the customer relationship life-cycle (from acquisition of the product through to usage and ownership and eventual disposal). As every customer is different and has changing needs, it is crucial that the value proposition for each customer is clearly and individually articulated and cognizant of the customer's lifetime value. Thus the economic value of customer segments to the organization informs decisions about the value proposition. This topic is addressed later in this chapter.

A structured method for developing value propositions, originated by consulting firm McKinsey and Co. and further developed by others,[17-21] is comprised of two main parts: *formulation of the value proposition* and profitable delivery of this value proposition by means of a *value delivery system*.

Formulating the value proposition

Formulating the value proposition forms the first part of the value proposition concept. Some examples of value propositions, based on work by consultants Michael Lanning and Lynn Phillips,[22] are shown in Figure 3.6. The approach followed in developing these value propositions involves determining:

- the target customers
- the benefits offered to these customers
- the price charged relative to the competition, and
- a formal statement of the value proposition.

Figure 3.6 Examples of value propositions for various industries

Company/ product	Target customers	Benefits	Price	Value proposition
Perdue (chicken)	Quality-conscious consumers of chicken	Tenderness	10 per cent premium	More tender, golden chicken at a moderate price premium
Volvo (estate car)	Safety-conscious 'upscale' families	Durability and safety	20 per cent premium	The safest, most durable estate car your family can travel in at a significant price premium
Domino's (pizza)	Convenience - minded pizza lovers	Delivery speed and good quality	15 per cent premium	A good pizza, delivered hot to your door within 30 minutes of ordering, at a moderate price premium

The value proposition approach suggests companies should adopt a three-step sequence of:

- analysing and segmenting markets by the values customers desire
- rigorously assessing opportunities in each segment to deliver superior value
- explicitly choosing the value proposition that optimizes these opportunities.

Step 1: Analysing markets based on value

This first step involves understanding the price/benefit opportunities that exist within the market and here the value map can prove a useful tool. Value maps provide a graphical presentation of the relative positions of different competitors in terms of the benefits and price attributes that relate to customer value.

Figure 3.7 shows a value map for the airline industry past and present based on a study undertaken by a group of New York University researchers.[23] It depicts a value frontier that incorporates the price/benefit positions of the major carriers. If all competitors are in a similar position on such a map, commoditization and reduced profitability would probably result. This situation is apparent with many players in the airline industry. On the other hand, highly successful companies tend to establish differentiated positions on the value

Figure 3.7   Value map for the airline industry (past and present)

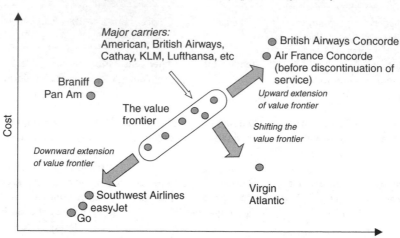

frontier. If companies fall consistently in the underperformer region of the map their future survival is questionable.

These researchers suggest three generic strategies for developing differentiated value propositions on the value map:[24]

1. *Extend the value frontier towards the low end of the value map* – the strategy adopted by Southwest Airlines in the USA and by easyJet and Go airlines in Europe.
2. *Extend the value frontier towards the high end of the value map* – this strategy was adopted by British Airways and Air France with their Concorde fleets before they were retired. Pursuit of this strategy is often based on technological innovation.
3. *Shift the value frontier* – the strategy adopted by Virgin Atlantic with its 'upper class' service, offers first class facilities and a highly distinctive personality based on a business class fare structure.

High-performance companies characteristically focus on the development of superior value propositions in order to take advantage of new growth opportunities and identifiable, premier customer groups.

Step 2: Assessing opportunities in each segment to deliver superior value
When a critical review of any market is undertaken it soon becomes obvious that the idea of a single market for a given product or service is highly restrictive. As we discussed in the previous chapter, all

markets are made up of market segments, or groups of customers with the same or similar needs. Reaching the most profitable and suitable market segments is a matter of evaluating the opportunities and limitations in each segment for delivering superior customer value. Even where the offer made to customers is technically identical to competitors' offers, efforts to differentiate the total or 'package' offer in terms of relationships and branding can reap significant rewards.

Many companies that have adopted a market aggregation or macro-segmentation strategy in the past are now actively addressing new ways of appealing to customers at lower levels of segment granularity. In considering new attributes that may form part of an enhanced offer made to more specific customer segments, companies will find it useful to use the 'supplementary services' approach illustrated in Figure 3.2 as a creativity tool.

Value maps may also be constructed at the market segment level to enable very specific price/benefit opportunities to be evaluated within them, thus highlighting the most promising ones and the most appropriate propositions for these segments. Assessments of potential opportunities for delivering superlative value should involve a rigorous analysis of cost, competitive offers and, importantly, organizational 'fit' on both strategic and operational levels. Part of this exercise should include a formal assessment of the market attractiveness and business strengths within each segment. Frameworks such as the directional policy matrix[25] can be used to do this analysis.

Step 3: Explicitly choosing the value proposition
Having identified the target market segments, the next priority is to create a value proposition of winning relevance. The characteristics of the segments that form some markets may vary so radically that different value propositions will be required for different segments. For example, in the automotive industry, the needs and preferences of customers in the luxury segment who buy Rolls-Royce cars are clearly distinct from those of customers in the trendy youth segment who buy Smart cars or VW Beetles. Businesses that justifiably exhibit less marked differences between their product and service offers may benefit from approaching the value proposition issue by developing a generic value proposition for the market as a whole and then developing more specific variants for each specific segment.

Once formulated, value propositions should be carefully reviewed to confirm that they are truly distinctive and appropriate. The check-

Figure 3.8   A checklist to review your value proposition

1. Is the target customer clearly identified?
2. Are the customer benefits explicit, specific, measurable and distinctive?
3. Is the price, relative to competition, explicitly stated?
4. Is the value proposition clearly superior for the target customer (superior benefits, lower price or both)?
5. Do we have, or can we build, the skills to deliver it?
6. Can we deliver it at a cost that permits an adequate profit?
7. Is it viable and sustainable in the light of competitors and their capabilities?
8. Is it the best of several value propositions we considered?
9. Are there any impending discontinuities (in technology, customer habits, regulation, market growth, etc) that could change our position?
10. Is the value proposition clear and simple?

Source: Adapted from Lanning and Michaels[19] and Lanning and Phillips[21]

list in Figure 3.8 can be used to determine whether a superior value proposition has really been developed.

The value delivery system

The means by which the value proposition is delivered represents the other half of the value proposition concept. The importance of having a system, or framework for value delivery stems from the realization that focusing on the traditional physical sequence of 'make the product/service and sell the product/service' is suboptimal. The value delivery system emphasizes that companies need to shift from a traditional view of seeing their business as a set of functional activities to an externally oriented view that sees their business as a vehicle for value delivery. The value delivery system consists of three parts as portrayed in Figure 3.9: choose the value, provide the value and communicate the value.

1. *Choose the value.* Choosing the most appropriate value proposition involves understanding the forces driving demand, customer economics, the buying process and how well the competition serves customer needs, particularly in terms of their products, service and prices charged.
2. *Provide the value.* Developing a product and service package that provides clear and superior value involves focusing on product quality and performance, service cost and responsiveness, manufacturing cost and flexibility, channel structure and performance and price structure.
3. *Communicate the value.* Engaging in promotional activity to persuade customers that the value offered is better than that of competitors not

Figure 3.9 The value delivery system

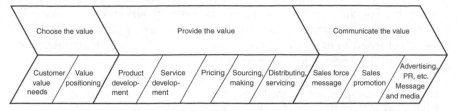

Source: Based on Bower and Garda[18]

only involves sales promotion, advertising and the sales force, but also the provision of outstanding service in a way that is recognized and remembered by the target audience.

Building the value proposition

Correct formulation of the proposition and building a value delivery system to ensure it has an impact on the customer base represent the two main elements of the value proposition. Much of the success of a value delivery system depends on the thoroughness and innovation with which value is both generated and reinforced throughout the supplier organization. 'Differentiating the winners is the extent to which this value proposition is echoed in the business system, through changes in branch service delivery, new products, systems that provide integrated information to customers and those serving them, relationship pricing, etc. Executing these changes is more difficult than choosing the value but also provides formidable obstacles to imitation'.[26]

British Telecommunications plc (BT), one of the world's leading telecommunications providers and one of the largest private sector companies in Europe, has developed a sophisticated approach to the development of value propositions with its corporate B2B customers as outlined below.

Case 3.1   BT: creating new customer value propositions – Case study overview

BT Retail has developed a formal approach to ensure that customers are receiving tailored offers that deliver real and sustained value to them. BT's approach to customer value creation has two main components: the value statement and the value proposition. The value statement describes the impact that BT can have on the market or on an industry segment. The value proposition is a customer specific proposal, usually using a value statement as a starting point, that is quantifiable in both value returned to the customer and revenue to BT. It is a clear statement of the value BT brings to a particular client.

This case examines how BT Retail is working to ensure that the company's propositions, products and services add continuing value to their customers. BT's emphasis on creating customer value is strongly echoed in BT Group's current three-year strategy – the cornerstone of which is customer satisfaction.

The full case study is at the end of this chapter (see p. 159)

The Zurich Financial Services Group is a leading provider of financial protection and wealth accumulation products and solutions for some 35 million customers in over 60 countries. They have a well-established reputation for serving the insurance and investment needs of B2C and B2B customers worldwide.

Case 3.2   Value propositions at Zurich Financial Services – Case study overview

Zurich Financial Services Group (ZFS) needs to manage customer relationships effectively across a diverse customer base. Competitive performance demands continuous innovation and dedicated attention to the ever-changing requirements and aspirations of customers. To ensure a profitable customer base ZFS has devised a new framework for developing value propositions. The catalyst for ZFS's refocus was the increased recognition that customers do not just want a whole range of products, but require solutions that are pertinent to their lives and needs.

This case describes the methodology adopted by ZFS's renewed focus on building value propositions with a more formalized and strategic emphasis. A key feature of the new methodology is its emphasis on customer feedback that is intended to be used to inform all decision making.

The full case study is at the end of this chapter (see p. 164)

Value assessment

To determine if the value proposition is likely to result in a superior customer experience, it is necessary to quantify the relative importance that customers place upon the various attributes of a product. A value assessment based on subjective judgements about the attributes and benefits that are important to the customer can fall prey to the assumption that the supplier and customer attach the same importance to the various product attributes – rarely do they.

Managers seeking to build customer-oriented offers need to know what specific combination of product and service features, relationships and brand are most important to the organization's key customer segments. This is the domain of value assessment. Value assessment can be undertaken by a company using its managers' perceptions of what customers view as important or by seeking this information directly from its customers.

Experienced and informed managers may have a reasonably accurate perspective regarding the product and service features and benefits that are most important to their customers, especially where these views are supported by other evidence. We have seen good examples of companies successfully using their manager's experience to identify key attributes by which customers make choices.

However, a frequent mistake made by companies is assuming customers attach the same importance to these attributes as do the company's own managers. Experience suggests that even when an organization correctly identifies most of those attributes which are most relevant to the customer, frequently the relative ranking of these by the customer and the supplier vary significantly. A much better way is to assess the offer from the customer's perspective and to take into account differences in customer perception across market segments.

Traditional means of customers' assessment of value

The most common means of discovering the perceived value of product attributes is to ask a representative sample of customers to rank them in terms of importance on a five, seven or ten point scale. Most managers are very familiar with this approach, which requests respondents to rank particular features or service attributes on a four or five point scale from 'very satisfied' to 'very dissatisfied' or 'very important' to 'very unimportant'.

However, where a large number of attributes are concerned, this method is impractical and offers little real insight. An alternative approach is to ask respondents to place a weight from 1 to 10 against each attribute while ranking them on a scale of, say, 'very satisfied' to 'very dissatisfied'. This approach is also prone to problems, particularly where respondents do not know the importance of some features, may be unwilling to disclose their opinions, may rate too many attributes as being very high in importance, or may be influenced by peer pressure, causing some features to be overrated.

Another approach is to request respondents to allocate a total of 100 points among all the elements identified. However, this can be a daunting task and can result in an arbitrary allocation of points. Dissatisfaction with such methods led researchers to develop a research technique called 'trade-off analysis'. This tool is a much more robust method for identifying the implicit importance that customers attach to key attributes.

Improving value assessment using trade-off analysis

A more realistic evaluation of customer value can be obtained by asking a representative sample of customers to rank the product's attributes and then, using an analytical tool such as conjoint analysis, or trade-off analysis, to apply a weighting system to discover the weight given to different levels of each attribute. Here advanced computer analysis is used to calibrate the importance 'weights', which can then be aggregated to provide an objective measure of the 'utility' that customers prescribe to each elements of customer value.

This technique is based on the simple concept of trading off one attribute against another. For example, the purchaser of a new car is likely to trade off a number of specific product attributes in agreeing the purchase price and specifications. Vehicle performance, petrol economy, number of seats, safety features, boot capacity, low price, and so on will have factored in his decision. Trade-off analysis can also be used to identify customers who share common preferences in terms of product attributes and may reveal substantial market segments with service needs that are not fully catered for by existing offers.

Trade-off analysis possesses several advantages over more traditional forms of value assessment, as it:

1. Employs measures of attribute importance that do not rely on direct rating by respondents
2. Forces a trade-off among very important attributes to determine which are the most important; and
3. Achieves this for each customer separately.

There are two forms of trade-off analysis. The 'full profile' approach presents respondents with a full-profile description of an offer and asks them to rate the offer's constituent elements. The 'pairwise' trade-off approach asks respondents to rank combinations of variants of two attributes, from the least preferred to the most preferred and then repeats this for a series of other pairs of attributes.[27]

The 'full profile' form of trade-off analysis is a more commonly used approach and is often deemed more realistic by researchers as all the product's aspects are considered at the same time. However, if the number of attributes is large then the judging process used for each individual profile in the 'full profile' approach can become very complex and demanding. For that reason other researchers prefer the 'pairwise' trade-off approach. The Robotic Components example (see box) demonstrates the use of the pairwise trade-off analysis. Specialist research texts provide more detailed discussion of these trade-off approaches including the full profile form.[28]

Robotic Components Inc. is a manufacturer of components for the growing industrial robot market. As part of a new CRM initiative they are examining various value propositions to improve their logistics to customers. For example, they believe that buyers might be prepared to sacrifice some decrease in stock availability for an improvement in delivery reliability of a day or two. They decided to undertake a value assessment, using the pairwise trade-off approach, based on the following options of stock availability, order cycle time and delivery reliability:

Stock availability:	75 per cent
	85 per cent
	95 per cent
Order cycle time:	2 days
	3 days
	4 days
Delivery reliability:	$\pm$ 1 day
	$\pm$ 3 days

With this pairwise form of conjoint analysis, the various trade-offs are placed before the respondent as a series of matrices. The respondent then completes each matrix to illustrate his/her preference for service alternatives. Thus, with the first trade-off matrix between order cycle time and stock availability, shown below, the most preferred combination would be an order cycle time of 2 days with a stock availability of

95 per cent (where the number 1 in the matrix represents the first preferred option). The last preferred combination is an order cycle time of 5 days with a stock availability of 75 per cent (where the number 9 in the matrix represents the ninth and least preferred option). For the other combinations the respondents complete the matrix to show their own preferences. An example of a typical response is given below for each of the three trade-off matrices:

Distribution service trade-off matrices

		Order cycle time		
		2 days	3 days	4 days
	75%	6	8	9
Stock	85%	3	5	7
availability	95%	I	2	4

		Order cycle time		
		2 days	3 days	4 days
Delivery	±I day	I	3	5
reliability	±3 days	2	4	6

		Stock availability		
		75%	85%	95%
Delivery	±I day	4	2	I
reliability	±3 days	6	5	3

Once these trade-off matrices are completed, computer analysis is used to determine the implicit 'importance weights' that underlie the initial preference rankings. For the data in the above example the following weights are identified for a given respondent:

Service element		Importance weight
1. Stock availability:	75%	− 0.480
	85%	0
	95%	+0.480
2. Delivery time:	2 days	+0.456
	3 days	0
	4 days	−0.456
3. Delivery reliability:	±I day	+0.239
	±3 days	−0.239

Thus, for this respondent, stock availability appears to be marginally more important than delivery time and both were in the region of twice as important as delivery reliability. Information such as this can be most useful. For example, in this case, a stock availability of 85 per cent with 2 days' delivery and a reliability of ± 1 day is seen as being almost equally acceptable as 95 per cent with 2 days' delivery and a reliability of ± 3 day (a combined weight of 0.695 [0 + 0.456 + 0.239] compared with 0.697 [0.480 + 0.456 − 0.239]). This suggests that a tightening up on delivery reliability might reduce stockholding and still provide an acceptable level of customer service.

Robotic Components then repeated this for different customers, identified key customer segments and used this information to create appropriate offers to different customer segments.

Source: Adapted from an example by Professor Martin Christopher and used with his permission

Trade-off analysis can be used to identify customers who share common preferences in terms of attributes. Experience of researchers and consultants working in this area suggests that this form of analysis may often reveal substantial market segments with service needs that are not fully catered for by existing product or service offers. Numerous studies using this approach have now been carried out by both consultants and market researchers. As a result its commercial acceptance as a means of value assessment has grown greatly.

Having completed our discussion of 'the value the customer receives', including its two main components – the value proposition and the value assessment – we now turn our attention to 'the value the organization receives'.

The value the organization receives

The value the supplier organization receives from the customer has the greatest association with the term 'customer value'. Customer value from this perspective is the *outcome* of providing and delivering superior value for the customer, deploying improved acquisition and retention strategies and utilizing effective channel management. Fundamental to the concept of customer value are two key elements. First, determining how existing and potential customer profitability varies across different customers and customer segments. Second, understanding the economics of customer acquisition and customer retention and opportunities for cross-selling, upselling and building customer advocacy. How these elements contribute to increasing customer lifetime value is integral to this view of value creation.

Customer profitability

We emphasized the importance of market segmentation earlier in this chapter. Carefully segmenting the market and developing an approach that maximizes the value of your most desirable customer segments and the corresponding lifetime value that these customer groups produce for your company, lie at the heart of the value creation process. Companies need to understand the existing profitability of their key customer segments (and, in certain businesses, the profitability of individual customers) and initiate action to realize the potential profitability of those segments and consequently improve customer lifetime value.

It is somewhat surprising that most companies focus on identifying the profitability of products rather than customers,[29] when it is customers who generate profits, not products. Products create costs but customers create profits. This distinction is not just semantic. We find that the difference between profit and loss is typically determined *after* a product is manufactured. The costs of storing, moving and supporting products are significant. Customers differ widely in their requirements for delivery service, in their ordering patterns and, indeed, in the products they purchase. Each product has its own unique profile of margin, value/density, volume and handling requirements. Similarly customers will order different product mixes, will have their own unique requirements as to the number of delivery points and, of course, the number of times they order and the complexity of their orders will differ. Putting all these factors together can produce widely differing cost implications for the supplier.

The 80/20 rule, or 'Pareto Law', suggests that 80 per cent of the total sales volume of a business is typically generated by just 20 per cent of its customers and that 80 per cent of the total costs of servicing all the customers will probably be incurred by only 20 per cent of the customers (but probably not the same 20 per cent).

The profitability of customers varies considerably whether we are examining this at the customer segment or individual, or one-to-one, customer level. Figure 3.10 shows the shape of the profit distribution

Figure 3.10   Customer profitability analysis

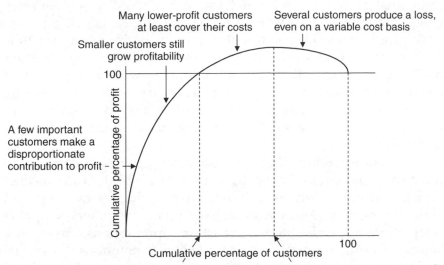

Source: Adapted from Christopher[30]

resulting from the uneven spread of profits across the customer base. From this example, it can be seen that there is a 'tail' of customers who are actually unprofitable and who therefore reduce total profit contribution. It is essential to understand which segment these customers fit into. The analysis in this figure, which is based on large corporate customers, applies equally at the customer segment level.

A key aim of CRM is to develop close relationships with customers in segments that are, or have the potential to become, highly profitable. So the ability to create customer segment profit and loss accounts at the appropriate level – segment, micro-segment or individual customer – is fundamental to a successful CRM strategy.

The problem is that traditional accounting systems make it difficult, if not impossible, to identify the true costs of serving individual customers. Companies often assume that there is an 'average' cost of serving a customer, thus forgoing the opportunity to target those customers or segments who have real potential for transforming their own bottom line.

Why customers differ in their real profitability

Customers' profitability may vary because different customers often buy a different mix of products with different gross margins. Also, there will usually be substantial differences in the costs of servicing individual customers. As noted above, profitability is frequently determined by what happens *after* the point of production.

The costs of service begin with the order itself: how much time does the sales person spend with the customer; is there a key account manager who spends their time wholly or in part working with that customer; what commissions do we pay on these sales, and so forth. Also there are the order processing costs which themselves differ according to the number of lines on the order, the number of orders and their complexity.

For physical products there are also transport costs, materials handling costs and often – particularly if goods are held on a dedicated basis for customer, such as with own-label products – inventory and warehousing costs. Further, for large corporate customers, suppliers often allocate specific funds for customer promotions, advertising support, additional discounts and the like. Promotions – a special pack for a particular retailer, for instance – will often carry additional hidden costs to the supplier. For example, the disruption to production schedules and the additional inventory holding cost is rarely accounted for or assigned to customers.

The basic principle of customer profitability analysis is that the company should seek to assign all costs that are specific to individual accounts. A useful test to apply when looking at these costs is to ask: 'What costs would I *avoid* if I didn't do business with this customer?' The benefit of using the principle of 'avoidability' is that many costs of servicing customers are actually shared among several or many customers. The warehouse is a good example: unless the supplier could release warehousing space for other purposes then it would be incorrect to allocate a proportion of the total warehousing costs to a particular customer.

Though it may be impracticable to undertake such analysis for individual accounts, organizations should be able to select a sample of representative customers in order to gain a view of the relative costs associated with different types of accounts, distribution channels and market segments.

What often emerges from customer profitability studies is that the largest customers in terms of volume, or even revenue, may not be the most profitable because they cost so much to service. So though these larger customers may gain bigger volume-based discounts, they require more frequent deliveries to more dispersed locations and they may insist on non-standard packaging, for example.

Understanding future profit potential

Once the enterprise has a clear view on existing profitability of its major customers or customer segments it then needs to consider their future profitability. We need to identify the potential to build and extend customer segment profitability further.

Don Peppers and Martha Rogers of Marketing 1:1 have developed a customer typology that helps businesses rank their customers and identify relevant strategies. They suggest ranking customers into five groups, or quintiles, in terms of their potential lifetime value and propose that emphasis is placed on three groups:[31]

- MVCs or *most valuable customers* are those customers which have the highest actual lifetime values. They represent the core of a company's current business and the CRM objective with regard to them is *customer retention*.
- STCs or *second tier customers* represent those customers with the highest unrealized potential. They could be a source of greater profitability for the company than they currently are and the CRM objective with regard to them is *customer growth*.
- BZs or *below zero customers* are those customers who will probably never earn sufficient profit to justify the expense involved in serving them. The CRM objective with regard to them is *customer divestment*.

A customer value typology such as this is useful in helping an organization reach appropriate decisions as to how it can best utilize its resources. Because of the high value that they already represent for a business the focus for MVCs is developing appropriate customer retention strategies. STCs may be similar to MVCs in terms of their potential profitability and lifetime value. Here the opportunity is to obtain a larger size of their wallet as they may be purchasing products from our competitors. BZs represent customers who usually cost more to serve than they are ever likely to return in profit to our company. If there is no potential for profit improvement, we need to consider how to divest ourselves of these customers provided it is ethically responsible to do this. Ideally we should persuade them to shift to one of our competitors where they can be equally unprofitable for them. This suggests we need to be careful to acquire only those customers that have the potential to be profitable for our enterprise.

Ideally the organization should seek to develop financial systems that routinely collect and analyse customer profitability data. Essential to such analysis is the need for organizational understanding of how customer acquisition, customer retention and opportunities for cross-selling, upselling and building customer advocacy contribute to profitability across different customer segments.

Customer acquisition and its economics

The role and relative importance of customer acquisition varies considerably according to a company's specific situation. For example, a new market entrant will be mainly focused on customer acquisition, while an established enterprise will be more concerned with customer retention.

The customer acquisition process is typically concerned with issues such as:

- acquiring customers at a lower cost
- acquiring more customers
- acquiring more attractive customers, and
- acquiring customers utilizing new channels.

The starting point in understanding customer value from the perspective of the supplier organization is to determine the existing customer acquisition costs within the major channels used by the company and to identify how these costs vary within different customer segments.

Customer acquisition at United Electricity plc

We can illustrate the economics of both customer acquisition and customer retention by using the example of United Electricity plc, a large UK electricity supplier. Since the late 1990s, the residential sector of the market has gone through substantial changes as electricity companies, for the first time, could sell electricity outside their traditional geographic boundaries. United Electricity faced competition within their own territory from other electricity providers, but also could now market their services outside their traditional geography.

A market segmentation of United Electricity's customer base identified four key market segments, each of which displayed different characteristics in terms of socioeconomic grouping, expected switching behaviour and customer profiles.[32]

The data needed to undertake an analysis of customer acquisition and customer retention economics at United Electricity, at the segment level, were collected. This included the number of existing customers within each segment, annual customer acquisition targets with reference to the total UK customer base, the cost of acquisition (per customer) and estimates of gross profit per customer per annum for each segment. The likely annual retention rates in the new competitive environment were considered. Different levels of retention for each segment were estimated; one scenario of the broad characteristics of these segments is shown in Figure 3.11. Some figures have been changed to protect proprietary information.

Figure 3.11 Customer segment data template for United Electricity plc

	Segment	No. existing customers (S)	Acquisition target (N)	Cost of acquisition (C)	Annual retention rate (α)	Profit per customer per year (K)
Group 1	Struggling empty nest super-loyals	421 300	500	£110	99%	£6
Group 2	Older settled marrieds	618 000	66 000	£70	97%	£9
Group 3	Switchable middles	497 900	110 000	£55	94%	£18
Group 4	Promiscuous averages	459 600	220 000	£30	90%	£22

United Electricity estimated the acquisition costs per customer at the customer segment level shown in Figure 3.11 as follows:

- Segment 1 – 'struggling empty nest super-loyals' £110
- Segment 2 – 'older settled marrieds' £70
- Segment 3 – 'switchable middles' £55
- Segment 4 – 'promiscuous averages' £30.

To enable a comparison of acquisition costs, the expected profitability of the average customer in each segment and the overall profit potential of each segment overall were also considered.

When the customer acquisition cost is divided by the profit per customer per annum, the number of years required to break even is identified. The annual profit per customer in Segment 1 (the 'struggling empty nest super loyals') was £6, making a break-even of 18.3 years. As this segment comprises elderly people, many of the customers will die before they break even! In the case of Segment 4 (the 'promiscuous averages'), the annual profit per customer was £22, making a break-even of 1.36 years. This segment appears highly attractive in terms of acquisition economics, especially if CRM strategies successfully to retain customers are put in place.

We have observed that many B2C organizations do not differentiate their CRM activities at the segment level. They contact each prospect with the same frequency (as United Electricity had done since their establishment) instead of applying a level of effort consistent with the cost of acquisition and profit potential. Their unrefined use of resources not only leads to wasted investment but can cause annoyance among customers who are either being oversupplied or undersupplied with attention. This situation highlights the importance of understanding acquisition economics at the segment level.

Acquisition within different channels

Having determined the acquisition costs for different segments, the enterprise then needs to review how acquisition costs vary across different channels. The advent of web sites and electronic communication channels has enabled companies to acquire customers at a fraction of the cost of using more traditional channels such as direct mail.

Companies also need to understand the relative costs of customer acquisition in different channels such as using direct mail, television advertising, a direct sales force and e-commerce. The apparent high cost of certain channels does not mean that they should be disregarded. For example certain companies have found a direct sales approach to households an effective way to generate sales despite its higher costs as a channel.

Further, customers acquired in different channels may be different or may behave differently. For example, frozen food retailer Iceland supplemented its traditional retail channel with an Internet site. As a result it acquired customers from a more affluent segment – one that was not well represented within its existing customer base. Additionally, the average order size of these Internet customers was higher and more profitable than for traditional customers who physically shopped in its retail branches. We examine channels in greater detail in the next chapter.

Improving acquisition activities

Even companies with high retention rates lose customers, so they also need continually to acquire new ones. When customer acquisition costs and how they vary at the segment and chan. levels are properly understood, companies can then identify how improve acquisition activities. This may involve acquiring a greater number of customers or more attractive customers, or getting them at a lower cost. In many instances customer acquisition can be improved through acting on insights from the value proposition and value assessment described earlier. Well targeted promotional campaigns and the encouragement of customer referrals can also attract customers who meet the company's criteria. First Direct, the leading UK bank, boasts the highest levels of advocacy in the retail banking sector. Approximately one third of all its customers join as a direct result of 'word-of-mouth' or customer referral – with the bonus of reducing its average customer acquisition cost by one third.

Customer retention and its economics

Although many companies recognize that customer retention is important, relatively few understand the economics of customer retention within their own firm. Since the start of the 1990s research has identified the financial benefits of customer acquisition versus customer retention.

(For example, Fred Reichheld and Earl Sasser, a partner at consulting firm Bain & Co and a professor at the Harvard Business School, published revealing research which demonstrated the financial impact of customer retention.[33] They found even a small increase in customer retention produced a dramatic and positive effect on profitability: a five percentage points increase in customer retention yielded a very high improvement in profitability in net present value (NPV) terms.)If the customer retention rate was increased from, say, 85 to 90 per cent this represented an average NPV profit increase of around 40 per cent. Figure 3.12 shows this NPV varied from 35 to 95 per cent among the businesses studied.

These results have had a significant impact in drawing attention to the critical role customer retention has to play within CRM strategy. However, as Reichheld has observed, the economics of retention are often lost in the shadows of traditional accounting. This is because changes in defection rates may have little effect on this year's profits, but the resulting effect on long-term profit and growth can be enormous.

Figure 3.12   Profit impact of a five percentage points increase in customer retention for selected businesses

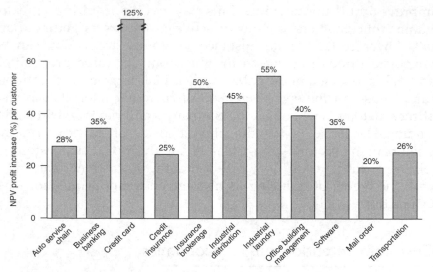

Source: Adapted from Reichheld and Sasser[34]

Customer retention at United Electricity plc

In the United Electricity plc example above we now consider the impact of improvement in customer retention. Experienced executives estimated the potential improvement in customer retention that could be achieved through a CRM strategy based on improved service, given the relative attractiveness of the four segments. These resulted in the following improvement targets: Segment 1 – 1 per cent, Segment 2 – 2 per cent, Segment 3 – 5 per cent and Segment 4 – 9 per cent, based on a service strategy. Using these increases in retention rates for each segment we modelled the increase in 'gross' profit in five and ten years' time and compared it with the base case.

The results in Figure 3.13 show a significant increase in overall gross profit, before costs of improved service, of 48 per cent at year 5 (from £21.7 m to £32.2 m) and 71 per cent at year 10 (from £23.8 m to £40.6 m). The results within each of the four different segments varied significantly because of differences in improvement in retention rates and other inputs to the model. We have found relatively few organizations who undertake evaluation of segment profitability in this way. However, the broad approach is straightforward – understand the profit potential in each segment (gross profit less costs) and selectively manage the segments to maximize profits.

Figure 3.13 Profit projections for improved retention at United Electricity

Segment	Existing retention rate		Retention rate with improved se	
	Profit in 5 years (£m)	Profit in 10 years (£m)	Profit in 5 years (£m)	Profit in 10 years (£m)
1	2.697	2.089	2.848	2.331
2	4.477	5.112	5.347	6.692
3	6.377	7.586	9.343	12.704
4	8.167	8.989	14.663	18.828
Total	21.718	23.776	32.201	40.555

In considering CRM initiatives, it should be emphasized that the costs of improving customer retention are not necessarily substantial. The most attractive CRM initiatives are those that are of high value to the customer but are of low cost to the supplier. Organizations should first consider a reallocation of the existing expenditure such that greater emphasis is placed on those segments that have the greatest potential for increasing net present profitability. This may involve no significant increase in costs. For example, if United Electricity was mailing each of its customers seven times per year it may wish to reduce the expenditure greatly on the one million plus customers in Segments 1 and 2 and apply this to customers in Segments 3 and 4.

The organization can next identify where additional incremental expenditure should selectively be placed on the most relevant market segments. The objective of this activity is to ensure the overall cost–benefit of the increased expenditure significantly enhances profitability.

Why retention improvement impacts profitability

The reasons why retention has such a significant effect on profitability have been highlighted by Reichheld and Sasser:

● acquiring new customers involves costs that can be significant and it may take some years to turn a new customer into a profitable customer
● as customers become more satisfied and confident in their relationship with a supplier, they are more likely to give the supplier a larger proportion of their business, or 'share of wallet'
● as the relationship with a customer develops, there is greater mutual understanding and collaboration, which produces efficiencies that lower operating costs. Sometimes customers are willing to integrate their IT

systems, including planning, ordering and scheduling, with those of their suppliers and this further reduces costs
- satisfied customers are more likely to refer others, which promotes profit generation as the cost of acquisition of these new customers is dramatically reduced. In some industries, customer advocacy can play a very important role in acquiring new customers, particularly when there is a high risk involved in choosing a supplier
- loyal customers can be less price-sensitive and may be less likely to defect due to price increases. This is especially true in business-to-business markets where the relationship with the supplier becomes more valued and switching costs increase.[35]

However, despite these findings, research suggests that managers have been slow to implement changes in marketing activities to emphasize customer retention.

Acquisition and retention activities in practice

A number of studies have pointed out that many companies are still more strongly focused on the acquisition of new customers than on development of their existing customer base.[36] For example, a survey of UK financial services carried out by Berry Consulting and AT&T showed that expenditure on customer acquisition (48 per cent) was more than double that spent on customer retention (22 per cent).[37]

In a survey we carried out of the marketing practices of 225 UK organizations, in a wide range of industries, there were similar results. We found the greatest proportion of marketing budgets – 41 per cent – was spent on customer acquisition, while only 23 per cent was spent on customer retention. Given that the majority of firms surveyed in this sample were in mature industries, the research suggests to us that economics of customer retention and customer acquisition are poorly understood and hugely under-exploited.

Figure 3.14 presents data from a further study by KPMG that show results for a range of different industries. This figure shows that the marketing budgets in most sectors emphasize acquisition more than retention. Marketing expenditure is particularly heavily slanted towards the acquisition of new customers in the insurance and Internet and telecoms sectors. The bias towards acquiring new customers in the latter sector is less surprising given the recent emergent nature of many new companies in this sector.

Figure 3.14 Expenditure on customer acquisition and customer retention

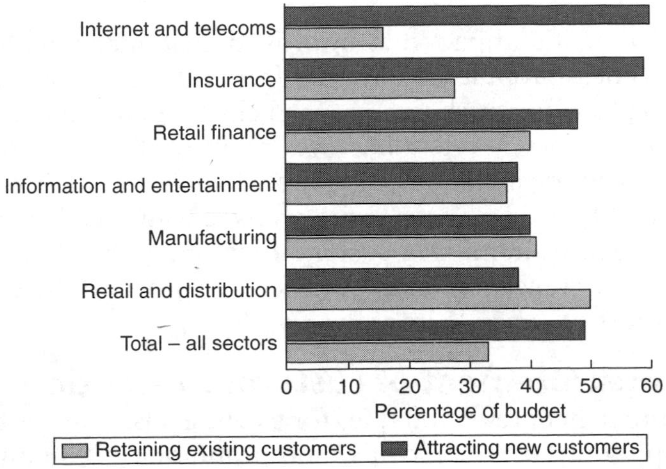

Source: Adapted from KPMG[38]

Different companies will need to place different emphasis on customer retention and customer acquisition. So a conclusion regarding the relative amounts being spent in both these areas needs to be drawn according to the individual circumstances of that enterprise. Research by the author has found that many organizations are not placing the optimal balance of expenditure on acquisition and retention activities. In a study of 200 large UK organizations we found a significance misallocation in the amount of money spent on customer acquisition and customer retention. The study identified three categories of organization – 'acquirers', 'retainers' and 'profit maximizers through CRM'.

Acquirers spent too much on customer acquisition activities at the expense of customer retention activities. The majority of firms, 80 per cent of them, were in this category. Retainers, by contrast, spent too much on customer retention activities at the expense of customer acquisition – this group represented 10 per cent of firms. The 'profit maximizers through CRM' represented only 10 per cent of firms in their survey. Only this last category considered they had identified the appropriate balance in spend between acquisition and retention activities.

Taken together these studies show a significant underemphasis on customer retention. We are not suggesting that new customers are unimportant, indeed, they are essential for sustained success. However, a balance is needed between the marketing efforts directed towards existing and new customers. CRM activities need to emphasize customer retention improvement more strongly.

˙amework for customer retention improvement

Given the dramatic impact that improved customer retention can have on business profitability and the fact that many organizations continue to place too much emphasis on customer acquisition at the expense of customer retention, we now outline a structured approach which organizations can follow to enhance their retention and profitability levels. Three major steps are involved in such an approach: the measurement of customer retention; the identification of root causes of defection and key service issues; and the development of corrective action to improve retention.

Step 1: measurement of customer retention

The measurement of retention rates for existing customers is the first step in improving customer loyalty and profitability. It involves two major tasks – measurement of customer retention rates and profitability analysis by segment.

To measure customer retention, a number of dimensions need to be analysed in detail. These include the measurement of customer retention rates over time, by market segment and in terms of the product/service offered. If customers buy from a number of suppliers, share of wallet should also be identified.

The outcome of this first step should be a clear definition of customer retention, a measurement of present customer retention rates and an understanding of the existing and future profit potential for each market segment.

Step 2: identification of causes of defection and key service issues

This step involves the identification of the underlying causes of customer defection. Traditional marketing research into customer satisfaction does not always provide accurate answers as to *why* customers abandon one supplier for another. All too often customer satisfaction questionnaires are poorly designed, superficial and fail to address the key issues – forcing respondents to tick pre-determined response choices.

The root causes of customer defections should be clearly identified, for it is only by understanding them that the company can begin to implement a successful customer retention programme. Often this research task needs to be undertaken by very experienced market researchers.

Step 3: corrective action to improve retention

The final step in the process of enhancing customer retention involves taking remedial action. At this point, plans to improve retention become highly specific to the organization concerned and any actions taken will be particular to the given context. Some key elements include marshalling top management commitment, ensuring employee satisfaction and dedication to building long-term customer relationships, utilizing best practice techniques to improve performance and developing a plan to implement customer retention strategy.

Organizations are now recognizing that enhanced customer satisfaction leads to better customer retention and profitability. Many organizations are now reviewing their CRM strategies to find ways to boost retention rates as a means of improving their business performance. Achieving the benefits of long-term customer relationships needs a firm commitment – from senior management and all staff – to understanding and serving the needs of customers. It also requires a clear understanding of the potential benefits in terms of customer segment lifetime value.

Customer segment lifetime value

Customer lifetime value is defined in many ways. In some instances companies use sales revenues, in others they use contribution, gross profit or net profit. Some consider lifetime value in terms of what the customer will contribute in the future, others in terms of what the customer has contributed in the past, while some think about the value of all purchases – past and future.

Let us start by considering a simple description of lifetime value in terms of revenue. The person who has purchased four cars from a car dealer over the past ten years with an average cost of $40 000 may be viewed as a $120 000 customer. However, more relevant is the fact that this customer, if retained over the rest of their car purchasing life of 25 years, may buy ten more cars. If they cost the same amount this represents $400 000 in terms of lifetime revenue.

However, this future lifetime revenue does not represent the real value to the dealer. The revenue needs to be adjusted by a profit margin to obtain a lifetime profit. It also needs to be adjusted in a number of other ways. First, a discount rate needs to be applied to all future profits to reflect the time value of money. Second, other purchases such as servicing the car may need to be taken into account. Third, opportunities to cross-sell the customer other related products such as insurance, extended warranties and leasing need to be taken into account. Fourth, opportunities to upsell the customer into more expensive models in the future need to be considered. Fifth, if the dealer delivers outstanding service, the customer may become an advocate of that dealership and recommend many friends and business colleagues to them. Dealers like Sewell Village Cadillac in Texas and Fletcher Jones Mercedes-Benz dealers in California have developed a legendary and international reputation for outstanding customer service and as a result have developed an outstanding asset in terms of the lifetime value custom of their customers.

In B2B relationships there is a further dimension – reference value. It is not enough for an enterprise to have profitable and well-regarded customers; they should also benefit from them as reference sites. Efforts need to be directed at identifying and motivating business customers to act as these reference sites. Finnish consultants and researchers Kaj Storbacka and Jarmo Lehtinen discuss a large software designer who used an important customer as a reference:

> Potential future customers were, with the company's permission of course, informed about what kind of system had been delivered and how the delivery had been handled in collaboration with the customer. The corporate customer's CEO was also often asked to give presentations about the partnership. This often occurred at small seminars to which potential customers had been invited. The software designer's customer was happy to describe this joint effort. He was very credible since he also addressed issues which were problematic. The CEO was pleased to talk at these seminars since, as he said himself, this meant that he had to reflect on certain issues, but he was probably also pleased to receive the recognition of being an expert in his field.[39]

Defining the role of customer lifetime value

Richard Lowrie of IBM points out that 'there is no single definition of customer lifetime value ... However, many organizations in a variety of customer-centric industries are creating strategies around the concept of customer lifetime value and loyalty'.[40] To calculate a customer's real lifetime value an enterprise needs to look at the projected future profit over the life of the account.

We define customer lifetime value (CLV) as the net present value of the future profit flows over the lifetime of the customer relationship. This represents the entire expected profit flow, adjusted by an appropriate discount rate, over a customer's lifetime including the elements outlined above including cross-selling, upselling, advocacy and, where relevant, reference effects. The CLV should be calculated at the level of segmentation granularity appropriate to that business. Care should be taken to be sensibly conservative when making future estimates.

Customer lifetime value is difficult to measure because of the difficulties in putting quantification on future events. However, although there are a number of different ways of calculating lifetime value and difficulties in measurement this does not mean the concept should be rejected. Peppers and Rogers point out that:

> Statistical models of individual customer lifetime values are only as good as the data and analysis that go into them ... and even with perfect data they can never provide perfect predictions. With a reasonable amount of care, nevertheless, such a model will serve your purpose. You don't need an exact figure. What you need is a means of comparing the advantage of one marketing program or selling strategy with another. You need figures that can provide usable information.[41]

It should not be assumed that companies will wish to retain all their customers into the future. Some customers may cost too much money to service, or have such high acquisition costs in relation to their profitability, that they will never prove to be worthwhile and profitable in terms of CLV. Clearly, it would be inadvisable to invest further in such customer segments. It is likely that within a given portfolio of customers, there may be some segments that are profitable, some that are at break-even point and some that are unprofitable in terms of their CLV. Thus, increasing customer retention does not always yield positive increases in CLV. In some instances, increasing the retention of such unprofitable customers will create negative CLV. It should be recognized, however, that some 'unprofitable customers' may be valuable in their contribution towards fixed costs and overheads and considerable caution needs to be placed in the allocation of fixed and variable costs to ensure that customers who make a contribution are not simply discarded.

In the future, it is very likely that calculations of customer lifetime value will be carried out using complex computer models generated by heuristic software systems (i.e. systems that incorporate a significant degree of intelligence and can 'learn' from experience) and will therefore become far more accurate and manipulable.[42]

Calculating customer lifetime value

A simple example of the calculation of customer lifetime value is given in Figure 3.15. This customer has no revenues or profit in the first year and then generates a profit of $1 000 000 in year 1, increasing steadily to a profit of $5 000 000 in year 5.

Figure 3.15   Calculation of customer lifetime value

Year	Future profit ($000s)	Discount factor Based on 10%	NPV ($ 000s)
Year 1	1000	0.91	910
Year 2	2000	0.83	1 660
Year 3	3000	0.75	2 250
Year 4	4000	0.68	2 720
Year 5	5000	0.62	3 100
CLV			10 670

We use here a discount rate of 10 per cent as profit made in the future which is not as valuable as profit made today. The discount rate is used to reduce these future profits down to their net present value (NPV) to make future profits values comparable to any current profits or costs. The formula used for the discount rate is:

$$D = (1 + i)^n$$

where i = the market rate of interest including risk and n = the number of years.

The discount rates may be calculated from this formula or are readily accessible in the discount tables published in most financial textbooks. Here we use discount factors relevant to an annual interest rate of 10 per cent. By multiplying the profit for each year by the relevant profit we calculate an NPV profit for each year. Added together these give a customer lifetime value of $10 670 000 over a 5-year lifetime. More detailed mathematical formulations can be used to show the calculation of customer lifetime value for more complex examples. Those wishing to look into such mathematical formulation should see the work of Northwestern professor Robert Blattberg[43] or Cape Town University professor Mike Page[44] and their colleagues.

Research has highlighted the need for managers to develop a stronger emphasis on customer retention and identify its impact on CLV. Some companies are now starting to build comprehensive models that enable them to measure CLV at the segment level. Such models can be used to depict the trade-off between acquisition and retention strategies in specific businesses. They enable the CLV profit impact of changes in customer retention, customer acquisition and other variables to be measured at the aggregate, segment, micro-segment and individual customer levels.

However, few organizations have reached the stage of fully understanding their existing acquisition economics and retention economics, let alone gone beyond it. Those that have can move on to modelling future profit potential for each market segment. Modelling of future profit potential takes into account that customers may be persuaded to buy other products, or more of an existing product over time. By enhancing their predictive modelling capability the firms can identify ways to increase 'share of wallet' as well as market share, especially through more creative exploitation of channel structures such as the Internet.

Building profit improvement

In seeking to build future profitability, companies need to develop an integrated programme that addresses customer acquisition, customer retention and other related activities that can improve CLV. One framework for reviewing such profit opportunities is the ACURA model, shown in Figure 3.16.

The acronym ACURA stands for: acquisition, cross-sell, upsell, retention and advocacy. Only rarely do companies systematically build CRM strategies that focus on all the elements within this ACURA framework. While companies may seek to improve customer acquisition and customer retention, they also need to exploit cross-selling, upselling and advocacy opportunities.

When organizations model their potential future profit they need to take into account the fact that individual consumers may be persuaded to buy other products – cross-selling, or more of an existing product over time – upselling. Also, corporate customers tend to buy from a range of suppliers. By improving its service the supplier may be able to increase 'share of wallet' as well as market share, especially through exploiting alternative channel structures such as

Figure 3.16   The ACURA framework

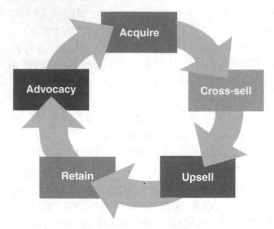

Source: Payne[45]

the Internet. Companies such as McDonalds and American Express are excellent at cross-selling and upselling and Virgin and First Direct excel at creating advocacy within their customer bases.

Earlier in this chapter we emphasized how companies should manage customer acquisition and retention to improve their profitability. To become even more profitable, they need to develop integrated programmes that also address related activities, such as cross-selling and upselling, that can improve customer lifetime value.

For each element of ACURA companies can usefully review potential strategies to improve profitability by market segment and then identify their potential profit impact. The main steps involved in applying the ACURA framework are as follows:

1. Identify key segments and their characteristics. Select two to four segments with the greatest long-term profit potential
2. Determine generic ACURA strategies
3. Decide which ACURA strategies relate to which segments and make rough estimate of profit potential
4. Identify key metrics for each segment and overall profit potential
5. Determine critical factors for success in CRM implementation, investment required and strategy for selling internally.

An overview of an exercise for strategies to improve cross-selling in a supermarket is shown in Figure 3.17.

The supermarket first identifies generic strategies to improve each element in the ACURA model. In the example in Figure 3.17, the

Figure 3.17 ACURA model cross-selling template for a supermarket

Cross-sell	Segment			
	1	*2*	*3*	*4*
Wider product range		$$$		
Linked offers				
Special offers		$$		$
Loyalty cards		$		
Train staff to link products	$			
Shelf design	$		$$	
In store promotions		$	$	
Buy in bulk		$$$		$
Oven ready convenience foods			$	

generic cross-sell strategies that may be relevant to a number of segments include developing a wider product range, making linked or special offers, introducing loyalty cards, etc. The profit potential of applying each of these strategies for each customer segments is then considered. An estimate of this is represented by the number of $ signs for each segment strategy. Appropriate metrics which measure the impact of cross-sell strategies are then identified. Finally, each relevant strategy is considered in more detail including the investment required to implement each strategy and the likely return in each segment.

The potential of the ACURA framework is highlighted when McDonalds is considered. McDonalds have a systematic approach to upselling and cross-selling that typically results in a customer having a 'Big Mac' rather than a standard hamburger; being asked if they want fries to go with the hamburger; then 'will that be a large fries?' and 'would you like a drink to go with that?' and 'will that be a large coke?'. The combination of successful upselling and cross-selling, if carried out where it is relevant to customer needs and on a consistent basis by all employees, has the potential to make a huge improvement in profitability when compared with an organization that does not emphasize these key elements of enterprise customer value.

Summary

The value creation process is crucial to transforming the outputs of the strategy development process in CRM into programmes that both *extract* and *deliver* value. An insufficient focus on the value provided for key customers, as opposed to the income derived from them, can seriously diminish the impact of the offer in terms of its perceived value. Only a balanced value exchange will ensure that both parties enjoy a good return on investment, leading to a good (long-term and profitable) relationship.

Achieving the ideal equilibrium between giving value to customers and getting value from customers is a critical component of CRM and requires competence in managing the perception and projection of value within the reality of acquisition and retention economics. To anticipate and satisfy the needs of current and potential customers, the supplier organization must be able to target specific customers and to demonstrate added value through differentiated value propositions and service delivery. This means adopting an analytical approach to value creation, supported by a dynamic, detailed knowledge of customers, competitors, opportunities and the company's own performance capabilities.

In mature markets and as competition intensifies it becomes imperative for organizations to recognize that existing customers are easier to sell to and are frequently more profitable. But although managers may agree intellectually with this view, the practices within their organizations often tell a different story. They can take existing customers for granted, while focusing too much of their attention and resources on attracting new customers. There are many examples of organizations that have invested too heavily in unselective customer acquisition only to find they have attracted a significant proportion of their customer base that is marginal or unprofitable.

Increasingly sophisticated approaches to customer segmentation, value propositions development and lifetime value calculation will help companies better to understand how value should be created for the customer and the enterprise. However, this will only be realized by ensuring a superior customer experience within and across all the channels in which the company interacts with its customers – the topic of the next chapter.

Checklist for CRM leaders

CRM leaders need to review the following issues about the *Value Creation Process*.

The value the customer receives:

1. The value the customer receives gets as much attention from senior management as the value the latter receive by way of revenue and profits
2. We have a clear view throughout the organization regarding the nature of the 'core' and 'augmented' offer made to our customers
3. At least annually we review whether further supplementary services should be added to our offer to increase the value received by our customers
4. Customer relationships and the impact of the brand are fully understood and managed within my organization
5. My organization recognizes the importance of maximizing the number of customer 'advocates' and taking action to minimize customer 'terrorists'
6. My organization has developed a written value proposition identifying the value offered to customers
7. Our value proposition is tailored to different customer segments
8. My organization assesses customer value and end-user customer satisfaction and quantifies overall satisfaction with specific attributes such as responsiveness, accuracy and timeliness
9. We set targets using comparative data drawn from high-performing organizations
10. We measure complaints and other key indicators of customer (end-user) dissatisfaction (e.g. returns, warranty claims), record these indicators by cause and act on them.

The value the organization receives:

1. We utilize an appropriate level of segmentation based on satisfaction measures, sales, profits and other relevant historical information
2. My organization has identified how acquisition costs and annual profit earned per customer vary at the segment level. We have identified our most profitable customers and calculated our share of their wallet
3. We measure customer retention rates at the segment level and have quantified the profit impact of improvement in retention rates
4. The organization has identified profitable and non-profitable segments and adjusts the style and cost of campaigns, win-back strategies, customer service and support accordingly

5. We have identified the amounts we spend on both customer acquisition and customer retention at the aggregate and segment levels and have confirmed these are well-balanced
6. We have identified targets for customer retention improvement at the segment level and have developed plans to achieve them
7. The organization understands the value that each customer segment brings to the company in terms of lifetime value
8. We have calculated the relative potential profit improvement from acquisition, cross-selling, upselling, retention and advocacy at the segment level and have plans to realize these profits
9. We use a comprehensive set of metrics to measure customer acquisition, retention, profitability and lifetime value at the segment level and these are reported to senior management at least quarterly
10. We regularly review competitive activity and quantify how this activity may impact on our customer value metrics; any significant changes are always communicated to senior management.

Each issue should be considered in terms of:

Rating for our organization (5 = applies fully; 0 = does not apply at all)
Importance to our organization (5 = very important; 0 = no importance)

Case 3.1   BT – creating new customer value propositions

The company

British Telecommunications plc (BT) is one of the world's leading telecommunications providers and one of the largest private sector companies in Europe. It is the principal trading company of BT Group plc and the prime channel to market for the Group's separate main businesses: BT Ignite (retail broadband networks); BTopenworld (retail Internet); BT Retail (retail telecoms); BT Wholesale (wholesale telecoms network); and BTexact Technologies (advanced research and development organization).

Based in London, with offices throughout the UK and ventures in more than 40 countries, BT is the UK's main telecommunications provider. Its core activities include local, long distance and international telecommunications services, Internet and broadband services and IT solutions. It also provides network services to other licensed operators. In 2002, the company employed over 100 000 people and had an annual turnover of £18.4 billion.

BT Retail had some 28 million customer lines equating to a UK market share of approximately 73 per cent of the residential voice market and 45 per cent of the business voice market in 2002. In addition, BT Retail delivers tailored information technology solutions for small and medium enterprises and larger organizations in the public and private sectors. BT Retail strives to enable its business and residential customers to communicate easily with the world around them, using an extensive product and service portfolio covering voice, data, Internet and multimedia, as well as managed and packaged communications solutions.

The challenge

Over the past few years, competition in the telecommunications market has accelerated. Under these conditions of increased competition it has become increasingly important for BT to develop a greater focus on delivering value to its customers.

BT Retail has for many years been concerned with delivering value to its business and residential customers. It has done this by focusing on helping its customers communicate easily with the world around them, using an extensive product and service portfolio covering voice, data, Internet and multimedia, as well as managed and packaged communications solutions. However, what is needed is a more formal approach to ensure that customers are receiving tailored offers of direct relevance and that deliver real and sustained value to them.

The solution

BT Retail has taken up this challenge by implementing a customer-centric strategy with the intention of becoming recognized as the telecommunications industry's customer service champion. Under the leadership of Pierre Danon, Managing Director of BT Retail, the business is integrating traditional products and services with new wave technologies to provide carefully developed customer value propositions.

In 1999, a project on proposition development was initiated. This initially focused on the Major Business division of BT Retail. Danny McLaughlin, Managing Director of Major Business stated its objective: 'I want Corporate Clients to be judged by the value we bring to the customer, not just as a supplier of telecoms. What we have to offer is a value proposition. We have to use our understanding of the customer to create a compelling value proposition.'

BT regards a customer proposition as the combination of products and services offered to a customer based on an accurately identified set of customer needs. It recognizes that becoming totally customer focused depends on first defining customer needs and then allowing them to drive the development of winning value propositions and world-class communications and e-business solutions which fulfil the proposition and deliver the value promise. BT shares the view that business today revolves around the needs being served, not the products being offered.

Through this concentration on proposition development, BT intends to improve the quality of its service delivery and enhance customer satisfaction while, at the same time, reducing costs by cementing efficiencies and driving greater productivity. This commitment to customer value marked a significant change in BT's business approach, from one which is product and technology-led to one which focuses on understanding customer needs and building value-based revenue streams.

BT's propositions project works at unifying the value system, integrating three core elements of the organization: the Customer (*Sell-side*); the Enterprise itself (*In-side*); and Suppliers and Partners (*Buy-side*). BT sees the following activities as key to providing this integration and delivering an excellent value proposition:

- Having an excellent understanding of the customer's industry
- Having an excellent understanding of BT's own industry
- Building excellent relationships with clients
- Being excellent at what BT does with its industry and global partners.

These aims are reflected in six proposition areas:

1. *Customer relationship management*
CRM solutions are those that provide our clients with the ability intelligently to handle their customer contacts, resulting in more efficient management

of resource and enhanced customer relationships. Example: system to improve call handling (e.g. call centre).

2. *Supply chain management*
Allows seamless interaction between suppliers, internal functions and customers to promote efficiency and flexibility. Example: electronic procurement/catalogues.

3. *Knowledge management*
Gaining commercial advantage through the active management of Intellectual Capital: the way we develop, share and exploit our knowledge. Example: web site which allows knowledge sharing across departments (e.g. Intellact – an intranet used internally within BT).

4. *Organizational effectiveness*
Improves work processes and styles. Example: remote working, HR outsourcing.

5. *Flexible working*
Work anytime and anywhere solutions, from mobility to conferencing and including ancillary support devices and services which maximize the benefits of moving customers towards the vision of a virtual organization.

6. *eBusiness*
eBusiness is fundamental to each theme area, both at a strategic level and in terms of proposition development, solutions delivery and how BT communicates its capability.

BT's approach to customer value creation has two main components: the *value statement* and the *value proposition*.

The value statement describes the impact that BT can have on the market or on an industry segment. It is a general statement of intent that is applicable to the customer's business sector. The value statement is used to position BT and generate interest and takes the following form:

(*Customer*) will be able to (*improve what*) through the ability to (*do what*) as a result of (*BT enabler, technology and/or service*).

The value proposition is a customer-specific proposal, usually using a value statement as a starting point, that is quantifiable in both value returned to the customer and revenue to BT. It is a clear statement of the value BT brings to a particular client and answers the questions:

● How much value (financial benefit to the customer)?
● How soon can the value be realized (timing)?
● How sure is the value (risk)?
● How will the value be measured (value return)?

The value proposition builds on the value statement and takes the following form:

(*Customer*) will be able to (*improve what*) by (*how much and/or what percentage*) through the ability to (*do what*) as a result of (*what BT enabler, technology, and/or service*) for (*what total cost – tangible and intangible*). By (*time factor*) BT will be able to demonstrate the delivery of value by (*a specific, quantifiable measure*).

The strongest value propositions should therefore have at their core a financial linkage from an initiative to a measurable improvement in the business, especially around critical issues.

BT Retail understands it can no longer rely on perceived value to win contracts. Says Danny McLaughlin, 'If we can quantify our value, we will be better positioned to command premium margins based on our value, rather than based on our cost or our competitors' prices. And we can avoid 'impact gaps' which arise if the value expected by the customer is not realized'.

McLaughlin emphasizes that throughout the sales cycle the value of the business issue and the offering must be continually quantified so that the customer believes in and owns the value proposition. 'It is important to get the customer to understand the financial impact of their problem. The customer is more likely to quantify pain early in the sales cycle. If we can keep our customers focused on a clear statement of BT's net value, the higher our success rate and revenue will be.'

BT Retail is working to ensure that the company's propositions, products and services are all supported by economic value equations which give examples of the value that they can add to major business's customers. These sources of value include quality levels, customer satisfaction levels, productivity of assets, people and capital, employee satisfaction – turnover; headcount reduction, financial measures – ROI, new revenue streams, expense reduction, market share, reducing risk, timeliness of getting product to market and variety and quality of products. These value formulas are based on sources of value relevant to individual customers, as defined by detailed analyses and customer profiling.

The results

BT's proposition approach has been enthusiastically supported by the marketing community. The value proposition themes mean that the focus of both marketing and sales is on the customer need, which is resulting in a better understanding of customer requirements and their reasons to purchase. In addition, product development is now driven by this understanding of customer need, moving BT towards a market-led rather than product driven approach. Propositions are now developed against a specific set of customers and therefore messages are not only more relevant but only customers who have the need are communicated with, resulting in better customer satisfaction and less confusion. The learning from the programme has led to the development of a formal proposition development tool – the BT Playbook, which has been adopted as best practice across the BT Group and the evolution of the value proposition themes into even more customer focused – for instance 'Interacting with Customers' – rather than the more technology orientated Customer Relationship Management.

BT's emphasis on creating customer value is strongly echoed in BT Group's current three-year strategy. The cornerstone of the new strategy is customer satisfaction and BT aims to be the most customer-focused and efficient communications company in the markets in which it operates. BT's new chief executive officer, Ben Verwaayen, summarizes the approach: 'We are going to act as one company focused on our customers. If we can get our customer satisfaction right, introduce new and innovative services, manage our costs and cash effectively and unite our people, we can deliver real value to our shareholders'.

This strategy responds to the growing challenge of maintaining competitive advantage in an ever-changing marketplace. With traditional business models of 'buy and sell' being replaced by value-based negotiations, companies such as BT are looking to new and innovative ways of convincing customers to choose their products over those of competitors. The development and use of carefully constructed value propositions, such as those outlined above, will enable companies both to deliver superior value to their customers and to achieve competitive advantage.

Case 3.2   Building new value propositions at Zurich Financial Services

The company

The Zurich Financial Services Group (ZFS) is a leading provider of financial protection and wealth accumulation products and solutions for some 35 million customers in over 60 countries. Founded in 1872, ZFS has a well-established reputation for serving the insurance and investment needs of individuals and companies worldwide. ZFS's industry stronghold was confirmed in 1998 through the merger of the Zurich Group with the financial services business of BAT Industries.

Based in Zürich, Switzerland, ZFS's key markets are the USA, UK and Switzerland. In addition, the company is growing businesses in select markets around the world. UK subsidiary operations include Eagle Star Insurance, Allied Dunbar Assurance, Zurich Insurance and Threadneedle Investments.

The Group concentrates its activities in four core businesses: non-life, life, Farmers Management Services and asset management. These business divisions are organized into four regions – Continental Europe; UKISA (United Kingdom, Ireland and South Africa)/Asia Pacific; North America Consumer/Latin America; and North America Corporate – and one global asset management business.

Managing customer relationships effectively across this diverse customer base and comprehensive product/service portfolio is an ongoing challenge for ZFS. Competitive performance demands continuous innovation and dedicated attention to the ever-changing requirements and aspirations of customers. In an effort to retain its high market-responsiveness, entrepreneurialism and expertise, ZFS has centred its business focus on the design and delivery of superior customer value propositions.

A formidable framework

To ensure a profitable customer base and high-quality outcomes, ZFS has devised a framework for developing value propositions. The inputs to proposition development constitute a description of the business opportunity and a detailed outline of the needs of the selected customer segments concerned. The outputs comprise all the components required to deliver the new value proposition, such as product literature, IT systems, business processes, training and licensing and sales support tools. The value proposition framework, given in Figure following, consists of a series of five processes.

Zurich Financial Services Value Proposition Framework

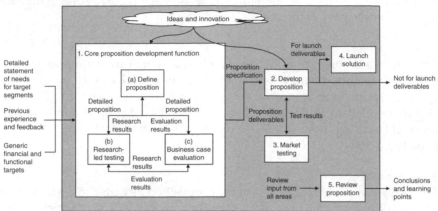

1. *Core proposition development function*

The initial process is concerned with the detailed specification of the proposition to be developed. It normally involves cross-functional collaboration and some or all of the constituent sub-processes. For example, a major new product development may require several iterations of all three sub-processes, whereas a simple re-pricing is unlikely to require any testing.

(a) Define proposition – turning the outlined business opportunity into an articulated specification, covering (as appropriate): product, service, distribution, communication and pricing. The amount of work entailed depends on the nature of the customer requirement. Clearly, creating a new proposition is more involved than modifying an existing one.
(b) Business case evaluation – determining the business rationale for the defined proposition, incorporating a financial evaluation. This activity is carried out alongside other processes and several iterations may be necessary before a viable proposition is reached.
(c) Research-led testing – using various test methods, such as focus groups and customer surveys, to examine one or more aspects of a prospective value proposition. For example, testing the demand for specific benefits or investigating the degree of price sensitivity. This process is invoked as and when necessary and is usually conducted in partnership with third party specialists.

2. *Develop proposition*

The next process encompasses the cross-functional activities involved in actually creating the deliverables of the planned value proposition. It will vary in scope and content, depending on the proposition, but may include developing or amending business processes, IT systems, training material, marketing material and product literature. The process may be carried out in stages over a significant period of time. For example, a new product may have deliverables that are not required for launch but are needed in time for the first anniversary of the policy.

3. Market testing

This process involves offering the developed value proposition to a representative selection of target customers in a controlled way, in order to test specific aspects of it. The process is applied where necessary and is generally more relevant in the context of a service-based proposition than of a product-based proposition. As with step 1(c), third party specialists are usually involved.

4. Launch solution

This is the process of making the value proposition available to customers on a full-scale basis. Again, it covers a range of activities, not all of which will be relevant in every instance. These include: training and licensing distributors; producing and distributing literature; implementing IT systems; and equipping and managing administrators.

5. Review proposition

This review process is carried out once for each proposition at an agreed period of time after launch. All aspects of proposition development are examined and performance is compared to forecasts. Resultant learning acquired from the insights and analyses generated is then fed back into management and decision-making processes to inform future activity in the areas of Client Acquisition, Customer Segmentation and Proposition Development.

The early stages

ZFS is in the process of testing a couple of value propositions developed on this basis. Arvind Malhotra, Director, Customer Strategy & Segmentation, explains: 'For each target segment we seek to define a single value proposition which encompasses our offering to them over the lifetime of our relationship with them. We then deliver this proposition through the solutions we build to meet their needs'.

As an example within the 'small business' segment, the company has identified the customer need to manage personal finances and business pressures concurrently as a key area of development. By centralizing expertise, ZFS is able to offer an integrated solution that jointly addresses both concerns in a simple, straightforward manner. Similarly for the 'family' segment, recognizing that moving home is a key event in the customer's life stage and a very stressful one, Zurich is developing a readily available solution which offers customized flexibility. The proposition to the customer is one of 'convenience and choice'.

The winning feature of the new methodology is seen as its emphasis on customer focus. ZFS proactively asks its customers what they want. Customer feedback is intended to be used to inform all decision making. Prior to the introduction of the framework, value propositions were organized on product lines and the company delivered several individual products. The catalyst for ZFS's refocus was learning that customers do not just want a whole range of products, but require solutions that are pertinent to their lives and needs. Furthermore, this customer intelligence is not self-contained within Proposition Development, but is actively channelled to sales advisers, customer communications managers and other functions. 'Traditionally, we operated product silos. Now we work across these silos to create solutions', comments Malhotra.

A promising approach

ZFS's approach to developing value propositions shows significant sophistication. First, the framework recognizes the imperative of specificity – the need to target the specific requirements of specific customers. Experience has shown that a casual or broad-brushed attitude to market segmentation and problem definition is inadequate. Secondly, the framework emphasizes the iterative nature of value – value can be tailored, augmented and improved. Feedback points are evident at the top and sides of the framework, enabling valuable ideas, learning and market intelligence to be integrated into future proposition development activity. Thirdly, the framework considers time – a fundamental prerequisite and critical success factor of any strategic process. For the right value propositions to be created for the right customers, decisions must be based on meaningful information and tested and refined in a real environment. The investment of time is one of the most important resource allocations, as inept or inaccurate decisions can be costly in both the short and the long term.

ZFS's renewed focus on building value propositions in a more formalized and strategic manner is an effective means of tackling some of the competitive challenges that lie ahead in the retail financial services sector. 'We are not badging the exercise as CRM', says Malhotra, 'but regard it as part of a wider initiative to become more customer focused'. ZFS's move to elicit customer feedback and inject customer perspective into proposition development is providing a powerful launch pad for that process.

Chapter 4

The multi-channel integration process

The strategy framework for CRM

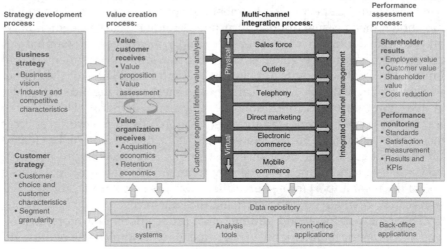

Information management process

The multi-channel integration process has a pivotal role to play in CRM as it takes the outputs of the business strategy and value creation processes and translates them into value-adding interactions with customers. These include all pre-sales communications, the sales interaction, post-sales service and support with the customer.

This process involves making decisions about the most appropriate combination of channel participants and channel options through which to interact with your customer base, how to ensure the customer experiences is highly positive within those channels and, where the customer interacts with more than one channel, how to obtain and present a 'single unified view of the customer'. Put simply the multi-channel integration process is concerned with two key questions:

1. What are the best ways for us to get to customers and for customers to get to us?
2. What does a perfect or outstanding customer experience, deliverable at an affordable cost, look like?

Multi-channel integration involves all the contacts and interfaces between the customer and the organization supplying them. There are now a large number of channels through which customers and suppliers may interact in a variety of communications, sales and service situations. Integrating these channel participants and channel options is the key to success. Many large organizations are now starting to think about implementing a multi-channel delivery capability in an integrated way.

This chapter reviews the *multi-channel integration process* with the objective of providing an understanding of integrated channel management and the role of the six channel categories in the CRM strategy framework. In order to consider the optimal nature of the enterprise's customer interface in a multi-channel environment the following issues are addressed in this chapter:

- the nature of channel participants and channel options
- the structure of industry channels
- the types of channel options and channel categories
- the channel strategies a business can select from
- the nature of the customer experience
- the development of an integrated multi-channel strategy.

Channel participants and channel options

Channel participants (or *channel members*) refer to the intermediaries such as wholesalers, retailers and value-added resellers (VARs) through which a supplier reaches its final customers. *Channel options* (or *channel media*) refer to the means by which the supplier (if selling directly to the end customer), or its intermediaries, interacts with customers. Sales forces, retail branches, call centres and the Internet are examples of channel options. Collectively the term channel is used here to include both channel participants and channel options. This multitude of channels creates enormous opportunities for improving the scope and strength of customer relationships but great challenges in managing the complexity of channels in a successful and cost-effective manner.

To establish a strong customer relationship, both supplier and customer must have ready and reliable communications, interactions and access to each other. Thus ensuring that effective and efficient two-way (and where appropriate, one-way) contact exists with the customer is a priority issue for successful CRM.

The development of electronic channels

Of particular importance is the recent development of electronic channels. In today's environment costs within many traditional channels, such as in sales forces and branch networks, are increasing at an alarming rate. As a result, there is increasing pressure on organizations to move to electronic channels and seek to develop customer self-service strategies in order to reduce cost.

Many customers in both B2C and B2B sectors are now embracing self-service. Self-service enables customers to order products or services, seek information and solve problems at the time and place their needs dictate. This is made possible through a combination of personalized web sites and contact centres. Benefits to the customer can be identified through regular customer satisfaction tracking surveys. In B2C markets there are an increasing number of companies such as Amazon and CDnow that have successfully developed self-service models. Consumer markets, with relatively simple product offers, especially lend themselves to the use of Internet self-service. However, not all companies should or will move to full self-service models.

In B2B markets, for example, important interactions such as major sales are likely to be encouraged in face-to-face encounters while various more routine transactions are handled via the e-channel. By channelling low value and less complex transactions through electronic routes, scarce resources, such as an account manager's time, can be much better deployed. In B2B markets rarely does an electronic channel fully support its own business case – it needs to be seen in the overall context of the full channel mix. For example, in online purchasing, business customers will generally want to speak to someone to purchase the services they require so the integration of call centre and web becomes essential. Also, the overall economics of individual channels needs be considered in the context of the economics of the overarching full channel mix. For example, reductions in head count for face-to-face sales support the investment for desk-based teams and the electronic channels.

However, as companies seek to introduce such cost savings, it is essential that there is not a significant reduction in customer value as the result of the introduction of a new channel. The dramatic decline of the technology stocks listed on stock exchanges at the start of this decade caused an increased focus on electronic channel solutions that address real customer needs and create significant customer value and are based on sound business models. Thus a more sophisticated approach to using electronic channels is emerging – one that seeks increases in customer satisfaction and increases in sales and profits, as well as reducing the cost of sale.

Reviewing industry channel structures

A review of the existing industry structure and its channel participants, as well as likely future shifts in it, needs to be undertaken prior to addressing how multiple channels should best work together. While this review is typically undertaken as part of the strategy development process discussed in Chapter 2, it needs to now be considered at a more detailed level within the multi-channel integration process.

Channel participants

The existing industry channel structure needs to be reviewed and documented. This involves a study of the current channel participants and their roles. There are a number of channel participants through which a company may seek to serve the final customer, some of which are illustrated in Figure 4.1. The channel structure that will be appropriate for any given organization will depend upon

Figure 4.1   Alternative industry structures in terms of channel participants

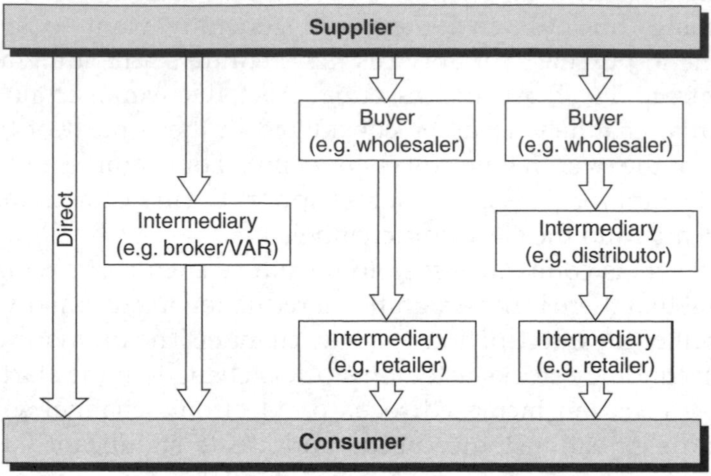

which approach can best attract the final customers in the target segment, which in turn will depend upon the organization's and intermediaries' ability to create value relevant to those customers' needs.

Of increasing importance in B2B markets is one type of intermediary – 'business partners'. In the IT sector, for example, such business partners range from being small niche operators or value added resellers (VARs) to large system integrators. A number of IT software suppliers have found their competencies lie more in software development than customer relationships and for this reason, or because of capacity problems and implementation weaknesses, have turned to this type of partner.

The choice regarding channel alternatives should be made following a determination of the value proposition relevant to the final customer in the desired segments that a company wishes to serve and may involve a combination of those shown above. Central to these decisions will be an analysis of the value of these customer segments to the organization, based on the economics of segments. This topic is discussed in Chapter 3.

Reviewing channel alternatives

In the context of rapid technological change, the role of channel participants should be subject to regular scrutiny as circumstances change and new opportunities present themselves. There is now an increasing recognition that for a firm to be successful it needs to create a demand chain that is more effective than that of its competitors. Therefore it is demand chains or market networks that compete, rather than just companies. Thus the task that needs to be addressed is how to create superiority in what has been termed the *value delivery network*.[1]

As well as considering target customers' current buying behaviours and motivations, it is important for a company also to consider how these might change over time, particularly with respect to the impact of developing technology. Over the last decade, the traditional channel structures of many industries have been dismantled and reconfigured in response to new electronic technologies that have opened new paths to market.

In the future, organizations will develop new channel management teams who map channel coverage for new propositions and products as they come to market. Such teams will manage changes in the channel mix, based on consequent shifts in margins, as products move through their life-cycle.

Understanding structural change – the role of intermediaries

Thus managers responsible for channel strategy need to understand both the nature of their industry channel structure now and how it is likely to alter in the future. Valuable insights into emerging trends within channel structures can be gained from understanding the previous evolution of the industry channel structure as well as examining the experiences of other sectors or other industries on a global basis. Of particular relevance are the opportunities and threats that result from two forms of structural change: disintermediation and reintermediation.

Disintermediation
Disintermediation is where changes in the current business model or advances in technology mean that a company ceases to need to use intermediaries to create the value sought by end customers.

Numerous examples of disintermediation can be found in businesses that have utilized e-commerce channels or have adopted call centre technology and computer telephony integration (CTI), rather than utilizing more traditional branch-based intermediaries.

Disintermediation in the computer industry

Dell Computers provides an excellent example of successful disintermediation. Michael Dell realized he could purchase computer components, assemble them and sell them directly to the final customer. This strategy enabled him to bypass the traditional channels of distribution favoured by the established computer manufacturers and offer them at a significant discount. Dell now sells over four million computers each year. The Internet channel has played an increasingly important role for Dell and the astonishing $1 million per day in sales achieved in 1997 has multiplied many times since then as the Internet's use as a sales and service channel has increased.

Disintermediation in the insurance industry

UK insurance company Direct Line initially utilized call centre technology and IT, and later the Internet, to create additional value for their target market compared to the channel structure consisting mainly of retail insurance brokers that had dominated the insurance industry until then. Focusing on individuals with low insurance risk, the company was able to offer them even lower premiums by enabling customers to deal directly with the company, so eliminating the need to factor costly brokerage commissions (and the overheads associated with supporting a broker network) into the prices of policies. Moreover, by dealing with their customers directly, the company was able to develop a fuller understanding of them, enabling Direct Line to develop new products tailored to their needs and proactively pursue cross-selling opportunities.

Reintermediation

Reintermediation is where changes in the current business model or advances in technology result in the emergence of new types of intermediary that can create more value than was possible in the previous channel structure.

A good example of reintermediation exists on the web in the form of so-called 'infomediaries', or web-enabled information agents. Rather than the customer having to spend considerable time researching the possible alternatives when considering purchasing a type of product, the infomediary performs that function on their behalf.

These may take the form of simple so-called buying engines where the customer enters their specific purchase criteria and the agent searches the offers available from different suppliers that meet those criteria. It then provides the consumer with details of products meeting the criteria they entered along with comparative prices, where they can be purchased, etc.

Infomediaries also exist as 'buyer collectives' where consumers wishing to purchase a particular product are able to combine their purchasing power to secure volume discounts from suppliers of that product.

Reintermediation in the automobile industry
Some infomediaries are developing additional services, such as the supply of general information about a particular product category or products meeting a series of different needs based around general life events. For example, Autobytel.com, a web-based car sales intermediary, started by offering customers general information about cars, which helped them in identifying their search criteria, and the ability to research dealers from whom they could purchase the specified vehicle. The company now assists customers with financing, insurance and service scheduling, increasingly performing many of the functions previously undertaken by dealers and taking ownership of the long-term relationship with the customer.

Benchmarking structural change

Benchmarking structural changes in analogous industry sectors may be especially useful in understanding opportunities and threats within your own industry. In considering experiences in other sectors, the role of mediation in them warrants careful examination. In some industries, intermediaries are becoming more valuable channel members, while in others the value of intermediaries is being challenged. Unless the intermediary is adding value to the customer relationship, it may prove to be an unnecessary cost and may be by-passed. Many organizations are now finding that in order to build stronger relationships with final customers they need to change the emphasis and expenditure at different channel levels or, alternatively, refocus the existing expenditure in ways that build deeper and more sustained relationships. The example of Amazon.com below illustrates some of the issues of mediation in an industry where there has been profound structural change.

Amazon.com: disintermediation or reintermediation in the bookselling industry?

By providing their bookselling service on the web, Amazon.com avoided the need for expensive high street outlets and were able to pass on the cost savings to customers in lower prices. Added value was offered in terms of customer convenience, for customers could order a book at any time of the day or night from their own home or office computer. The use of sophisticated web and database technologies greatly enhanced the company's customer intelligence, enabling them also to recommend books to individual customers and to notify them of forthcoming releases within their areas of interest.

However, unlike major retail book chains that order direct from the book publisher, Amazon use book wholesalers extensively. Some observers cite this as an example of disintermediation, however, in this context it can be considered an example of reintermediation as an extra channel layer has been added when compared to a company that deals directly with book publishers. However, Amazon are potentially well-placed to deal directly with book authors and sell their books, possibly in electronic form, thus organizations like Amazon may disintermediate the book publisher and book wholesaler out of the channel chain in the future.

Orientation of intermediaries

In addressing structural change, the orientation of existing and future intermediaries needs to be considered. One can categorize intermediaries according to their 'allegiance'. Some are clearly allied to selling a specific company's products. In contrast, buying engines have no such allegiance. Their role is not to sell a particular company's products; it is simply to provide consumers with information on those products that best meet their need, regardless of who supplies them, and secure consumers the lowest price. In between these two extremes, one can identify channel members that are neutral in their orientation. Thus a traditional retailer stocks a range of goods. While it has an interest in selling goods and supporting the most profitable price possible, it does not have any vested interest in selling one company's products more than another's.

The difference in allegiance clearly comes from who controls the channel member. Thus seller-oriented members will typically be owned by the seller or rely on the seller for most of their income. Thus the seller enjoys a high degree of direct control. In contrast, buyer-oriented ones rely on the buyer for their income (e.g. through subscriptions or the volumes of buyers they are able to attract and thus the advertising revenue or commissions they can secure). Hence their allegiance is with the buyer. Neutral channel members rely on both buyers and sellers and thus their allegiance is neither on one side nor the other.

These differences in the relative degree of control of intermediaries require the company to understand their orientation and motives fully and to adopt different strategies to engage with the different types of channel member.

Buyer-oriented intermediaries

The Internet has given rise to a large increase in new buyer-oriented intermediaries, so these are worthy of further discussion. There are two major categories of buyer-oriented intermediaries: buying engines and communities.[2]

Buying engines simply offer users the means of reviewing different companies' offers on the basis of cost. They are typically only relevant to buyers with a thorough understanding of the product area in which they are purchasing and a clear specification of what they require. The clear threat is that such intermediaries may lead to downward pressure on prices to buyers and hence commoditization. Except for companies that can enjoy cost leadership in their industries, the only response open to companies facing the emergence of such intermediaries is CRM – extending individualized relationships to customers and creating value so that it is hard for such commodity-based intermediaries to compete.

Communities on the other hand serve buyers with greater information and support needs. Those that prove popular will impact strongly on customers' buying decisions. They will potentially have considerable control over the relationship with the end customer. Faced with the emergence of such an intermediary, enterprises need to examine how they can create partnerships with them to add to the value created for their users.

Developing market structure maps

The existing industry structure and the role of channel participants can be better understood by means of a market structure map that shows how products or services flow from the producer through

Figure 4.2   Market structure map

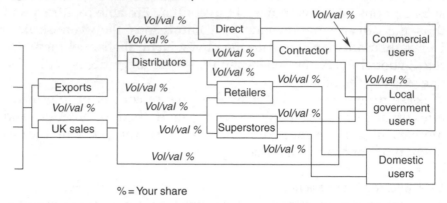

% = Your share

Source: Based on McDonald and Dunbar[3]

various intermediaries to the final customer. The market map identifies the volumes of product and services sold and the sales values associated with them. An example of a market map is shown in Figure 4.2.

A market map is constructed by plotting the various stages in the channel structure. It identifies all stages from the production of goods or services by the enterprise (and its competitors), through the various channel members to the final users. Quantification of the volumes or values at each of these stages is a key element in the process. Where possible changes in volumes and values over time should be identified on the market map so the dynamics of channels can be better understood. Ideally margins retained by each channel member at each stage of the market map should be identified as well as how these may have changed over time. As the market map is developed further refinements are made to it including the addition of information about specific market segments and different purchasing procedures encountered by channel members.[4]

Market maps help evaluate the success of existing channel participants and the amount of CRM effort directed at different groups and consideration of alternative future structures. The analysis of the industry and competitive environment, discussed as part of the strategy development process in Chapter 2, will provide very useful input into a consideration of what structural changes may occur. In particular, the eight forces industry analysis, discussed in Chapter 2, can be used to help identify future structural changes.

You can start by reviewing whether removing one of the intermediaries or adding a new type of intermediary would result in better optimization of information flows, physical flows as well as volumes, values and profits. If so, then one has grounds for expecting such a change may happen in the future or consider introducing such changes for your organization – if your role within the industry structure enables you to make these changes.

For example, the current structure of the car industry is such that manufacturers supply myriad dealers who in turn supply product information, test drives, servicing, sales and financing to the customer. However, such an approach has tremendous inefficiencies and costs built in such as having huge numbers of cars sitting on dealer forecourts throughout the country. Many changes and structural shifts are occurring in this industry at present. In Europe, some are being driven by the new 'block exemption' regulatory environment, some by the rise of new competitors such as car supermarkets and others by changes in customer purchasing behaviour with an increasing number of customers shopping on the Internet. Further changes may occur such as the use of more centralized distribution from which cars are delivered direct to the end consumer, reducing the high levels of stock carried in the dealer network.

Channel options and categories

Equipped with a sound understanding of the key issues underlying selection of the appropriate channel participants, managers can then examine and evaluate the channel options (or channel media) available.

Channel categories

These options fall into six main channel categories, as shown in the CRM strategy framework. Although there are many individual channel options, we have found it convenient to group them into these six categories. Thus options such as retail branches and kiosks are included within 'outlets' and the Internet and digital TV within 'e-commerce'. Electronic commerce and mobile commerce (e-commerce and M-commerce) are addressed separately, as the ubiquity of the mobile device, the rapid development of WAP (wireless application protocol) and newer technologies such as generation (3G) mobile services and the ability to tailor information based on the customer's physical location, justify the latter being considered in its own right. The six channel categories are:

- Sales force (including field account management, service and personal representation)
- Outlets (including retail branches, stores, depots and kiosks)
- Telephony (including traditional telephone, facsimile, telex and call centre contact)
- Direct marketing (including direct mail, radio, traditional TV, etc., but excluding e-commerce)
- E-commerce (including e-mail, the Internet and digital TV)
- M-commerce (including mobile telephony, SMS and text messaging, WAP and 3G mobile services).

Figure 4.3 summarizes the general characteristics and functionality of these different channel types and indicates the kinds of customer needs they can satisfy.

Mobile commerce as a separate channel category

Before discussing the integration of these channel options, some commentary should be made on the decision, for the present, to consider mobile commerce as a separate channel category. There are two reasons for this. First, M-commerce is not only time independent, it is also place independent. E-commerce has made a major impact because the customer can obtain information about a company's offerings or purchase its products at whatever time they choose, irrespective of the company's opening hours. With M-commerce the customer can obtain information or make a purchase any time and they can do it from anywhere using their mobile device in a much more convenient way.

Second, M-commerce can utilize global positioning technology on the customer's mobile device to relate the position of a customer relative to a supply of what the customer is seeking. This opens up a multitude of new opportunities to add customer value ranging from finding a local parking space, identification of the closest petrol station or Italian restaurant, to location-based dating services based on two people meeting mutually programmed criteria.

Figure 4.3 General characteristics of the different channel options

Channel option	General characteristics and functionality
Sales force	The interactive nature of face-to-face communication with customers means that sales staff can deal effectively with complex non-standard queries. They are also well placed to determine an individual's specific needs and to make purchase recommendations. Sales force automation systems (SFAs) can be used to individualize customer service further by ensuring that those handling sales enquiries have the necessary knowledge and skills to respond to customer's individual information needs. Using printed materials or product samples, sales representatives can also convey large amounts of information and demonstrate product features. However, sales staff offer limited customer access, partly because they generally only work during office hours and partly because they are limited in the number of customers they can serve at any one time. Personal selling via sales representatives therefore tends to be an extremely expensive form of marketing channel.
Outlets	The physical presence of stores and other outlets offers a number of benefits. As well as being reassuringly visible, they allow for the physical inspection of products and the return of unwanted sales. Customers can browse among products at liberty and can gain large amounts of information, both via product displays and through conversation with sales assistants. Moreover, assuming staff are well trained, in-store conversations can be used to resolve complex non-standard queries. However, accessibility is limited by restricted opening hours and the requirement that customers make the journey to and from the store. Further, the level of individual attention the customer receives in the store (according to their specific needs and value to the organization) can be difficult to achieve on a mass scale. To provide further scope for individualizing service, some retailers are installing kiosks to provide a web-based service channel in-store. Online search and service facilities can also be tailored to the customer according to the customer's contact history and purchase profile. Moreover, the capture of purchase information in-store via electronic point of sale (EPOS) and loyalty cards can also be used to develop individual customer profiles to drive tailored activity in other channels, such as direct mail.
Telephony	In principle, call centres can offer access to a company 24 hours × 7 days. The service provided to a customer via this channel can be tailored cost-effectively to their particular interests and their value to the organization by using company records to guide the script brought up on the operative's screen and by directing their call to suitably skilled personnel via automated call routing systems. By affording human dialogue, the telephone channel is well suited for dealing with complex, vague or unclear questions from customers. It also enables the information conveyed to be adapted in real time according to the customer's earlier responses during the interaction. However, the amount of information

Figure 4.3   (continued)

Channel option	General characteristics and functionality

that can be exchanged is limited by the extent to which it can be conveyed verbally and can be retained by a listener. The telephone is best suited to providing responses to specific queries from a customer, i.e. it does not readily offer the customer an opportunity to 'browse' or the call centre representative to 'sell' a complex proposition. Nor does it enable the physical inspection of a product. By its 'virtual' nature this channel is more subject to engendering customer mistrust, unless the customer has a familiar and comfortable relationship with the company built through other channels.

Direct marketing   When based on full and accurate database records of the customer, including their contact and purchase histories and customer profile, direct mail can offer a reasonable degree of service customization. Mailings can be tailored to the customer's individual interests and life events. (The advent of digital printing has made small print runs far cheaper than was previously possible under lithographic printing, enabling far more mail pieces to be targeted at far smaller segments.) Large amounts of information can be relayed through text and graphics, allowing many products to be featured, such as in a product catalogue. Customers are offered the opportunity to browse through the company's products and perhaps also to place an order via post.

However, direct mail does not represent a fast and flexible medium in terms of its customer responsiveness. Information sent via telephone or Internet can be more easily and quickly adapted to customer feedback – with mailings one has to send a mail piece, wait a number of days for the customer's response (if there is one) and then despatch another progressively updated item. Moreover, direct mail offers the customer little access to a company and limited opportunity for the company to deal with customer queries – again requiring the recipient to complete a response device, mail it to the company, have it processed and so on (unless of course a company integrates another channel to handle the response, such as allowing customers to respond by phone). Mail offers no means of physically inspecting a product (unless a sample of the product is enclosed). While the tangible quality of the mail piece can provide a degree of customer reassurance, there is the potential for customer mistrust if the customer is not already familiar with the company through using other channels.

E-commerce   The web truly offers customers 24 × 7 access to the company and the company unique access to its users. Clever web site design can enable the company to recognize individual users through log-in procedures or 'cookie' technology. The information conveyed to users via the site can be tailored or personalized to their particular interests, purchase history and value to the organization, in real time, based on a 'memory' of their previous visits to the site. Trading over the Internet supports

Figure 4.3 *(continued)*

Channel option	General characteristics and functionality
	the development of 1:1 relationships with customers on a mass scale. Moreover, the volume of information that can be conveyed is potentially infinite, considering the sophisticated facilities of multimedia and hyperlinks to other sites. The customer can readily browse the company's products online and can revisit the information by saving it on computer or printing it out for later reference. However, while the medium deals well with simple standard queries via tables of FAQs, non-standard or more complex queries will need to be dealt with by a human operative (via e-mail in the case of the former or telephone in the case of the latter). In addition, physical inspection of the actual product is again impossible. The 'virtual' nature of e-commerce may generate customer mistrust unless the customer is already familiar with the company via other channels.
Mobile commerce	Wireless Application Protocol (WAP) has faced a number of limitations. Its ability to convey information is in part limited by the ability to exploit bandwidth capacity. However, the new generation of G3 phones offers the capability of being able to deliver full colour displays, audio and video. This offers higher levels of accessibility than the web, enabling users to access information or perform transactions from any place as well as at any time. Added value in terms of customization is possible because as well as taking account of a customer's previous purchase history and contact with the organization, M-commerce enables offers to be extended according to an individual's location at a particular point in time. For example, BT introduced some years ago FindMe, where a company can offer a user information about their facilities in the area by identifying the physical location of the user. In addition, as Bluetooth and similar technologies develop, mobile devices will be able to function as a micropayments system enabling a customer to check out of a hotel, for instance, simply by walking past a detector and entering a payment code into the mobile device rather than having to queue to see a member of staff.

Source: Payne and Frow[5]

Numerous applications using mobile technology are being explored not only in B2C markets, but also in B2B markets. One of the early pioneers in the B2B market was Ideal Boilers who developed an M-commerce solution for plumbers.

Case 4.1:   Ideal Boilers: Case study overview

Ideal Boilers, a leading gas boiler manufacturer based in the UK and part of the Caradon group of companies, supplies almost a fifth of domestic boilers and almost half of all commercial and industrial boilers in the UK market. Ideal sells boilers to an extremely fragmented and disparate installation community, with some 40 000 companies employing 90 000 installers. Dealing successfully with the smaller installation companies, who constitute over 50 per cent of operators in the domestic heating market, was a challenge. In particular, there was a requirement to ensure that information on installation instructions, new products, fault finding and special promotions is passed to the user customer base.

In September 2000 Ideal launched the Heating Information Service Project, a pioneering initiative to exploit mobile technology for mutual business benefit. Ideal joined up with BT Cellnet (now O₂) and Improveline.com to develop a new Mobile Internet service that will save busy heating engineers valuable time and money by providing them with access to technical information and diagnostic support on-site using WAP-enabled phones. Mobile phones were provided free of charge to approved heating installers to replace or supplement their existing mobile handsets. The phones incorporated Caradon's Heating Information Service, giving the handset operator direct and immediate access to vital information by entering a PIN security code.

By using a mobile phone to get information to and from its customer base, Caradon was the first among its industry peers to communicate via a medium that has become an everyday tool of heating installers. Further, the effectiveness of its information service was not dependent on a customer's proximity to a PC or propensity to use the Internet. The Ideal initiative won exceptional praise at the Computer Weekly Awards for E-business Excellence where both project and project champion scooped major awards.

The full case study is at the end of this chapter (see p. 218)

While a detailed review of studies in this area by specialist industry researchers such as Durlacher[6] and CRM Group[7] (now Vectia Ltd.) justifies a distinction between e-commerce and M-commerce, device convergence is likely to make such distinctions less important in the years ahead.

Integration and the channel categories

Faced with the necessity of offering consumers different channel options to meet their changing needs, there are two integration imperatives that must be addressed if a company is to deliver a consistent individualized relationship to customers, create the maximum value for them and provide an outstanding customer experience. These are to integrate the activities within a given channel and to integrate the activities performed across the different channels during different stages of the customer's relationship with the enterprise.

Insight into the impact that can be achieved through such effective integration of channel activity can be gained by contrasting the experience of customers using a channel option of a company whose activities are not integrated (too often the reality) with that of a customer using a channel where the company has achieved integration.

Sales force

Non-integrated

An international bank in Hong Kong responded to a tender for a large piece of business from a major corporation. The customer was visited by two senior managers from different departments in the bank on the same day each with a response to the tender. Unfortunately, each was unaware that the other was seeing the client. Although both presented similar proposals with respect to content, the fees they quoted for the work differed by 25 per cent. This resulted in considerable embarrassment at the bank and considerable amusement in the local financial community – neither bid won the business.

Integrated

In a company that has integrated its channels with its customers, there is an IT system that enables them to identify previous contact with the customer. This is typically achieved with a sales force automation system. Moreover, not only is relevant and up to date information held about the individual customer, but processes are in place to use it to ensure staff tailor their activities based on any previous contacts the customer has had with the organization. Any contact with the customer is logged on the system regardless of whether the channel is personal contact, a letter, a telephone call or an e-mail.

Outlets

Non-integrated

A customer learns of a new product their bank has launched through receiving a direct mail piece. Their interest was particularly aroused because the mail piece said the product was in line with the bank's mission to provide outstanding service and make life easier for its customers. However, on visiting their local branch during lunchtime, they find they have to queue because most counter staff are on their lunch break. When they do finally reach a representative, they find they have received no training in the product and are not familiar with it. Moreover, they seem disinterested and unhappy in their work. And, of course, the computer system is down.

Integrated

McDonalds ensures its restaurants consistently deliver the customer service promised in its advertising through rigorous training of its staff in a prescribed mode for customer interaction. The staff member first smiles, establishes eye contact and greets the customer. Then after taking the order, they make suggestions of additional items the customer may want to accompany their meal. As well as ensuring all of its customers are consistently made to feel welcome, this approach also maximizes the cross-selling and upselling opportunities for the company.

Telephony

Non-integrated

Consider the most recent calls you have made to a call centre. How many have been positive experiences for you? You are not alone in being disappointed. All too often even major business clients find themselves having to wait for long periods of time while ironically being repeatedly told that 'Your call is important to us' by a pre-recorded voice. Frequently the person eventually answering their call does not have the skills to deal with their query and the caller again finds themselves put 'on hold' while they are passed to yet another department. Interestingly, many large organizations with advanced call centre technology fail to exploit its functionality.

Integrated

A corporate customer calls a company's call centre. Call Line Identification (CLI) helps identify them by recognizing the telephone number of the incoming call (or if the customer is calling from someone else's phone, they are recognized by the PIN number they are invited to enter, with the same effect). Upon recognition, the customer is automatically shifted from call 120 to number 5 in the queue and is answered within 30 seconds. In addition, the customer's records are brought up onto the operators screen and, depending upon the time or the day of the week, rules-based procedures may configure the screen with the items most likely to be of relevance to that customer's call on the basis of the caller's history of contact with the organization.

Direct mail
Non-integrated
Many of us are familiar with receiving a constant barrage of unsolicited materials that have little relevance to us. Indeed, we may even be bombarded by solicitations from a company to take up a product that we have already purchased from them. However, to add insult to injury, this time there may be a special offer that was absent when we purchased it. Moreover, the barrage may consist of offers from different departments of the organization with no apparent guiding logic. In addition, they may be completely incompatible with information we have already supplied to the organization via other channels (e.g. via a conversation with a call centre or a staff member in the branch).

Integrated
If customers receive information that is highly relevant to their interests, they do not perceive it as junk mail but as a valued communication. Rover Cars was among the first automotive companies to understand this. Many years ago, it produced 'Catalyst' a unique magazine that allowed customers to choose a significant part of the contents based on their individual lifestyle interests including gardening, cooking and sports. Many different versions reflected the customer's profile. This programme was carefully integrated with other points of channel contact. Each issue contained a questionnaire to update the customer's details and, to integrate with their campaign management, identify where they were in their 'purchase window'.

E-commerce
Non-integrated
Any regular user of the Internet will be only too familiar with the exasperating experience of using badly thought out and poorly constructed web sites. In spite of company's positioning their e-commerce presence as a means of giving customers added convenience, many of our encounters with these sites are frustrating. In particular, registration processes and purchasing procedures seem designed to deter usage with many organizations requiring so much information that the customer is put off and never completes the process. Alternatively,

if a mistake is made in completing fields, it can be impossible to identify where that mistake is and how to correct it. Moreover, there is frequently no phone number or e-mail address through which one might sort out problems.

Integrated

By contrast users of Amazon.com have a far more positive experience. When they use the site, it is personalized to them using collaborative filtering organization to provide recommendations of other books likely to be of interest to them, based on what previous purchasers of that book have also bought. Moreover, the fulfilment process is integrated with the ordering channel and the brand identity is highly uniform across the different points of contact. Items purchased not only arrive in a timely manner; they are well packaged and have a range of useful enclosures, e.g. bookmarks. The effect is to reinforce the customer's positive impressions of the company formed through their previous interactions with it.

M-commerce

Non-integrated

Customers who have to contact their mobile service provider have widely different experiences depending on the identity of their service provider. Some companies' skills seem to be in sales and branding, rather than customer service. Customers experience great frustration when they have to wait exceptionally long times in a queue or, if they are prepaid customers who are topping up their balance, find their credit card not authorized through a fault in the system. Further, early adopters of mobile phones incorporating WAP and 3G have often had an experience inconsistent with the promise made. Poor communication to customers has contributed to these problems as much as bad design and limitations in the bandwidth.

Integrated

As experience grows and subsequent generations of mobile technology emerge there are great opportunities to deliver positive customer experiences, provided that the fundamental limitations of this channel are effectively communicated to and understood by the customer. A significant number of customers who understand these limitations are delighted with services available. This is true both for business customers, whose time is scarce and who are required to be very mobile and for individual consumers who wish to be updated frequently on the news, weather and activities of their football team. Some companies such as banks have been successful in integrating their M-commerce solutions with other channels.

Combining channels

These main channel categories can be represented as a continuum of forms of customer contact ranging from the physical (such as a face-to-face encounter with a company sales representative) to the virtual (such as an e-commerce or G3 or WAP phone transaction). Clearly, employing a combination of the channels most appropriate to the target customer base and company structure will provide the greatest commercial exposure and return. In many instances, different types of channels can be used concurrently. Thus there will be an increasing convergence of channel options into what has become known as a 'contact centre'. These contact centres can integrate, for example, telephone, e-mail and web contact. Newer developments such as 'voice over IP' (voice over Internet protocol) integrate both telephony and the Internet in a more interactive way.

Land's End provides a good example of a B2C organization that has integrated different channels to increase the value created for the customer.

Landsend.com

The web site of online fashion retailer Landsend.com contains a series of features to provide an individualized service. Users can enter details on their physical build, hair colour, face shape, skin tone, etc. and receive fashion advice on screen tailored to these aspects. Moreover, these details can be used to create an on-screen avatar so that the user can see what different outfits would look like on someone with their build and features, in part creating the means of 'trying on' clothing one can perform in a physical shop. Even the experience of going to the shops with a friend can be replicated by allowing two different users to move through the site together and view the same pages at the same time from different PCs.

However, what is difficult to replicate on a site is the function of a sales assistant with the inherent ability of human conversation to deal with complex or unfocused non-standard queries. To deal with this, the site is integrated with the company's call centre. By clicking the 'Land's End Live' button, users can opt to be phoned by a company representative or interact with them in a chatroom using IRC (Internet Relay Chat). Areas in which they might seek such assistance include how to find a particular item, how to use the site or simply to discuss possible outfits with another person. Moreover, the call centre staff can tailor their advice to the individual's situation both by being able to view the same pages as them or by examining their past purchase history to suggest items that might be of interest to that user or that might match items they can see are already in their wardrobe.

By bringing these two channels together in this way a greater range of the customer's needs can be met and more value created for them in the interaction than would be possible were the customer to deal with either channel separately.

Deciding which channels to use and in what combination (including at what time and with which segments), is a matter of being aware of the channel members and channel options available and then evaluating them in the context of the company's business situation. This necessarily requires a full understanding of the nature of each channel type, including how it functions and what benefits and limitations it offers. It also requires an honest appraisal of the company's capabilities as well as the needs and potential of its market segments. Customers' needs during the sales cycle will vary according to the product involved and the nature of the segment to which they belong. Such an evaluation will lead to a consideration of the most appropriate channel strategy.

In B2C markets the evaluation and choice may be relatively simple. However, in B2B markets, where there is complex account management and a large product portfolio, there will inevitably be the need for a more detailed evaluation and for a wider range of channels to be utilized. An extra level layer of complexity can occur here because of the channel hand-off required as the product or proposition moves through the sales cycle from demand generation to fulfilment.

Channel strategies

The basic decisions relating to a firm's strategic channel decisions have been identified by researchers such as professor Burt Rosenbloom of Drexel University who identifies six key areas for decisions:

1. What role should channels play in a firm's overall objectives and strategies?
2. What role should channels play in the marketing mix?

3. How should the firm's marketing channels be designed to achieve its distribution objectives?
4. What kinds of channel members should be selected to meet the firm's distribution objectives?
5. How can the external marketing channel and partners be managed to implement the firm's channel design effectively and efficiently on a continuing basis?
6. How can channel member performance be evaluated?[8]

These six areas provide a powerful checklist for a company to consider its strategic channel decisions.

Channel strategy options

The starting point in addressing channel strategy options is to consider objectively who should dictate channel strategy – the customer or the supplier. In general, the customer's needs are the ones that should be considered. If customers in the firm's target segments have demands that can be satisfied best through a particular channel strategy, this should be emphasized in the firm's CRM strategy. However, circumstances including capacity, competencies and capabilities and business ambitions may dictate a more supplier-oriented and less customer-oriented, approach.

Companies usually select from one of the following broad channel strategy options:

A *mono-channel provider strategy* is based on customer interactions through one main channel. Direct Line and First Direct both started as telephone operations, while in the online environment companies such as Amazon and CDnow adopt single channel Internet strategies referred to as 'pure play'.

A *customer segment channel strategy* recognizes that different customer groups may wish to interact with different channel types. Zurich Financial Services use different channels and brands to appeal to particular market segments. Thus their brands such as Allied Dunbar, Zurich, Eagle Star and Threadneedle use different routes to market including a direct sales force, independent financial advisers (IFAs) and a telephone contact centre in order to serve 18 customer groups with differing needs and attitudes.

A *graduated account management strategy* is based on the existing and future potential value of customers. Many business-to-business companies have implemented a graduated approach where important commercial customers are served by key account managers, medium-sized businesses through telephone-based account managers and small customers through a call centre.

A *channel migrator strategy* is concerned with migrating customers from one channel to another. This strategy may be driven by the potential within a new channel to serve more lucrative customer segments or the opportunities to reduce cost or increase customer value. Low cost airline easyJet commenced selling tickets solely through a call centre, but is now encouraging customers to purchase their tickets through the Internet. They have used a combination of financial incentives and reduced levels of service in the call centre successfully to encourage their customers to buy online.

An *activity-based channel strategy* recognizes that customers may wish to use different channels in combination to undertake different tasks. Thus a customer purchasing a computer may visit a branch physically to inspect it, use the Internet to select the exact specification of the computer and use a call centre to confirm this specification will meet their specific needs and to order it.

An *integrated multi-channel strategy* involves utilizing the full range of commercially viable channels to serve customers and integrating them without attempting to influence the channel that the customer wishes to use. Banks such as Intelligent Finance and Woolwich in the UK and Merita bank, now part of the Nordea group, in Scandinavia are examples of successful implementation of multi-channel approaches. In the telecommunications industry BT in the UK is responding to their corporate market demands by deploying an integrated multi-channel strategy. Here the business should seek to capture all customer information across all channels and integrate it within a single data repository so the business can recognize previous interactions with the customer, regardless of the channel in which the interactions took place, and use this to enhance the customer experience.

The role of a multi-channel strategy

Given the range of channel strategies outlined above, why are more and more businesses adopting multi-channel integration? Is not the appropriate strategy for some companies to create and build businesses based on only one channel?

While some businesses may choose a single channel strategy, many more will benefit from a strategy based on the integration of multiple channels. For example, firms trading solely on the Internet may have much to gain from adopting a multi-channel approach. Joanna Marsh, a director at McKinsey & Company and a leader of the firm's e-tail practice, believes a combined approach is vital in e-commerce. 'To be successful, online retailers need to exploit other marketing channels simultaneously, such as in-store and catalogue sales, as well as private labels. Our study shows that multi-channel players can increase their share of wallet, as many customers are already browsing on the web before buying in the store.'[9]

A multi-channel strategy offers greater scope for respecting customers' channel preferences and propensities of use, therefore enhancing the company's attractiveness and, ultimately, responsiveness to customers. In today's business arena, customer service is regarded not only as the key to differential advantage but also as a baseline requirement to compete. Excellent customer service sees customer choice as a right, not a privilege and this extends to allowing customers to use whatever channel they wish (such as mail, phone, fax, Internet, face-to-face, etc.) for whatever reason motivates them to contact the company (such as to place an order, ask a query, register a complaint, track a fault, request a service, respond to a promotion, etc.). Likewise, it also respects how customers wish to be contacted by the company to receive notifications, such as payment reminders or special offers, or to contribute to value enhancement, such as participating in market surveys or enabling after-sales service fulfilment.

Understanding the customer relationship life-cycle

Discussions about channel options are often dominated by considerations relating to making the sale. However, for strategic CRM the channels need to be considered in the context of the whole interaction over the life-cycle of the customer relationship, not just in terms of the sales activity. Customer understanding needs to go beyond traditional market research, which tends to be descriptive and aggregate results together and drill down at a micro-level into the characteristics of the customer value chain for key customer types, or segments. In other words, we need to understand the processes that customers engage in – running an assembly line, an airline, or a professional services firm – and then identify the opportunities to create value within those processes. We create value either by making those processes more effective, doing them better or more efficiently, doing them more cheaply.[10]

To help businesses identify such value-creating opportunities the stages of a customer relationship can be considered under the three broad headings of acquisition, consolidation and enhancement, as shown in Figure 4.4.

Figure 4.4   Understanding the nature of customer encounters

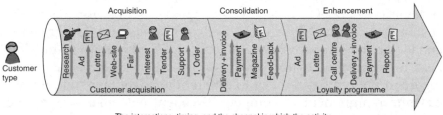

The interactions, timing, and the channel in which the activity
takes place need to be closely integrated

Source: Vectia Ltd.[11]

These stages can be broken down into more specific elements which will vary depending on the business being considered. For example, a computer manufacturer selling to business customers identified the following key elements:

- marketing communications
- prospecting and lead generation
- sales qualification
- proposal generation
- pre-sales activity
- selling
- installation
- post-sales service
- ongoing account management.

A similar approach has been suggested by Sandra Vandermerwe, a professor at Imperial College, who proposes mapping the 'customer activity cycle'.[12] Its objective is to gain a deep understanding of what customers 'do' (including activities before and after the 'doing') through a detailed mapping of the stages in these customer processes. When these activity cycles are mapped, the next step is to understand where the opportunities lie to create further value. For example, it may involve which elements of that activity cycle are the most complex, uncertain, frustrating or time-consuming; or those elements with which the customer is most dissatisfied.

Within these typical stages, a great number of interactions occur between the customer and the organization across different channels. Understanding the nature of different customer encounters within a multi-channel environment is essential if the organization's CRM activities are to be fully effective. Also, there needs to be a clear understanding of the costs associated with each stage of the relationship life-cycle as well as the likely margins delivered by customers at each stage of the life-cycle. Further, customers' needs during the customer relationship life-cycle phases will vary according to the segment to which they belong and the product or service involved. Thus determining the most appropriate forms of channel options for specific customer segments is also critical. The channel approach adopted by a supplier should be developed in a way that enables the company to meet different customer segments' needs over the life-cycle and to maximize the value it creates for them.

Understanding the customer experience

Faced with the necessity of offering customers different channel types to meet their changing needs during the sales cycle (pre-sale, sale and post-sale), it is increasingly imperative to integrate the activities in those different channels to produce the most positive customer experience and to create the maximum value. Competitive advantage today is not just about selling products and services to customers; it is about delivering world class service and building long-term and profitable relationships with customers, which are founded on mutual benefit and trust. To succeed, therefore, the company must consistently seek to offer an individualized relationship, where economically feasible, in every customer interaction through whatever channel is being used.

With the accelerating pace of technology, it is increasingly impossible to maintain competitive advantage merely through the attributes of individual products. Product life-cycles are now so short that soon after launch a company is likely to find competitors or new entrants imitating any new innovation – hence the logic for

CRM. Rather than merely producing discrete products for a mass market, the company pursues ongoing relationships with its most profitable customers. The value to the customer resides not in any single product but in the reassurance that the company will continue to offer them a stream of products tailored to their particular needs. In a sense, the company becomes the trusted supplier for the customer. By continually offering superior customer value to the customer in an extended relationship, the financial or psychological cost to the customer of switching to another supplier rises dramatically. The result is increased levels of customer retention and profitability and a potential decrease in customer sensitivity to price.

The customer experience and emotional goodwill

However, if a company is to succeed in this endeavour, it needs to ensure that it continues to offer the customer the same individualized relationship over time and across all points of contact. In other words, the structure and flow of activity in the different channels through which the company and customer interact must be integrated so that the channels, both individually and collectively, consistently deliver the value proposition in the eyes of the customer. The provision of a 'seamless and consistent customer experience' at every juncture will engender trust, which in turn will reinforce the relationship and perhaps propel it towards a higher level of opportunity and return.

The collective experiences a customer has developed into what is termed 'an emotional reservoir of goodwill' towards the supplier, shown in Figure 4.5. High quality experiences increase emotional goodwill and the likelihood of the customer giving their supplier further custom. In contrast, failure to deliver on the individualized-relationship value proposition can leave the customer disappointed and frustrated, leading to dissonance in the relationship and, worse, to the ultimate defection of the customer to a competitor.

Evaluating the customer experience

In evaluating the customer experience a five-point customer satisfaction scale is often used. Assume the satisfaction labels attached to the scores are as follows:

5 – perfect/outstanding
4 – satisfied
3 – average/mediocre
2 – poor
1 – terrible.

Figure 4.5   The emotional reservoir of goodwill

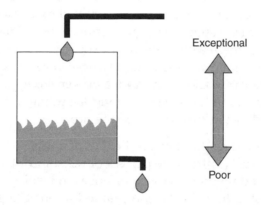

Findings in a number of studies have confirmed the importance of seeking high levels of satisfaction. For example, a study by Jones and Sasser[13] on loyalty and customer satisfaction reached two major conclusions. First, only highly delighted customers (e.g. a '5' on the 5-point scale) can be considered truly loyal. Second, customers who are just satisfied (e.g. a '4' on the 5-point scale) are only slightly more loyal than customers who are thoroughly dissatisfied (e.g. a '1' on a 5-point scale).

Because of the great importance of a 5/5 customer experience, the channel strategy should seek to ensure such an experience occurs within channel *and* across multiple channels. The channel experience needs to be considered, in the context of a company's industry sector and its important customer segments, by asking three questions:

● What is the typical and perfect customer experience *within* channels?
● What is the typical and perfect customer experience *across* channels?
● How do we sustain and *improve the customer experience* within channel, across channel and substitute an existing channel for a better one?

The customer experience within channel

We recently investigated over 1000 customers' views of their experiences within channel including the Internet and call centres and asked the following questions:

- What percentage of telephone calls you have made to a call centre over the past two months have resulted in a perfect/outstanding customer experience? Contrast these with those where you have experienced delays, poor interactive voice response, multiple hand-offs, etc.
- What percentage of the visits to web sites you have made over the past two months have resulted in a perfect/outstanding customer experience? Contrast these with those where you have not been able to complete the registration process or experienced unreasonable requests for information at registration, poor layout, broken linkages, poor navigation structures, computer lock-up (apparently due to the web site), or unnecessarily long delays in moving around the site.

Over 70 per cent of respondents indicated only one in ten experiences in contacting a call centre were perfect or outstanding and more than 60 per cent said only one in ten experiences in visiting web sites were perfect or outstanding. Many complained about the poor customer experience within these channels. Given such poor results, companies need to understand, within their industry, what constitutes an outstanding and what constitutes a typical customer experience among their key customer segments and how they can improve it.

However, improved customer experience must be achieved at an affordable cost. The concept of segmented service strategy is important here. Improvement should be based on the profit potential of different customer segments and service strategies and investment decisions should be made with the knowledge of this profit potential. Where a customer interacts with multiple channels, which is increasingly the case, the customer experience needs to be considered cumulatively across all channel interactions.

The customer experience across channels

The customer experience commences with the communications activities undertaken as part of the company's acquisition programme and continues through all subsequent forms of customer interaction. In communicating with the customer, a company is likely to use a combination of different channel options or media, such as advertising, direct mail, sales promotions, public relations, and so on. If the company is to be successful in forming a particular perception of itself in the mind of the customer and in building a relationship with them on that foundation across channels, it must ensure consistency in the messages conveyed by these different means. Any incoherence or conflict in the messages in different channels will confuse the customer, who may then misinterpret or 'draw a blank' about what the company stands for and what it is offering. This confusion across channels can seriously diminish the customer's view of the company and possibly instigate negative word-of-mouth.

The 'touch-points' where the customer interacts with the supplier in multiple channels represent the most crucial opportunities to leverage advantage. It is here that the planned marketing communications meet the reality of what the customer actually experiences when they interact with the company. The customer's 'experience' of the company will probably be a composite formed through using different types of channel. It will be based, for instance, on how the customer's call is handled when they phone the company, how efficiently their orders are processed, how professionally their complaints or service queries are dealt with and whether the visiting sales representative listens to them and responds appropriately.

If the customer's experience of the company falls short of what they have been led to expect, their disappointment will probably show as frustration or a withdrawal of trust in the company. Unless the resultant quality gap or damage to the relationship can be quickly and fully redressed and the customer reassured, the company's espoused position will be undermined. The danger is not just that the company will lose a customer, but that it will effectively hand the customer to a competitor. At the other extreme, if the customer's experience of dealing with the company meets or indeed surpasses their expectations such that their experiences are outstanding (or better), then the company's reputation will be given a boost and the relationship will be strengthened.

Improving the customer experience – the role of technology

Technology can make a major contribution to achieving a perfect or outstanding customer experience. For example, within a call centre,

CLI (caller line identification) can identify the caller and rules-based systems can accelerate important customers up a large queue of calls; interactive voice response (IVR) can assist a customer to find the most appropriate person to speak to without multiple hand-offs; CTI (computer–telephony integration) tools, in conjunction with CLI, can enable a customer's computer records to be called up instantaneously and be shown on the call centre operator's screen. Together with an empathetic and well-trained company representative, these technologies can dramatically improve the customer experience, in this case in the contact centre environment.

The advent of increasingly sophisticated database technologies has greatly enhanced the ability of companies to target and differentiate their products, customers and customer communications. Special search, analysis and tracking features also enable companies to monitor the effectiveness and efficiency of marketing activity and thus to maximize the return on marketing expenditure. By recording the customer's responses to different messages sent through different communication channels, the company can learn progressively more about its individual customers and how they (and others like them) are likely to respond to certain communications. Based on this information, the company can develop models to use in predicting the customer response behaviour of different segments to various types of communication. These educated projections can then be employed to help marketers evaluate alternative communications programmes and the probable return on investment these might achieve. As a result more informed multi-channel strategies can be developed.

However, ironically those companies that achieve high ratings in terms of the customer experience, both within a channel and across channels, often do not have superior or proprietary technology. Rather they typically achieve their superiority by *how* they utilize the technology solution and through the quality of staff at the customer interface.

The 'perfect' customer experience

All enterprises need to consider how they should 'engineer' their customer experience. The objective for most businesses should be to offer an outstanding or 'perfect' customer experience at an affordable cost. We define outstanding or 'perfect' in this context as achieving a 5/5 score on customer satisfaction. Note the word perfect is in quotes, for it needs to be considered in context of the nature of customer expectations relating to that offer. To achieve a 5/5 score on a first class flight with Singapore Airlines or British Airways costing say $8000, expectations are likely to be very high. However, a similar 5/5 score in customer experience may be achieved with a low cost airline such as Southwest Airlines or easyjet with a fare of, say, $80. Here expectations are that the staff are pleasant, the plane is clean and it departs and arrives on time – even though the seats are cramped and the food minimal or non-existent.

There are many aspects to achieving an outstanding or perfect customer experience. Perhaps the most important one is a deep knowledge of customer needs and the criticality of ensuring CRM operates across the business in a cross-functional manner. However, this cross-functional working is the exception rather than the rule. For example, Evert Gummesson, a professor at Stockholm University, describes Lee Iacocca's first impressions when he took over the failing Chrysler Corporation over two decades ago: 'Nobody at Chrysler seemed to understand that interaction among different enterprise functions in a company is absolutely critical. People in engineering and manufacturing almost have to be sleeping together. These guys were not even flirting… The manufacturing guys would build cars without even checking with the sales guys. They just built them, stuck them in a yard, and then hoped that somebody would take them out of there. We ended up with a huge inventory and a financial nightmare.'[14]

We consider the use of the term 'perfect' can help engage all staff, across all departments and business functions, in delivering an outstanding product or service. TNT Express Services are a good example of an organization in the B2B sector that uses the concept of the perfect customer experience to ensure all employees have a deep knowledge of customer needs, operate in an aligned manner across functions and in all customer encounters and deliver superior customer service.

TNT – Creating the Perfect Customer Transaction

TNT Express Services UK & Ireland is part of the global TPG Group, which employs 148 000 employees in 64 countries and has an annual turnover of £8 billion. They provide an excellent example of an organization dedicated to creating and delivering a perfect experience for every customer, every time.

In 1978 the company employed 500 staff in the UK with a sales revenue of £5 m, while today it has grown to some 9500 employees with a sales revenue of £630 m. Although this growth was dramatic, senior management recognized that in an increasingly competitive market with over 4000 parcel courier companies, simply delivering customer satisfaction was not enough.

In 1999 TNT undertook research that showed very high levels of customer satisfaction. Some 90 per cent were satisfied, with the balance being neutral or dissatisfied. However, they concluded that those customers who were merely 'satisfied', as opposed to those that were 'very satisfied' could be in danger of defection, especially if they had some subsequent reason for dissatisfaction. The company recognized that it was imperative to improve the experience of these customers, shifting them to being highly satisfied and thereby increasing their loyalty and profitability.

TNT did further research and found that by asking whether customers had any problems with the service that they received from TNT, they obtained a much clearer picture of the customer experience and how it could be improved. TNT then launched a radical programme aimed at creating the 'Perfect Transaction' for all customers. The 'Perfect Transaction' includes the chain of events from when a customer requests a collection, to the time that payment is received for the consignment – as shown in Figure 4.6.

Figure 4.6   The 'Perfect Customer Transaction' at TNT

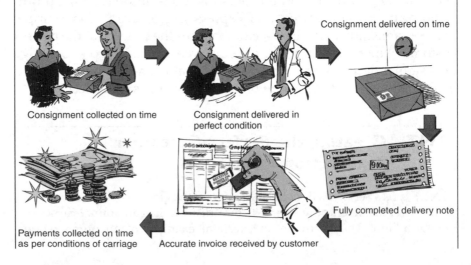

Consignment delivered on time

Consignment collected on time

Consignment delivered in perfect condition

Fully completed delivery note

Payments collected on time as per conditions of carriage

Accurate invoice received by customer

The first step was to understand where improvements could be made to the customer experience. TNT started by asking customers, in much greater detail than had been done previously, about what they wanted. Then, using this information, a list of areas where the customer experience could be improved was developed. Before any performance enhancements were made, statistical modelling was used to prioritize this list. Costs associated with these improvements were carefully considered. TNT senior managers recognized that outstanding customer service had to be delivered at a reasonable cost – both in terms of cost to the customer and to the company. Next, the opportunities for improvement were analysed by weighting the frequency of occurrence with the impact of the problem to pinpoint enhancements that really mattered to the customer. This led to the identification of the key areas which would lead to the perfect transaction.

High on the list of priorities, customers asked for one point of contact when they called into TNT in order to avoid excessive call transfers, too many contact points and long telephone holding. As a result, the customer services department was strengthened. Instead of multiple points of contact, a customer who now calls in deals with one individual who can handle any enquiry. Employees have greater ability to respond to customer queries through wider knowledge, greater authority and enhanced technology. The result is that the customer gets better and faster service. Implementation is ongoing with the list of improvements continually being added to and modified. Always, service enhancement is driven by feedback from the customers.

TNT has also found that employee satisfaction has dramatically improved – employees enjoy giving better service to the customer and become frustrated when they lack the skills and authority to do so. The extensive customer service training includes an innovative programme called 'The perfect transaction'. Here employees are trained to understand that they play an important role in delivering the customer experience. Teamwork is essential with each person sharing in the responsibility of achieving perfection in each step of the transaction. This can only be achieved if employees share a positive attitude – striving to beat their previous best performance.

In 2003, TNT won the transport industry award for 'best use of Internet/e-commerce'. This award was in recognition of the company's work in developing new applications to enable customers to monitor the location of their parcels. The new multi-channel applications enable customers to track more than 750 000 consignments each week from collection to delivery, through a range of different channel media.

Although TNT had provided Internet tracking for their customers for more than five years, the new application means consignments can now be monitored via a wide range of communication devices. This gives customers the ability to check the whereabouts of their goods via mobile phones, handheld computers, e-mail, web browsers and even conventional touch-tone phones.

The results of this strategy have been enviable. The UK & Ireland operation is the largest in the TNT Express group, representing approximately one quarter of group sales and is the highest profit contributor. The global Express business profits now represent nearly 6.5 per cent of the Express turnover of more than £2.8 billion – a dramatic improvement from the late 1990s. In recognition of its achievements, the company has been awarded numerous industry awards for service excellence and customer care.

The concept of the perfect customer experience is not restricted to B2B – it is equally relevant to the B2C sector. The case study on Guinness outlined below provides a good example from the FMCG (fast moving consumer goods) sector. The case highlights again the importance of cross-functional involvement and the need for customer education to ensure the ultimate consumer has an outstanding experience.

Case 4.2:   Guinness – Case study overview

Guinness is one of the most well recognized global brands and has a loyal following of consumers. Their special brewing skills are at the heart of every one of the 10 million glasses that Guinness customers enjoy every day across the world. However, producing a consistently high quality product was one of the key problems facing Guinness.

Research suggested that consumers often were presented with a less-than-perfect pint at the point of consumption. Guinness recognized this as a major challenge, involving the total management of the supply chain. Achieving this lay beyond the remit of any one department. To ensure a perfect consumer experience at the point of delivery they formed a special cross-functional process improvement team charged with the job of delivering the 'Perfect Pint'.

The 'Perfect Pint' team found that, often, problems developed once the beer arrived at the licensed premises. The team undertook considerable work to ensure consistency of quality in the final stages of the supply chain. This included guidelines for the publicans on all aspects of the 'pub dispense quality' and recognizing the important role of both pub staff and consumers in ensuring the 'Perfect Pint' was delivered. Detailed instructions and training ensured the 'Perfect Pint' was pulled properly and drunk correctly by consumers.

This strategy, based on the cross-functional involvement of all aspects of Guinness' operations, has successfully delivered the 'perfect' customer experience. This initiative has helped propel Guinness to achieve its highest ever share of the total draught market.

The full case study is at the end of this chapter (see p. 222)

Building a multi-channel strategy

Building a multi-channel strategy involves a channel design that offers the greatest value for the customer and the company. This involves assessing the value created for the end consumer by different channels structures, understanding the economics of different channel structures and determining the channel strategy that will create the maximum value for consumers and the greatest profit for the company.

Developing a multi-channel strategy that delivers an appropriate customer experience for a company's main customer segments includes a number of key activities:

- develop strategic multi-channel objectives
- understand the needs and concerns of key customer segments
- undertake a strategic review of industry structure and channel options
- understand shifts in channel usage patterns
- review channel economics
- develop an integrated channel management strategy.

Drawing on earlier discussions, each of these activities is now reviewed.

Develop strategic multi-channel objectives

The starting point for formulating a multi-channel strategy is to determine the key strategic objectives. The overall objective of multi-channel integration is to provide a significantly enhanced customer experience that results in higher customer satisfaction and increased sales, profits and share of wallet. Ideally, this should be accompanied by a lower cost to serve, through alternative channels, lower in the value chain, e.g. from direct sales force to desk-based account management or a shift from desk-based account management to the adoption or increase in the use of electronic solutions.

Specific strategic objectives should be developed by a company to reflect the earlier CRM strategy development and value creation processes.

For example, the broad objectives set for a new multi-channel strategy by a leading company for its major business clients included:

- improve the customer experience
- increase account coverage
- improve revenue growth
- decrease operating expenses
- utilize the full skills and resources of our business and its employees.

These objectives then should be translated into more specific quantified ones. This may require a benchmarking exercise by understanding experiences of similar companies or undertaking a pilot project better to quantify potential targets. The objectives are likely to be further refined as a result of the additional steps outlined below.

Understand the needs and concerns of key customer segments

It is crucial that a market-driven approach should determine channel choice. This choice, of course, has to be mediated by the relative economics of different channel options from both the customer's and the organization's perspectives. This step will also involve reviewing the value propositions at the market segment level as well as researching customers' channel preferences. The needs, wants and concerns of customers should be a primary force in considering the design of marketing channels. Central to understanding these needs and concerns is a detailed segmentation analysis that is typically undertaken as part of the CRM strategy development process.

However, as mentioned previously, consumers will have different needs at different stages of the relationship life-cycle. Thus channels need to be considered in the context of the whole interaction with the customer over the whole of this cycle, not just at the point of sale. It is a company's activities in this wider context that determines the value it creates for the customer and the relationship it develops with them, both over a single sale and over the series of subsequent activities that make up the customer relationship.

The acquisition or sales activity can be broken down into three phases: pre-sale, sale and post-sale. The initial pre-sale stage may be characterized by the consumer initially gathering information to learn about the product area and identify and evaluate possible alternatives. They may have specific questions they wish to find answers to; some of these may be routine and some complex. They may require help to determine what version of a product would best meet their needs. Then there follows the sales phase. Here the process needs to be easy from the customer's point of view with accurate and reliable information meeting the customer's needs. Following the sale comes the post-sale phase. For example, the customer may require support in using the product. This may be in the form of general advice on how to use the product or assistance if it develops a defect or arranging servicing. In some cases, the customer may need physically to return the product either for repair or to receive a replacement.

Naturally, the needs customers will have over the sales cycle will vary according to the type of product and the customer's experience with it. Thus for some products, all the consumer may require is that it is readily available when desired. For example, the channel strategy of Coke is simply based upon ensuring that a can is always within 'an arm's reach of desire'. For others, customers may have far more complex needs. For example, when buying a computer a customer requires a great deal more in the pre-sale, sale and post-sale phases. Similarly, the needs may differ by customer segment. First Direct's cash-rich, time-poor consumers need to be able to perform transactions at any place at any time of the day. In contrast an old age pensioner may value the social interaction and exercise involved in a visit to their bank branch between 9.00 a.m. and 4 p.m. Having 24-hour telephone or Internet access would offer them little additional value.

This activity should result in an understanding of the needs and concerns of the company's different customer segments at different stages of the life-cycle. In addition, as customers are likely to have several needs at any given stage of the cycle, one must also determine the relative importance they attach to those needs. This can be established through standard research techniques such as observing customer behaviour, questionnaire research or using focus groups of segment members.

Undertake a strategic review of industry structure and channel options

The review of the industry structure will involve the identification of the channel participants described earlier. This will involve a review of the channel alternatives currently being used by the company as well as those used by their competitors and, in addition, the potential for structural change by means of disintermediation or reintermediation. This task can be assisted using a tool called channel chain analysis which considers how a combination of channels is used at different stages of the customer interaction with their supplier.

Figure 4.7 provides an example of channel chain analysis which shows an analysis for the B2B personal computer market offered by competitors at different points in time. In this case the traditional key account management structure on the left is now mainly used only for large computers or large accounts, as other channel chains now offer better channel economics. The direct model in the middle was introduced in the mid-1990s and was pioneered by Dell, with press advertising being the major promotional activity, additional information being supplied by product brochures and call centre

Figure 4.7   Channel chain analysis for personal computers

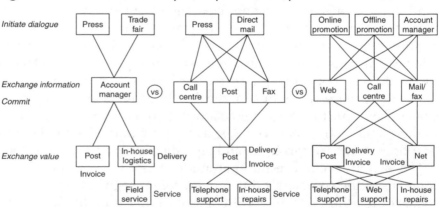

Source: Wilson and McDonald[15]

employees. Here the order could be placed by a variety of means – often through a traditional means such as a fax or mail order sent to the accounts department. More recently the Internet has been added to the channel mix, as shown on the right.[16]

Having understood past and present models, future channel chain diagrams can be constructed and experimented with to consider other options. As Cranfield academics Hugh Wilson and Malcolm McDonald, authors of this approach, note:

> the next step is to consider possible future channel chains. This requires experimentation with channel chain diagrams to think through not just how the sale is to be made, but also how every other aspect of the customer's needs will be satisfied. Will a mobile phone purchaser buying over the web be able to return a faulty phone to a nearby store? Will an e-hub be able to handle not just price negotiations, but also information flows on stock levels, complaints, returns and product development – and if not, what additional channels will be needed? ... There is a timing issue to be considered as well. Even if a channel chain offers a theoretically better proposition to customers, they may not yet be ready for it. A channel chain innovation, like a product innovation, is likely to proceed along the lines of the diffusion of the innovation curve.[17]

This analytical framework should be used creatively, getting input from different groups of company executives. It is also of value to seek the views of analysts, consultants and industry experts as well as benchmarking experiences in analogous industry sectors.

Understand shifts in channel usage patterns

The consideration of possible channel options can be assisted by an understanding of how shifts will occur in channel usage patterns. Figure 4.8 illustrates the relative increase in usage of newer electronic channels.

An exploration of past trends and future forecasts in channel usage should be considered with respect to the company's customer segments. Also, the relative importance of different channels at different customer relationship life-cycle stages for the product or proposition needs to be considered. Usage of different channels by different customer segments may vary considerably and, if this is the case, the potential adoption curves for key segments should be estimated.

Figure 4.8   Interactions shift to new channels

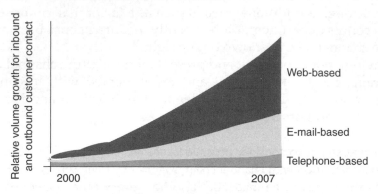

Review channel economics

The next step is to review channel economics. In some industries marketing channel costs may represent as much as 40 per cent, or even 50 per cent, of the price paid by the customer, so these often represent a prime opportunity for cost reduction. However, alternative channel structures and channel options have widely differing economics in terms of transaction costs, infrastructural costs and relative usage.

Transaction costs across different channels vary so markedly that they are frequently the primary area of focus in discussions on channel adoption. Figure 4.9 provides an illustration of relative transaction costs across electronic, call centre and field sales channels, based on an Institute of Directors report.[18]

Not surprisingly many businesses have rushed into the online channel because of its low transaction costs. However, while channel transaction costs are important, other aspects of channel economics must also be explored. The apparently low transaction costs involved in selling on the Internet need to be considered alongside other considerations such as marketing, web site development, fulfilment and other costs.

A study undertaken by McKinsey & Co. and Salomon Smith & Barney found the economics of selling on the Internet varied greatly. Their study focused on sectors within five industries and determined the online retail categories showing the highest customer net present value were, in order: groceries, prescription drugs, speciality

Figure 4.9 Transaction costs by channel

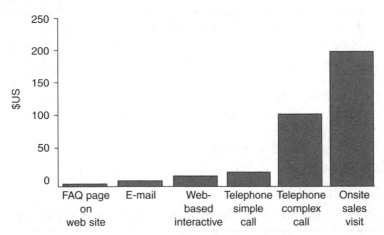

apparel, department store apparel, direct mail apparel, pure play books, pure play toys and pure play apparel.[19]

Economics of the online retail toy market

Their examination of pure play toy retailers illustrates how full economic costs need to be taken into account, as well as transaction costs. For this sector, they concluded that even if a contribution to gross income of $11 per order was received (which is extremely ambitious given high fulfilment costs), the company would need more than a $1 billion in revenues to support the $130 million dollars cost it would have in warehouse, web site, marketing and overhead costs. Such a company would need to capture an extremely high 5 per cent of the total US toy market to be viable. This highlights in particular the difficulty for later market entrance into a pure play world.

Economics of the online grocery market

In the grocery sector the study found the average online grocery order generated only $9 of gross income. With a typical online customer buying groceries on the web site, say, 30 times per year the overall net present value can be calculated. Order frequency drives the net present value of an online grocery customer to $909 dollars over a 4-year period according to the study data.

For many grocery retailers seeking to create an online business, either new entrants or existing grocery retailers, the building of special dedicated warehouses with low cost of order picking appears attractive. The approach adopted by supermarket chains such as Tesco of having their staff pick customers' orders from a normal store has been dismissed as too expensive. However, the approach taken by Tesco Direct, now the largest online grocery store in the world, has been vindicated. New online grocery retailers using dedicated warehouses have failed to develop viable business models. The huge order volume needed to justify economically using expensive dedicated warehouses has still not yet been achieved by Tesco. Only now that order volumes are starting to approach economic levels are plans to develop dedicated warehouses being addressed.

Develop an integrated channel management strategy

This step involves making decisions regarding how the company's strategic channel objectives will be achieved through a properly integrated channel management strategy. The choice of the appropriate multi-channel strategy will depend upon the desired customer experience for the key target segments, the complexity of the channel interaction and the channel economics. The economics of channels and the relative degree of use of alternative channels by different customer segments will have significantly different profit outcomes. Understanding the different profit contributions of customer segments and successfully exploiting this is a factor of superior channel management.

Developing an integration channel management strategy gives rise to the following issues:

1. How to achieve brand consistency in the formal communications programmes of different channels.
2. How to achieve consistency in how customers experience the company when they deal with its various channels.
3. How to ensure the communications and services a customer receives through different channels are coordinated and coherent, tailored to their particular interests and cognizant of their previous encounters with the company.

As noted earlier the nature of the total customer experience across different channels needs to be carefully addressed. The concept of customer experience design is a relatively new concept. However, two recent books on experience design and managing customer experiences[20,21] have made a significant contribution to our thinking in this area.

The relative complexity of the interactions leading to the sale and the costs of serving the channel also need to be fully considered. Companies such as BT and Xerox together with leading consultants such as Marketbridge[22] are pioneering new approaches to multi-channel integration. Figure 4.10 provides an illustration of this in a business-to -business sector.

These channel options need to be considered in the context of the channel participants or channel members that are used. Selection of appropriate channel members, discussed earlier in the chapter, can result in different industry structures that may include business partners, value-added resellers and other intermediaries as well as direct sales models. Each channel member should utilize the most appropriate range of channel alternatives.

The channel alternatives shown in Figure 4.10 have different advantages and challenges. Each element of customer interaction needs to be analysed to ensure the appropriate channel is being engaged for that activity. While the face-to-face channel used in much account management is costly, it is necessary for complex tasks and important customer segments. However, less complex

Figure 4.10 Channel alternatives based on cost and the complexity of sale

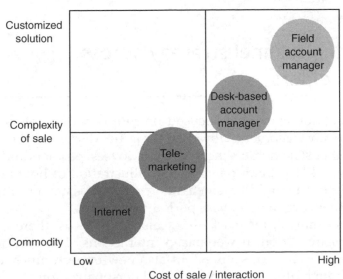

tasks may be handled for the same key customers through other lower-cost channels. Desk-based account management might involve a highly experienced salesperson who can immediately access customer information and use it in a highly interactive and customized manner, while telemarketing may deal with more routine sales, service and queries. The Internet and electronic channels provide the opportunity for high quality personalized self-service. However, the development of this channel of will be dependent on high quality portals and customer education and acceptance.

Leading companies are now driving considerable cost out of their account management structure by introducing innovations in this area. The creation of a differentiated and superior value proposition hinges on the provision of open and responsive interactions and dialogue with customers. This means actively recognizing what are the best channels for reaching individual customers and what channels individual customers prefer to use for different tasks, how they use them at present and how their usage in the future may change.

The benefits of deploying an integrated multi-channel approach are considerable. Marketbridge point out the benefits: 'All activities combined, enabled by CRM processes and technologies, lead to a more complete view of the customer that allows deeper understanding of account buyer behaviour and consistent customer interaction through shared account information. These benefits spawn opportunities to cross-sell and upsell, and thus increase sales growth and market share'.[23]

Planning channel strategy across stakeholders

The discussion above has focused on multi-channel integration in the context of customers. However, the issues discussed above apply also to other stakeholders including employees, partners and suppliers. Figure 4.11 provides a simplified illustration of how one company might plan to shift their channel mix with customer, employees and partners over a three-year period.

In this example, for marketing, sales and service there is a high degree of migration to web-based interactions. This not only can create significant cost savings but also new opportunities to create value through utilization of web-based personalization.

Figure 4.11   Channel mix change matrix for customer, employees and partners

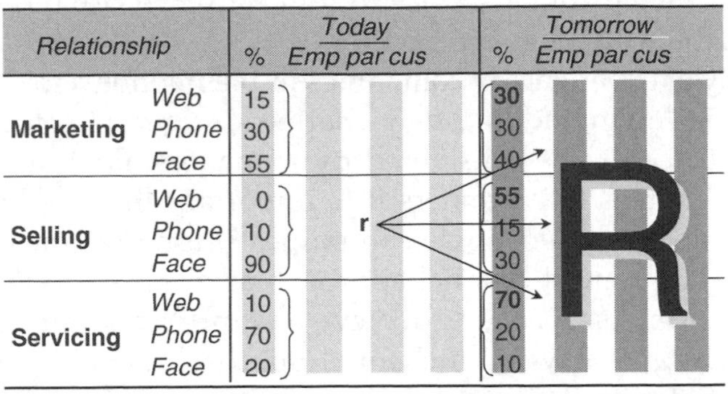

Relationship		Today % Emp par cus	Tomorrow % Emp par cus
Marketing	Web	15	30
	Phone	30	30
	Face	55	40
Selling	Web	0	55
	Phone	10	15
	Face	90	30
Servicing	Web	10	70
	Phone	70	20
	Face	20	10

Source: based on Broad Vision

Companies in a wide range of industries have already taken steps to implement new channel strategies that improve both efficiency and effectiveness in their stakeholder relationships. For example, Walmart and Tesco have developed highly integrated electronic channel strategies with their suppliers and Oracle have saved a huge amount of employee administration costs by migrating these activities to the web.

Summary

This chapter has examined the role of the multi-channel integration process in customer relationship management. A comprehensive multi-channel integration strategy that has the support of both management and staff is essential for any company that wishes to maintain a first-class level of customer experience within and across its channels.

Providing quality products and services in new as well as traditional channels is important for companies wishing to meet the expectations of today's customers. However, many companies do not seem to recognize the need to maintain equally high standards of service *across all channels*. The quality of a company's service is only as high as the weakest link in their channel offer and the enterprise needs to uphold the same high standard of service and customer experience in all channels. If one of the channels does not function, the customer will be disappointed. For example, if the booking service with a mobile phone does not work properly the customer will be upset and it will make no difference to the displeased customer that the customer service in a face-to-face situation is exemplary and the web site is superb.

A review of experience of companies implementing a multi-channel approach involving adding new channels, suggests some practical issues that need to be considered by managers. First, in offering a range of channels to customers it is important that the benefits do not seem too one-sided. Some companies emphasize the benefits to themselves of a multi-channel approach as opposed to the benefits to their customers. Second, extensive communication to staff of the reasons why the new multi-channel approach is being adopted is essential. Sales staff, in particular, need to be taken through the economic arguments as well as an explanation of any likely impact on their work role and their remuneration. Third, companies should be aware how staff in one channel may seek to sabotage other channels.

Of critical importance is the technology required to support integration of the offline and online channels. This can only be prescribed once a single clear understanding of the business processes and associated channel 'maps' are determined across marketing, sales and service. Here the information management process, the subject of the next chapter, has a key role to play.

Checklist for CRM leaders

CRM leaders need to review the following issues about the *Multi-Channel Integration Process*.

Channel options and strategies:

1. Our senior management have considered the future role of both existing and potential channel participants in our industry
2. We have a clear view on the future impact of electronic channels in our industry
3. Possible structural changes in our industry (disintermediation or reintermediation) have been fully considered
4. We fully understand the advantages and disadvantages of the major channel categories (sales force, outlets, telephony, direct, e-commerce, mobile, etc.) when developing our channel strategies
5. Our organization formally reviews the range of channel strategy options every year

6. My organization understands the channels our customers wish to use at different stages of their relationship with us, e.g. pre-sales, sales and post-sales
7. We know how customer channel preference varies at the segment level across different products or services sold by our company
8. We utilize appropriate analytical tools such as market structure maps to identify the value and volume of goods and services passing through different channels for our company and for our competitors
9. Changes in our customers' channel usage and preferences and general trends in channel usage are reviewed regularly
10. The organization has an agreed set of metrics for measuring channel performance.

Customer experience and multi-channel integration

1. The organization has a strategy for integrated channel management
2. We monitor the customer experience within channel and across channels and compare our performance with that of our competitors
3. The organization has identified what constitutes an outstanding (or 'perfect') customer experience and strives to deliver it
4. The customer experiences consistency in 'look, touch and feel' across channels and this experience is in keeping with our brand image
5. The organization collects information on all relevant types of customer interactions (e.g. calls, faxes, mail, e-mail, web-based and EDI transactions) to ensure that customer requirements and targets are met
6. The economics of different channels are thoroughly understood
7. The organization is effective in adding new channels to complement existing channels
8. New channels are integrated with existing channels so that an individual is recognized as the customer regardless of the channels used
9. Customer-affecting applications, such as order handling, work across all our channels. Products purchased in one channel (e.g. the Internet) can be returned through other channels (e.g. a retail outlet)
10. We consider channel integration issues for our employees and partners as well as our customers.

Each issue should be considered in terms of:

Rating for our organization   (5 = *applies fully; 0 = does not apply at all*)
Importance to our organization (5 = very important; 0 = no importance)

Case 4.1   Ideal boilers: a mobile solution for plumbers

The company

Ideal Boilers is a leading gas boiler manufacturer based in the UK. This well-known brand supplies almost a fifth of domestic boilers and almost half of all commercial and industrial boilers in the UK market. Ideal is one of the businesses within Caradon Plumbing (CP), which was divested by Caradon plc, a leading supplier of products to the home improvement, building and construction markets in 2001. With this restructure, Caradon Ideal Boilers retained a shortened name – Ideal Boilers – under the new ownership of HSBC Private Equity.

Ideal is a traditional company serving a solid customer base in the heating and plumbing industry. Its business-to-business customers include heating engineers, heating contractors, plumbers and British Gas. Boilers are typically sold to these installation customers via merchants.

At the start of the new millennium, like many other companies, Ideal was under pressure to improve its products and customer support provision in an environment of increasing pan-European competition. Ideal and its merchant retailers and installers needed to comply with increasingly complex legal and trade requirements, while at the same time upholding traditionally high levels of safety and service. To succeed in being a company that was easy to do business with, that added value and increased shareholder profitability, Ideal needed to maintain a direct customer relationship with all its customers, including those who buy its products via an indirect channel.

The challenge

Ideal sells boilers to an extremely fragmented and disparate installation community, with some 40 000 companies employing 90 000 installers. Understandably, Ideal and its competitors in the heating marketplace struggle to manage relationships effectively with this vast pool of customers. Whereas communications and interactions are relatively straightforward with large companies such as British Gas, dealing successfully with the smaller installation companies, who constitute over 50 per cent of operators in the domestic heating market, is a challenge.

Because a very high proportion of Ideal's products are sold via the top, national builder's merchants, there was a requirement to ensure that information on installation instructions, new products, fault finding and special promotions is passed to the user customer base. Identifying and supplying relevant information to this army of heating installers is problematic for they are expensive to access via traditional methods and as individual operators, they tend to order small quantities on a less regular, needs basis. They are also characteristically loyal to brands, so any proposition to win them over from competitors needed to be innovative, compelling and part of a long-term acquisition and retention strategy.

The typical profile of this elusive target market can be described as a one- or two-man company that operates from a van and is heavily reliant on a mobile phone for accessing information, ordering stock and generally coordinating projects while on-site or in transit. The unique nature of each installation means that the customer often needs to check product/installation specifications and delivery times while quoting for a job or installing a heating system.

Clearly, the ability to obtain technical information and advice via a mobile phone would be a distinct advantage. However, seeking assistance by phone costs time and money in terms of both the customer's phone usage and the requirement for customer support back at Ideal's offices. So the location and transmission of requested information was an additional consideration in Ideal's quest to own a direct communication channel with customers.

The solution

In September 2000 Ideal launched the Heating Information Service Project, a pioneering initiative to exploit emergent mobile/WAP technology for mutual business benefits. Ideal joined up with BT Cellnet (now O$_2$) and Improveline.com to develop a new Mobile Internet service that will save busy heating engineers valuable time and money by providing them with access to technical information and diagnostic support on-site using WAP-enabled phones.

BT provided more than 8000 WAP phones free of charge to Caradon-approved heating installers to replace or supplement their existing mobile handsets. The phones incorporated Caradon's Heating Information Service, giving the handset operator direct and immediate access to vital information by entering a PIN security code. In return, BT raised revenue from the call costs as it ensures the installers use BT Cellnet instead of the rival network they may have used previously.

Plumbers and heating engineers were also to be notified of new work opportunities via their mobile phones through links to www.improveline.com, an online home improvement referral site which matches homeowners with accredited contractors in their area. In this way they can opt to bid for new jobs through their handset from pre-defined criteria. Marshall King, Chief Executive of Improveline.com noted: 'This is a tremendous opportunity to bring undoubted benefits of WAP technology to a significant area of the UK workforce, with a package of online services that will make the heating installer more effective in the field. It combines perfectly with the web technology which we are using to assist thousands of homeowners every month as they plan their home improvement projects'.

The results

By using a mobile phone to get information to and from its customer base, Caradon was the first among its industry peers to communicate via a medium that has become an everyday tool of heating installers. Further, the effectiveness of its information service was not dependent on a customer's proximity to a PC or propensity to use the Internet. The move, said Ideal's Managing Director, Neil MacPherson, 'supports Ideal Boiler's key strategic initiative of leveraging technology to develop stronger relationships with the installer community and improve the end-to-end customer experience'.

The scheme involved an initial £30 000 investment, a year's development work and months of testing with target customers. The scheme offered significant benefits. For the first time, Ideal had a direct communication route to its roving customer base. The mobile phones also provided a valuable marketing tool for targeted campaigns as well as positioning the company as an industry expert, available for consultation at all times.

Ideal's Installer Director and project champion, Simon Kujawa, highlighted the solution's strong logic: 'We sell to merchants who sell on to contractors. These are people who use our products and need information. They have "right now" questions to do with technical issues, safety or government regulations. The bottom line is that the more information we can get out, the more they are likely to use our products. These people spend 99 per cent of their time in vans or on site and they are heavy users of mobile phones. Mobile was an ideal opportunity as we can proactively get information to them'.

The service was fully hosted and managed by BT, who designed the phone offer to be more cost-effective than any other arrangement available to the user, thus assuring initial take up of the scheme. The flexibility of BT Cellnet's Mobile Internet services enabled Caradon to tailor applications to specific industry needs.

The attraction for the plumbing and heating engineers was that they had self-access to business critical data and could order literature and resolve common faults through their handsets, maximizing time and cost savings and service enhancement. The partnership with BT also meant that they had handset access to the World Wide Web and an e-mail facility, while the link with Improveline.com afforded admittance to job leads that could be converted to sales.

The Ideal initiative won exceptional praise at the Computer Weekly Awards for E-business Excellence in October 2000, where both project and project champion scooped major awards. MacPherson was delighted with the tribute: 'The scheme has already been tremendously successful with our customers and the recognition that these awards represent confirms our belief in the project'. He continued: 'Ideal is constantly seeking to develop its customer communications to ensure that they receive the information they need, when they need it and in appropriate form. We see this project as only a first in a long line of developments to further improve and fine tune our communications with both customers and suppliers'.

This project represents an early innovation in developing an enhanced multi-channel offer through the use of the mobile channel. Since 2002 Ideal Boilers have gone through a number of structural and operational changes. They are currently owned by funds managed by Montagu Private Equity. By 2002 BT had completed the demerger of mmO_2, comprising their mobile assets in Europe including O_2 UK, formerly BT Cellnet.

Case 4.2   Guinness – Delivering the 'Perfect Pint'

The company

Guinness was founded in Ireland by Arthur Guinness in 1759. Within a short period of time the dark rich beverage was brewed so well that it ousted all imports from the Irish market, captured a share of the English trade and revolutionized the brewing industry. By 1825 Guinness Stout was available abroad and by 1838 Guinness' Irish Brewery was the largest in Ireland. In 1881, the annual production of Guinness brewed had exceeded one million barrels a year and by 1914, St James's Gate was the world's largest brewery.

Guinness is now also brewed in over 35 countries around the world. All of these overseas brews must contain a flavoured extract produced at the St James's Gate brewery in Dublin. Hence the special brewing skills developed at Arthur Guinness' brewery remain at the heart of every one of the 10 million glasses of Guinness enjoyed every day across the world.

Today, Guinness, part of Diegio plc, is one of the most well recognized global brands and has a loyal following of consumers. However, producing a consistently high quality product was one of the key problems facing Guinness.

The challenge

Product quality is recognized as a critical factor in building loyalty among consumers – especially in converting occasional drinkers into loyal consumers. Research suggests that acquiring a taste for thick dark beer requires the product to meet consumer expectations on every occasion. In each brewery, manufacturing processes are carefully controlled. Ingredients are rigorously checked with every brew containing a special ingredient, which is brewed in Dublin.

Each day Guinness' trained tasters do taste tests on dozens of samples of beer. All the company's products are tasted at regular stages throughout their life-cycle to ensure they are in top condition for their consumers. These tasters score the beer for its aroma, flavour and head quality, as well as detecting any problems or deviation in product quality.

However, producing a standard product is not enough to ensure that every customer enjoys the same 'Perfect Pint' every time – anywhere. Research in the UK during the 1990s suggested that consumers often were presented with a less-than-perfect pint at the point of consumption. Guinness Brewing GB recognized this as a major challenge, involving a total management of the supply chain. Hence they needed to address the challenge of ensuring a consistently perfect consumer experience at the point of delivery.

The solution

Achieving this lay beyond the remit of any one department. To ensure a perfect consumer experience at the point of delivery they formed a special cross-functional process improvement team charged with the job of delivering the 'Perfect Pint'.

The team carefully mapped and measured the entire product delivery process, from brewery to consumer. The team drew up a detailed programme which when implemented would consistently deliver the 'Perfect Pint'. The control of the supply chain, which Guinness calls the 'quality chain', involves four main stages:

- ensuring quality of the raw materials being supplied to Guinness
- ensuring quality within the brewing and packaging processes
- ensuring that the publican serves the 'Perfect Pint'
- ensuring that the customer is educated in enjoying the final stages of consumption.

During the first two stages quality control involved rigorous purchasing and checks on manufacturing standards. Dedication to quality at Guinness starts with suppliers and purchasers working together to meet these standards, while manufacturing involves world-class techniques and Total Quality Management. All employees are educated to share the 'quality vision' and are trained to understand how every person plays a vital role in the quality chain. During the brewing process samples are tested at every stage. Even the loading into kegs, cans and bottles is carefully controlled to ensure that beers are more consistent in flavour and appearance in the glass.

However, the 'Perfect Pint' team found that often problems developed once the beer arrived at the licensed premises. Guinness, like other cask beers, is a 'live' product and needs to be handled carefully. Frequently the beer was not stored and presented correctly and even though this was not directly within the control of Guinness, it was critical to the quality delivered to the consumer.

The team undertook considerable research to ensure consistency of quality in the final stages of the supply chain. Results of their work include guidelines for the publicans on all aspects of the 'pub dispense quality'. These guidelines include advice on the correct gas mixture when pulling the pint, the ideal dispensing temperature, cleaning beer lines, washing glasses and the perfect presentation.

Guinness put considerable research and development effort into the areas of dispensing equipment and methods employed in pulling pints. For example, the current tap used by pubs to dispense Guinness was developed at a cost of over £1 million. The tap has been designed so that it is easy to operate and so it ensures that every pint is perfectly presented. Other developments include the introduction of a new gas-blending programme for pubs selling draught beer. The installation of such initiatives helps ensure consumers experience a 'Perfect Pint' on each occasion.

Training of bar staff has not been neglected. The 'Perfect Pint' team recognized the important role of staff that pull the 'Perfect Pint' and deliver the experience. The famous 'two-part pour' requires practice. Detailed instructions and training were provided by Guinness to ensure the 'Perfect Pint' was pulled properly and drunk correctly by consumers:

> Hold the glass at a 45 degree angle close to the spout to prevent large bubbles from forming in the head. Pull the tap fully open and fill the glass 75 per cent full. Allow the stout to settle completely before filling the rest of the glass. The creamy head will separate from the dark body. To top off the pint push the tap forward slightly until the head rises just proud of the rim. Never allow the stout to overflow or run down the glass.

Every Guinness employee is trained to recognize their responsibility in ensuring that 'The Perfect Pint' is enjoyed everywhere. Employees learn how to execute the two-part pour and are encouraged to check the pouring technique, and test the depth of the head and temperature of the pint in licensed premises. Employees can alert the 'Perfect Pint' support team if a problem is encountered, so that the publican can be offered further advice or training.

The results

But achieving the 'Perfect Pint' does not stop there. Research showed Guinness that consumer education was also important if the consumption experience was going to be consistent – every time. Guinness needed to communicate to consumers their part in securing the 'Perfect Pint'. Point of sale laminated cards were used which explained, on one side, how to pour the Perfect Pint and on the reverse side, the correct serving temperature and a ruler that allowed consumers to measure the correct thickness of the head on their pint.

Consumers were also targeted with a highly successful advertising campaign that extolled the virtues of waiting for a perfect pint – as it takes between 90 and 120 seconds for a perfect pint of Guinness to settle. Thirsty customers now wait patiently for their Guinness. They have become part of the process and are now convinced that if it's worth having, then it's worth waiting for. Even the core customers have learnt to deal with the wait

Figure 1   Pouring the 'Perfect Pint' of Guinness

involved. As one pub owner observed: 'The old timers finish their pints in three sips. They re-order right after the second sip; by the time they finish the last sip, a fresh one will arrive. They're hearty men'.

This customer experience strategy propelled Guinness to achieve its highest ever share of the total draught market. Guinness recognized that the presentation of beer is critical in terms of ensuring repeat purchase – and this requires a total integration of all aspects of the supply chain – including the consumer. The 'Perfect Pint' project has been so successful that the approach has been applied worldwide to improve the presentation and quality of draught Guinness.

Chapter 5

The information management process

The strategy framework for CRM

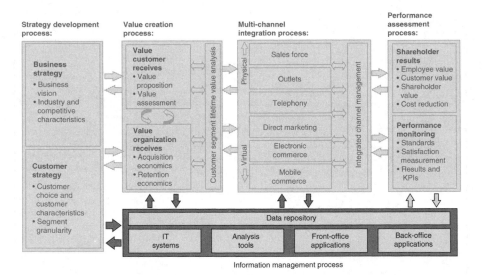

Information management process

The information management process is concerned with two key activities: the collection and collation of customer information from all customer contact points and the utilization of this information to construct complete and current customer profiles which can be used to enhance the quality of the customer experience, thus contributing to the value creation process. As companies grow and interact with an increasing number of customers through an increasing diversity of channels, the need for a systematic approach to organizing and employing information becomes ever greater. Two questions are of special importance in the information management process:

1. How should we organize information on customers?
2. How can we 'replicate' the mind of customers and use this information to improve our CRM activities?

Where customer information is spread across disparate functions and departments, interactions with the customer are based on partial or no knowledge of the customer, even though the customer may have been with the organization for years. This fragmentation of customer knowledge creates two major problems for the company. First, the customer is treated in an impersonal way, which may lead to dissatisfaction and defection. Second, there is no single unified view of the customer upon which to act and to plan.

In an effort to keep pace with escalating volumes of data, the tendency has been for organizations to create more or bigger databases within functions or departments, leading to a wealth of disparate silos of customer information. Companies are thus left with a fragmented and often unwieldy body of information upon which to make crucial management decisions. The elevation of CRM from the level of a specific application such as a call centre, to the level of a pan-company strategy requires the integration of customer interactions across all communication channels, front-office and back-office applications and business functions. What is required to manage this integration on an ongoing basis is a purposefully designed system that brings together data, computers, procedure and people – or what is termed an integrated CRM solution. This is the output of the information management process.

The information management process can usefully be thought of as the engine that drives CRM activities. It consists of several elements that need to work closely together. Information should be used to fuel, formulate and facilitate strategic and tactical CRM actions.

As the figure above shows, the other processes that make up the strategic framework for CRM all depend on the information management process. The *strategy development process* involves analysing customer data in different ways to provide insights that could yield competitive advantage. The *value creation process* utilizes customer information to develop superior value propositions and to determine how more value can be created for the organization. The *multi-channel integration process* is highly dependent on the systems that capture, store and disseminate customer information. The *performance assessment process* requires financial, sales, customer, operational and other information to be made available to evaluate the success of CRM and identify areas for improvement.

To appreciate fully the significance of the information management process within strategic CRM, it is important first to be clear about the role of information, information technology and information management in CRM.

The role of information, IT and information management

Information

CRM is founded on the premise that relationships with customers can be forged and managed to the mutual advantage of those in the relationship, or all relevant stakeholders. However, suppliers and their value chain partners cannot interact and nurture relationships with customers they know nothing or very little about. While having information about customers is therefore essential to relationship building, it is not alone sufficient. Of much greater importance is being informed and making informed decisions. In other words, the real value of information lies in its use, not in its mere existence. This simple truth is evident in the fact that many companies possess vast amounts of information on their customers, but few fully exploit this treasure trove for greatest benefit.

IT

Many equate CRM with IT. For instance, the bigger your database, the more advanced you are in CRM. This notion of a direct correlation between the two is misleading for CRM is a management approach and IT is a management tool. Further, in the terms in which we define CRM, it is possible to have highly sophisticated CRM without having highly sophisticated IT. For example, the traditional corner shop proprietor built intimate relationships with his regular customers by recognizing their individual needs and circumstances and tailoring his service accordingly. Historically, he did not log their buying habits and preferences in an electronic database as no such thing existed, but he referred to his own memory of customers and applied it conscientiously. The shopkeeper knew which customers were most valuable and how to retain them by delivering appropriate value.

Businesses today compete in a much more complex environment and potentially with millions of customers they have never actually met, so IT has become a vital feature of managing customer relationships. However, the corner shop principle still applies, in that a working 'memory' of customers, supported by two-way dialogue, is what enables effective customer relationship management. Thus it is important to keep the technological aspect of CRM in the correct perspective: as the means to an end and not the end itself.

Information management

Information management is about achieving an acceptable balance between operating intelligently and operating idealistically. Consider the following scenario. The heart surgeon may have all the latest equipment, superlative training and a genuine commitment to saving the life of his patient, but if he operates on the basis that he is replacing a valve in a serious but routine procedure, rather than working to rectify the multiple complications he finds once the patient's chest is opened, he will probably fail in his efforts to help and possibly with fatal consequences. So who will be to blame? The surgeon for not knowing enough about his patient's unique needs and condition and not being prepared for the unexpected, or the patient for not forwarding more information about the patterns or progression of her illness? Often we do not know what it is we need to know to address a problem, or by the same token, what we really do not need to know. Clearly, neither the undersupply nor oversupply of information is satisfactory. The quest is therefore to find the right information and at the right time. Learning that the patient has a family history of a rare coronary disease after she has fallen into a coma on the operating table is of little comfort or benefit.

This analogy serves to emphasize the constituent dimensions of information: quality, quantity, relevance, timing, ownership and application. The function of information *management* in the CRM context is to transform information into usable knowledge and to apply this knowledge effectively and ethically in the creation of customer value. The right information in the wrong hands or at the wrong time has little constructive value. Further, the 'perishable' quality of information demands that it needs constant updating and replenishing. The management of information therefore encompasses the organization (capture, storage, dissemination), utilization (analysis, interpretation, application) and regulation (monitoring, control and security) of information.

The information management process

The information management process should be considered in two stages. First, the CRM strategy (or the relevant component of it) needs to be reviewed in the context of the organization's information management needs. Second, the technological options needed to implement the agreed strategy have to be determined. The first stage will involve a strategic review of the current condition, capability and capacity of the information management infrastructure, in relation to the customer, channel and product strategies defined in the preceding CRM processes.

We discussed in Chapter 2 how each organization, depending on the core business and a number of related strategic issues, needs to consider precisely which CRM strategy is appropriate now and in the future. Figure 5.1 reintroduces the CRM Strategy Matrix, discussed in that chapter, which identified four broad strategic options facing organizations – product-based selling, customer-based marketing, managed service and support and individualized CRM (or what Peppers and Rogers term '1 to 1 Marketing'[1]). The latter is the most sophisticated – it requires collection and analysis of extensive information about customers and also the desire and ability to give customers individualized service.

Here the strategic issues to be reviewed will include: Is customer information extracted from each interaction or transaction regardless of the channel the customer uses? Is this information centralized and leveraged and exploited across all functions and channels? Is the information technology platform deemed appropriate for the present and for the future? The results of such a review will highlight the

Figure 5.1   The CRM strategy matrix

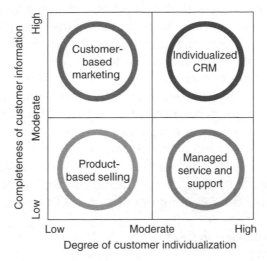

strengths and weaknesses of existing information management provision. Importantly, it will help clarify the completeness of information (how much customer information is held and how sophisticated is the analysis of that information) and the degree of customer individualization (the extent to which customer information is used to provide customized service).

As the number of channels increases with the development of newer electronic channels such as webTV and third generation mobiles, the information management process will become even more central to the management of customer relationships and thus to the achievement of customer-centric strategic goals. A key role of the information management process is to ensure the customer centricity and relevancy of the organization by embedding the customer perspective in all business activity. In effect, the firm must be able to 'replicate the mind of the customer' if it is to provide the kind of individual or customized service that will attract, retain and grow profitable customer relationships. Thus the emphasis in this process needs to be on how we can use information in a proactive way to develop enhanced relationships with the customer, rather than on the elegance and sophistication of the technology. The design of the technological components of CRM should therefore be driven not by IT interests, but by the organization's strategy for using customer information to improve its competitiveness.

With this in mind, an information management infrastructure that will support and deliver the chosen CRM strategy should be developed. For most companies, this will involve the incorporation of specific technologies. As depicted in the CRM strategy framework at the start of this chapter, the main technological components of the information management process comprise the data repository, analytical tools, IT systems, front-office applications and back-office applications. These five components contribute to building better customer relationships by making the organization 'market intelligent', 'service competent' and 'strategy confident'. Development of the technological framework should take account of the following issues, which include recognition of the limitations and evolution of technology as well as the five component parts of this process:

- the technical barriers in CRM
- data repository
- analytical tools
- IT systems
- front-office and back-office applications
- challenges posed by emerging technology.

The technical barriers in CRM

The technical barriers in CRM are highlighted by the gap between expectations and results. When our growing expectations of technological tools are not matched by their capacity to meet those expectations, the tools become, in our perception, barriers rather than enablers. In reality, the 'obstacles' are less a matter of tool malfunction than they are our own misalignment of strategic 'will' with tactical 'way'. Where once our IT tools were considered adequate, our demands on them have changed because our requirements and expectations are different. Managing customer relationships effectively at one time meant getting customers' address details correct on mass mailings and ensuring that everyone received a copy. Today it means understanding customers' individual buying habits and contact preferences and strategically targeting communications via a multitude of channels. What is required to overcome these technical barriers is a more accurate understanding of what we wish to achieve and a more appropriate means of achieving it. The experience of the automobile industry is a case in point.

A study of the UK's leading car manufacturers, importers and dealers by Cap Gemini several years ago found that most computerized customer databases have serious gaps or deficiencies. The databases did not support the recording of customer lifestyles or interests and could not record essential demographic information. Even when customer data were captured, they were not always accessible to marketing or other customer-facing functions. The business implications of these problems were summarized as follows: 'The defects are said to be causing strategic problems in the companies' sales and marketing programmes, frequently making them unable to track either customers or prospects efficiently, to target advertising accurately or to develop effective personalized direct marketing campaigns'.[2] Despite improvements over the last few years these problems are still commonplace in the automotive sector and other sectors.

This serves to illustrate how poor customer information can limit the success of CRM and other strategic initiatives. When we encounter such problems, we are forced to ask ourselves some basic questions. Are we really capturing the customer information we need? Is customer information being made available to the people who can use it to increase sales and add customer value? Are we getting the most out of the information we collect, or does our data analysis capability need to be improved?

The data repository

To make an enterprise customer-focused, it is not sufficient simply to collect data about customers, or even to generate management information from individual databases, because they normally provide only a partial view of the customer. To understand and manage customers as complete and unique entities, it is necessary for large organizations to have a powerful corporate memory of customers – an integrated enterprise-wide data store that can provide the data analyses and applications.

The role of the data repository is to collect, hold and integrate customer information and thus enable the company to develop and manage customer relationships effectively. We use the term data repository here to refer to all of an organization's databases, data marts and data warehouses combined. Before exploring the selection and combination of these as technology options for CRM we will first consider the key elements of a data repository.

The data repository for a large organization dealing with many customers is typically comprised of two main parts: the *database* and the *data warehouse*. There are two forms of data warehouse: the conventional data warehouse and the operational data store.

Databases are computer program software packages for storing data gathered from a source such as a call centre, the sales force, customer and market surveys, electronic points of sale (EPOS) and so on. Each tactical database usually operates separately and is constructed to be user-specific, storing only that which is relevant to the tasks of its main users. Management and planning information drawn from a single database is therefore limited in value because it provides an incomplete view of customer-related activity. However, the value of databases extends well beyond their function as a collection of data about customers from which we can understand current customer relationships and develop prospective customer relationships. If properly exploited, databases can provide a 'reality check' to help us become more *relevant* to those customers and prospects.

The data warehouse is a collection of related databases that have been brought together so that the maximum value can be extracted from them. A data warehouse is a single data store containing a complete and consistent set of data about an organization's customer and business activities. In this chapter we will use the term 'data mart' to describe a single subject data warehouse and the term 'data warehouse' to describe an enterprise data warehouse system. Although the principle of the data warehouse is simple, the process of creating one can be quite complex due to the fragmented nature of the databases from which data are copied and the large scale of the task. Thus it is necessary to use a data conversion process to coordinate the conversion task. Technically the data warehouse is structured for query performance.

The operational data store (ODS) is a special form of data warehouse, much smaller than a conventional data warehouse, storing only the information necessary to provide a single identity for all customers, regardless of how many identities they have in different back-office systems. Technically the ODS is structured for transactional performance. This is used mainly by front-office systems and processes to provide a single view of the customer. For example, it enables call centres, sales force automation and e-commerce solutions to have a consistent view of customer activities.

The data conversion process copies data from tactical databases to the data warehouse in such a way that data duplication is minimized and inconsistencies between databases are resolved. The process makes use of an enterprise data model, which describes the contents of each tactical database and includes rules for combining data from different databases after appropriate data cleansing and deduplication. The main benefit of using an enterprise data model is that the rules for copying and integrating data are all kept together, making them easier to manage than the copy programs that connect individual pairs of databases together for creating decision support systems (DSS) or data marts. These centralized rules make the task of integrating databases easier for IS staff, reducing the cost and effort of providing complex information for tasks such as CRM.

When a successful data warehouse implementation is achieved, analytic tools can be used in conjunction with it to develop opportunities to create value for both the customer and the organization. The case study on Barclays' use of an SAS data warehouse and analytics illustrates how improved financial performance can be achieved through innovative use of technology.

Case 5.1   Barclays – Case study overview

Barclays plc is a major UK-based global provider of financial services, with a presence in over 60 countries. Personal Financial Services (PFS) is an important division of Barclays' operations providing customized products and services to upwards of 19 million personal and small business customers. In 2000, Barclays PFS required a tool to sell mortgages against a background of ambitious targets. The challenge for PFS was how to get the appropriate information into the sales people's hands at the point of customer contact.

This technology solution that was adopted gave authorized users interactive telephone access to information in the Credit Risk Management Data Warehouse via a fixed or mobile phone. The project was developed with SAS®, who built the Credit Risk Management Data Warehouse and Periphonics, who delivered and maintained Voice solutions on multiple Barclays sites.

Within six weeks of going live, Barclays achieved £1 million (1.6 million) in extra new sales, entirely attributable to the new solution. ROI was achieved in eight weeks. By April 2001 Barclays had already attributed £70 million in pure new sales to the new solution. Expenditure on the system was recouped in six months. The project's exceptional success financially was mirrored in the delight of PFS employees and customers. Sales staff were making more sales and completing each sale in less time. Customers expressed high satisfaction with the simpler, faster service.

The full case study is at the end of this chapter (see p. 275)

Selecting and combining technology options for CRM

We have pointed out that the CRM technology approach adopted will be highly dependent on the organization's CRM strategy. There are four broad alternative technology options for facilitating different degrees of development of CRM strategy in terms of data repository. These include:

- a tactical database with decision support systems
- data marts (or single subject data warehouses)
- an enterprise data warehouse, and
- integrated CRM solutions.

These options, which progressively extend the range of CRM applications available, are outlined in Figure 5.2.

Figure 5.2   Technology levels for CRM

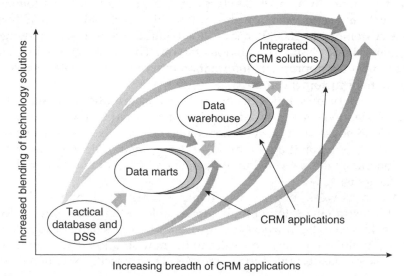

It is not necessary to choose one of these four technology options to the exclusion of others. On the contrary, most large organizations will need to blend these solutions creatively as they progressively adopt more sophisticated forms of CRM, as they migrate from product-based selling to individualized relationship marketing on the CRM Strategy Matrix shown in Figure 5.1. We now describe how these technology options can be used to assist in CRM. As we discuss these options we will refer back to the strategic positions on the CRM Strategy Matrix.

Tactical database and decision support systems

Most organizations already have some form of 'product-based selling' – i.e. various forms of marketing databases, sales databases and associated decision support systems. At the most basic level they have a marketing database which holds the names and addresses of customers. This may have a basic application package associated with it and the database can usually be extended to include basic segmentation information on, for example, geography, job title and size of organization. The database and software technology used is often on a personal computer.

It is common to develop a database to support specific needs like mailing lists or for simple but specific analysis and reporting. The database typically can only retain data for a short time and does not have a link back to the customer. It is often built, owned and managed by the marketing department. The structure of a tactical database is shown in Figure 5.3.

Figure 5.3 Tactical database and decision support systems

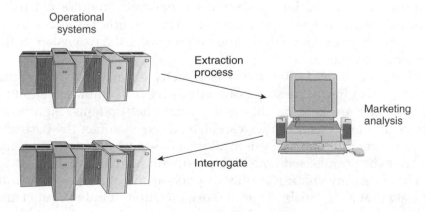

In addition to the database used in marketing, different parts of the organization often build up their own; the commercial department might have one for general mailings and the sales department might have their own for contact management purposes. In this way lists can be developed for mass mailings to customers in isolation or through merging of these lists.

Advantages

These systems can be quick to establish and require very little investment in terms of IT. However, even at this level, more in-depth analysis can provide significant benefits, such as better targeting of direct marketing activity or a better understanding of market buying behaviour.

The use of modern query and reporting tools or more advanced analysis tools (referred to as 'online analytical processing' (OLAP) or data mining tools) can help to identify new sales and marketing opportunities. These end-user tools provide multi-dimensional views of the data which better reflect the business and provide advanced user interfaces that allow the users to interact directly with the data.

These analysis tools are important elements of any technology solution used by a marketing organization for CRM purposes, because they will help it to unearth the 'nuggets of gold' in the data and help analyse customers either as individuals, or in product-based segments.

Disadvantages

However, using such simple systems will severely limit the sophistication of the sales and marketing strategies that an organization can deploy. Tactical marketing databases inevitably require extensive manual work to load and maintain. This diverts resources away from the key role of analysis and often makes the extension of the system prohibitive.

Using query and analysis tools directly on existing operational systems also limits the scope of analysis, i.e. it is impossible to link data which are kept on different operational systems. Significant query and analysis activities can also adversely affect the performance of the operational system themselves and therefore may not prove to be popular with the IT department maintaining them.

However, any analysis is only as good as the quality and breadth of data that are available from the organization. If only product and financial data are available then this may be useful for reporting sales or identifying products which are selling well. However, it does not help the company build up a consolidated 'single view of the customer' so that every department in the business sees the 'same picture' in terms of data on customers enabling it to identify and execute appropriate relationship marketing strategies.

Data marts

It is the ability of computers to act as an enormous memory and capture all the information on a customer that has been the driving force behind the adoption of CRM IT applications. This ability, coupled with the rapidly decreasing cost but increasing power of computers, has lowered the entry point for many organizations and has made the applications affordable.

Moving from 'product-based selling' to 'customer-based marketing' requires a more advanced CRM system. Users need more complex analysis power and the business needs a much more structured approach to the collection, sorting and storage of data regarding the customer. This typically involves building what is termed a data warehouse. This is separate from the operational systems which currently hold the data and it is built solely to 'warehouse' all the data that need to be collected in order to support a CRM system. The simplest form of data warehousing is called a data mart.

A data mart is technically a repository for information about a single source. In other words it is a 'single subject' data warehouse, implying it is not as grand in scope as its big brother – the enterprise data warehouse (discussed in the next section) – which is built for the entire organization. Data marts are a natural extension of the database (enabled by more developed technology). So far as marketing is concerned, the single subject would be typically based around the customer. A simple representation of data marts is shown in Figure 5.4.

Data mart solutions can be purchased as part of a packaged application or as an integral suite of software which allows the extraction of data from operational systems. However, the sorting, organizing and design of that data are done in a form which is optimized for analysis of data not for running business operations. Thus, additional software products may be needed so that data can be presented in simple-to-use graphical forms which enable users to understand them.

The data mart package may also include query and analysis tools to enable the analysis of that data. Some tools allow the user to analyse

Figure 5.4   Data marts

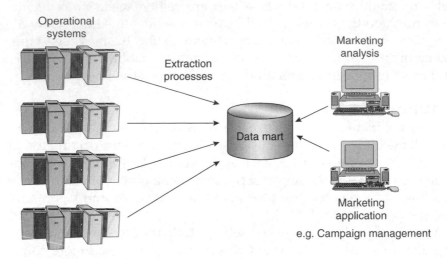

data directly form older legacy systems. However, while this is useful, these tools are often limited in terms of their power of analysis.

Advantages
The data mart will typically run on a departmental server technology rather than on a PC. This permits a vast number of users to connect to it and use information from it.

Data marts are proving popular for organizations with departments (or lines of business) that want to respond quickly to a new market or business opportunity. Other organizations may introduce a data mart to get a pilot system up and running quickly and achieve easily identifiable paybacks.

Disadvantages
Organizations must be careful that multiple, unconnected data marts do not spring up in many areas of the company making a 'single customer view' across multiple systems difficult to achieve.

In order to achieve a customer-centric view across the entire organization, multiple subject data must be held (i.e. financial and transactional data on the customer). This implies that an enterprise data warehouse will ultimately need to be constructed that brings all relative customer information into one consistent store.

Many data warehouse solutions start as data marts forming part of a pilot scheme, with the aim of achieving an initial win within the organization. However, it is important that, although on the surface they are a data mart, they should from the start be architected as a data warehouse.

Any analysis is only as good as the quality and breadth of data that are available. If only product sales and financial data are available then this may be useful for recognizing the best customers and their profitability, but it does not help the company build up a consolidated 'single view of the customer' so every department in the business sees the 'same picture'.

It is the 'single customer view' across an organization which will help drive the identification of true customer value (including 'share of customer' and 'customer lifetime value') and will also ensure that appropriate customer service is provided. This can only be achieved by the adoption of more 'business-critical' computer solutions and database technology which can grow in size and scope. These business-critical solutions are often classed as data warehouses even though, as far as the common definition of the term is concerned, they may be called data marts, albeit very large ones.

Enterprise data warehouse

As business shifts from product-based selling to more developed forms of customer-based marketing or managed service and support (see Figure 5.2), there is a requirement for more data and greater integration of data, both from the front office (call centres, customer-facing applications) and the back office (general ledger, human resources, operations). As the volume of data expands and the complexity increases, this may result in many databases and data marts. Therefore, it is much more logical and beneficial to have one repository for data. For CRM systems this is an enterprise data warehouse, shown in Figure 5.5.

Once the data warehouse is created with cleansed, 'single version of the truth' data, the appropriate query and analysis tools and data mining software can be applied to start to understand better customer behaviour and the organization can plan more advanced CRM strategies.

The data warehouse can then evolve into a multi-tier structure where parts of the organization take information from the main data warehouse into their own systems. These may include analysis databases or dependent data marts (single subject repositories which are data-dependent on the central version of the data warehouse).

Until now we have not discussed other customer databases which may also be used to support a call centre or any other customer

Figure 5.5　Enterprise data warehouse

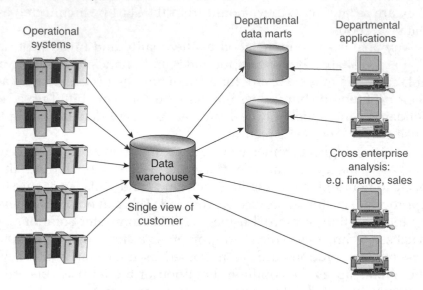

service application. These relate to the 'managed service and support' strategies in the bottom right-hand corner of the CRM Strategy Matrix in Figure 5.1. Here customer data are typically captured as part of the system running the customer service application. Initially this may continue to run as a stand alone application. However, as the CRM strategy takes shape within an organization and a data warehouse is put into operation, data from applications such as a call centre need to be captured and enhanced by the data warehouse.

In the early stages this may involve file transfers of information (e.g. from call centre to data warehouse), a file containing changes to customer details or products purchased (e.g. from data warehouse to call centre), lists of customers being developed for outbound telemarketing offers, or 'flags' being created for credit rating.

As the data warehouse evolves and the organization gets better at capturing information on all interactions with the customer, so does sophistication of the CRM strategies employed. This is possible because the data warehouse can track customer interactions over the whole of the customer's lifetime.

Advantages
Using a data warehouse has several advantages. First, it stops complex data analysis from interfering with normal business activity by

removing a heavy demand on the databases. Second, the data in a data warehouse changes only periodically (e.g. every 24 hours), allowing meaningful comparisons to be made on stable sets of data which exist in between updates of the data warehouse. If databases were used for analysis, analyses made at different times would produce different results, making it impossible to compare, for example, the sale of different products or the volume of sales in different regions. The further advantage of the enterprise data warehouse approach is the fact that an organization can refer to one 'single version of the truth' which can then feed numerous data marts with consistent data.

Disadvantages
Enterprise data warehouses are large and complex IT systems that require significant investment. This may result in lengthy lead times to implementation.

As the business may not be able wait for the data warehouse to be implemented, it needs to make decisions today and a cheaper, less appropriate solution may be adopted.

Integrated CRM solutions
In addition to computer and database memory capabilities, Internet technology is becoming increasingly pivotal for most organizations. The Internet can potentially connect any individual to any other individual or organization around the globe. The attraction of using this as a customer relationship management tool is obvious.

However, electronic commerce web sites are at widely differing levels of sophistication – some of them are relatively simple, some of them are highly sophisticated. The most advanced use their web site regularly to collect information from the customer and provide highly individualized service back to the customer. This technology-enabled approach to CRM has created greatly increased opportunities to interact with large numbers of customers on a one-to-one basis.

However, in order to use the Internet effectively for sophisticated CRM applications the organization must have integrated its e-commerce systems with a customer-orientated data warehouse which is able to push and pull customer intelligence from the Internet. An organization usually cannot conduct sophisticated electronic commerce without first installing some form of data warehouse.

If an organization, because of its marketing ambitions to utilize a new channel or its desire to be first in attracting a particular customer group, uses the Internet as a mechanism to service their customers, a more advanced set of CRM technologies needs to be introduced. Figure 5.6 shows an outline of the final stage of CRM development – an integrated CRM solution.

Figure 5.6   Integrated CRM solutions

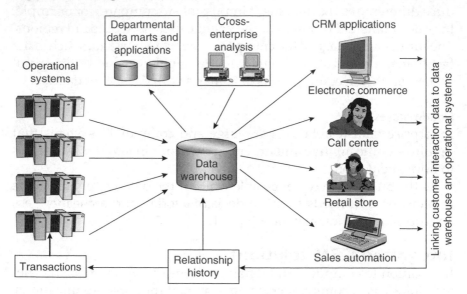

To implement such a solution, the organization does not need to add further data marts or data warehousing technology. In fact, the business may have all the data and sophisticated architecture that is needed, but it has to deal with them in a more intelligent way. However, it does need to add, to the top of the existing data marts and data warehousing architecture, a range of integrated CRM applications. This can mean using an interactive electronic commerce application, allowing the customer to interact with the company's web site and make purchases in real time.

The backbone to this approach is the enterprise data warehouse which serves both as a capture device and as the memory for the system, enabling the customer to be given a totally individualized and coordinated service across all CRM interfaces. Several components are needed. These include a specially designed web front-end for interacting with the customer, sophisticated application software for the capture, navigation, processing and matching of customers to products and services, a link to other customer systems such as the call centre and field sales support systems and links to the main operational systems.

To achieve total integration means linking this tightly into both the front- and back-office applications. Complete systems that provide this high level of integration are now improving in capability. They provide organizations with the potential for a quick implementation path for the adoption of CRM and significantly reduce the potential development risks.

Advantages
An integrated CRM solution will enable an organization to move towards the top right-hand corner of the CRM Strategy matrix, i.e. 'individualized CRM' in Figure 5.1. A range of sophisticated CRM strategies can be adopted which are appropriate for the organization without being handicapped by existing IT. The business opportunities are significant for those who can get to this position first.

Disadvantages
Like the enterprise data warehouses, integrated CRM systems are complex and require significant investment in both the warehouse and operational systems. Organizations need to reduce the risk and cost of these systems by buying packages where available and working with established and proven technology suppliers.

There are now numerous examples of organizations that have adopted such electronic commerce mainstream solutions including Amazon.com, CDnow, E*trade – electronic share trading – RS Components and most airlines for their ticket purchases, to name but a few.

Electronic commerce web sites are at widely differing levels of sophistication. The most advanced use their web site to collect information from the customer and provide highly individualized service back to the customer. This advanced technology-enabled approach to CRM has created greatly increased opportunities to interact with large numbers of customers on a one-to-one basis.

The choice of technology options
In considering the choice of these technology solutions, managers who are currently using a tactical database typically ask questions such as: 'When do we need simple query and analysis tools and when do we need a data mart? Why do I need a data warehouse when I have a satisfactory query and reporting tool on my data base?'.

If all an organization needs to do is to query its existing database (and it is getting the ease of use and the answers that it wants from the query and reporting tools that it has), then it does not need a data mart or a data warehouse. It clearly has the technology solution that it currently needs. If, however, it needs to access information from more than one system, or if the end users question their capability to correct a query which goes across two different proprietary systems (e.g. data on an individual customer's name may be stored in different ways in different data sources) then a simple database may not be suitable. Also if the organization wants to look at additional information, such as historical data, then a data mart is needed.

A data mart may be the appropriate solution if an organization has a requirement for only one data mart. However if the sales, finance and marketing functions in an organization all require one, then problems can develop. The data mart solution for these multiple business functions may not be easy to manage technically and it does not scale easily (any changes on the operational or the business side need much work to be done on them in terms of transformation and extraction routines). In this situation a data warehouse will provide a more satisfactory solution.

From a practical perspective it will be appropriate, especially in large organizations, to combine the above technologies creatively. For example, a more complex CRM may include a strategic application with dependent data marts on a data warehouse, together with a tactical application which allows staff to build independent data marts for more tactical solutions. A tactical data mart may be needed quickly for a particular business activity – one that does not need integrating with the rest of the organization.

In choosing technology solutions, 'scalability' is an important consideration. The business needs to create flexible technology architecture suitable for both present and future needs. It needs to take account of the building blocks in place at present as well as requirements which may exist in two years' time. Managers may not yet know what will be needed and perhaps the technology does not exist at present. It is also necessary to create an architecture which will be responsive to the increasingly sophisticated requirements of CRM in the future.

One key to success will be the ability to 'think big and start small'. The organization needs to have a vision of what it wishes to achieve and what will be required in the future and then break this down into appropriate components.

By undertaking a scoping study it can ensure that the key to ensuring that the solutions decided on are extendible, scalable and manageable. The best approach is to plan ahead for the integration of the future business-based solutions that will be needed. This may involve evolutionary deployment of one or more dependent data marts with the type of architecture outlined above, with the aim of maximizing the benefits and minimizing the risks to the organization.

The topic of data warehousing is a vast one. Author and consultant Ron Swift[3] provides a good description of data warehousing in the context of CRM. Further books by Agosta[4], Inmon and his colleagues[5] and Kelly[6] deal with this topic in much greater detail.

Analytical tools

The analytical tools that enable effective use of the data warehouse or other elements of the data repository can be found in both general data mining packages and in specific software application packages. Data mining is a discovery method applied to vast collections of data, which works by classifying and clustering data, often from a variety of different and even mutually incompatible databases and then searching for associations. It is primarily a form of statistical analysis but may also include artificial intelligence. Data mining can be used to reveal meaningful patterns about customer buying habits, lifestyle, demographics and so on, which would otherwise remain hidden and thus provides indications of how customer relationships can be improved. More specific software application packages include analytical tools that focus on such tasks as campaign management analysis, credit scoring and customer profiling. These task-specific software packages combine several of the general functions of data mining with support for the task that will not be found in standard data mining software.

While data mining technologies are extremely powerful and can lead to some profound insights into customer behaviour, some of them have historically been difficult to use and require considerable experience to be of real benefit. However, this drawback is beginning to disappear as analytical tools are incorporated into task-specific packages that make them easier to use.

Standard data mining packages will typically include some, or all, of the following techniques:

● visualization: histograms, bar charts, line graphs, scatter plots, box plots and other types of visual representation

- clustering/segmentation, prediction, deviation detection and link analysis
- neural networks and decision trees.

Task-specific software packages combine these general types of data analysis with specific marketing support, resulting in analytical tools such as:

- market segmentation analysis
- affinity grouping
- churn management
- customer profiling
- profitability analysis.

Online analytical processing (OLAP) tools are data reporting rather than data mining tools, but they can also be used to analyse data held in a data warehouse.

It is worth considering each of these analytical techniques briefly to gain an appreciation of the scope and scale of technology available.

Standard data mining

Visualization tools

Visualization tools enable complex data analyses to be represented in simple form. This not only enhances understanding by providing a manageable view of data, but also aids the accurate interpretation of various aspects of the data. For example, a column graph emphasizes the values of items as they vary at precise intervals over a period of time, while a pie graph emphasizes the relative contribution of each data item to the whole. Such presentation graphics make group discussion of data analyses easier by ensuring everyone is working from the same 'picture'.

Segmentation, prediction, deviation detection and link analysis

Segmentation involves dividing data on the basis that some database entries have similar characteristics (e.g. some customers buy similar items at the supermarket). Segmentation can be controlled by the user to test how well defined existing clusters really are, or it can be done automatically in order to identify new clusters.

Prediction involves developing a model (e.g. of customer behaviour) and applying it to historic customer data to estimate the

impact of a change, such as an advertising campaign or the introduction of a new product. A predictive model might be built using
responses to a customer survey. If, for example, a survey provides
data on gender, age, occupation, PC ownership, home and work
Internet usage and newspaper and magazine subscriptions, a model
could be derived to estimate the likely uptake of an online service
and to target advertising in the conventional media.

Deviation detection tools extend segmentation tools by analysing
data that fall outside of well-defined clusters. These tools can be
used for a variety of tasks, ranging from identifying unusual questionnaire responses to spotting unusual transaction patterns for
fraud prevention. Neural networks can be used for some types of
deviation detection and statistical analysis can be applied to determine the significance of deviations once they have been identified.

Link analysis finds relationships between sets of data entries in a
database. It can be used to discover relationships between the purchases that customers make over time and, in a form known as *market basket analysis*, can be used to work out which products shoppers
buy in combination, so that the products can be positioned together
in supermarket aisles.

Link analysis is based on the idea that events relate people, places
and other things together. When you fly from London to New York,
for example, the plane links the two cities together and 'being a passenger' links you to the plane. Similarly, when you make a telephone
call, you are linking together two (or more) telephones. Most data
analysis techniques ignore link information, focusing instead on single objects (e.g. customers), rather than the relationships between
them. Understanding these links can, however, provide important
insights into the nature of customer interaction, making link analysis
a valuable tool.

Link analysis is quite expensive and can place a heavy demand on
databases. One example, which has potential value for e-commerce,
is the use of link analysis to find online communities on the Internet.
This approach examines hyperlinks between web pages to identify
groups of resources that are linked together and pages that are
linked to most often. Interlinking of web pages suggests that the web
pages represent common interests, while many links to a single page
suggest that that page is an important resource for the community.
Although not widely utilized, link analysis of the Internet can provide insights relevant to the targeting and placement of online
advertising and other marketing activities.

Neural networks

Neural networks are computer models that are based on some processes in the brain. They are essentially statistical processes that have built-in feedback mechanisms so that they can 'learn'. These tools are readily available in off-the-shelf software packages and have been used for quite a wide range of business processes. Neural networks are capable of identifying different types of relationships, including the detection of clusters. As the internal mechanism of the network adapts automatically, however, neural networks do not explain relationships. This is one of their weaknesses, which can be overcome by using the neural network to identify relationships and then applying other data mining techniques to explain why they exist.

A neural network is trained by providing it with a range of different examples, all described in terms of inputs and outputs. We could, for example, describe customers in terms of their age, gender, income and other factors and describe their outputs in terms of the banking services they use. We then provide the neural network with 'inputs' from existing customer data. The neural network predicts the banking services for each customer. If it predicts wrongly, the neural network adjusts itself. Over time, it becomes more accurate at making predictions. When a neural network has been trained, it can be used on new customer information to make predictions that marketers and other decision makers can act upon.

Neural networks are potentially very powerful tools for making predictions about customer behaviour. They must be used with some caution, however, as they only predict based on the data inputs that are provided. If, for example, 'number of children' were an important variable in the use of financial services, the neural network would only be effective if it was programmed to include number of children as an input. Another limitation is that neural networks work best when the relationships between the inputs and outputs are stable. On occasion, customer behaviour can change quite significantly. Neural networks will adapt to a limited degree but do not change radically once programmed. If business conditions change dramatically, neural networks will be less effective and should be replaced by other more appropriate analytical tools.

Decision trees

Decision trees structure data according to well-defined rules. They are popular because, unlike neural networks, they explain why a particular outcome is recommended. Decision analysis tools classify existing data in order to identify rules that lead to valid recommendations. These rules can then be used to support business decision making.

Automated tools for constructing decision trees work by splitting data in a way that spreads all items (products, customers, transactions, etc.) most evenly. If, for example, a group of customers is 90 per cent male and 50 per cent single, then marital status would be used first to classify the data. The aim of forming the tree is to split the items into groups with similar characteristics. When an effective decision tree structure has been formed, which classifies individual cases accurately, the tree can be converted into decision rules and used to support decision making.

For a more detailed discussion of data mining see the books by experts such as Groth[7] and Berry and Linoff.[8]

Task-specific analysis tools

Market segmentation analysis

Market segmentation was discussed in some detail in Chapter 2.[9] Customers can be segmented according to their basic characteristics, such as geography and job title, without using any special analysis. We simply specify the postcodes or job titles of interest and extract the relevant customers from the database. This kind of segmentation is very limited and does not help us to gain insights into the preferences and buying habits of customers. To do this, we must analyse detailed historical information about sales. If we succeed in identifying a meaningful cluster of customers, we can target this cluster with a particular offer that is likely to attract their attention. This can help stimulate extra sales and gain customer loyalty by developing products and services that better suit their requirements. Two types of analysis tool can help in identifying new segments using customer data in the data repository.

The first option is visual analysis, as described above. By plotting graphs using different dimensions, we can sometimes see groupings of customers with similar characteristics. If we plotted customer age against purchases of coffee, for example, we might find that certain age groups consume more filter coffee, while another age group consumes most decaffeinated coffee. Unfortunately, visualization is only useful for analysing two or three dimensions. On many occasions, we will need to identify clusters using many different pieces of customer data. In these cases, the second approach of using automatic cluster detection is the preferred option.

There are several different types of automatic cluster detection. One of the most common (K-means) will split a database into a number of segments specified by the user. This method is best suited to working with numerical data, although it can be used with other data in a limited way. An alternative approach, known as agglomeration, begins by treating each entry in a database as a cluster (of 1 record) and combines similar clusters until only a small number of clusters remains. Alternative techniques can be used for dealing with non-numerical data, such as counting the number of data fields that match in a set of customer records. Clusters can also be identified using some kinds of decision tree and neural network methods.

Affinity grouping

Affinity grouping is used to identify individual data items that tend to be associated with one another. A typical application is analysing supermarket purchases to discover items that are bought together so that store layouts can be improved (it is for this reason that affinity grouping is sometimes called *market basket analysis*). The data mining technique underlying affinity grouping is the generation of *association rules* using link analysis procedures (described above). An association rule takes a form such as, 'People who buy nappies on Friday also tend to buy beer or wine'. This suggests two possible courses of action: displaying nappies near the alcohol section (on Fridays) and putting snacks, such as crisps and nuts, near to the nappies to 'remind' customers to buy their wine or beer. These techniques can be used on entire data sets to find general relationships or on small data sets to find more localized rules (e.g. to identify sales trends specific to stores in urban and suburban areas).

Churn management

In highly competitive industries where customers are able to change suppliers at little cost, companies will be continually losing some customers to competitors and gaining others. This is known as churn in industries such as telecommunications, or attrition in industries such as banking. In some industries, churn is a serious problem. Some estimate that in the mobile telephone market, churn rates are around 25 per cent in Europe, while attracting a new customer costs an average of $400. Improving customer retention (or reducing churn) by even a small amount can clearly lead to substantial cost savings. Customer retention is examined in some detail in Chapter 2.

The first stage in churn management is to measure existing churn and to understand churn in the context of the entire distribution network, which may include a number of channels. The aim should be to identify particular trouble spots that can be targeted for direct action. The use of OLAP tools to create performance indicators is usually sufficient and is supported by many dedicated churn management packages. These tools enable churn rates to be correlated with geographic areas, dealers, service plans and so on. High correlations will indicate, for example, that some dealers have much higher churn rates than others. These tools also support the identification of customer segments that have both high churn rates and high potential value. These segments can then be targeted with customer retention campaigns. Some tools use neural networks and decision trees to identify customers likely to churn and to explain why.

With churn analysis data, two approaches to churn management can be used: reactive and proactive. The reactive approach involves providing churn analysis data to customer service representatives so that they can offer appropriate incentives to customers who are threatening to switch to a competitor. The proactive approach involves identifying problem customer segments and targeting them with direct mail or telephone calls.

Customer profiling

Customer profiling uses predictive analysis tools to model customer activity so that in future, value propositions can be tailored more closely to customers. Models can be created that are based on customer needs, behaviours and profitability and, by drawing upon a large volume of data about customer segments, can be used to predict how customers will react to new situations. Marketing campaigns, for example, can be enhanced by using predictive customer profiles to estimate the likely responses of different customer segments.

Profitability analysis

Traditionally, companies have focused on the profitability of their products and services. Recently, improved understanding of the costs of customer acquisition versus customer retention have suggested that measuring and managing the profitability of individual customers can be a more effective strategy. Hence, we now often try to determine customer lifetime value (discussed in Chapter 2).

Effective customer management is now expressed in terms of satisfying profitable customers so that they will not switch suppliers and
migrating unprofitable customers to a profitable position.

Profitability analysis involves improving data integration and data
capture at a number of points. First, integrating customer databases is
essential for determining the total number of products and services
that a customer has bought. This requires integration of departmental
databases, usually by data warehousing. Second, data must be captured on the cost of servicing each customer. This may involve using
CRM tools that capture the amount of time spent by operators who
answer the customer's calls and reply to letters and e-mails.

Without such specific data, the costs of providing customer service
are simply averaged over all customers, disguising the fact that some,
seemingly valuable, customers are actually unprofitable because they
use up disproportionate amounts of customer service time. Once
such data are collected, profitability of individual customers can be
determined and customers segmented according to a combination of
their profitability and other characteristics. These segments can be
used as the basis for developing customer migration strategies, as
well as for identifying valuable customer segments that need to be
protected from competition.

In some industries, the growth of online marketplaces (or 'market
spaces') has greatly reduced profit margins. Adapting profitability
analysis tools to this problem has made it possible for suppliers to
determine which requests for quotes (RFQs) are likely to be profitable
and at what level bids in online auctions no longer promise a profit.[10]

Online analytical processing (OLAP)

OLAP is an advanced data reporting tool, which provides more
advanced facilities than the query tools described earlier. It is not
strictly a data mining tool because it provides summary data rather
than identifying patterns in data. Nevertheless, OLAP tools are powerful and quite easy to use. They can make a significant contribution
to extracting value from customer databases, adding to the value of
data mining applications, rather than replacing them.

OLAP tools have advanced graphical interfaces that make it possible
for users with little statistical knowledge to explore large volumes of
data. Underlying this interface is a new database (sometimes called a
cube) containing data from the data repository that has been stored
using a special structure to make the 'slicing and dicing' of data
quicker and easier. Whereas conventional reporting tools can take

hours to gather data, OLAP tools can provide reports in only a few seconds. It should be noted, however, that achieving this fast response comes at the expense of losing some precision in the storage of certain types of data.

The key differences between data mining and OLAP are best summarized by considering the kinds of management issues they each address. Data mining is more forward looking, providing insights into the best ways to manage different groups of customers. It is intended to support decision making. OLAP reports have a more historical focus, summarizing the data on, for example, recent sales performance and highlighting trends. An OLAP analysis of past sales, for instance, may show that some products sell best on a particular day. It does not, however, tell us why this is the case. A data mining technique, such as affinity grouping, may provide some insights to explain this trend. Another use of OLAP is for visualizing the results of data mining analysis. Perhaps one of the more important contributions of OLAP, however, is that its ease of use makes data analysis accessible to a much wider range of people within the organization.

Analytical tools are instrumental in sorting data and extracting meaning from it to guide the development of management strategies. In identifying customer and market trends, techniques such as data mining can help to clarify budget inefficiencies and the most useful allocation of resources. Segmentation and predictive modelling can be used to identify new customer groups to enhance propositions, or to provide an early warning system. Importantly, the ongoing development and utilization of the data warehouse also facilitates the exchange of information and knowledge between the enterprise and customers.

IT systems

IT systems refer to the computer hardware and the related software and middleware used within the organization. Hardware consists of the pieces of physical equipment (desktop PCs, laptops, database servers, web servers, mainframe computers, key boards and other peripherals) on which software, or computer programs, are run. Middleware are programs that serve as intermediaries between clients requesting information and server programs providing requested data, where the client and server are operating on different computing platforms.

For CRM to be effective, IT systems must be able to deliver the information needed on customers both now and in the future and to accomplish an array of other administrative duties such as billing, processing, distribution, stock ordering etc. These tasks represent an enormous dependency and demand on the technology. As the number of customers and customer transactions escalate, the organization's capacity to scale existing systems or plan for the migration to larger systems without disrupting business operations becomes critical. So too is the integration of data from highly contrasting systems, such as structured databases and rich multi-media networks.

Normally, an organization's IT systems are developed over a period of time and in response to particular departmental needs. Thus different, and often incompatible, computing systems – both hardware and software – are utilized in different parts of the business. While new IT systems tend to be based around open technical standards, reducing compatibility problems, old legacy systems can be very difficult to integrate. In some cases, replacing the legacy hardware and applications may be a more attractive option.

Where separate IT systems do arise, hardware and systems software integration must take place before databases can be connected to the data warehouse and user access can be provided across the company. The integration of disparate IT systems into a holistic architecture represents a major undertaking, requiring substantial investment. It is therefore crucial that proposals for systems integration be firmly based on a robust CRM strategy (which has taken account of IT infrastructure) and a thorough strategic review of IT systems. The agreed IT architecture should be designed to integrate or replace existing IT systems and to provide flexibility for future changes and expansion.

A constant challenge when planning IT architecture is matching hardware with the demands of users. There are various options available, including client-server, server-based (or host) systems and internet/intranet solutions. These options can be combined to form IT networks that satisfy a range of different needs.

Selecting hardware

When introducing CRM into the organization, it is likely that at least some users will require new computer hardware. For some users, this will be a standard desktop PC. For those working in the field, a laptop or other mobile data solution will be required. For call centre workers, some form of computer-telephone integration (CTI) may be used to improve worker productivity. The range of technical options is enormous and continues to increase. Choosing hardware requires a focus on user needs and consideration of how users work and under what conditions.

For many managers, their existing desktop PC will be sufficient to run CRM software. Indeed, as more CRM software is web-enabled, most machines with web browsers will be adequate for basic reporting and data analysis. For business analysts and users performing complex data mining, more powerful machines are likely to be needed. These may be high specification PCs or specialist workstations, depending upon the volume of statistical analysis and the use of visualization tools. These machines will have larger high quality displays than normal PCs, more memory and a faster processor. The choice of PC or workstation will depend upon the infrastructure and technical support available in your organization, as many workstations will use operating systems other than Microsoft Windows (such as Unix). The cost of having a small number of workstations is high because they will require different network hardware and IT staff will need to be trained in how to support them.

The choice of mobile equipment for users in the field is even more problematic than for business analysts, as both the interaction with the customer and the security of the remote connection must be taken into account. Considering interaction between, for example, the salesperson and customer is particularly important when selecting hardware. A standard laptop PC can take several minutes to boot-up and, because of its size, act as a barrier to normal communication between people. Smaller handheld devices are much lighter and less obtrusive but use different versions of software to a laptop computer. This may mean that CRM tools on the handheld will have fewer features, so care should be taken to ensure that the device will support the key tasks performed by users.

With continuing advances in mobile telephony, the option is now available for workers in the field to connect their computer directly to the company's data repository, rather than using copies of customer data. This makes it possible to change customer details, place orders, check stock availability and so on. There are two approaches to providing online solutions in the field. The first option is for the user to dial-in directly to a computer in the company. This option is intrinsically quite secure because data are passed down a direct telephone connection, with the user connecting to the network using the same user ID and password as he/she does in the office. The second option is to use the portable computer to connect to the Internet and provide access to CRM tools via a secure web browser. This option raises some additional security risks because the CRM server is publicly accessible. For this reason, extra security measures, such as using encryption and firewalls, are required.

For the call centre and help desk, standard PCs may be fitted with CTI hardware. CTI hardware connects the computer to the telephone line, so that the caller's number can be used to help identify the caller. This makes it possible automatically to retrieve the customer's details from a customer database ready for the operator to answer the call. Similar technologies can also be used for providing interactive voice response services, where customers press numbers on their keypad to select options offered to them by a computerized voice. Over the next few years, it will become increasingly common to use the Internet for placing telephone calls. This technology makes it possible for customers and call-centre operators to talk to each other while viewing the same web page on their PCs. This collaborative browsing technology requires the integration of Internet and telephone networks and thus will involve gradual change in the telephone and computer networks in the organization.

Front-office and back-office applications

Front-office applications are the technologies used to support all those activities that involve direct interface with customers, including sales force automation (SFA) and call-centre management. These applications are used to increase revenues by improving customer retention and raising sales closure rates. *Back-office applications* support internal administration activities and supplier relationships, involving human resources, procurement, warehouse management, logistics software and some financial processes. Some marketing activities, such as campaign management, are difficult to classify because they are customer facing, but do not directly support interactions with the customer.

The growth of enterprise-wide systems and e-business is also blurring the distinction between front office and back office and challenging the structure and operation of existing information management processes. Goods tracking, for example, has traditionally been a back-office system used by employees who do not have any interaction with the customers. Many companies are, however, providing customers with direct access to goods tracking software via the Internet so that they can track their own orders. In this case, goods tracking must be regarded as a front-office system because its performance affects the customer's perceptions of the organization.

The overriding concern in CRM about front- and back-office systems is that they are sufficiently connected and coordinated to optimize customer relations and workflow. It is essential that they combine to support all stages of interaction between the customer and the organization. This can be difficult to ensure because there can be dozens of applications spread throughout the organization which have evolved over time to meet departmental needs. Often, departments have been organized around products/services or business functions, rather than being designed to support the customer relationship. For this reason, it is useful to review existing applications from the perspective of customer interaction so that the adequacy of applications can be assessed. By identifying the organization's key activities and mapping existing IT support onto them, it is possible to identify areas where new applications are required or where existing applications need to be connected together or integrated to provide seamless customer service. Performing such an analysis ensures that customer needs drive technology solutions, rather than the other way around.

Recently, attention has focused on the implications of e-business strategies that put customers and business partners into direct contact with databases. This increased access to operational data can create new challenges for CRM, which may demand changes in the approach to data warehousing and the organization of front-office and back-office applications. One such challenge is the pressure e-business creates for a 'real-time' marketing response, which requires all customer interactions to be conducted with an enterprise-wide view, rather than just the marketing planning activities. In some cases, this change may lead to pressure for data analysis to use real-time data, rather than a data warehouse that is only updated periodically.

Front-office applications

Front-office applications can be used to improve the value created for customers and the value delivered by customers. They provide a means for increasing sales closure rates, improving customer service and enhancing cross- and upselling. Thus they are key to raising levels of customer retention and customer profitability. The most common front-office applications are:

- sales force automation
- call-centre and help-desk management
- product configuration
- marketing automation and campaign management.

Sales force automation

Sales force automation (SFA) refers to sales and marketing systems which are loaded onto laptop computers to link salespeople in the field directly to their office base via a modem or mobile phone. SFA enables rapid order processing and order status enquiring. The incorporation of forecasting and reporting tools ensures that customer information is accurate and up-to-date, which enhances sales forecasting. Most of the leading CRM vendors offer products in this area, often as part of their CRM packages. This has a key advantage in that sales force, customer service and marketing activities are viewed and updated with the same set of integrated customer information.

SFA tools offer most benefit when they are applied to inefficient sales processes, particularly administrative tasks, where time and resources are consumed consolidating sales information which has been stored and reported in different ways. Some organizations have embraced SFA as an opportunity to change their sales approach altogether.

When introducing SFA software, it is important to focus on the management of customer information flows. Primary consideration should be given to deciding what information needs to be captured and where, and who is responsible for examining, processing and updating the data. Particular attention should be paid to locating and resolving any duplicated activities or areas where information falls down a 'black hole'.

Call-centre and help-desk management

Call centres have escalated in importance over the last decade as many companies have reduced their high street presence and launched Internet channels. Although communication and transactions can be conducted via the web site, customers still demand the option to speak with a human representative for technical and process assistance. The telephone is both a channel in its own right and an important form of support for other channels. As telephone and data technologies converge, the role of the call centre will continue to expand, both as a customer interface and as an internal information resource. The case study on Hallifax's adoption of E.piphany real time solutions provides an excellent creative example of how the call centre can be leveraged to create customer value.

Case 5.2   Halifax – Case study overview

Halifax Bank, a subsidiary of HBOS Group, is the largest home mortgage lender in the UK and offers a diverse set of financial and asset management services, including retail and business banking, consumer credit, savings products, pension products, life insurance and other investment-related products.

The continuing rise in the number of inbound calls to Halifax's contact centre offered tremendous scope for enhancing value creation. In order to harness the full sales and relationship-building potential of each telephone interaction, the bank needed to be able to demonstrate individual customer knowledge and relevance in real time. Determined to capitalize on the growing dialogue with its customers, Halifax deployed marketing solutions from E.piphany, Inc. to meet its cross-selling objectives. This provided real-time decisioning to allow for the construction of a consolidated customer profile and the delivery of a personalized product offer. Using the Real-Time system, the call-centre agents could rapidly access a customer's information and match it to directly relevant offers in the course of conversation.

In 2000, Halifax piloted E.piphany Real-Time software with 160 of its call-centre agents to support cross-sell development. Within six months of introducing the system to the call centre, investment costs had been recouped and offer acceptance rates among some of the top-selling agents had increased by more than 55 per cent. By adopting a phased approach, the company was able to measure performance improvement and economically reinvest incremental return. Building on the success of the pilot project, Halifax has rolled out the system to all 750 retail bank outlets.

The full case study is at the end of this chapter (see p. 279)

The ability to deliver effective customer service from a call centre depends on the availability of full and accurate customer information, as well as product and service information. This requires the integration of customer data across the organization, so that call-centre workers are able to deal with most enquiries by themselves, only redirecting the customer to another employee when particular expertise is required. The integration of customer data is also required to support multi-channel integration, which focuses on the call centre. Call-centre operatives already handle telephone calls, faxes and e-mail messages. Increasingly, they will also interact with the customer via shared web pages and Internet telephony. To maintain the quality of service provided, the organization will need to retain a single view of the customer regardless of what channels the customer uses. Integrated IT systems will also need to ensure that customer communications are prioritized according to need, rather than according to the channel used. Software to support call centres is improving in quality and multimedia management is increasing as new Internet technologies become available.

Help-desk software has been used for some time by IT departments for tracking problems within the organization. These tools are now being adapted to help customer service representatives handle problems raised by customers. These packages typically support the tracking of orders, accounting and billing and the calculation of the customer's cost of ownership. Some of them also support the identification and sharing of best practice in dealing with customer problems. For those organizations that provide on-site customer support, specialized field service software is available. These systems manage the dispatch of field service personnel, spare parts inventory and repair depots. Perhaps the most important feature of these systems, however, is that they help bring together customer data from multiple legacy systems so that customer service and sales staff have access to a complete customer history.

Product configuration

Product configuration tools use a database to track the features and prices of a broad collection of products. They are particularly useful where a product, such as a PC, has many components (e.g. disk drive, memory and monitor), which can be configured to a customer's exact requirements. These tools usually have graphical interfaces and are quite easy to use. They can be run on a laptop computer (particularly useful for sales staff in the field) or via the Internet. Using a configuration tool can save the salesperson from having to search through product catalogues, select the right components and calculate the cost of each customized item. Product configuration and cost calculations are performed automatically, which also reduces the chances of producing inaccurate quotes. Configuration tools also safeguard against unworkable product configurations, such as putting more memory into a computer than it is physically capable of holding. Product configuration tools are provided online by a number of computer and car manufacturers and in the field by companies such as Renault; they are not only useful where products are complex but can help with complex pricing structures for commodity products by providing salespeople with an accurate database of, for example, the different volume discounts offered by each of a retailer's suppliers.

Marketing automation and campaign management

Growing profitable customer relationships involves developing customized value propositions and delivering them to the customer. (We discuss value proposition development in Chapter 3.) Marketers must have ready access to up-to-date information in greater volumes and in more diverse formats than ever before. Marketing automation involves taking organized manual marketing processes and automating them through the use of defined business rules and executing them electronically. For example, many aspects of the following marketing processes can be automated: prospect qualification, customer segmentation, contact management, customer value measurement and the development of behavioural models for testing planned marketing campaigns.

Most campaign management tools enable the marketer to specify the steps involved in the marketing campaign and to calculate costs and commercial returns. They also support 'what-if' analyses on customer segments. These tools help the organization to target its marketing at customers who are valuable to the company and likely to respond to campaign offers. By automating some tasks, they can also make communications with the customer more cost-effective.

Campaign management typically begins with market segmentation analysis and extends this by using the segmentation information to help develop personalized marketing messages. In some CRM systems, initial segmentation for campaigning is performed using OLAP analysis. Customer profiles/models are then created and used to feed information into campaign management software. This software is then used to design a campaign designed to gain responses from each of the target segments and to communicate details of the campaign to all employees (and business partners) who will come into contact with the targeted customers. This ensures that interaction with the customers is consistent across channels during the campaign. The campaign management software is then used to direct the marketing campaign and to assess its impact. Where campaigns use the Internet as a communications channel, e-mail messages and web sites can be personalized for customers in the target segments. Some of the tools for developing personalized web sites learn customer preferences by analysing the customer's use of the web site. As more preference data are collected from the web site, the personalized pages are improved in real-time.

A key part of campaign management is assessing the response to the campaign. Support for response assessment is typically offered in the form of tools for monitoring web site activity and for monitoring customer databases for changes. Some tools monitor customer responses through all channels, making it possible to identify changes in customer behaviour with particular marketing efforts on specific channels. This is an increasingly important facility as companies adopt a multi-channel approach to customer relationship management (see Chapter 4). Taking response assessment further, some campaign management packages use neural networks or other forms of analysis to build models of customer behaviour using the new response data and other data sources. The reporting functions of campaign management include a range of standard reports and, in many cases, OLAP functionality, as described earlier.

Back-office applications

Back-office applications streamline internal business processes and include general ledger and financial systems, inventory management and human resources. In many cases, they are legacy systems or software packages using specific databases. Some companies are using enterprise resource planning (ERP) systems to provide integrated back-office systems, also adding the benefits of data warehousing and providing additional management and control tools. Difficulties in implementing e-business strategies have shown that there is also a strong need for integration between back-office and front-office systems. For this reason, many ERP vendors are opening up their systems to front-office CRM applications, or developing CRM features to add to their existing ERP packages.

Many of the vendors in this area offer integrated applications that use an open standard, known as XML (or possibly an XML meta standard such as XBRL, ebXML, BPSS, WSFL or Xlang), for data interchange, making it easy for business partners who use different systems to exchange data.

Another area of back-office technology of growing importance is the use of mass customization technologies, which we discussed in Chapter 2. These are increasingly seen as the key to competitiveness in manufacturing and service industries. These technologies can give the customer direct input into the value creation process. Ford Motor Company, for example, launched a mass customization initiative that enables customers to choose which accessories they want to be fitted to their new car. This benefits Ford because the add-ons are mostly high margin items, such as alloy wheels. It also benefits the customer because the add-ons are covered by Ford's warranty and can be included in the financing package for the car.

For mass customization technologies to operate efficiently, it is essential to achieve a high level of integration between back-end systems (such as production scheduling) and front-end systems (such as product configuration tools). In manufacturing, integration may also be required with suppliers to ensure that stocks of components are replenished in line with fluctuations in demand. By connecting production scheduling to customer service systems via the Internet, it is also possible to provide the customer with delivery dates and order-tracking facilities. For example, Dell Computers has expanded its mass customization activities by inviting customers to configure their PCs online. Dell's system accepts orders from its web site, which features the different computer options available, such as increased memory, extra disk drives and so on. Once online payment is confirmed, the order is immediately scheduled for construction to the customer's exact requirements.

Opportunities offered by emerging technology

Developing a customer-focused information management process requires both an enterprise-wide data warehouse and the integration of the software applications supporting all channels. We describe the combination of these, in addition to the CRM analysis and support tools, as an integrated CRM solution. With the growth of e-commerce, integrated solutions increasingly involve the joining of the data warehouse and/or the operational data store with Internet applications, as well as with call centres and sales force automation. The emergence of other channels, including mobile and interactive digital TV, will drive the need for more complex solutions. Keeping pace with technological innovation and applying it discriminately will be constant concerns. This is in addition to the CRM requirement of being able to understand, satisfy and anticipate the needs of an increasingly discerning and diverse customer base.

Business process outsourcing, business service provisioning and application service provisioning

Intensifying commercial and competitive pressures, exacerbated by the availability of promising new technologies, has led many companies to consider Business Process Outsourcing (BPO) and/or use of a Business Service Provider (BSP) and/or an Application Service Provider (ASP).

Engaging external vendors and service providers can be beneficial where the requisite expertise does not exist in-house or the costs would otherwise be prohibitive (in terms of both the investment of resources and the diversion of certain skills away from other crucial tasks). However, it is imperative to the success of strategic CRM that responsibility for customer relationship management be retained within the organization. While the vendor or vendors may be perfectly capable of fulfilling their customer care duties and contractual obligations, the realities of business dynamics mean that customer needs and competitive climates can change quickly. The organization must be able to respond swiftly and appropriately. It must monitor marketplace fluctuations and the performance effectiveness of its vendors. The organization knows best what its customers want and how to ensure their expectations are met. This is the role of the performance assessment process examined in the next chapter.

Implementing a CRM solution is likely to be costly and often requires expertise for customizing the software. Particularly if a company is working on leading-edge CRM activities, such as personalized customer portals, implementation can take many months.

Up until recently, the choice for companies that want to reduce their business process costs has been simple and involved either BPO or an ASP.

Business process outsourcing (BPO)

This involves delegating an entire business process such as the call centre, direct marketing or tele-marketing to an external service provider leaving the company to focus on its core business. However, as a result it may lose some control over the business process. There are many companies providing these services including shared service centres, systems integrators and IT vendors.

In many cases it is difficult to keep BPO providers focused on key metrics such as customer satisfaction when they are placed under immense pressure to reduce costs. Minimizing operational costs normally involves reorganizing for the efficiency of the BPO provider – not the customers. This normally results in most customers waiting in 'call groups' to speak to a call desk representative. It can result in call desk representatives being measured on how many calls per hour they can process rather than how many customers were happy with the outcome of their call.

Application service provider (ASP)

Here the company runs the CRM processes themselves but buys access to a CRM solution. The ASP will develop, customize, implement, manage and support the CRM solution, which is still run by a company's own marketing department. As a free-standing CRM package this is an ideal solution. It is quicker, cheaper and easier to get up and running than a conventional software solution. However, there is still no integration of CRM into the day-to-day cross-company business processes. The company still has to bear the costs of time, effort and money in integrating these business processes.

An ASP provides CRM facilities for an organization usually for a flat monthly fee per user. In some cases, the benefits can be considerable. Westbourne Electric, for example, estimated that in-house implementation would cost $350 000 and take at least two months, in addition to ongoing maintenance and support costs. When introduced, their ASP solution cost $200 per user per month and was operational in just four days.[11]

Business service provider (BSP)

For many companies, neither BPO nor ASP solutions are optimum. Choosing either solution could leave companies with partially optimized business processes. By using 'Web Services' to automate the delivery of business processes and enabling companies to perform transactions themselves, the BSP model solves many of the limitations of the ASP and BPO models.

A web service is a re-usable application component providing some business functionality for utilization by other applications over an Internet connection.[12,13] Web services involve offering companies discrete modules of business functionality such as doing a credit check, doing a post code check, identifying the propensity of customers to buy a given product, etc.

Business service provision goes beyond cost reduction and operational enhancement. It enables true process transformation by incorporating business knowledge and technology and helping companies with issues such as:

- Collaboration: enabling integration and optimization of business processes within the company and also between the company and its suppliers, partners and customers
- Process integration: enabling the maximization of synergies across processes
- Self-service: empowering the end user (the employee, supplier, partner and customer), reducing errors and increasing satisfaction
- Human expertise: allowing people the freedom to use their knowledge and expertise while providing transparent and ongoing process support.

Leading analysts such as Gartner conclude such advantages of BSP may enable most business processes ultimately to be candidates for BSP.

Selecting a CRM solution

CRM software is complex, expensive and still in its early stages of development. This creates problems at all stages of developing an integrated CRM solution, from identifying CRM needs, through vendor selection, to training users to get the most out of the new systems.

In terms of selecting CRM software, there are integration and best practice issues which emphasize the importance of careful outsourcing. Beginning with the choice of CRM software, it is important to note that most CRM products initially focused on specific tasks, such as sales automation or mass e-mail promotions. Consequently, they have some core strengths but there are weaknesses in other areas. For this reason, it is important when selecting a CRM vendor to have a clear understanding of your CRM needs and where you require particularly strong CRM support. If no single vendor has key strengths in your key areas, you may need to select more than one vendor and integrate components of the CRM products.

As the range of available software applications illustrates, many organizations now have a multitude of complex databases and software applications. These applications provide valuable support for a range of business activities. They can make life difficult, however, by creating islands of information that cannot readily be connected together. For this reason, a pressing concern in many organizations is to improve the level of integration. Support for this is available in the form of middleware, sometimes known as an Enterprise Messaging Layer, which provides customized links between ERP, CRM and other software applications in a process called *enterprise application integration* (EAI). In the future EAI is likely to be undertaken using a web services interface.

One risk of using multiple CRM vendors is that it can build more islands of information, rather than achieving an integrated CRM solution. In some cases, using different software for sales, marketing and customer service has resulted in each function having its own customer database and business rules.

Some form of middleware is often required when a business finds that its CRM needs can only be met using several pieces of CRM software from different vendors. If a single view of the customer is required across these islands of information then an operational data store will also be required.

In order to make informed decisions about BPO, ASP and/or BSP, or CRM solutions in general, whether establishing new partner arrangements or reviewing existing ones, the company should evaluate potential candidates against specific criteria. Some fundamental questions relating to vendor/partner selection include:

- Does the firm possess the requisite core competence and have a successful track record to prove it?
- Does the firm have experience of working similarly in partnership with other organizations and have those relationships been trouble-free/extended/deepened?
- Does the firm offer compatibility in terms of technology, philosophy, practice?
- Does the vendor demonstrate assurance in terms of quality, reliability, integrity (i.e. does it have the internal control and capacity to deliver)?

- Does the firm compete in a populated market or does it represent a niche market (i.e. is the choice of vendor limited by number of vendors operating in our problem areas)?
- If the vendor is to be one of several vendors engaged, is it willing and able to work collaboratively in the best interests of the employing organization?
- Does the firm represent a justifiably cost-effective option (i.e. does it have and will it provide the scalability and flexibility to accommodate change)?
- Does it have proof of delivery on time and on budget for similar projects.[14,15]

Data protection, privacy and codes of practice

Issues of data protection, privacy and security should be a major item on the corporate agenda. As the technological interface between customer and company extends, the trust becomes then to protect. Many commentators have pointed out that greater transparency among companies and customers, which is designed to create stronger relationships between them, means that a much greater amount of intimate business or personal details is collected and is potentially more widely accessible. Posting company information on the web or buying a product electronically over the Internet, for example, runs the risk of it ending up in inappropriate hands. Controlling access to information therefore forms a major part of the information management process.

There is increasing focus on data protection of personal information throughout the world. Different countries have taken different approaches so there is no uniform procedure. However, there is increasing pressure to work together to protect the rights of consumers as personal information crosses international borders. Genevieve Findlay, Merlin Stone and their colleagues have compiled a very useful overview of current trends in data protection. Drawing on CMAT data (discussed in the next chapter) they conclude:

- only 15 per cent of companies have clear and published data standards for imported data
- only 26 per cent comply fully with the terms of list rental agreements
- only 30 per cent consistently store the source of their customer data on the custom database, for each new record added
- only 17 per cent could demonstrate complete understanding of data protection legislation

- only 7 per cent have comprehensive and clear customer information quality standards
- only 7 per cent give proper incentives to relevant staff concerning customer information quality
- only 10 per cent document core customer information in such a way that relevant non-systems people can understand it
- only 7 per cent formally validate customer records once a year or more often
- only 20 per cent have a clear policy for archiving customer information.[16]

This represents an extremely poor picture of data use and archiving. These researchers conclude that most companies' problems with compliance with data protection laws arise from not paying close enough attention to their data infrastructure including the processes by which customer data are gathered, maintained and supplemented and the systems on which they are held.[17]

Timing of technology introduction

One of the key aspects of managing information effectively using integrated technologies is adopting the right technology at the right time. Clearly, software technologies provide a tremendous aid in automating common processes and in identifying, prioritizing and managing customer relationships. Web technologies have the potential dramatically to enhance communication with customers as well as the quality and range of service offered. The rise of mobile telephony, location-based services and interactive digital TV will no doubt also prove invaluable in bonding commercial relationships. However, decisions relating to technology upgrades or installations should take account of what degree of technological intervention is required to create and deliver customer value. Is the technology appropriate to the customers and the requirements of the business? Companies must be wary of investing in technology that far outreaches the organization's capability and the needs of premium customers.

Additionally, is the technology capable of delivering what and when its vendors promise? Technology has advanced considerably in recent years. At present, the web tools offered by some CRM vendors make it possible to provide customers with access to their personal information and to view order status information and service requests. They also support the development of Internet portals with personalized content. However, few companies have so far succeeded in using this functionality fully to support online customer self-service.

Summary

The information management process is playing an increasingly critical role in CRM, in supporting the collection, analysis and use of enormous volumes of complex customer data. Since customer data have a limited shelf life, it is crucial that it is accumulated, updated and deployed in an organized and integrated manner to provide a current and comprehensive view of customers. The ability to 'replicate' the mind of the customer and use it to improve the customer experience is a central tenet of CRM.

Selecting the appropriate IT hardware, software and systems to achieve this can be a challenging task, given the constraints of legacy systems, the enormous range of technology options and the uniqueness of every business situation. The growing variety of CRM tools and services on offer from IT vendors further complicates the questions of what constitutes the best CRM solution and whether to source the IT infrastructure externally or to construct it using internal expertise. Whatever option, or combination of options, is pursued, the underlying principle is that the IT infrastructure should create a 'nerve centre', integrating disparate customer data into customer interactions that create superior customer experiences.

Through the effective use of analytical tools, such as data mining and market segmentation analysis, the data warehouse can be used to help identify the most promising customers and to assist in developing strategies to retain them and enhance their value. Data warehouses are particularly valuable to organizations whose sheer scale of operation may mean they are losing touch with individual customers. More importantly, once created, the data warehouse can support the monitoring of customers and provide a mechanism for testing and refining customer strategy. This capability is increasingly significant as markets become ever more dynamic and personalized services and one-to-one marketing become more commonplace

Organizations should, however, also be aware of the potential drawbacks of data warehousing. Data warehouse functionality is limited by the quality and comprehensiveness of the data it contains.

Further, the more open the data warehouse, the more vulnerable it is to attack from hackers and viruses and data theft. As the building of customer relationships relies heavily on consumer trust, confidentiality restrictions and privacy acts must be visibly upheld and the organization held accountable for any breaches of trust. Data protection should be given a high priority.

To ensure that technology solutions support CRM, it is important to undertake IT planning from a perspective of providing a seamless customer service across channels, rather than planning activities from a departmental or functional perspective. Such a customer-centric approach to IT planning will ensure that customer information is used effectively to maximize customer value and the customer profitability. Furthermore, data analysis tools, such as those outlined above, make it possible to measure business activities to determine whether new ways of managing customer relationships might be advantageous in increasing shareholder value. This analysis provides the basis for the performance assessment process, the subject of the next chapter.

Checklist for CRM leaders

CRM leaders need to review the following issues about the *Information Management Process*.

The data repository and CRM architecture:

1. Where data on customers reside in different databases we know their location, accuracy and completeness
2. We have created a central data warehouse and have a single view of the customer. Information in the warehouse is accurate and complete
3. Our organization has an appropriate structure for its data repository (data warehouse, data marts, etc.) given our present and planned customer data requirements
4. Our data structure reflects our business and customer strategies in terms of segment granularity and personalization requirements
5. Our customer information links with the company's existing systems such as fulfilment, service and finance
6. We have an appropriate strategy for our IT systems including hardware and software. We have taken account of the potential of developments such as web services, business process outsourcing, and/or use of a business service provider, and/or use of an application service provider

7. We effectively utilize general data mining tools for customer insight and task-specific analysis tools for market segmentation, customer profiling, profitability analysis, predictive modelling, etc.
8. We have identified and utilized appropriate front-office systems for CRM and considered integration issues with back-office systems
9. We realistically appraise and address significant systems integration, people, processes and training tasks associated with introduction of any new CRM system, e.g. sales force automation
10. We fully investigate and budget for change management, project management and employee engagement issues associated with any proposed new CRM systems we plan to introduce.

Information and customer knowledge management:

1. My organization has introduced processes to provide relevant data and information for all appropriate staff
2. Our organization ensures the integrity of the data it collects in terms of relevancy, accuracy, currency and objectivity
3. We ensure security of all sensitive customer data (e.g. credit-card numbers and personal information)
4. We verify that all individuals who have access to sensitive and proprietary data understand the security requirements and protocols
5. My organization has implemented processes to prevent the unauthorized use or alteration of sensitive and proprietary data
6. We regularly consider opportunities to introduce new e-commerce applications to improve customer service or to reduce costs
7. There is an integrated plan agreed across all channels and functional departments for the collection and use of customer information
8. My customer information system allows information about individual customers to be recognized and used to produce summary information about the customer for use in customer applications and campaign management
9. My company uses customer analysis techniques to provide proactive customer information for cross-selling and upselling purposes
10. The company makes effective use of analytical techniques, such as predictive modelling, that use customer information to develop greater customer profitability and increased lifetime value.

Each issue should be considered in terms of:

Rating for our organization (5 = applies fully; 0 = does not apply at all)
Importance to our organization (5 = very important; 0 = no importance)

Case 5.1 Barclays introduces the 'intelligent sell' with SAS® technology

The company

Barclays plc is a major UK-based global provider of financial services, with a presence in over 60 countries. From its traditional foundations 300 years ago, Barclays has grown to become the largest UK online banker, serving more than three million online customers. In 2001 the company achieved pre-tax profits of £3.61 billion and had total assets of £357 billion.

Personal Financial Services (PFS) is an important division of Barclays' operations. PFS provides customized products and services for upwards of 19 million personal and small business customers and has as its mission 'to deliver value to shareholders by placing the customer at the centre of all activities'. This case study examines the launch of an innovative CRM project in 2000 and its subsequent development over the next two years.

The acquisition of Woolwich Mortgage Bank in November 2000 further strengthened the UK position of Barclays' Personal business, giving the company a portfolio of £56 plus billion of secured loans by 2002 which is managed by the Credit Risk function. It is the task of the Credit Risk Management department to optimize the mortgage asset quality through its complex lending expertise, policy management and advanced business technology solutions. The route to profitability in a lending environment is to increase the volume of lending while, at the same time, reducing the risk of default or non-payment. Key to managing and monitoring portfolio performance within PFS is the use of a mature data warehouse known as the 'Credit Risk Management Data Warehouse'.

Based on SAS® technology, the data warehouse holds Pre-Approved Mortgage Limit (PAML) figures on more than nine million customers – information that is of vital interest to PFS sales staff. The PAML figures are derived from several types of customer data (Property, Financial, Transactional, Personal and Application) obtained from core systems. Data marts drive aggregation of the data to create customer and household views, enabling the determination of which customers are composite to a household. SAS analytics then perform a series of credit risk calculations to determine how much can be lent to each customer within an acceptable risk framework. The SAS environment holds the limit calculation engines and business rules processing and financial caps and algorithms, allowing Barclays to optimize its lending position.

The challenge

In early 2000, Barclays PFS required a tool to sell mortgages against a background of ambitious targets. 'The sales staff were screaming for tools to help them achieve their mortgage sales targets and an important element in the equation is the ability to make a firm proposition', says Pankaj Mistry, Head of Risk Systems at Credit Risk Management. The challenge for PFS was how to get the PAML information into the sales people's hands at the point of customer contact, as PFS has thousands of sales staff based at hundreds of offices or out in the field. A solution needed to be found quickly which would be easily accessible anytime, anyplace and anywhere, but not via a PC or terminal as these were not available at all sales locations.

The solution

After careful evaluation, Credit Risk Management undertook a pilot project to build and implement Pre-approved Mortgage Limits-Interactive Voice Response (PAML-IVR). This technology solution gave authorized users interactive telephone access to information in the Credit Risk Management Data Warehouse via a fixed or mobile phone. The project was developed in collaboration with companies familiar to Barclays: SAS built the Credit Risk Management Data Warehouse and Periphonics, the voice services arm of Nortel Networks, delivered and maintained Voice solutions on multiple Barclays sites. Bringing together the two different technology partners carried its own unique challenges: common ground had to be found and rules of engagement had to be firmly established.

SAS is the market leader in providing a new generation of business intelligence (BI) software and services that enables businesses to make informed decisions and to develop more profitable relationships with their customers and suppliers. For 25 years, SAS has been giving customers around the world *The Power to Know*™, being known as a vendor that completely integrates data warehousing, analytics and traditional BI applications to create intelligence from vast numbers of data. Periphonics offers a complete suite of the advanced voice processing and speech technology products and services that are driving the next wave of e-Business. Its sophisticated IVR portfolio, for example, allows customers to self-service via touchtone, speech and web-enabled applications.

The PAML-IVR solution represents an unprecedented convergence of SAS applications and IVR technology. The SAS software handles all the data transactions, calculates the customers' credit limits and facilitates interfaces with other requisite technology. The Periphonics telephony technology ensures speedy and secure transactions. The security application was devised as a part of the telephone scripting, enabling users to register and validate themselves, obtain a personal identification number (PIN) and change it if necessary, over the telephone, thus negating the need to administer thousands of PIN numbers manually. The salesperson simply dials in to one of 30 dedicated lines to the IVR server, gives their PIN and staff numbers, their sales outlet sort code and their customer identification numbers and specifies whether their request involves one or two mortgage applicants. The IVR server then feeds the salesperson's telephone request through to SAS data sets that are refreshed on a monthly basis with the latest information from the Credit Risk Management Data Warehouse. SAS communication software feeds back the PAML data which, in turn, are converted into voice output, giving the salesperson instant information on the size of the loan that can be offered. As Mistry explains: 'Access to this information gives the salespeople a tremendous advantage because they don't need to worry about a mortgage being declined after an offer has been made. They know exactly what the customer's limit is'.

The prototype phase of the project began in July 2000 and took 30 person-days' effort (ten from Barclays staff). Components of the PAML-IVR solution included: a telephone line and hub; the IVR server and software; telephone scripting; a security application; the data server and software; and the interface program. After three months' development, the prototype system was tested with 30 pilot users at various UK locations over a 90-day period. The trial focused on the system's performance and, more importantly, the impact on the sales process of making the rich PAML information readily available.

The results

Credit Risk Management successfully met the challenge to devise a delivery mechanism to rapidly access PAML information from the Credit Risk Management Data Warehouse. 'Although some of the technology components were completely new, the solution proved itself to be very robust and could support a 24 × 7 operation', concludes Mistry. 'Within six weeks of going live, Barclays achieved £1 million (1.6 million) in extra new sales, entirely attributable to the new PAML-IVR solution. ROI was achieved in eight weeks'.

The project's exceptional success financially was mirrored in the delight of PFS employees and customers. Sales staff were making more sales and completing each sale in less time. A 15- to 30-minute reduction in form-filling and financial history assessment during a customer interview was possible because the amount Barclays was prepared to lend the customer had been predetermined using the PAML-IVR solution. Customers also expressed high satisfaction with the simpler, faster service. They were no longer required to complete a 12-page form just to start the application process – doing the groundwork the company should be doing – and they could depend on receiving a straightforward, definitive response. All told, the solution enabled PFS to provide a 24 × 6 service Monday to Saturday with minimal downtime (Sundays being reserved for system maintenance) and to deliver a more profitable and positive customer experience.

Impressed by this boost to revenues, sales force productivity and customer satisfaction, the Personal Executive gave the go-ahead in November 2000 for an extension of PAML-IVR leading to a national roll out to 4000 salespeople. By April 2001 Barclays had already attributed £70 million (111 million) in pure new sales to the PAML-IVR solution and the conversion rate of applications to actual completions had increased from 40 to 45 per cent. Expenditure on the national system was recouped in six months.

Apart from the direct tangible results, Mistry highlights the more profound benefits in relation to the organization's mission. 'The customer feels he has received a great service without paperwork: an immediate decision without the need to produce evidence. PAML-IVR helps make the customer feel that our service revolves around his/her needs as an individual. And that obviously helps to create shareholder value.'

Barclays' pragmatic approach of starting small and proving the concept ensured flexibility and a quick and measurable impact – minimizing risk and maximizing return. The creative integration of its customer knowledge and PAML risk methodology, deployed at the point of sale, has given the company a leading edge over competitors. Since IVR has never before been applied in this way, no other financial services providers have the benefit of being able to deliver such a technology-enabled, user-efficient and customer-intelligent service.

A constructive change in attitude accompanied the technical triumph. Whereas Credit Risk Management was traditionally viewed by Sales and Marketing as very prudent, conservative and unsupportive of ambitious sales and marketing activity, it was now actively encouraging Sales and Marketing to pursue initiatives and to target pre-approved and risk-vetted customers who represent ideal prospects from a credit risk management perspective.

The PAML-IVR solution has helped PFS in achieving customer-centricity, while strengthening the Barclays Group strategy of leveraging customer knowledge to deliver business advantages for the benefit of the customer and the organization. Barclays' successful adoption of this forward-looking technology suggests that the 'hard sell' is obsolete, having been superseded by a more informed and insightful approach – the 'intelligent sell'.

Case 5.2 Halifax gives extra value with E.piphany Real-Time solutions

The company

Halifax bank, a subsidiary of HBOS Group, is the largest home mortgage lender in the UK and offers a diverse set of financial and asset management services, including retail and business banking, consumer credit, savings products, pension products, life insurance and other investment-related products. With over £300 billion in total assets, Halifax manages a network of 750 branches, more than 700 financial agencies and intermediaries and approximately 400 estate agencies. The company registered an annual profit of £3 billion (before tax and exceptional items) in 2001 and continues to build on a legacy of well-earned confidence.

The merger of Halifax plc and Bank of Scotland as HBOS in September 2001 marked a challenge to the 'Big 4' clearing banks. HBOS has a substantial customer base, comprising personal, business and corporate customers. Its breadth of reach in existing markets represents significant commercial opportunities and these are fast being realized through an active focus on personalized customer solutions. James Crosby, HBOS Chief Executive, summarizes the Group's strategy: 'We seek to be more productive, sell more and hold on to our customers by giving them real value and superb service'.

The challenge

A prime contributor to the HBOS brand, Halifax has led from the front in turning strategic intent into business initiative. In late 1999, a group of Halifax executives seized upon an opportunity to drive steeper profit and revenue growth by managing customer relationships more proactively. The continuing rise in the number of inbound calls to Halifax's contact centre offered tremendous scope for enhancing value creation. The bank received in excess of 24 million calls in 1999 and forecast that call volume would increase by more than 25 per cent through 2002. 'We knew we were missing revenue opportunities with each inbound call and wanted a system to generate personalized offers to customers', says Ruth Southern, Manager of New Sales Solutions, Retail Sales Development at Halifax. 'We also knew that customer loyalty and profitability would grow with each product sold to an existing customer.'

In order to harness the full sales and relationship-building potential of each telephone interaction, the bank needed to be able to demonstrate individual customer knowledge and relevance in real time. Intense competition and the rapid evolution of the financial services industry had elevated customer responsiveness from a desirable characteristic to a crucial factor. Moreover, 'responsiveness' was now defined by the quality, not just the quickness, of response. The use of multiple channels and, particularly, web-enabled media whose self-service dimension emphasizes ease and expedience, had set new standards of customer convenience and service coherence. Customer value was unmistakably the key driver of shareholder value.

Halifax had already made a significant investment in call centre infrastructure and inbound calls were being handled with the utmost efficiency. However, the call centre technology (a home-grown, agent desk top application) did not possess the sophisticated analysis tools to cross-sell and upsell effectively the company's array of financial products. Halifax had a separate system for reviewing customer information and a centrally controlled marketing system for developing and presenting customer propositions. In addition, it was Halifax's ultimate aim to enhance the value of interactions across all customer touchpoints, including the bank's branches, agencies and interactive voice response (IVR) system. Clearly, new tools and resources were required if these immediate and longer-term customer relationship management (CRM) goals were to be achieved.

The solution

Determined to capitalize on the growing dialogue with its customers, Halifax chose to deploy marketing solutions from E.piphany, Inc. to meet its cross-selling objectives. E.piphany is a leading provider of CRM software to the largest global enterprises. Major businesses use the vendor's integrated CRM suite, E.piphany E.6™, to enhance their customers' experience, enable organizational effectiveness and drive value.

In Q2/3 2000, Halifax piloted E.piphany Real-Time software with 160 of its call centre agents to support cross-sell development. E.phiphany Real-Time provides real-time decisioning to allow for the construction of a consolidated customer profile and the delivery of a personalized product offer. Using the Real-Time system, the call centre agents could rapidly access a customer's information and match it to directly relevant offers in the course of conversation. In this way, they were able to demonstrate thorough knowledge of Halifax's products and customers, resolve callers' problems quickly and easily, recommend new or upgraded products where appropriate and close sales with assured customer satisfaction.

In a next step, Halifax deployed E.piphany Real-Time to its Halifax Direct IVR system, which provides targeted messages to callers using its automated 24-hour telephone service for balance enquiries, bill payments and other standard transactions. The E.piphany solution expanded the self-service capability by leveraging customer information to deliver personalized offers, thus generating new product and service sales. For example, customers would be offered the opportunity to upgrade their bank account, based on an understanding of the amount of monthly credits made to their existing account. If the customer chooses to accept the offer, they are provided with an option to connect directly to an agent to fulfil their request. Activation of the targeted message is guided by a record of the last time the customer accessed the IVR and whether or not they have previously been offered a campaign via the IVR system.

The results

Halifax's initial deployment of E.phiphany Real-Time exceeded expectations. Within six months of introducing the system to the call centre, investment costs had been recouped and offer acceptance rates among some of the top-selling agents had increased by more than 55 per cent. More importantly, customer acceptance across all campaign types (mortgage, personal loan, savings and current account) has risen considerably to an above industry average of 7.6 per cent. The success of the system was measured against internal product sales targets and the volume of business generated; it surpassed even the most optimistic performance predictions.

In addition to delivering impressive financial results, the E.piphany system had an empowering effect on staff. With accurate and instructive information at their fingertips, call centre agents were able to communicate with customers more effectively and with a greater sense of confidence. Even those who were apprehensive about selling sophisticated financial products found that the user-friendly screen prompts provided the reassurance to overcome their fears and develop their skills as sales people. As Southern explains: 'When agents became more comfortable with the system, they became more opportunistic about additional sales'. This direct and positive impact on staff morale helped ensure a smooth transition to the new system.

Potential resistance to the organizational changes required was diminished also by new-found competencies. Because E.piphany Real-Time is a self-learning solution (meaning it becomes demonstrably smarter through use), the system can recognize the key characteristics of customers who are most likely to accept a particular offer based on a knowledge of customers who have previously shown an interest in that product. This ability to distinguish purchase proclivity and act on it immediately enables the campaign conversion rate to be higher than would otherwise be the case.

Prior to deployment of E.piphany Real-Time, the company's cross-selling techniques leaned towards generic marketing or hopeful guesswork. Call centre agents were often led, unknowingly, to suggest products that customers already had or would not need. Now, fully aware of which products match which customers at the point of sale, agents make offers that are deeply relevant. The reaction of Halifax customers to the CRM initiative has been likewise encouraging. Customer feedback shows it is a welcome change and a move in the right direction. This is borne out by the fact that 10 per cent of all sales prompts now generate a lead and a substantial 50 per cent of those leads close a sale.

By adopting a phased approach, testing E.piphany Real-Time first within the call centre and then extending it successfully to the Halifax Direct IVR system, the company was able to measure performance improvement and economically reinvest incremental return. 'We started small, we proved the case and rolled out our system', says Southern. 'We've generated growth that otherwise would not have occurred and we've created much greater customer loyalty. Now, we intend to continue expanding these capabilities further utilizing the E.piphany system.'

Plans are in place to use E.piphany Real-Time to heighten the capabilities of Halifax's online banking services and enable the generation of personalized offers as customers navigate the company's web site, www.hbosplc.com. The move will allow the now highly individual nature of customer propositions to be maintained while augmenting customer value in terms of channel choice.

Building on the success of the pilot project, Halifax has rolled out the system to all 750 retail bank outlets. This is giving counter tellers the customer insight to manage their customer relationships more personally and profitably. There are also plans in place to implement the same system in agencies and to expand the system to support Bank of Scotland branch and call centre operations. Graeme Morgan, Product Manager at Halifax Retail Bank IT, is delighted with the mutual benefit provided by the implementation. 'Our staff can have total confidence to sell our financial products, based on the fact that all the information they have is the most up to date available. From entering the customer account number it takes a fraction of a second for the E.piphany software to prompt the staff on the appropriate product offering. This has already given us a strong advantage in our branches, driven product uptake and helped maintain customer and employee satisfaction.'

Halifax's adoption of the E.piphany CRM solution has helped reinforce its claim of 'always giving you extra' – extra value for money and extra reason for doing business with Halifax. Designed to help manage customer relationships better, the E.piphany CRM solution is now key to enhancing customer service and cross-selling opportunities throughout the retail bank operation.

Chapter 6

The performance assessment process

The strategic framework for CRM

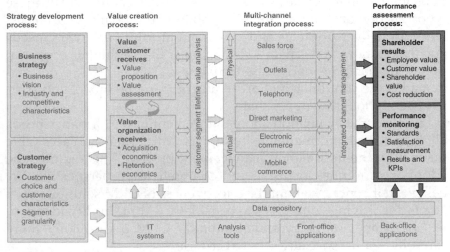

Information management process

The *performance assessment process* is the final process in the Strategic Framework for CRM. The purpose of this process is to ensure that the organization's strategic aims in terms of CRM are being delivered to an appropriate and acceptable standard and that a basis for future improvement is firmly established. As shown in the above figure the process has a dual focus on *shareholder results*, which provides a 'macro-view' of the key drivers of CRM performance, and on *performance monitoring*, which involves a more detailed 'micro-view' of the key descriptors of CRM performance. This process involves focusing on two key issues:

1. How can we create increased profits and shareholder value?
2. How should we set standards, develop metrics, measure our results and improve our performance?

Together these issues provide an understanding of how CRM delivers shareholder results and how CRM performance can be measured and thus further enhanced.

As emphasized throughout this book, CRM breaks with traditional management practice in that it involves the whole organization and emphasizes avoiding functional divides. In so doing CRM embraces a new logic for commercial relevance: business success ultimately derives from the creation of customer value, which is achieved through the skilful management and development of customer relationships involving all key stakeholders. Market leaders will be those who can demonstrate an unfailing ability continually and consistently to deliver products and services that fulfil customers' needs and expectations and can do so in a manner that highlights organizational competencies and cost-effectiveness. This is a tall order and demands the coordinated effort of all company members and partners throughout the supply chain.

Likewise, the evaluation and enhancement of performance needs all the required information to be supplied in a timely and accessible manner by the information management process. This requires the adoption of a more inclusive and comprehensive perspective. We believe that concerns about the effectiveness of CRM solutions are a key factor driving companies to consider CRM in this broader context of business strategy and to monitor CRM performance more carefully against specially selected criteria.

The need for a systematic approach

Historically, firms have tended to organize themselves in terms of functional responsibility and thus performance measures have reflected the individual objectives of departments or strategic business units. For example, Finance has been driven by profit, Sales by volume and Marketing by customer acquisition. The movement towards greater convergence and consolidation in many industries has blurred the distinctions among the aims of traditional allocations of organizational responsibility. More collaborative work practices have necessitated more consultative measurement and monitoring systems. In short, a redefinition of the business model requires a recalibration of business performance. Because CRM is a cross-functional activity, CRM performance measurement must use a range of metrics that span the gamut of processes and channels used to deliver CRM.

As yet, there is no universally recognized system for measuring the success of CRM. This is partly due to the fact that every CRM programme is unique and cannot be judged identically and partly because formalized CRM is a relatively new discipline. Although customer relationship management is often considered the remit of marketing as it builds on the tenets of relationship marketing, in practice it forms part of the job of every employee in every department. This sharing of customer responsibility compounds the difficulty of agreeing specific measures that will accurately reflect CRM performance and strategic progress.

Early attempts to measure marketing performance were largely directed at monitoring financial outputs. These included profit, sales and cash flow. In the 1980s, there was a realization that non-financial measures also played a part in delivering the overall performance of marketing. Organizations began to recognize that variables such as brand equity, customer satisfaction and customer loyalty were very important in transforming marketing inputs to organizational outputs. During the 1990s, the emphasis switched to the use of multiple measures that would together provide a more complete picture of marketing performance. However, this method raises difficult issues for managers, including which measures should be included in performance monitoring models and how to account for the interrelationships between measures.

Clearly what is needed for the 2000s is a more definitive framework that identifies the principal measures of CRM performance and how these measures organize into a system that can be used continually to monitor, track and improve performance in support of the CRM vision. The performance assessment process, highlighted in the figure above, provides a structure for developing such a system based on the following key actions:

1. Understand the *key drivers of shareholder results* and the significance of the linkages between them

2. Identify the *appropriate standards, metrics and KPIs* against which the various CRM activities can be measured
3. Establish an *effective CRM performance monitoring system* to apply these measures on an ongoing basis.

Each of these key actions is now examined in turn.

Understanding the key drivers of shareholder results

To achieve the ultimate objective of CRM – the delivery of excellent shareholder results through an increase in shareholder value – an organization must maximize the main sources of revenue, profit and growth within the context of both business and customer strategy. The four main elements are:

- building employee value
- building customer value
- building shareholder value
- reducing costs.

The first three elements impact of three key stakeholder groups, while the latter is a potentially significant means of directly improving profits. The development of the 'linkage model' or 'service profit chain',[1] shown in Figure 6.1, confirms the relationship correlation between value creation and profitability, as well as the linkage between employee value, customer value and shareholder value.

The linkage model suggests that an improvement in leadership and management behaviour has a positive impact on employee attitudes and employee satisfaction. The more satisfied and motivated an employee, the longer they are likely to stay with an organization and the better they will do their job. This will have a positive effect

Figure 6.1   The linkage model

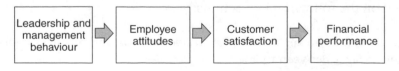

on customer satisfaction, so customers will stay longer and generate higher sales for the company. The result is stronger profitability and increased shareholder value. This model provides a key logic to the broader perspective of CRM. We will return to the model later in this chapter.

Shareholder value, customer value, employee value and cost reduction

Many organizations now recognize the importance of improving their performance by managing the value input and impact of each major stakeholder group. It is obvious that certain stakeholder groups are more important than others. While this importance will vary to some extent from organization to organization, three stakeholder groups, shareholders, customers and employees have emerged as the core focus for most organizations in terms of value management and performance improvement. Frederick Reichheld of consulting firm, Bain & Company, points out that these three key stakeholders – the 'forces of loyalty' – are pivotal in achieving commercial success.[2] These key drivers of shareholder results are shown in Figure 6.2. This figure emphasizes the need to consider each of these stakeholders from the perspective of the value of the stakeholder group to the organization *and* the value of the organization to that stakeholder group.

It is useful to make a subtle distinction between building shareholder value and achieving shareholder results. In this context, *shareholder value* creation may be viewed in a more narrow sense as being concerned with identifiable value in terms of returns on capital that stem from initiatives such as improved customer satisfaction and increasing customer retention, excluding stock market measures. *Shareholder results* include how shareholders and the stock market respond to these improvements in shareholder value: that is, they reflect the stock market perspective. Research shows that shareholders take a range of non-financial measures into account when valuing companies. For example, the 'Measures that Matter' study[3] suggests that on average 35 per cent of an investment decision is driven by non-financial data. Hence, issues such as communicating a coherent and well-planned CRM strategy may have a significant part to play in achieving improved shareholder results.

Figure 6.2   Key drivers of shareholder results

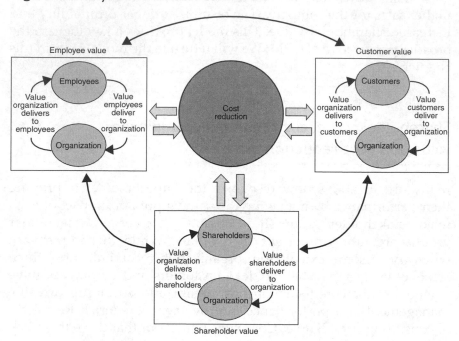

Cost reduction is an obvious source of potential increase in profits and shareholder results. Improving efficiency and the use of lower cost channels are common means of achieving cost reduction. However, as we will discuss shortly it is important that this is not done at the expense of lowered levels of customer satisfaction and customer value.

Employee value

In addressing CRM performance it is tempting to focus immediately on standards for CRM, metrics and key performance indicators (KPIs). However, the need first to focus on the drivers of shareholder results should be emphasized.

John McKean in his book *Information Masters*[4] made a critical observation that typically 92 per cent of the historical investment in CRM expenditure goes into data and technology, but these aspects only represent 25 per cent of the competency determinants for success. Organizations need also to make sure the other most critical elements that represent 75 per cent of the competency determinants for success, such as people, processes, organization, culture and leadership actively support CRM activities in a relevant manner. McKean's research indicates that a total of 60 per cent of the competency determinants for success involve people, organization, culture and leadership. Thus the people element is absolutely critical in making CRM work. These issues are discussed in more detail in the next chapter.

Employee value needs to be considered from two perspectives – the value employees deliver to the organization and the value the organization delivers to employees. Further, a motivated employee can add value to the customer.

The value employees deliver to the organization is usually measured against a number of performance objectives. Often these represent short-term goals, where employee performance is appraised against performance targets. Employee value of this form is closely linked to employee retention, for long-tenured employees are more likely to know their jobs and the goals of the organization and are thus able to be more productive.

The value the organization delivers to its employees comprises the benefits the work force receives in exchange for the opportunity cost, time and labour expended in performing their jobs. This bundle of benefits includes the internal service quality created by management practices, encompassing reward and appraisal policies, training and development opportunities and the motivation and empowerment of employees.

Linking employee remuneration to specific customer objectives, such as customer satisfaction and customer retention, supports the creation of value for both the employees and the organization.

How the company's leadership, human resources and culture are organized are therefore key factors in determining employee value which, in turn, has a significant bearing on customer and shareholder value. This is evident in the types of measures used to monitor the value delivered by employees, for example, product quality measures, employee turnover, recruitment costs and employee satisfaction.

Customer value

Customer value is concerned with both *the value the organization receives from the customer* and *the value the customer receives from the organization*. As the topic of customer value has been already discussed in Chapter 3, only a brief recap is given here.

The value the organization receives from the customer is determined by the profits obtained from the customer over the lifetime of their relationship with the organization, or their 'customer lifetime value' and the economics of customer acquisition and retention.

The value the customer receives from the organization is defined by the perceived benefits of the offer made to the customer, which extend beyond the core product or service. These higher-level benefits, or 'added values', emanate not from basic product features but from intangible factors, such as the provision of better customer service or association with a quality brand image. A number of measures are used to monitor this aspect of customer value including customer retention, customer acquisition costs, customer satisfaction and customer profitability.

The key issues relating to customer value, discussed in Chapter 3, include:

The nature of 'the offer' a company makes to its customer – Customer value is an inherent part of the product or service offer which the company can actively manage to benefit the customer. Customers do not buy goods or services, but rather a bundle of benefits in the form of product features and added value. This total offering – or 'the offer', as it is commonly called – represents the value that customers get when they buy goods or services.

The use of relationships and branding to increase customer value – Building better relationships with customers through offering superior customer service is one way of securing competitive advantage. The use of customer service as a more important competitive weapon derives from increasingly sophisticated customer requirements and the demand for ever-higher standards of service. Developing greater customer involvement with the company's products is a good way to use the brand to enhance customer value. The Harley-Davidson Owners Group, discussed in Chapter 3, provides a good illustration of this.

The value proposition – The value proposition comprises three key steps: choose the value, provide the value and communicate the value. Success rests on the thoroughness and innovation that goes into developing the value proposition and communicating it throughout the supplying organization.

The value of customers to the company – To calculate a customer's real worth, the company must look at the expected profit flow from the customer over the customer's lifetime, rather than the results this year: the longer the customer relationship, the greater the profit per customer.

Shareholder value

The growing power and influence of financial analysts has driven many company boards to regard the creation of shareholder value as their primary business objective. However, the emphasis is frequently placed on quarterly results rather than the longer term. Balancing long-term and short-term returns and communicating this balance to shareholders, is therefore becoming a priority.

Shareholder value is created by achieving a favourable rate of return on capital invested. This can be accomplished in a number of ways. Ian Cornelius and Matt Davies[5] have summarized the five principal strategies that can lead to the creation of shareholder value. These are:

1. increasing the return generated on existing capital invested
2. investing more capital where the rate of return exceeds that required
3. divesting assets which generate a return lower than that required, thus releasing capital for more productive use
4. extending the period over which returns above the required rate are generated
5. reducing the cost of capital.

These strategies require a 'value based management' approach that emphasizes creating and maximizing the wealth of shareholders in every aspect of the business. Such an approach involves measuring and managing the following key financial variables, or 'value drivers':

- the opening amount of capital invested
- the rate of return generated on capital
- the rate of return that investors require
- the growth in the value of capital invested
- the time horizon over which returns are expected to exceed those required by shareholders.

Most of what has been written on shareholder value focuses on the *value the organization delivers to shareholders*. Over the last decade there has been particular emphasis on tools that measure shareholder value creation and shareholder results, including economic value added (EVA), shareholder value added (SVA), market value added (MVA) and cash flow return on investment (CFROI). A summary of key measures of shareholder value is shown in Figure 6.3.

Figure 6.3   Shareholder value measures

Company	Shareholder value product
LEK/Alcar Consulting Group	Shareholder value added (SVA)
Stern Stewart & Co	Market value added (MVA)
	Economic value added (EVA™)
McKinsey & Co	Various methods
Marakon Associates	Various methods
Braxton Associates	Cash flow return on investment (CFROI)
The Boston Consulting Group	Cash flow return on investment (CFROI)
	Cash value added (CVA)
Holt Value Associates	Cash flow return on investment (CFROI)

Source: Based on 'Metric Wars'[7]

Although there is an ongoing debate as to which technique most accurately measures shareholder value, what is important is to consider shareholder value in the context of the whole business and, in particular, in relation to customer value. The specific measurement of shareholder value is complex and beyond the scope of this book. (The interested reader should consult the detailed report by Cornelius and Davies.[6])

Although the issue of the *value the shareholders deliver to the organization* is emphasized much less, the loyalty of shareholders and other investors is an issue of considerable importance. Frederick Reichheld points out that shareholder churn in the average public company in the USA is more than 50 per cent per annum and argues that managers find it very difficult to pursue long-term value-creation strategies without the support of loyal and knowledgeable shareholders. He notes that many of the world's leading companies (in terms of high customer loyalty and high customer retention) are either privately owned, 'mutual' or public companies, where there is a high shareholder loyalty and thus a high value delivered by shareholders to the organization.

Delivering value to shareholders is an increasing concern of CEOs. However, an obsession with maximizing shareholder value has sometimes led to the neglect of other stakeholder groups, causing high employee turnover, poor quality products and services and ultimately reduced shareholder value. It is therefore crucial that shareholder value be viewed as a balance between immediate financial return and longer-term sustainability. This will be discussed in the following chapter.

Cost reduction

Cost reduction can represent a good source of increase in profits and shareholder results.

Opportunities for cost reduction lie in:

1. exploiting economies of scale
2. benchmarking best practice within and outside the industry
3. outsourcing non-core activities
4. leveraging shared activities across the organization
5. improving CRM efficiency and effectiveness.

Better information management can be a primary source of cost reduction in CRM. For example, one large US investment bank found they could redeploy 45 per cent of their staff in marketing, sales and service because the time required to undertake these activities was significantly reduced through gaining a higher level of information competency.[8]

Deploying electronic systems, such as automated telephony services, which lower costs by enabling reductions in staff and overheads, is an attractive potential source of cost reduction. However, an over concentration on cost reduction as a means of delivering shareholder results can be counterproductive if it *decreases customer value*. For example, the creation of a central call centre in a bank will help reduce costs but may disenfranchise customers who prefer to interact with bank employees whom they know. Dealing with bank representatives who are unfamiliar with their individual circumstances and banking habits can be regarded as an affront to their long-standing status as loyal customers. A large UK bank recently had to reverse its new policy of customers only being able to speak to a central call centre, rather than directly to their branch, as a result of many complaints from angry customers. Thus, any cost reduction strategy needs to be considered in the context of its effect on customer value.

The utilization of new electronic channels, such as online self-service facilities on the Internet, which lower the costs of customer acquisition, transaction and servicing offers a further opportunity for cost reduction. With its innovative web site Dell places much of the buying process in its customers' hands. Using the benefits of web self-service, discussed in Chapter 5, customers can configure own product and place their own orders. This dramatically speeds up the buying process, improves accuracy, decreases costs of correction and problem resolution and is considerably less labour intensive for Dell. Further, storage and distribution costs are cut because of more timely and efficient stock management and delivery.

Achieving a productive balance between cost reduction and customer satisfaction means understanding the value that may be created or sacrificed in the management of the customer relationship. This value factor constitutes a central element of CRM, for it is what drives success in the organization. A well-managed value process will lead to a better quality of workforce, in terms of the organization's ability to attract and retain highly motivated, committed and appropriately skilled employees. Such a dedicated workforce is more likely to deliver a better customer experience, which in turn will deliver better shareholder value through increased sales, repeat orders and customer referrals.

The importance of an appropriate value exchange is clear: concentrating on how much value (in the form of profits) an organization can extract from its customers, without understanding what customers value from the organization in order to provide it satisfactorily, is not a sustainable strategy in today's competitive environment. Nor is a strategy of profit improvement through cost reduction where cost savings are made at the expense of customer value. Thus, an integrated approach is needed to optimize the contribution of each stakeholder group and the opportunities for cost reduction, as well as to exploit the *linkages* between them.

Linking shareholder value, employee value, customer value and cost reduction

In addition to the profit-enhancing potential of each group's value contribution, there is potential contained in the linkages between them. There is also an obvious connection between cost reduction and the three key stakeholders discussed above. As Figure 6.3 suggests, cost savings can be used to increase employee value (e.g. through investing in staff training or job incentives), increase customer value (e.g. through augmenting the value proposition) or increase shareholder value (e.g. through improving 'the bottom line').

Conversely, improvement in these value areas can result in substantial cost reductions. For example, an improvement in customer value may drive increased customer satisfaction, resulting in high levels of advocacy among the customer base and consequent savings in marketing costs. This knock-on effect is evident in organizations such as First Direct, the UK bank, which acquires a third or more of its customers through customer referrals rather than through traditional marketing activities. Thus its acquisition costs for each customer are significantly reduced.

We have noted above the linkage between three areas: employee value, customer value and shareholder value – but how are they related? The linkage model shown in Figure 6.1 gives insight into the logic but not the specific relationships between variables within these areas. It is not clear for most organizations how much one variable needs to improve to achieve a given level of improvement in another variable. For example, if employee attitudes and satisfaction increase by a measurable amount, what specific impact will this have on customer satisfaction and resulting profitability?

As discussed shortly, some leading companies are using advanced modelling approaches to verify the exact nature of the linkages between these sources of added value in their businesses and use them to improve shareholder results. As the search for new and improved ways of measuring the performance of key variables *across* these critical linkages continues, organizations are recognizing the importance of addressing these higher-level drivers before determining CRM standards, metrics and key performance indicators (KPIs).

Developing appropriate standards, metrics and KPIs

Despite the increasing focus in businesses on customer-facing activities, there is growing concern that the standards and metrics generally used by companies for assessing CRM performance are not as advanced as they should be. In particular, more detailed standards, measures and KPIs are needed to ensure CRM activities are planned and performed effectively and that a feedback loop exists to maximize organizational learning and improvement.

As shown in the Strategic Framework for CRM, assessing CRM performance involves a consideration of the contribution and interaction of multiple processes. The five interrelated and cross-functional processes common to all commercial organizations are:

- the strategic development process
- the value creation process
- the multi-channel integration process
- the information management process
- the performance assessment process.

These processes centre on how the organization delivers value to the customer while enhancing the value received by the company in terms of shareholder results. While these processes have universal application, the extent to which they are emphasized will vary according to the situation of the organization concerned.

Companies need simultaneously to consider what standards and metrics should be used by them and what are their CRM priorities, given their specific circumstances. Organizations can benefit from first learning about existing standards and metrics used by other organizations before reinventing what others have already done.

Standards

The lack of an internationally recognized set of standards for CRM has hindered efforts to measure and benchmark best practice – a prerequisite to helping achieve improved performance in CRM. Few companies as yet have developed their own integrated and detailed processes for measuring CRM performance. The complexity of measuring the many processes contributing to the success of CRM makes this a potentially daunting task.

However, the increasing importance of CRM measurement has recently resulted in a number of organizations developing CRM standards for more general use. These standards typically relate to either a complete view of CRM activity or a specific part of it. Two of the leading initiatives are the QCi Customer Management Assessment Tool used as a general CRM review and the Customer Outsourcing Performance Centre (COPC) standards for customer service centres.

The QCi Customer Management Assessment Tool (CMAT)

CMAT™ is a proprietary assessment tool for understanding how well an organization manages its customers. It is carried out by trained assessors who are experienced CRM practitioners within QCi Assessment Ltd,[9] a specialist CRM consultancy, or one of its partner organizations.

The model is based on the following elements:

1. analysis and planning
2. the proposition
3. people and organization
4. information technology
5. process management
6. customer management activity
7. measuring the effect
8. the customer experience.

Each of these elements is further sub-divided into component parts. For example, 'people and organization' covers:

- organizational structure
- role identification
- competencies definition and gap analysis
- training requirements and resources
- objective setting and monitoring
- supplier selection and management.

CMAT uses over 250 questions to assess the organization's perform-ance. Each question in the assessment is based on known and demonstrable good practices from the clients of QCi and from accepted industry benchmark organizations. A 'scoring based on evidence' approach is taken to answering each question and a broad range of people, from senior directors to operational level practition-ers, are interviewed. The approach is specifically designed to iden-tify *clear plans*, *real delivery* and an *identifiable effect* of each of the practices questioned. In this way the all too common gap between senior management perception of the situation and the 'front line' reality is often identified.

Figure 6.4 provides data for 'United Bank' in term of its overall performance and eight component measures of the CMAT model. It

Figure 6.4   CMAT performance benchmarking for 'United Bank'

	Overall average	United Bank	Insurance	Other finance	Retail banking
Overall scores	32	40	28	30	41
Analysis & planning	28	28	27	19	37
The proposition	30	26	26	24	36
People & organization	38	54	31	40	49
Information & technology	37	36	32	38	46
Process management	29	36	27	36	35
Customer management activity	31	37	26	30	37
Measuring the effect	35	60	29	36	49
The customer experience	28	40	20	16	42

Source: © QCi Assessment Ltd, used with permission

also compares it with the overall average across all industry sectors and also more interestingly within more direct competitors in banking, insurance and other finance businesses. Thus United Bank can compare itself with its competitors and also best practice across all industries.

The output of the assessment is a report and Board-level presentation that positions the organization against a relevant benchmark of other organizations. It also provides a quartile positioning for each of 27 CRM areas into which the sections of the Customer Management model are divided. The assessment has been carried out in over 100 organizations worldwide so provides a rich set of data for a company to benchmark its performance against.

The objective of the CMAT tool is to provide an objective and quantitative assessment of how well the organization currently manages its customers with a score that correlates to business performance and benchmarks the organization against a relevant set of other organizations. This is especially beneficial when the company can compare itself against competitors in its own vertical industry sector, such as shown in Figure 6.4. It also forms a clear 'baseline' against which improvements delivered by a CRM programme can be measured and provides a broad-based check that all the necessary CRM foundations are in place before investing in specific programmes or technology.

Customer Operations Performance Centre (COPC) Standard

Other standards focus on particular aspects of CRM in more detail. One such approach is the *COPC Standard* developed by users of customer service centres, call centres and fulfilment services in the USA. It was initiated by representatives of a number of leading companies – including American Express, Dell Computer Corp., Microsoft, Novell and L.L. Bean – in response to their concerns about the performance of call centre providers.

The developers of this standard believed that improvement standards could help augment service quality within a service environment, just as has been seen in manufacturing industries that employed similar quality measures. Although some service providers used existing standards such as ISO 9000, these were orientated towards manufacturing industries and failed to give the operational benefits that were needed in service businesses.

The COPC-2000 standard[10] is awarded to companies successfully completing a formal audit measuring the effectiveness of their internal customer-facing operations. Among its aims is to distinguish between excellent service providers and those that are mediocre, enabling companies who are outsourcing call or service centres to use this information before they make their purchasing decision. The standard includes developing process specifications based on customer requirements, so service delivery processes are customer and not operationally driven.

The COPC standard is based on a number of well-recognized criteria used in the Malcolm Baldridge Quality Award. There are four key areas used within these standards.

- *Performance standards*, includes customer satisfaction, product and service quality, employee satisfaction and supplier performance
- *Processes*, includes process control, supplier management, internal quality audits and product development
- *People*, includes recruitment and development, compensation, recognition and the work environment of employees
- *Planning and leadership*, includes leadership, planning and performance review.

Although COPC does not set specific performance objectives that every call centre must meet, it does require that all performance metrics are tracked by linking them to customer satisfaction drivers. This information is then used to improve overall call centre performance.

The aim of the COPC standard is to improve performance of all outsourced call centres through widespread adoption of the standards. The measures have been widely accepted and, although call centres have often chosen not to pursue accreditation; many employ the performance metrics.

While COPC is supported by many call centre providers, only a small number have as yet been certified. The process is difficult and costly, so some organizations are choosing to adopt the standards and use these to benchmark their performance, without going through the accreditation process.

While the COPC standards are designed for specific types of organizations with a strong emphasis on customer service delivery, they are useful as an example of an integrated approach to measuring effectiveness within a key area of CRM.

Metrics

The identification of appropriate metrics is another challenge for companies seeking to evaluate and enhance their CRM performance. The main problem lies in determining the critical measures of CRM-related activity that are most appropriate to the organization and managing them effectively.

It is important at this stage to note the distinction between metrics and KPIs. *Metrics* involve all those CRM-related activities that should be measured. *Key performance indicators* are the high-level measures that are critical to the success of the business and that should be monitored closely by the Board and top management.

We consider four main categories of CRM metrics are especially important – customer metrics, operational (employee and process) metrics, strategic metrics and output and comparative metrics. These key metrics represent the 'vital statistics' of healthy CRM, signalling the strength or weakness of the underlying CRM processes. Other more specialized metrics may also be needed to meet specific company requirements. In any event, these CRM metrics should be applied regularly to provide an overall appraisal and monitoring of CRM effectiveness.

Customer metrics

Customer metrics measure both the value delivered by the organization to the customer and the value delivered by the customer to the organization. They are focused around measures of customer attitude and behaviour.

Customer metrics are used to measure:

1. customer acquisition and customer retention rates
2. customer satisfaction measures
3. customer lifetime value
4. customer experience within channel and across multi-channels
5. customer complaints and seriousness of them
6. segment and micro-segment profitability
7. 'share of wallet'
8. product density (number of products and services used by a customer)
9. customer recommendation and advocacy measures
10. increase in customer value through cross-sell and upsell.

People and process metrics

People and process metrics focus on how well the organization's resources are managed to optimize CRM at an operational level. People metrics are concerned with standards used to monitor the skills and motivation of employees in delivering the customer experience. Process metrics reflect the efficiency of the organization in delivering CRM, including cost savings secured through process enhancement.

People metrics are used to measure:

1. employee performance against customer service standards
2. employee satisfaction
3. employee attitudes and motivation
4. employee productivity
5. staff absenteeism
6. employee retention and employee tenure
7. recruitment costs.

Process metrics are used to measure:

1. customer service levels
2. order fulfilment
3. supplier performance targets
4. variation within key customer processes
5. new product/service development targets
6. time to market
7. process improvement targets.

Strategic metrics

Strategic metrics measure the organization's success in achieving its business objectives within the strategic approach to CRM that has been adopted. They measure, for example, the extent to which the business strategies meet the required shareholder value targets and strengthen the organization's position in the marketplace.

Strategic metrics are used to measure:

1. shareholder value added/market value added
2. profitability and cash flow
3. returns on net assets, sales, CRM investments, etc.
4. growth rates
5. expense ratios
6. market positioning
7. innovation
8. brand equity
9. specific targets for other stakeholders.

Output and comparative metrics

Output and comparative metrics measure the output of the organization's CRM strategy, especially in relation to competitor activity and recognized best practice. These comparative measures are frequently more important than absolute measures. Sole reliance on internal metrics can be dangerous for they provide an isolated and insular view of the situation. For example, a market share of 20 per cent may be advantageous if the largest competitor has a market share of 10 per cent; however, it may be risky if the two largest competitors have market shares of 30 per cent each. Similarly, high levels of service quality and customer satisfaction are generally only beneficial if they are higher than those of the competition.

Output and comparative metrics are used to measure:

1. relative profitability
2. relative market share
3. relative customer satisfaction
4. relative customer retention
5. relative employee retention and satisfaction
6. relative product or service quality
7. cost reduction
8. improvements in employee value (in terms of employee retention and satisfaction)
9. increased competitive differentiation.

Special metrics

Special metrics are sometimes used in conjunction with the four main categories of metrics outlined above. For example, companies with intermediaries may need to implement customer performance measures at different channel levels. Businesses with a strong e-commerce component may need to address the different characteristics of an Internet channel by developing specific e-metrics. Interestingly, despite the availability of data from web channels, relatively few companies use these data to measure and monitor the effectiveness of their e-CRM activities.

Special e-metrics are used to measure:[11]

1. stickiness (the web site's ability to hold visitors' attention and to get them to become repeat users of the site)
2. focus (the scope and intensity of site visitor behaviour)
3. personalization index (how well the e-business uses personal customer data captured during site visits)
4. lifetime value (the contribution to company profits over the duration of the customer relationship. Measuring lifetime value is particularly important as less valuable customers using other channels can be moved to improved levels of profitability through using the web channel)
5. loyalty value (this includes visitor frequency, visit duration, number of pages viewed per visit, time elapsed between the user's first visit and most recent visit)
6. freshness factor (how often content on a web site is reviewed and renewed versus how frequently users visit the site).

Key performance indicators

As noted above, it is necessary to make a distinction among the metrics outlined above. Some of them will be relevant at an operational level and some important at a strategic level. The latter metrics are the key performance indicators that are critical to the success of the business and which need to be monitored regularly at Board level.

Tim Ambler, a leading researcher on performance metrics, made the following comment about high-level KPIs. 'Large companies have too many measures … Ten to 20 external metrics, plus two to five for the internal market (employees), are enough for the Board of a large company … Metrics and managing for value, taken together, give the Board the information it needs.'[12, 13]

Figure 6.5   Commonly used key marketplace metrics

Metric	% of firms using measure	% that reach the top board
Awareness	78.0	28.0
Market share (volume or value)	78.0	33.5
Relative price (market share value/volume)	70.0	34.5
Number of complaints (level of dissatisfaction)	69.0	30.0
Consumer satisfaction	68.0	36.0
Distribution/availability	66.0	11.5
Total number of customers	65.5	37.4
Perceived quality/esteem	64.0	32.0
Loyalty/retention	64.0	50.7
Relative perceived quality	62.5	52.8

Source: Based on Ambler[14]

The outcome of Ambler's research into the most commonly used marketplace KPIs is summarized in Figure 6.5.

This research is of particular interest because it not only measures companies' use of these KPIs but also the percentage of companies where these KPIs reach the Board. The research findings raise concern as key aspects of CRM, such as customer satisfaction and customer retention, only reach the Board in 36 per cent and 51 per cent of companies, respectively.

Decisions regarding which CRM metrics and high-level KPIs should be adopted for measuring the effectiveness of CRM processes and activities should not be taken casually. Using the wrong measures or measuring the wrong things is clearly self-defeating. Many companies will therefore need to establish a formalized system for monitoring CRM performance in order to ensure that the right metrics are used to manage activities at operational level and the right KPIs drive strategic decisions at Board level.

Multiple measures and linkage models

A relatively new development in measurement and metrics is the use of multiple metrics and measures and efforts to identify relationships between them. There has been a growing recognition of the importance of considering multiple measures as traditional financial accounting measures were prone to giving misleading results. Proposals for a more balanced presentation of both financial and operational measures have begun to proliferate.

A range of other models has been proposed for measuring different aspects of enterprise-wide performance. These include the Malcolm Baldridge award, the European Foundation for Quality Management (EFQM) Award and The Balanced Scorecard. These models represent systems of measures for monitoring and controlling enterprise performance; additionally they act as communication devices. In particular, they emphasize the importance of measuring employee satisfaction, customer satisfaction and business results in monitoring business performance.

However, there are drawbacks with some of these models. For example, although the Baldridge and EFQM quality models encouraged organizations to measure their performance in terms of employee satisfaction, customer satisfaction and financial results, the measures are not systematically linked together so as to identify the *relationships* between them.

The balanced scorecard

One of the most popular attempts to provide cross-functional measures is the balanced scorecard approach developed by Robert Kaplan and David Norton.[15] Their approach advocates the combination of four different perspectives of performance:

1. *the customer perspective*, which focuses on how the customer sees the organization
2. *the internal perspective*, which identifies what an organization must excel at
3. *the innovation and learning perspective*, which focuses on how an organization can improve and create value and
4. *the financial perspective*, which considers how an organization appears to its shareholders.

The 'balanced scorecard' has become an important part of many organizations' CRM activities as it contains a customer outcome dimension. However, the mixed focus of the scorecard approach can lead to inadequate levels of customer-responsiveness and lethargic change-management initiatives. The developers of this model also point out that companies need to create their own unique scorecards which reflect the nature of their own businesses and key priorities. In the same way, CRM performance measurement needs to be approached in an appropriately tailored way. Later in this chapter we show how the balanced scorecard criteria can be used to create a tailored success map for a specific organization.

Linkage models and the service-profit chain

Linkage models illustrate the relationships between employees, customers and organizational performance. The service-profit chain model shown in Figure 6.6, the best-known version of the linkage model, establishes the relationships between profitability, customer loyalty and employee satisfaction, loyalty and productivity. The researchers have described their model, as follows:

> The links in the chain, which should be regarded as propositions, are as follows: Profit and growth are stimulated primarily by customer loyalty. Loyalty is a direct result of customer satisfaction. Satisfaction is largely influenced by the value of services provided to customers. Value is created by satisfied, loyal and productive employees. Employee satisfaction, in turn, results primarily from high-quality support services and policies that enable employees to deliver results to customers.[16]

The service-profit chain model has shown how the linkages between these metrics are related and how KPIs can be leveraged to secure improved results. Advances in economic statistical modelling can now enable companies to identify the various relationships with greater accuracy and determine where improvements can most profitably be made. This work has been pioneered by the international consultancy CFI Group,[18] founded by University of Michigan econometrician Claes Fornell.

Figure 6.6   The service-profit chain

Internal service quality → Employee satisfaction → Employee retention / Employee productivity → External service value → Customer satisfaction → Customer loyalty → Revenue growth / Profitability

- Workplace design
- Job design
- Employee selection and development
- Employee rewards and recognition
- Tools for serving customers

- *Service concept:* results for customer

- Retention
- Repeat business
- Referral

- Service designed and delivered to meet targeted customers' needs

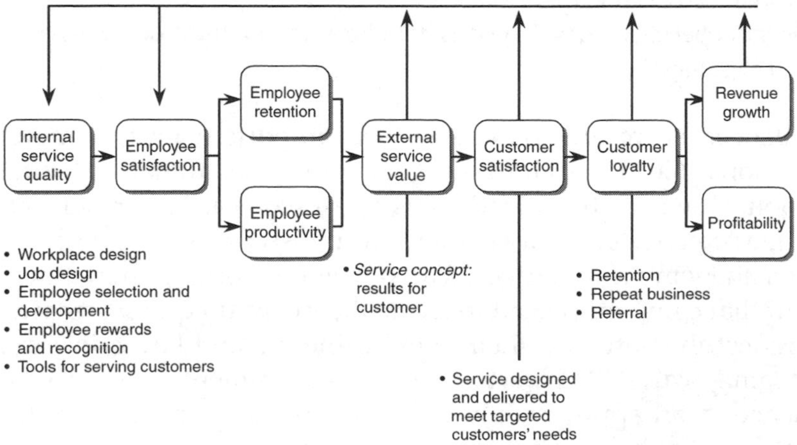

Source: Based on Heskett et al.[17]

However, although the concept of using a linkage model is potentially very attractive, there are still relatively few examples of companies who could be described as 'advanced' in terms of adoption of such an approach. This finding may not be surprising as very few of the companies involved in the original service-profit chain research had explored *all* the linkages across the model, let alone used causal techniques of measurement. The two case studies in this chapter show examples of leading companies who have pioneered this approach – one from the business-to-consumer sector and one from the business-to-business sector.

The first case study on Sears, Roebuck & Company, the leading US department store, is one of the most outstanding exemplars of the use of this approach. Sears used a modified version of the service profit chain to predict and manage performance and shareholder results.

Case 6.1   Sears, Roebuck & Company – Case study overview

Sears has held a position of eminence in the US retail sector for over 100 years. During this period, it has become a household name, with Americans associating it with quality and value. However, over the last decade or so, Sears has had to fight hard to overcome the difficulties of a mature market and adverse trading conditions.

This case study examines events over the last ten years. It focuses on how the senior management approached the situation facing the company in the 1990s, when Sears faced gigantic financial losses. Their remedy included adopting a new approach to managing business performance. They developed a model that links the performance of management, employees and customers directly to company profits and so provides some important insights into the value of adopting CRM.

This case study shows how effective CRM depends not only on managing relationships with customers, but also with other important stakeholders. It describes the roles played by three stakeholder groups: employees (including senior management and employees), customers and suppliers. The CEO and his top team recognized that to implement successful CRM, it was necessary to change the behaviour of its senior managers. The leadership skills of managers were responsible for the culture of Sears and this had an important impact on revenues.

Sears acknowledged that successful relationships with customers are dependent upon successful management of employees. Senior management identified key profit indicators which allowed them to manage their business more efficiently. Three key areas were monitored involving many metrics, including 25 employee measures, 20 customer measures and 19 financial performance indicators.

The full case study is at the end of this chapter (see p. 319)

The second case study that illustrates the use of this approach is Nortel Networks, the Canadian telecoms company. It illustrates how such CRM approaches can be extended to the business-to-business sector.

Case 6.2   Nortel Networks – Case study overview

Nortel Networks operates in the global telecommunications market. Although Nortel suffered badly from the dramatic downturn of the telecoms sector at the start of the 2000s, the company's use of performance assessment is highly developed. This case describes how Nortel developed a sophisticated CRM performance assessment process.

Understanding how value is created and delivered has played a critical role for the company as Nortel changed from being a manufacturer of equipment to a primarily service organization offering network solutions. This change in focus required very different skills and resources, putting pressure on the organization to be extremely flexible while continuing to deliver high quality customer service.

Initially Nortel focused on the key role of employees within the value creation process. It then directed attention to understanding how customer satisfaction and shareholder value are linked. Nortel understood that its relationships with customers would be threatened unless the company understood its value creation process. To achieve this, senior management identified that they needed to put in place a sophisticated measurement system. This allowed close monitoring of the value created by people and processes so that managers could allocate appropriately the investment resources of the business.

Nortel found that employee satisfaction accounts for 52 per cent of customer satisfaction, making this measure critical to successful CRM; so the company developed an appropriate employee recognition and reward system that was closely linked to business results and customer loyalty.

The full case study is at the end of this chapter (see p. 324)

Although the underlying ideas behind the service profit chain reflect the practices of many leading service organizations, very few companies have sought to develop detailed metrics to understand the linkages between employee value, customer value and shareholder value and how they contribute to corporate success.

The companies in these two case studies have had significant challenges confronting them, which has affected their recent performance. In common with many retailers, Sears' performance has been hit by the adverse economic environment of the early 2000s, intense competition and the aftermath of terrorists' threats and the second Gulf war. Nortel Networks was confronted by the worst downturn there has been in the history of the telecoms sector. However, they remain among the best examples of the development and use of advanced linkage models in their respective sectors.

Establishing a CRM performance monitoring system

As a company gains a good understanding of existing CRM standards, as well as CRM metrics and models in general use, it should also be considering its own requirements. This involves determining the key CRM standards, metrics and KPIs needed for its business and putting a CRM performance monitoring system in place.

CRM starts with the strategy development process. A key aspect in this process is agreement on the high-level goals and strategy of the business. This can then lead to the development of a strategy map or a success map that captures the performance model underlying the business strategy.

Developing strategy maps and success maps

Experts in performance measurement have identified a significant barrier to improved measurement: the need for senior management to agree on the business performance model for their firm *before* a comprehensive system of performance measurement can be developed.

A number of authors have pointed out the benefits of developing strategy, or success, maps. A success map provides a graphic outline of the highest-level goals the organization is striving to achieve and the current progress status. By juxtaposing the proposed end goal and the existing position, it is possible to identify the metrics necessary to ensure that the goal is achieved successfully. This process can be used to distil a wide range of measures down to those that matter most.

Kaplan and Norton have developed one of the best-known versions. Their *strategy map* involves identifying a chain of 'cause and effect' logic that connects the company's strategy with the drivers that lead to commercial success. It incorporates each of the four perspectives of the balanced scorecard.[19] Andy Neely and his colleagues have developed an extension of the strategy map, the *success map*, to emphasize the need for a broader perspective on stakeholders and a resolute emphasis on end goals.[20]

These mapping techniques can be extremely helpful in determining the most appropriate metrics and KPIs for monitoring CRM performance at any given time. Success maps may be complex or relatively simple.

Sears, Roebuck's performance model was built using data from over 800 stores.[21] It used 20 customer measures, 25 employee measures and 19 financial performance indicators by store (these included measures of productivity, revenues, margins, payroll costs, number of transactions, etc). Although the approach to measurement used by Sears, Roebuck involves many individual customer, employee and financial measures, these can be summarized in a relatively simple success map based on Sears' three key strategic objectives – to become:

- a compelling place to shop at
- a compelling place to work at
- a compelling place to invest in.

Sears attached to each of these strategic imperatives (aimed at the three main stakeholder groups: customers, employees and shareholders) a set of high level metrics which when agreed became the KPIs. A summary of the Sears' success map is shown in Figure 6.7.

A further example of a success map is shown in Figure 6.8. In this case, it is based on perspectives from the balanced scorecard and uses the financial, customer, internal and learning perspectives.

This approach provides the business logic for understanding the explicit levers that top executives need to manage and monitor for success.

Figure 6.7 Simplified success map for Sears, Roebuck

Strategic imperatives	Metrics
➤ Compelling place to shop	• meeting customer needs • creating customer satisfaction • retaining customers
➤ Compelling place to work	• achieving personal growth and development • empowered teams
➤ Compelling place to invest	• return on assets • sales growth • sales per square foot • operating income margin • inventory turnover

Development of metrics and KPIs for your business

From an examination of the success map and the lists of metrics above, the most relevant KPIs for your businesss can be identified and used to develop a monitoring system. Wherever feasible,

Figure 6.8 Success map based on the balanced scorecard

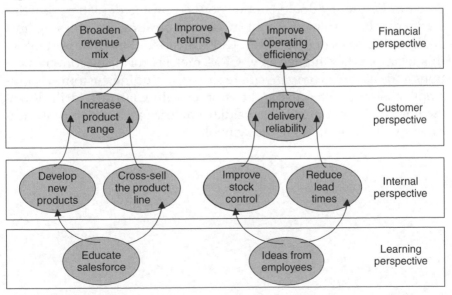

Source: Based on Neely[22]

metrics and KPIs should be consistent across the functions, business units and territories of the business. While existing measures may be available in many areas of the business, it is essential that these are complemented by new KPIs and standards that thoroughly assess the relationship with the enterprise's customers and which enable benchmarking of operational efficiency against competitors and other relevant organizations. Self-assessment, benchmarking and comparisons with external standards such as QCi and COPC are useful to gain this broader perspective.

One approach to metrics endorsed by a number of CRM senior executives is to get a broad picture of overall CRM activity but then to focus down in a much more detailed way on the most critical areas for the company. As one financial services executive said: 'I want to have a micro view of how we are doing compared to our competition across the full gamut of CRM; but I also need a summary dashboard of the really important KPIs that I need to focus on'. This is a pragmatic solution as it addresses the need to have an enterprise-wide view of CRM and to focus on the key performance areas to achieve targets in terms of profits and shareholder value. Once the relevant metrics have been identified, it is important that these are communicated clearly and in a visually engaging manner to management.

The example of a customer experience scorecard visualization given in Figure 6.9 demonstrates how a graphic depiction of CRM status can be a powerful tool in communicating progress against goals on the basis of those CRM KPIs considered most important. In this example, key higher-level CRM metrics for a telecommunications and cable TV company are reported, including customer acquisition, customer retention and customer value. Further 'drill-down' facilities into more detailed subsidiary metrics are available, as indicated by the magnifying glass symbol.

Figure 6.9 Example of a customer experience scorecard visualization

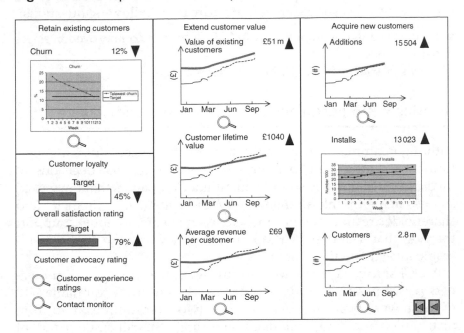

Source: Neely et al.[23]; based on Accenture and Telewest Communications

Other formats can also be used. One performance monitoring system used by companies such as GE involves developing a strategic 'route map', which gives the overall direction to be followed, together with a metrics 'dashboard' that reports the key performance measures, often using a 'stoplight' colour scheme of green, yellow and red to indicate whether each key metric is on target or otherwise.

Evaluating and communicating CRM return on investment

In addition to defining and applying the right standards, metrics and KPIs, an effective CRM performance monitoring system must be capable of measuring and communicating the return on investment (ROI). Because CRM places considerable emphasis on the use of IT in managing customer relationships, it is a potentially costly management option, in terms of both required IT expenditure and inherent adjustments to internal infrastructure and existing systems.

Given the number of reported CRM failures, the business case for investing in CRM should therefore address the following questions:

- Is an investment in improving CRM likely to lead to improved business performance?
- How can investments in CRM be measured?

Relating CRM performance to business performance

Although common sense would suggest that successful CRM performance should lead to improved business results, decisions to invest in CRM must be soundly justified. Companies that have used success maps to link a range of key CRM metrics to financial and shareholder results, such as those used by Sears, Roebuck, support the view that well-based CRM initiatives are worth the often considerable investment they entail.

A QCi study showed CMAT results correlate strongly with business performance. The study examined data from 21 companies (12 of these were from financial services, two from utilities, two from distribution and three from manufacturing). A panel of independent experts assessed the business performance of each organization against a broad range of measures such as sales growth, profitability and asset growth. The assessors did not know how well each organization had performed in its CMAT assessment.

The ranking of the organization's business performance was then compared to its ranking in terms of CMAT score. Figure 6.10 shows the results of the study in terms of CRM performance (measured by the CMAT score) and business performance.[24]

Figure 6.10 Comparison of CRM performance to business performance

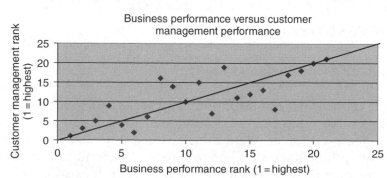

Source: © QCi Assessment Ltd, used with permission

This research supports the view that CRM performance is related to overall business performance and concludes that the most important factors are:

- people and leadership
- measurement and deployment processes to action needed results, and
- implementing appropriate CRM practices such as targeting high lifetime value customers.

These findings are encouraging and reinforce what experienced practitioners and knowledgeable consultants already know: attention to the 'people' element, implementation of customer-oriented practices and proper measurement systems constitute the critical success factors (CSFs) for CRM. However, given the incidence of CRM problems, further research is needed in this area.

Measuring CRM return on investment

A further issue of concern is measuring the return on CRM initiatives. A Cranfield Research Report[25] examined how companies measure the payback on their investment in CRM projects and found that the following four criteria are typically used when evaluating the success of investments in CRM activities. These criteria carry advantages and disadvantages.

1. *Improvements in customer service, satisfaction and retention*
   These metrics are of greatest value when specifically linked to approaches that show their impact on profit and shareholder value. We have noted earlier that customer retention of your best customers has a critical impact on profitability.
2. *Return on investment (ROI) on the CRM systems adopted*
   Measuring ROI on CRM systems is beneficial where there are specific investments in certain CRM applications, such as sales force automation (SFA) or campaign management systems which can be directly linked to customer metrics, or where there are identifiable efficiencies or cost reductions. However, it is important to ensure customer satisfaction is not adversely affected as a result of introducing such systems.
3. *Changes in overall company performance*
   Changes in overall company performance as a result of investment in CRM may be difficult to evaluate as it can often be hard to tell what would have happened without the CRM investment. Performance

improvements, for example, could be the result of many factors such as decreased promotional activities by competitors.

4. *Increases in customer and segment profitability*

   Measuring increases in the profitability of customers and customer segments and understanding how this ultimately impacts on shareholder value is an area of growing interest. It involves a consideration of both current and future profit impact potential. Hence, estimates of potential customer lifetime value need to be calculated alongside existing customer lifetime value.

ROI measurement is an important element of CRM. As stressed throughout this chapter, CRM performance assessment should be viewed in the context of a strategic approach to CRM. The typical criteria for measuring CRM ROI listed above clearly embrace this company-wide view of CRM.

Summary

The performance measurement systems adopted by organizations in the past have tended to be functionally driven. Thus, financial measures were mainly the concern of the Board and the finance department, marketing measures the domain of the marketing department and people measures the responsibility of the HR department. Such a functional separation of performance measures is inappropriate for CRM, which involves a cross-functional and holistic management approach.

The performance assessment process in the Strategic Framework for CRM involves an evaluation of the success of CRM activities in order that gaps in performance can be identified and improvements made. It is this process which ensures that the organization's strategic aims in terms of customer relationship management are being delivered to an appropriate and acceptable standard. The key actions involve understanding the drivers of shareholder value, identifying the appropriate metrics and standards against which the various CRM activities can be measured, establishing an effective monitoring system to apply these measures on an ongoing basis and communicating and acting on resultant learning.

A number of approaches are open to organizations seeking to establish CRM metrics and KPIs for measuring, monitoring and benchmarking their CRM performance. They include use of external benchmarks such as the QCi and COPC standards and measuring and monitoring performance using tools such as the balanced score-card and linkage models. However, in order to improve the performance of its CRM activities, a company must develop its own composite set of measures based on its own success maps. Such efforts to develop individually tailored and relevant performance assessment processes are critical, given the high incidence of reported CRM failure and the impressive returns for those who achieve CRM success.

Developing a CRM strategy does not conclude with the performance assessment process – the last of the five processes in the CRM strategy framework. In the final chapter that follows we address *organizing for CRM implementation*. Here we consider the readiness of the organization to engage in CRM activities and the issues of change management, project management and employee engagement that play such a crucial role in CRM success.

Checklist for CRM leaders

CRM leaders need to review the following issues about the *Performance Assessment Process*.

Shareholder results

1. Our top management recognize the importance of leadership in creating employee, customer and shareholder value
2. The key drivers of shareholder results – employee value, customer value, shareholder value and cost reduction – are fully understood
3. We place sufficient emphasis in our organization on employee value
4. We rank ourselves highly in terms of recruiting, selecting, developing and empowering our employees
5. We place sufficient emphasis in our organization on customer value
6. We rank ourselves highly in terms of delivering superior customer value opportunities in every attractive customer segment
7. We place sufficient emphasis in our organization on shareholder value
8. We rank ourselves highly in terms of creating shareholder value compared with our major competitors
9. We take full advantage of all opportunities for cost reduction. Cost reduction strategies do not negatively impact customer satisfaction
10. We have developed, or are developing, a balanced scorecard or linkage model in our organization that addresses the relationship between employee satisfaction, customer satisfaction and business results.

Standards, metrics and key performance indicators

1. We have developed our own standards across all the areas of CRM that are important to us
2. We have adopted standards developed by others (e.g. CMAT or COPC standards) and used these to benchmark our performance against relevant external comparators
3. We have identified and put in place appropriate customer metrics
4. We have identified and put in place appropriate people and process metrics
5. We have identified and put in place appropriate strategic metrics
6. We have identified and put in place appropriate output and comparative metrics
7. A strategy map (or success map) has been developed that identifies the chain of 'cause and effect' logic that connects our company's strategy with the drivers that lead to commercial success
8. Our organization has identified the most important KPIs and these are reported to senior management on a regular basis
9. Frameworks such as the balanced scorecard are utilized to ensure there is a focus on all relevant areas of performance, not just financial ones
10. A CRM performance monitoring process is in place and attention has been given to making sure KPIs are communicated in a visually engaging manner to management and other relevant employees.

Each issue should be considered in terms of:

Rating for our organization   (5 = applies fully; 0 = does not apply at all)
Importance to our organization (5 = very important; 0 = no importance)

Case 6.1   Sears, Roebuck and Company

The company

Sears, Roebuck and Company has been a leading US retailer for over 100 years. A household name, Americans associate it with value and quality. When Sears was founded in 1886, there were only 38 states in the USA and most of its product deliveries were horse drawn. In the ensuing 12 decades, the company laid down a multitude of highly refined business processes and well-automated information systems. However, during the last twenty years Sears has had to fight hard to overcome the difficulties inherent in a mature market, to combat adverse trading conditions and to compete with Wal-Mart, a much larger competitor. Sears realized that its familiar ways of doing business were no longer enough to keep ahead of competitors.

The challenge

In 1992, Sears, Roebuck and Company reported massive losses of $3.9 billion on sales of $52.3 billion. This was the worst trading year in the company's history. This resulted from various trends, most of them directly related to the company's lack of focus. Over the 1980s Sears had diversified into other markets such as insurance, financial services, brokerage and real estate. At the same time other retailers such as Wal-Mart were focusing on the retail consumer and were taking market share away from Sears. Sears needed to refocus on its core business and to develop a performance model that would help drive a return to profitability.

The solution

A new CEO, Arthur Martinez, was appointed in 1992 to head the merchandise group and he undertook a streamlining of the business. He closed 113 stores and terminated the 101-year-old Sears catalogue, which was a household institution within the USA. He also set about changing the service strategy, focusing on women, who were the most important buying decision makers.

Martinez set up four task forces (customers, employees, financial performance and innovation) to define world class status in each specific area, identify obstacles and define metrics for measuring progress. The task forces spent months listening to customers and employees, observing best practice in other organizations and establishing measures against objectives. Gradually it became apparent that what was needed was a model to show *direct causation* from employee attitudes, through customer satisfaction to profits. The company needed to know how management action, such as investment in sales force training, would directly translate into improved customer satisfaction, retention and higher revenues. What was needed was an operationalization of what they termed *the employee-customer-profit chain*. The revised model of this is shown in the figure below.

Figure I   The revised employee-customer-profit chain at Sears

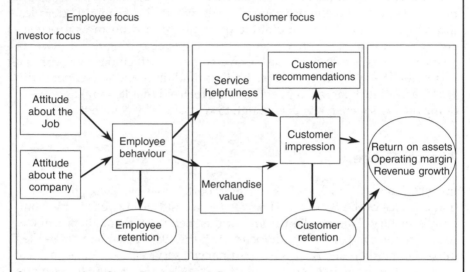

Source: based on Sears, Roebuck and Company.

Sears defined a set of measures based on its objectives. These were broken down into three objectives which focused on making Sears 'a compelling place to *work* at, to *shop* at and to *invest* in'. This represented a focus on three value domains: employees, customers and shareholders. Relationships between changes in key metrics were identified using causal pathway modelling. The econometric modelling of the relationships was undertaken by CFI Group.

Sears' enterprise performance model was built using data from over 800 stores. It used 20 customer measures, 25 employee measures and 19 financial performance indicators by store (these included measures of productivity, revenues, margins, payroll costs, number of transactions).

The results

The results of this work were impressive. Direct causal links were identified between employee measures, customer measures and revenues so total profit indicators for the company could be established. Employee attitude towards the job and company were found to be critical to employee loyalty and behaviour towards customers, while customer impression directly affected customer retention and the likelihood of recommendations. After further refinement, the model was used as a predictor of revenue growth: a 5 unit increase in employee attitude drives a 1.3 unit increase in customer impression, a 0.5 increase in revenue growth and a quantifiable increase in store profitability.

To implement the service-profit chain model successfully it was necessary for Sears to change the behaviour of its senior managers and encourage them to take responsibility for the company's culture and understand how this impacted on revenues. In addition, employee rewards needed to be aligned to the model for financial and non-financial measures.

Later, a further change was made by streamlining its CRM systems. Previously there were 18 separate legacy databases; there is now a single, integrated data warehouse of over seven terabytes, as shown in Figure 2.

Figure 2 The IT transformation at Sears

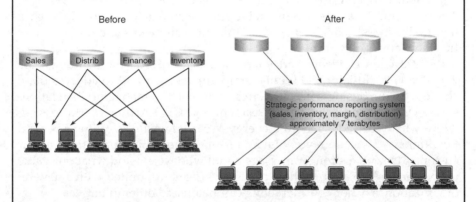

Source: R Swift, NCR Teradata

As a result, in 1993 the company reported a net income of $752 million – a dramatic reversal of fortunes for a mature company such as Sears. In the period following the implementation of the enterprise performance model, employee satisfaction at Sears rose by 4 per cent and customer satisfaction by almost 4 per cent. More than $200 million additional revenues were achieved through this value creation process.

Figure 3 shows the relative performance improvement on selected measures including profitability, customer satisfaction and associate (their term for employees) attitudes between 1992 and 1998.

Confidence in the data was such that Sears computed 30 per cent to 70 per cent of its executive compensation from these measures. Sears delivered earnings of US$1.3 billion in 1997. In terms of shareholder value, the

Figure 3   Sears, Roebuck – selected performance measures, 1992–1998

Source: Sears, Roebuck and Company.

total return to investors between September 1992 and April 1997 was 298 per cent. This was a remarkable improvement for a firm in such a mature business. Sears is now using this measurement system to improve future revenues and profits.

By 1998 a new challenge had emerged, the lack of sales momentum. Sears was in a very difficult and highly competitive sector and to address these challenges, the business needed a fresh approach to managing its relationships with customers. In 1999, President and CEO Arthur Martinez said, 'Now, what we need is renewed energy. We need what I'm calling a Second Revolution – a second revolution in our marketing communications to our customer to send a stronger message about who we are and what our value proposition is'. To address these challenges Sears responded with a new reorganization, a major new marketing campaign and other initiatives.

Martinez was also a driving force behind e-commerce activities at Sears. These began in 1996 with the launch of Sears.com and by 1999, it was rated by Nielsen as the fourth fastest growing shopping site. However, the site was not user friendly and in 2000 it was relaunched with enhanced capabilities. These included facilities that improved searches, smoothed navigation and simplified shopping. The results were very encouraging with Sears.com named the number one e-retailer in the world.

Another important development was the creation and development of GlobalNetXchange. This was launched in 2000 and was the first B2B marketplace for retail. Its success is due to uniting technology partners with retailers and in so doing, making the supply chain more efficient. Initially, the company has focused on the relationships of Sears and other retail giants, with their suppliers, partners and distributors. The exchange allows these companies to have a common place to buy, sell, trade or auction goods and services online. The result has been that companies have been able to buy more effectively and to manage their supply chain better. These advantages are passed on to the customer in creating a better value proposition. Sears knows that this is critical to driving sales and profits in the company.

In 2001 Alan Lacy, a new chief executive, was appointed. His radical new initiatives included the acquisition of Lands End, a $1.6 billion retailer and the largest catalogue and Internet specialty clothier in the USA, in 2002 and putting the profitable but troubled credit card division up for sale in 2003. The acquisition of Lands End was met favourably by financial analysts. However, analysts agree that the retail giant must continue focusing on a growth strategy to overcome the difficulties of this troubled sector. Central to their CRM strategy in the future will be performance measuring and management of critical relationships with employees, customers and shareholders.

Case Study 6.2   Nortel Networks

The company

Nortel Networks is a Canadian corporation operating in the global telecommunications market. The company had revenues in 2002 of can $10.6 billion and a staff of 35 000. In the 1990s the company saw rapid growth and this was achieved in market conditions of intense competition and rapid change. It was during this period that Nortel recognized that shifts in the market required it to move from being primarily a manufacturer of equipment to being mainly a service organization.

The challenge

Nortel recognized that it needed to understand how value was created and delivered within the business so that it could focus on the most critical areas. To achieve this, the company needed to develop its own model of value creation. Nortel's approach was influenced by work it had done on benchmarking leading organizations such as Xerox and Disney and from its work on quality where it was the winner of a number of quality awards. It had worked with leading external experts to develop aspects of its sophisticated model including Brad Gale, the CFI Group, Ray Kordupleski, and others. This work led to a recognition that value was created through a linked system of mutual benefit to shareholders, customers and employees. In order to identify the value creation process Nortel recognized that it needed a sophisticated measurement system.

The solution

The *Nortel business value cycle*, shown in Figure 1, was developed to link resources, internal and external processes and shareholders. Although the visual depiction of this model is different to the service-profit chain, it shows many similarities. However, it extends the model to incorporate the *processes* that create value. It also emphasizes the important role of leadership.

Logistically, establishing such a measurement system and then extending it across the global organization presented a major challenge. However, a significant outcome, made from the effort of establishing it globally, has been the sharing of knowledge across different parts of the business. For example, comparing the satisfaction ratings of a customer in one country with scores in another country has helped integrate management processes across the global operation. Also, initiatives to improve value creation which are tested in one country can, if successful, be adopted in other geographic areas.

Figure I   The Nortel business value cycle

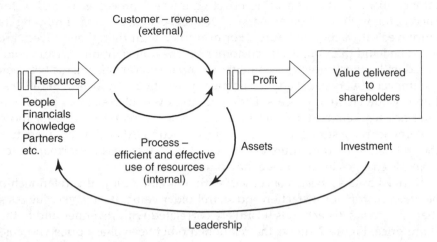

Source: Nortel Networks

The results

Nortel's use of a linkage model led to the company identifying many statistically valid relationships across its version of the service-profit chain. For example, it identified there are three key drivers of employee satisfaction: leadership, perceived customer focus of the business and the extent that an employee sees obstacles hindering job performance. Leadership accounts for 31 per cent of employee satisfaction and 18 per cent of customer satisfaction; so management recognized that developing the appropriate leadership style and supporting processes was vital. Leadership behaviour that every manager is required to demonstrate is clearly identified and regular appraisals evaluate performance. The organization emphasizes individual empowerment aligned to a carefully formulated and well-communicated business plan.

The value cycle model strongly emphasizes the key value of employees to the corporation. Critical to employee motivation are appropriate rewards that are linked to market factors. Nortel redesigned its recognition and rewards system, linking it closely to business results, customer loyalty and employee satisfaction. Seniority was dropped as a reward criterion. Employees were grouped into one of two teams. The first was a strategic development team that is rewarded on product 'time to market' and market success. The second was a customer-facing team that is rewarded by market share and 'share of customer wallet'. Rewards were therefore closely aligned to the value cycle model, so individual employees could understand their specific contribution to creating value for the business.

Nortel found that employee satisfaction accounts for 52 per cent of customer satisfaction. So, ensuring effective internal processes is critical for succeeding within customer markets. Nortel began a process of refining its employee satisfaction measures. For example, 'high flying' employees are identified and their impact on customer satisfaction is monitored and compared with other employee segments. Comparisons are also made between the impact of very satisfied, versus merely satisfied employees, in the customer value creation process. Different employee jobs, such as customer-interface workers and account managers, are compared to identify those that impact most strongly on customer satisfaction. Also, the data were further refined to predict future events, apart from business performance, for example changes in customer behaviour.

Nortel has also been concerned with understanding the relationship between customer satisfaction and shareholder value. Its analysis suggests that customer satisfaction is positively correlated with revenues and to the share price. Figure 2 shows the relationship between share price and customer satisfaction between 1993 and 1996. Share price continued to increase in 1997. An apparent later dip in share price at the beginning of 1998 was due to a board decision to split the shares and re-issue them on a 2 to 1 basis.

There have been many advantages gained for Nortel Networks from understanding and managing the linkages between employees, customers and shareholders through the application of a formal linkage model. Although the work we have seen does not measure causality, the correlations appear highly significant.

Figure 2   Nortel Networks – selected performance measures, 1993–1996

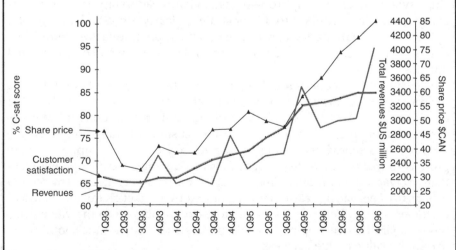

Source: Nortel Networks

Following a record year 2000 results in which adjusted net earnings increased by 61 per cent and earnings per share by 42 per cent, Nortel was hit by the dramatic downturn of the telco sector in the year 2001 when it started to sustain losses. This market was fast changing and players need to be agile to compete. For example, new products are frequently introduced into the market, often by smaller, innovative companies; these pose a considerable threat to the larger operators who struggle to change their technology.

Nortel responded by listening to their customers and developing new technology, but this resulted in massive investment that was not matched by customer spending. Many of Nortel's major customers, the telephone companies, were cutting back on their spending. Some weaker phone companies went out of business. Nortel was forced to lay off one half of its worldwide staff and lower its cost structure in efforts to return to profitability.

Sales fell from $17.5 billion in 2001 to $10.6 billion in 2002 and Nortel sought new leadership. John Roth, the CEO who has led the company through massive change, announced his retirement and Frank Dunn, the company's CFO and a 25-year veteran of Nortel, was appointed CEO. By 2003 Frank Dunn had completed much of the planned restructuring and he reported Nortel had stabilized their business model and ended the year with a very strong cash balance. The new CEO faces considerable business and CRM challenges that include winning new customers and keeping the loyalty of old ones in turbulent market conditions. The company's differentiation continues to be technology leadership and customer engagement. Its focus is on the delivery of multimedia services and network infrastructure that will allow its customers to grow their business and reduce overall costs.

Chapter 7

Organizing for CRM implementation

Key elements in organizing for CRM implementation

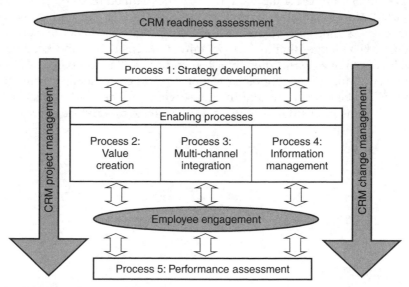

Source: Based on Payne and Frow[1]

In the previous chapters we examined in some detail the five key processes that comprise the Strategic Framework for CRM. In this final chapter we examine the key issues involved in organizing for implementation of a CRM programme. As the discussions and case studies throughout this book illustrate, the effective management of customer relationships involves many different and interlinked aspects. Understanding these factors and their implications is certainly critical to the success of any CRM initiative. However, simply thinking through the processes of CRM is not enough to ensure it is developed and implemented appropriately. Firms have to *organize* to deliver results from their CRM programmes.

The figure above sets the five key CRM processes addressed in the preceding chapters in the context of organizing for CRM implementation. Here they are positioned relative to four critical elements of a successful CRM programme: CRM readiness assessment; CRM change management; CRM project management; and employee engagement. This figure is an organizing model that represents the broad stages of progression. However, the model is recursive rather than linear in that its many activities need to be managed concurrently and some elements will need to be revisited as a consequence of later activities. Organizing for CRM involves systematically and interactively addressing each of these four elements as they relate to the five key CRM processes.[1]

Before a CRM strategy is developed, it is important to assess whether the organization is really ready and willing to implement customer-focused strategies and CRM initiatives. CRM is not an appropriate strategy for a company to adopt if it does not have the leadership of the enterprise engaged in supporting CRM and a board-level sponsor committed to its success. Thus, the cultural and leadership implications of CRM implementation must be fully understood if it is to have any chance of contributing to business improvement.

At the beginning of the book the essence of CRM was captured in the statement: 'CRM is information-enabled relationship marketing'. This concise description can be seen to hold much greater meaning now that we have examined many of the complexities and requirements of effective customer relationship management. CRM is indeed about leveraging relationships for mutual benefit through the skilful utilization of customer knowledge. But it is also about building stronger and more productive relationships with other stakeholders, particularly employees. This is evident in the fact that the main source of competitive advantage today is customer intimacy (discussed in Chapter 2) achieved through excellent customer service. Here employees have a critical role to play in its delivery.

We now consider how the elements of CRM readiness assessment, CRM change management, CRM project management and employee engagement come together to support the organization and implementation of a CRM strategy. We start by considering the CRM readiness assessment which helps the CRM sponsors and leaders assess the overall position in terms of readiness to progress with CRM initiatives and to identify how well developed their organization is relative to other companies.

CRM readiness assessment

In undertaking an assessment of CRM readiness we propose two tasks should be undertaken. First, an assessment should be made of overall CRM maturity relative to other companies that have embarked on the CRM journey and barriers to CRM success should be identified. This will provide a more general perspective to the company's current situation and help them benchmark where they are relative to other organizations. This is important as it provides the opportunity to assess relative competitive advantage. Second, a CRM readiness audit will help determine both how advanced your company is in its overall readiness to adopt or further develop CRM, and in which of the five processes in the CRM strategy framework your organization needs to place greatest emphasis. This audit will help the enterprise identify the key areas of importance in terms of CRM performance. Thus, a decision to adopt or enhance an enterprise's CRM activities should be based on understanding:

- its current stage of development and potential barriers to success
- its overall readiness to adopt CRM and
- the CRM activities that need to be addressed.

An assessment of these three elements through a CRM maturity assessment and a CRM readiness audit will assist the organization in deciding how to organize its CRM activities.

CRM maturity assessment

The emphasis an organization places on using data to help design and implement CRM strategies is reflected in the organization's stage of CRM development. In Chapter 2 we discussed how each organization should adopt a level of sophistication in CRM strategy appropriate to their competitive environment and their needs now and in the future. We identified four broad strategic options facing organizations – product-based selling, customer-based marketing, managed service and support and 'individualized' CRM; the latter requiring collection and analysis of extensive information about customers and the desire and ability to give customers highly individualized service. These options, considered as part of the strategy development process, now need to be considered in a much broader context of overall CRM implementation requirements. In particular, the degree of CRM development in other organizations provides a useful context for an enterprise to consider its own CRM initiatives.

Our research has shown that there are identifiable stages of maturity in CRM development. Each stage represents a level of CRM maturity characterized by the extent to which customer information is used to enhance the customer experience and customer-generated cash flows. However, each stage encompasses issues beyond choice of strategic options. More often than not CRM development requires wide-ranging adjustments within the firm, especially where marketing needs to shift from a product or transactional focus to a customer relationship focus. The kinds of organizational changes needed to embrace CRM can range from a revolution in mindset to a realignment of systems and processes. Special change management, project management and customer engagement activities are usually necessary to minimize disruption and risk and maximize performance. Strategies that do not take these dimensions on board are unlikely to succeed with their implementation of CRM.

To identify experiences and use of CRM the author and his colleague Lynette Ryals of Cranfield University undertook a study to investigate the development of CRM in organizations.[2] As our research showed that CRM is typically more advanced in the retail financial services sector than in other industry sectors, we focused on this sector in order to examine the stages of CRM development. Five levels of maturity in the development of CRM were identified:

1. Pre-CRM planning
2. Building a data repository
3. Moderately developed CRM
4. Well developed CRM
5. Highly advanced CRM.

Stage 1: Pre-CRM planning
The first stage is planning for the introduction CRM. This is the point at which organizations recognize the importance of CRM, however,

they have not yet progressed to a stage where the CRM project has been fully scoped. Organizations at this stage should particularly consider the implications for their organization of the four broad strategic options discussed earlier: product-based selling, customer-based marketing, managed service and support and 'individualized' CRM. Companies planning to introduce CRM especially need to undertake a CRM readiness audit – the structure of which is outlined shortly.

Stage 2: Building a data repository

The second stage of CRM is concerned with building an appropriate data repository – often in the form of a data warehouse. As covered earlier in Chapter 5, construction of the main data repository includes collecting and reviewing existing data and cleaning and de-duplicating customer records.

If the data repository is to be used predominantly for analytical CRM a data warehouse needs to be built to support the required analytical tasks. If the data repository is to be used primarily to support operational CRM then an operational data store (ODS) is required. This was also discussed in Chapter 5. Where companies need to address analytical and operational CRM, it is likely both forms of data warehouse may be required. Plans for the organization's data infrastructure are based on the data warehouse. Pilot data warehouses, an ODS or smaller data marts may be built as a preliminary step, prior to full implementation.

The key task associated with building a data warehouse is customer identification and data capture. Because of the data quality issues that emerge as companies begin to collect and centralize their customer data, organizations in the early stages of CRM development find they have to focus heavily on identifying *who* their customers are. We have found multiple records for a single customer and missing or out-of-date addresses are common problems. Managers find gaps, ambiguities and omissions in data they previously had assumed were complete and accurate. Often, enormous amounts of effort have to be expended in compiling accurate customer information. This typically involves collecting information from many separate databases and legacy systems.

Data integrity needs to be checked carefully. In one bank, a manager described how his organization was proud of the fact it had date of birth information for most of its customers. However, when the bank reviewed this information it found out that 10 per cent of the customer base appeared to have been born on 11th November 1911, or 11/11/11.

It was later discovered that some of the bank's data entry operators were too embarrassed to ask certain customers their date of birth and, pressured to fill the required data field, they found they could enter any number and the system would accept it. A series of '1's was the most popular choice. Such data integrity problems may require considerable efforts to rectify.

Stage 3: Moderately developed CRM

Organizations which are moderately developed in CRM are those which have typically progressed to a full data warehouse, although it may still be limited to a single business unit rather than being enterprise-wide. They begin to use tools such as sales force automation, call centres and computer telephony integration and campaign management in a more sophisticated manner but still on a 'stand alone' basis. At this stage, the CRM focus shifts towards data mining and identifying the value that can be extracted from the organization's existing customer information.

Having gathered and cleaned their data, these organizations turn their attention to the task of customer profitability analysis and segmentation and recognize the need to identify their most profitable customers, to profile them and to find more customers like them. However, few companies at this stage are able to generate fully satisfactory customer profitability analyses. In some cases initial customer profitability analyses were seen to challenge received wisdom. For example, one bank found that the most profitable 10 per cent and the least profitable 10 per cent of its customers had purchased almost identical numbers of the bank's products. Clearly, for this bank, their existing strategy of 'sell more products, make more money', was not always correct.

Some organizations at this stage change their approach to segmentation as a result of the development of their data warehouse. Previously, segmentation was viewed by them as a way to divide up the total customer base into more or less homogeneous groups. However, it was then difficult to determine which individual customers went into which segment. After the data warehouse became operational, managers were better able to identify their most profitable customers. They could then profile these individuals and focus efforts on acquiring more customers like them. In such cases, the segmentation approach shifted from one using a set of general customer characteristics to one incorporating the level of customer profitability or customer value.

Stage 4: Well developed CRM

'Well developed' suggests an organization that is moving towards an enterprise-wide data warehouse, widening its user base and increasing the number of users and further developing front-office tools such as sales force automation and contact centres. Such organizations will be more advanced in e-commerce applications. At this point, external proprietary data sources, such as Mosaic and GIS, are routinely fed into the data warehouse to enhance the company's own information.

A key task at this stage is customer prioritization. Gaining a deeper understanding of profitable customers becomes an important part of CRM activities. Use of increasingly sophisticated segmentation and profiling to do this becomes common. Customer prioritization also leads to strategies for reducing the cost of serving less profitable customers, such as encouraging customers to switch from using a counter service to using the telephone or Internet. Typically, the segmentation exercise also identifies undesirable customer groups.

Organizations in this group utilize much more effective campaign management by fully exploiting their data warehouses. One insurance company at this stage of development contrasted their current highly targeted approach with their previous practice of mailing one-twelfth of their database each month, irrespective of whether the products they were prioritizing were relevant to the customers they were mailing.

Stage 5: Highly advanced CRM

Organizations that have reached the highly advanced or 'best in class' status are fully integrated, offering extensive data warehouse access within the company across departmental functions. They may use advanced techniques such as neural networks and genetic algorithms to generate more refined data and continually learn from their customer information. They are highly advanced in terms of their market segmentation strategies and understanding of the required level of segment granularity. They routinely use predictive modelling. Because these organizations typically have a wide user base using their data warehouse, they also employ data visualization tools to present data in an easier-to-use chart format. Relatively few organizations have reached this level of CRM sophistication. American Express, USAA – the US insurance company, and MBNA America – the credit card company, are examples of companies that have reached this stage.

A task associated with such advanced usage of CRM is more active customer management in which organizations use tools such as campaign management to engage in an ongoing dialogue with a customer and to reap the maximum profit potential throughout the customer's lifetime. Such organizations with more developed CRM integrate a clearer understanding of the value of the customer with active customer management.

Reviewing your stage of CRM maturity

Organizations should use these guidelines on CRM maturity to review their own stage of development. Generally managers characterize their stage of development fairly accurately. However, we have found IT managers tend to rank their own organizations at a higher CRM stage than do their marketing colleagues. This is possibly because the IT managers have not understood how data are used by the marketing department and what their data requirements are.

Experienced CRM managers and consultants should already know which stage of CRM development a company is at. However, we have found several large corporations and many mid-sized companies with a surprising lack of knowledge as to how far they had progressed with their CRM, when compared with their competitors.

Thus a view should then be taken on the stage of development of competitors. This will require some research. Competitors' customers, industry reports, multi-client research studies and vendors who have provided solutions to a range of companies in that sector are good sources of this information. Submissions for industry awards and web sites of CRM vendors are often good sources of competitive information. If particular information on competitors is considered essential but difficult to find, some of the leading US strategy consulting firms have proved to be very successful in finding out such information – through very detailed industry interviews and other research methods.

Organizations in earlier stages of CRM development can also benefit greatly by benchmarking CRM activities of leading non-competitors who are at an advanced stage of CRM. We have led a number of benchmarking programmes in 'CRM best practice' and found companies in non-competing industries can be extremely generous in sharing their knowledge. CRM best practice workshops of around three days' duration typically involve a review of CRM maturity, a CRM readiness audit, visits to leading exemplars of relevant CRM practices and action planning. Such workshops are usually directed at senior management including the operations board and senior CRM managers. Our experience is that a short workshop can be very powerful in understanding the business benefits associated with CRM and in providing the business leaders with strong motivation to provide the leadership necessary to ensure successful implementation of CRM activities.

Identifying barriers to CRM success

When reviewing CRM readiness it is useful for companies to consider the barriers typically faced by other organizations in developing their CRM programmes. Our research has identified a number of common barriers to CRM success. Interestingly, the problems of existing legacy systems, which executives might expect to be a main source of difficulties and delays, appear to be less common than problems associated with internal attitudes and organizational structure.

Lack of skills

Lack of skills in building and using the new IT-based CRM system are a major barrier to the implementation of CRM. One CRM manager referred to a 'chronic technological skill shortage'. The organization for which he works was unable to recruit enough technically skilled people for a large-scale CRM implementation project. Other executives also highlighted the need for skills in operating the new system and several said that they relied on vendor training to meet this need, which was not always available quickly and was not of a uniform standard. Analytical skills in asking the right questions of the CRM system, was identified as being of special importance in making the most of the CRM investment.

Inadequate investment

Gaining adequate funding for CRM requirements is an important issue for organizations, particularly as many of the projects expanded dramatically in cost and sometimes in scope. Some organizations had overcome the problem of funding by adopting what was referred to as a 'quick wins' approach. By structuring their CRM implementation projects to deliver quick wins and visible benefits at incremental stages, such as improvements in customer service or higher response rates to campaigns, they were able to demonstrate immediate progress and returns. This helped to improve internal buy-in and motivate other parts of the business to extend the CRM systems within their own areas.

Poor data quality and quantity

Organizations at different stages of CRM development experience different issues with respect to data quality and data quantity. For companies at an early stage of CRM development data quality is a key issue. The extent of data quality problems and the amount of work necessary to remedy them surprised many managers. More advanced companies tend to have undertaken data cleansing and de-duplicating; for these organizations data quantity is a greater problem than data quality.

Failure to understand the business benefits

Low initial awareness of the benefits of a marketing database among senior management is also a barrier for companies less advanced in CRM implementation. This problem tends to be overcome as the data warehouse goes live and begins to deliver results. CRM managers point out that the data warehouse is perceived as a high cost and senior management often failed to understand the potential financial benefits in the earlier stages of the CRM project.

Functional boundaries

Managers at the functional or business unit level may be reluctant or unwilling to cooperate at the early stages of the CRM project. It may require considerable organizational effort to make functional and business unit managers aware of the benefits of greater company-wide operations and cross-functional working. This is a change management issue that we examine later in this chapter.

Lack of leadership and top management involvement

A lack of top management involvement and leadership of CRM activities is a further barrier to CRM success. Enlightened CEOs should view themselves as 'chief customer officer' also. Their role is to ensure a high level executive, ideally at Board level, acts as a sponsor and champion for the company's CRM activities and that the importance of transforming the company's relationships with customers through CRM is understood and shared by the Board and senior management. Leadership represents one of the key issues in change management and CRM sponsorship is discussed in more detail later in this chapter.

Inadequate measurement systems

CRM managers often point out how poor or inappropriate measurement and reward systems can hinder the initiation and fulfilment of CRM projects. Measures used to determine the success of CRM performance are often considered inadequate. Sometimes, the problem is that the organization is not clear about its goals or does not communicate its goals to its people. Issues of measurement were discussed in Chapter 6.

There are, of course, other issues that will impede successful CRM implementation, some of which are addressed later in this chapter. Any company undertaking CRM needs to understand these common barriers to CRM success and any more specific potential problem areas relevant to their particular business and consider the implications for their organization in advance of the introduction of customer management initiatives.

CRM readiness audit

Once the stage of CRM development and potential barriers to CRM have been considered, the company should then proceed with a more detailed assessment of its CRM readiness. The Strategic Framework for CRM explored in the previous chapters can be used by enterprises to assess their CRM readiness and to identify and address CRM priorities. As noted earlier, although these five CRM processes have universal application, the extent to which they are emphasized will vary according to each organization's unique situation.

Large customer-facing businesses are likely to need to review all these CRM processes and the key questions underpinning them in considerable detail. In such cases, key issues will include leadership and CRM sponsorship; how my company compares with other organizations; how satisfied my customers are with the products and services offered by my organization; and if we have the skilled and motivated people and appropriate IT systems to deliver an outstanding customer experience. However, smaller companies will have more limited resources and they may need to focus on a smaller number of more specific priorities. We now consider two forms of readiness assessment – the overview CRM audit and the comprehensive CRM audit. If an organization is in the early stages of CRM development, it may be useful to start with an overview audit to help get senior management understanding and buy-in at an early stage.

The overview CRM audit

The overview form of readiness audit can be used quickly to form an initial view on the key CRM priorities, to define the relative importance of these priorities and to determine where effort needs to be applied. The 'overview CRM audit' involves examining each of the five processes in the CRM Strategy Framework and determining the key areas of importance that need to be examined for your organization. First, the company's existing capabilities on the five key CRM processes should be considered. Second, the proposed change in emphasis should be determined.

To gain insight into an enterprise's adoption of CRM, it is valuable to have a cross-section of managers independently assess their organization's performance across the five processes outlined above in terms of the existing and proposed future emphasis. The results of such an exercise for a major retail bank are shown in Figure 7.1.

Figure 7.1 Present and proposed emphasis on CRM processes in a retail bank

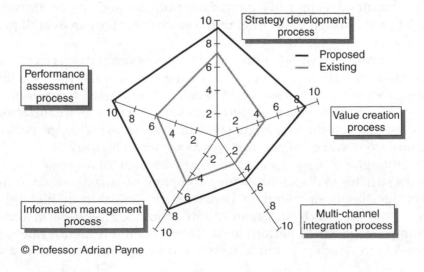

© Professor Adrian Payne

Priority initiatives are then developed to address each of the priority gaps that are identified.

We have used this mapping approach with many organizations and often found significant differences in the gap between the current position and the desired position and the relative emphasis on each process. In the case of this retail bank, changes were considered to be necessary in all processes, with the greatest improvement needed in the value creation and performance assessment processes. A number of important new CRM initiatives were identified and project teams were formed to implement them.

In one of Europe's largest service businesses we used this mapping process with 150 of its most senior staff including three divisional managing directors. Working in teams of six, each group identified current progress and the considerable challenges confronting their organization. There was a remarkably high degree of agreement from the 25 teams regarding the existing poor performance and the areas that needed improvement. This overview audit was instrumental in highlighting a number of key problems that had not been addressed and the high level of consensus amongst this senior management group galvanized it to agree a plan to rapidly focus on the CRM priorities identified as performance gaps.

A further example of a company's overview audit is shown in Figure 7.2 where nine areas, within the five CRM processes, are identified for attention. These are shown in this figure together with the key questions relating to each area. For each of the nine areas, the managers' responses to each question are scored against a set of agreed criteria using a five point scale from 'strongly agree' through to 'strongly disagree'. Averaging the scores provides an overall performance rating for each area.*

However, depending on the organization's specific objectives and situation, the relative importance of these may vary. If this is the case, a weight can be assigned to each area and used to compute a more representative overall performance score for the organization. The results can then be aggregated to give an overview of performance from a range of perspectives as shown in Figure 7.3.

Although simple in concept, the completion of this overview audit and a structured discussion with a company's managers around the scorings has been found to be extremely valuable in highlighting areas on which an organization should concentrate in order to improve its CRM performance. To extend the response rate it is possible to develop a simple web-based programme to collect and

Figure 7.2 Key areas for CRM focus in overview audit

Process	CRM measurement area
Strategy development	1. CRM leadership Does my organization demonstrate *leadership* in CRM? How do I compare with other organizations?
Value creation	2. Customer satisfaction How *satisfied* are my customers with the products and services offered by my organization?
	3. Customer lifetime value What is the lifetime *value* of my customers? How can I be more cost effective in delivering customer service to them?
Multi-channel integration	4. Customer access How effective and integrated is the *access* that my customers use to reach my organization?
Information management	5. Customer solutions and applications How effective are the customer *solutions* and *applications* that enable my customers to obtain my products and services?
	6. Customer information How do I manage the *customer information* used and generated at each customer contact to deliver the maximum value from my customers?
Performance assessment	7. Customer processes Does my organization have the *appropriate customer related processes* to deliver quality products and services?
	8. People standards Do I have the *skilled* and *motivated* people to deliver my products and services to customers?
	9. Performance reporting Does my organization have the appropriate *Performance Reporting* procedures to measure the impact of CRM strategy and operations on shareholder results?

aggregate the information from around the company, as can be done with a more comprehensive audit.

The comprehensive CRM audit

As with any organizational initiative, the success of a CRM programme depends very much on the existence of a sufficient level of preparedness within the organization. While the overview audit is a

Figure 7.3   CRM scores on overview audit

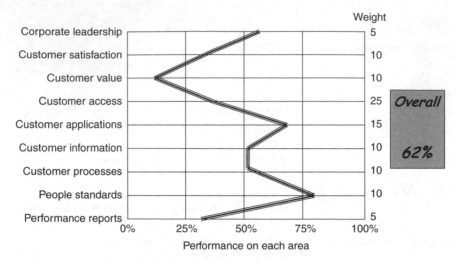

useful device to highlight opportunities and challenges and build consensus on the way forward, a more detailed insight into an enterprise's existing and potential use of CRM is usually needed. This involves a more detailed review of the five key CRM processes as well as a consideration of cultural, leadership and sponsorship issues. These latter factors are of particular relevance in preparing for a CRM programme and generating enthusiasm for it.

Each company will have different business priorities and market objectives. For this reason it is recommended that a tailored set of questions be developed for each of the major CRM processes. At the end of the chapter on each of the five CRM processes, we identified a number of 'issues for CRM leaders'. These are combined to form the 'comprehensive CRM audit' that appears in the Appendix at the end of this chapter. This audit includes a set of 100 questions, 20 on each of the five CRM processes. Although this generic audit can be used as it stands, we recommend it is adapted to suit the size and nature of the organization concerned. These questions should form the basis of an audit designed specifically to reflect the needs and circumstances of the enterprise.

In this comprehensive audit, the five CRM processes are broken down into two sub-sections each comprising ten questions. For example, the strategy development process is divided into business strategy (including leadership and sponsorship) and customer strategy;

the value creation process is divided into the value the customer receives and the value the organization receives and so on. There are two elements to score on a scale 0 to 5. These are: rating for our organization (5 = applies fully; 0 = does not apply at all) and importance to our organization (5 = very important; 0 = no importance).

An organization can approach a comprehensive CRM audit in two ways. First, it can develop its own audit tailored from the generic list of questions relating to CRM processes, shown in the Appendix. Second, other standardized CRM assessment tools can be used without modification.

If a tailored audit is required, we recommend a cross-functional team of executives, drawn from different functions including Marketing, IT, Human Resources and Finance, is used to develop an audit to suit the special circumstances of your organization. Managers wishing to use the comprehensive audit shown in the Appendix to this chapter, as a basis for their tailored audit, can obtain it from the author.[3] When completed and pilot tested, a cross-section of managers can then be asked to complete the audit using either a paper form or a web-based application. The data from this audit can then usefully be presented in a series of graphs or matrices that show the rating for the organization and the importance to the organization. This will help establish key CRM priorities. Such an audit covers quite complex issues. We have found completing the audit as part of one or more CRM workshops, with formal presentations that explain the concept of CRM in detail, helps ensure full understanding and a common vocabulary is used in the organization.

A number of other CRM assessment tools have also been developed, mainly by consulting firms. These are typically not tailored to the specific circumstances of an organization or industry sector and are not weighted to reflect the relative importance of specific CRM issues to the organization concerned. These audits vary greatly in detail and quality. Some are little more than a quiz and others show little evidence of thinking through the wide range of strategic issues relevant to CRM. Some audits like the CMAT assessment tool developed by QCi Ltd are more robust. We examined the CMAT assessment tool in Chapter 6 in terms of using it to understand how well the company is managing its customers.[4] It can also be used to consider CRM readiness more broadly. Although not specifically tailored to a particular enterprise, this tool has been developed as a result of exposure to a wide range of different organizations. QCi have accumulated a substantial number of data from a large number of businesses which enables comparisons to be made not only across all industries, but within relevant industry sectors. Because it is a proprietary tool, a company cannot use it themselves for a detailed self-audit; however, the overall cost of undertaking a CMAT assessment for a large organization is affordable.

Determining key CRM priorities

Regardless of the CRM readiness assessment audit used, the output of it should be the identification of the specific CRM activities and priorities that need to be addressed. These then need to be considered in the context of the strategy development process discussed in detail in Chapter 2. Companies' individual circumstances will dictate how they wish to consider their key CRM priorities. In one bank we worked with, twelve groups of employees identified an initial list of over one hundred activities and tasks that were considered worthy of more detailed examination. A group of senior managers then assessed these and categorized them using the matrix shown in Figure 7.4.

Each activity was then considered in more detail. On closer inspection some of them were related to each other so were reclassified and a significant number were rejected as being of minor importance. As a result of this exercise the number of activities was reduced. Issues

Figure 7.4   Classification matrix for issues identified in CRM audit

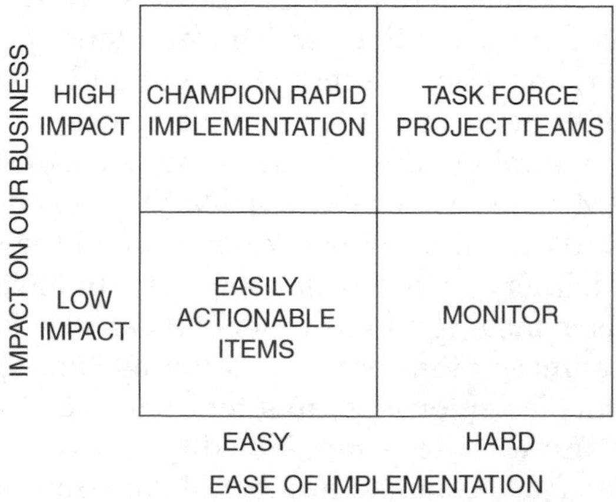

		EASY	HARD
IMPACT ON OUR BUSINESS	HIGH IMPACT	CHAMPION RAPID IMPLEMENTATION	TASK FORCE PROJECT TEAMS
	LOW IMPACT	EASILY ACTIONABLE ITEMS	MONITOR

EASE OF IMPLEMENTATION

that were considered to have a high impact on the business that were easy to implement were addressed immediately. A total of six projects that were hard to implement, but that potentially had a high impact on the business, were assigned to six task force project teams. Those that were hard to implement but had little expected payback were to be monitored over time to see if their importance changed in the future. A number of those activities that were classified as low impact but easy and inexpensive were proceeded with as they were considered likely to have a positive impact on employee morale.

A classification matrix such as this can make a major contribution to helping the enterprise form a clear view on its key priorities. Every organization starting a substantive new CRM programme needs to consider its overall readiness for a CRM implementation and what needs to be done to prepare the enterprise for it. Among the questions the enterprise should consider are: Is everyone in the organization aware of the objectives, requirements and 'strategic fit' of the proposed CRM programme and do they understand their own individual role within it? Will they accept their part with the necessary degree of commitment and cooperation? Are the requisite systems and processes in place to equip and support them in the endeavour? Will the CRM project be designed and developed to succeed, that is, has the organization fully considered the competitive context, the implementation time frame, the need for leadership and the dedication of resources in terms of both material expense and human expertise? These areas are ones where CRM change management and CRM project management play a critical role.

CRM change management and project management

Once a CRM readiness assessment has been undertaken and a decision has been made to proceed with new or expanded CRM initiatives, the key CRM processes examined throughout this book need to be addressed in a structured and integrated manner. The critical synergies generated by careful management of these five processes and the accompanying engagement of all employees, are highlighted by two activities which run in parallel with these processes – change management and project management.

We emphasized in Chapter 1 the wide range of CRM initiatives that may be undertaken under the heading of CRM. Within this book we have adopted a strategic perspective of CRM. This encompasses a myriad of possible initiatives ranging from improving customer care, a customer retention programme, more sophisticated market segmentation, introducing a data warehouse, adding a new channel, a global account management programme, introducing sales force automation – perhaps to thousands of employees, developing a balanced scorecard or a new performance reporting system. All of these can legitimately fall under the heading of CRM initiatives. However, the relative complexity of undertaking these initiatives varies as much as the activities themselves. The financial scale of such activities may vary from a few thousand dollars to one hundred million dollars or more!

We consider it is useful to distinguish between a CRM initiative, a CRM project and a CRM solution. We will use the term CRM initiative (or CRM programme) here to cover all the activities in an organization that are concerned with building customer relationships such as the ones listed above. We apply the term CRM solution (or CRM system) to an IT-based activity such as purchase of software to undertake customer segmentation or data mining, building a contact centre or introducing sales force automation. We use the term CRM project as an umbrella term to cover a more substantial CRM initiative (such as a contact centre or sales force automation) that involves significant project management activity. Typically this will involve one or more CRM solutions or systems.

Because of huge differences between the types of CRM initiative, not surprisingly, the consequences for change management and project management vary greatly. In the following sections we consider the nature of change management and project management and how they relate to CRM. We commence with a consideration of the multifaceted role of change management.

Change management

As the enterprise addresses each of the key CRM processes – strategy development, value creation, multi-channel integration, information management and performance assessment – it needs to consider the change management implications of them. For a large-scale and complex CRM initiative, companies will typically have to undergo substantial organizational and cultural change in order to implement it. A critical dimension of any large CRM programme, therefore, is an effective change management programme within the organization.

Change management is primarily concerned with people, systems and organizational change. We make a distinction here between change management which is concerned with strategic organizational change and employee engagement which we see as a more operationally oriented set of activities. They are of course closely entwined and activities relating to employee engagement, discussed later in this chapter, need to be carefully integrated with the change management initiatives. For example, training and management development activities can be associated with both change management and employee engagement. We discuss CRM training and development later in this chapter.

First, we review a framework that will assist in identifying the broad CRM change management activities that need to be addressed. Because CRM is potentially so wide-ranging in terms of the organizational ramifications, we need a robust analytical framework to help assist CRM leaders identify all the organizational change management issues in relation to a particular CRM programme. Second, we review three important and recurrent issues in CRM change management and implementation.

A framework for change management

The 'Seven S' framework, developed by strategy consulting firm McKinsey & Company, provides a powerful device for planning CRM change management initiatives. The framework, shown in Figure 7.5, consists of seven elements: strategy, structure, systems, staff, style, skills and shared values. Each of these is briefly described in this figure.

In addition to more traditional aspects of change – strategy, structure and systems – this framework highlights the need for organizations also to consider four other elements: style, staff, skills and shared values, if they are to be successful with a change management initiative. This framework can help organizations become more effective at CRM change management by carefully managing and orchestrating the relevant component parts of each element. Each of the seven elements should be aligned, like compass needles pointing in the same

Figure 7.5   The McKinsey 'Seven S' framework

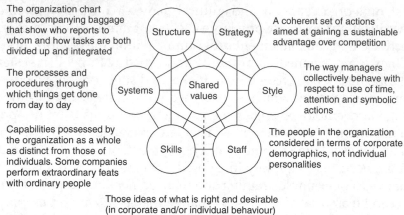

The organization chart and accompanying baggage that show who reports to whom and how tasks are both divided up and integrated

The processes and procedures through which things get done from day to day

Capabilities possessed by the organization as a whole as distinct from those of individuals. Some companies perform extraordinary feats with ordinary people

A coherent set of actions aimed at gaining a sustainable advantage over competition

The way managers collectively behave with respect to use of time, attention and symbolic actions

The people in the organization considered in terms of corporate demographics, not individual personalities

Those ideas of what is right and desirable (in corporate and/or individual behaviour) which are typical of the organization and common to most of its members

Source: Adapted from Waterman, Peters and Phillips[5]

direction, so that they support each other. The types of skills and breadth of knowledge required to make CRM succeed are quite different from those inherent in the traditional functional management model. Significant management development, cross-functional process management and leadership skills, for example, will be critical.

The Seven S summary shown in Figure 7.6 shows many dimensions of change management that are involved in changing the organization to process-oriented CRM. This is not intended to be a comprehensive list, but it is illustrative of the issues that emerge when using the Seven S framework. This suggests that a strategy to develop CRM must be supported by selected staff with appropriate skills along with a set of shared values, systems, management style and organizational structure.

This framework provides a means of viewing organizations as packages of key skills, or skill gaps. Hence, it can be used as a tool for analysing organizational deficiencies, building on positive skills and identifying new skills needed. An analysis can be undertaken by determining for each of the seven elements the key enablers to CRM, the key barriers to CRM and the new capabilities that need to be built.

The changes involved in making the transition to CRM are clearly profound. There are a number of potential obstacles to this transition, not least the entrenched interest in preserving the status quo. Understanding and acting on change management requirements is therefore a prerequisite to successful CRM implementation.

Figure 7.6   CRM change management issues

	From	To
Strategy	Market to major customer segments	Add value to individual customer relationships through tailored interactions
Shared values	Serve customers well	Service customers differently; serve best customers really well
Structure	Product orientation with focus on current period economics	Customer-segment orientation with focus on lifetime customer value
Skills	Analytical orientation with focus on current period economics	Ability to gather, analyse and interpret data and design systems to exploit a large, constantly evolving customer information base; ability to react at individual customer (or at least micro-segment) level
Staff	Marketing analysis managed statistically; information technology acts as support, but not as an active partner	Integration of marketing creativity with systems competencies to create capability that is both ideas-driven and analytically intense
Systems	Detailed, segmented, but relatively static decision support tools	Extensive, dynamic and flexible marketing support tools, programme management and execution systems, and operating links to support front-line actions
Style	Marketing plan orientation with emphasis on programmes for major segments delivered within standard period; mass media focus	Analytical approach and experimental attitude with emphasis on continuous learning (do, test, measure, fix) and value of data
Leading measures of success	Market share Current period profits	Share of most attractive customers (based on lifetime profit potential) Continuous learning/tailored marketing Large impact on a small set of customers

Source: Adapted from Child et al.[6]

Key issues in CRM change management

Given the great diversity of potential CRM initiatives, a general framework such as the McKinsey 'Seven S' framework is a powerful tool to help an organization identify those issues relevant to its particular context. These issues will typically vary from one organization to another. However, we have found three specific CRM issues that regularly need to be addressed in CRM programmes regardless of their nature. These include the need to establish a senior sponsor for CRM, to ensure an appropriate CRM vision and underlying set of values are in place and to have a supportive culture that facilitates improved cross-functional working within the organization.

Ensure senior CRM sponsorship

The attitude of the chief executive and senior management can be the determining factor in the success or failure of a CRM programme. Ideally, the chief executive should appoint a Board-level sponsor for CRM. The development of an organization totally focused on building profitable customer relationships usually requires intense effort on the part of senior management to shift existing employee attitudes towards developing a more customer-driven approach and using new technological tools. This requires the appointment of a strong leader and champion to oversee the organization's CRM activities – someone with vision, imagination, energy and persistence.

Without this person, the CRM programme can fail or degenerate into a situation where a limited number of employees are committed to the initiative. Bain & Company, the US strategy consulting firm has examined why CRM initiatives fail so often. Their research draws on examples from more than 200 companies across a wide range of industries. They conclude that one major reason that CRM fails is that most senior executives 'don't understand what they are implementing, let alone how much it costs or how long it will take'.[7]

The general skills of the CRM leader will include the following:

- in-depth understanding of business environment, markets and market segments
- credible at all levels within business
- knowledge of data management/data mining tools
- experience in dealing with complex IT issues
- financial skills

- comfortable operating at board level
- strategic thinker and planner
- excellent communication and leadership skills and ability to coordinate projects across functional departments
- familiarity with all operational areas of business.

The specific skills required in the CRM leader will vary from company to company according to the circumstances of the CRM project and the availability of internal human resources.

The commitment of senior managers and other employees to the CRM initiative will be heavily influenced by the visible behaviour of this CRM leader and champion, including the ways in which he or she communicates the worthiness of the CRM goals and the results obtained from CRM initiatives. CRM managers point out the difficulties of obtaining 'buy-in' to what are often very expensive projects. Having a board-level sponsor is vital, not only for initiating CRM projects but also for overcoming delays caused by passive resistance to change.

Establish a CRM vision

With a CRM leader in place, an early change management issue that needs to be addressed is the organization's shared values (see Figures 7.5 and 7.6). In a sense, these shared values are the 'glue' that holds the organization together. A clear and well-communicated CRM vision is an important means of building shared values. Earlier in Chapter 2 we explained that a business vision and its associated values form an important element of a company's strategy and we reviewed the research undertaken by Hugh Davidson into making vision and values work in organizations.

A CRM vision is a powerful means of creating shared values and a customer focus. Orange, the UK mobile service provider, is a good example of a company with a strong customer focus. Orange has always had a good reputation for customer service, but some years ago, following an appraisal of its operations, it developed a new vision, shown in Figure 7.7, that highlighted the importance of increased customer focus through the delivery of both rational and emotional needs that exceed customers' expectations. It is one that is memorable and motivating to employees.

Many companies score poorly on the development of a clear and strong vision because their visions are neither memorable nor motivating. Davidson has suggested the key issues an organization

Figure 7.7   Orange's CRM vision

'Our mission is to build strong enduring
relationships with our customers, thereby
increasing customer lifetime value and company
profitability and building sustainable competitive
advantage. We will achieve this through the
application of CRM strategies.'

'CRM is about building relationships to turn
customers into advocates, so that their decision to
stay with you becomes more "automatic"; they
buy more and spend more, and they tell their
friends and colleagues about your products and
services too.'

should address in order to overtake other companies in terms of
vision management:

- establish candidly who you are and what you stand for
- develop a future vision that excites and challenges
- involve all your people in developing vision and values
- communicate by action, signals and repetition
- embed vision and values into all practices, behaviours, processes and
  systems
- develop a distinctive brand proposition for your organization, which
  honestly reflects its substance and sets it apart
- regularly measure how well you are managing vision and values.[8]

Successful CRM implementation involves developing strong support for a customer orientation. A well-accepted vision will help
build commitment to CRM throughout the organization, but it needs
to be carefully and explicitly linked to the CRM project. CRM consultant Nick Siragher has emphasized how the CRM processes
should be defined so that end-users and non-technical personnel
understand what needs to occur from an operational point of view to
achieve the CRM vision:

> The process mapping must ensure a close and continuing relationship
> between strategic vision and the implementation of 'the solution'.
> Without this close relationship, CRM is nothing more than the imple-
> mentation of a few software tools and operational changes to achieve
> some process efficiencies. Consequently, the vision is lost ... To realize

the CRM vision, users must see the impact on how they work on a daily basis, and what achieving the vision means to them. The vision therefore needs to be explicit and understandable . . . The link between CRM vision and CRM solution is the very essence of the CRM project challenge.[9]

Supportive culture and improved cross-functional working

In this book we have emphasized that CRM is a cross-functional process. This approach requires cross-functional working and a major transition from the classic 'silo' mentality to a more 'customer-centric' view of the world. Successful CRM demands that members of different functions such as marketing, information technology and human resource management work together.

Research conducted at Cranfield University's CRM Research Forum confirms the importance of a set of clear pre-conditions necessary for effective CRM. As shown in Figure 7.8, these involve the organization having an appropriate marketing strategy, IT systems and organizational culture.

Figure 7.8   Marketing strategy, IT and cultural conditions

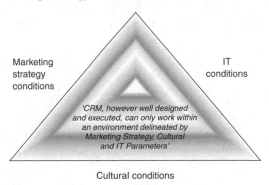

Marketing
strategy
conditions

IT
conditions

'CRM, however well designed
and executed, can only work within
an environment delineated by
Marketing Strategy, Cultural
and IT Parameters'

Cultural conditions

Source: Clark et al.[10]

Of particular relevance to change management are the organizational culture and climate conditions. This research showed four elements were important for effective CRM including:

● a positive organizational climate
● a market-oriented culture
● a strong culture
● a learning climate.

In many organizations there are inter-functional tensions that inhibit a positive customer-oriented organizational culture and climate and that prevent effective cross-functional collaboration. Conflict and anxiety between departments can arise for a number of reasons including differences in cultural or professional background, work perspectives, job tenure, age and level of understanding of the jobs performed by others.

One approach that is especially useful for surfacing the different perspectives and attitudes held by employees in different functions is the cultural web developed by British academic Gerry Johnson.[11] This provides a structure for auditing an organization's culture. It illustrates a number of interdependent subsystems including organization structures, power structures, control systems, symbols, stories and myths and routines and rituals, all of which are interconnected with the 'mindset', or paradigm – this is the set of common organizational assumptions and views held by most members of the organization or a department, function or unit within it.

Our experience suggests considerable divergence in organizational values and perspectives often exists between the IT function and the marketing function – the two groups most typically concerned with CRM implementation. Figure 7.9 shows the views of a group of IT managers in a large company with regard to their marketing colleagues. This figure shows how IT managers ascribe

Figure 7.9   IT's view of marketing

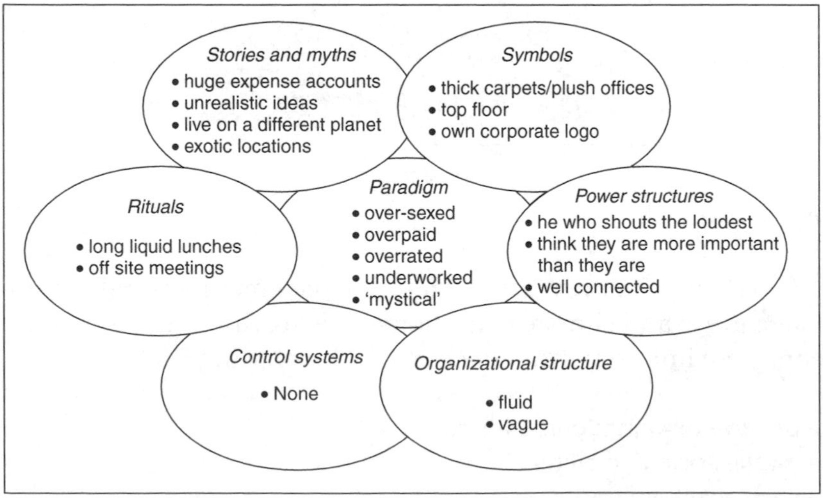

Source: Cranfield School of Management

a considerable number of negative sentiments with respect to the marketing managers in their organization. These include a general lack of respect: 'over-sexed, overpaid, overrated, underworked and mystical' and a belief that they do not contribute as much as they should to the organization.

Marketing managers also tend have clear stereotypical views of their colleagues in IT. In this organization, as shown in Figure 7.10, marketing managers viewed their IT colleagues as 'inflexible aliens' who spent vast sums and were rewarded on qualifications and skills rather than their contribution to organizational performance.

Figure 7.10 Marketing's view of IT

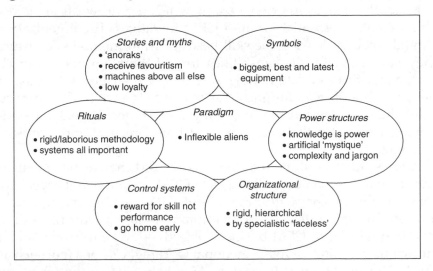

These views are clearly unhealthy. While such strong negative views of colleagues are not held in all organizations, such highly charged perspectives are by no means uncommon.

Other strong differences often exist between marketing (and IT) and other functional departments such as finance, human resources and general management. One study in a Fortune 500 electronics giant elicited the following opinions from groups of non-marketing staff: marketers are ' . . . naïve, conceited, insensitive, inexperienced and wrong; concerned only with advertising, promotion and enjoying themselves with customers; over-paid; largely unnecessary; lacking in business understanding; ignorant of financial matters; unnecessarily demanding; too often trying to change the company; uncontrollable; failing to achieve the wild goals they set; unwilling to learn from their mistakes; and a waste of funds needed by more important departments'.[12]

A good starting point in achieving better cross-functional integration is to surface the different views of functional departments held within the organization using a tool such as the cultural web and then to identify what needs to be done to reconcile any negative aspects so that the functions can work together in a more joined up way. Researchers suggest that change is likely to fail if it only focuses on one or two elements within the cultural web. Instead all the elements need to be considered together to form coherent change structures and systems, including the softer aspects such as symbolism and communication.

Establishing cross-functional teams which are drawn from across departments is essential for most CRM initiatives. The organization should work to develop the skill bases of team members to ensure they have the requisite capabilities for collaboration, including IT, marketing, finance, data mining and project management skills. In one organization, a multi-functional team was formed that was physically situated between the marketing and IT departments, a positioning which, for this company, had both practical and symbolic meaning.

Addressing these three key elements of CRM change management should help companies in all stages of CRM adoption, but especially those in the earlier stages. Successful CRM change management almost always needs a CRM champion, a clear vision (including clearly linking it to CRM business objectives and processes) and a culture that facilitates cross-functional working. Use of a tool such as the McKinsey 'Seven S' framework will help surface the other key elements that need to be addressed in a company-specific change management programme.

Project management

While change management is needed for virtually all CRM initiatives regardless of the scale of the CRM initiative, project management has increasing relevance as the size and complexity of CRM initiatives increase. In this section we briefly review the principles of project management before addressing specific issues relating to CRM projects.

CRM project management comprises two types of project. First, where a team of specialists is brought together on a temporary basis to address a particular project with a finite completion date. Second, where a cross-functional team is assembled with a remit of ongoing management of the enterprise's CRM initiative. (Some may argue that strictly speaking the latter is not a 'project' as it does not have a defined completion date.)

Projects are specific sets of activities designed to deliver specific outputs usually within defined timeframes. Successful CRM projects deliver against the CRM objectives derived from the corporate objectives and should be supportive of and complementary to the overall business strategy. Effective CRM project management is essential as experience has shown that CRM projects that overrun budgets and timescales can do considerable harm.

It is imperative for those devising and managing CRM projects to understand fully the particular role that IT plays in their specific CRM implementation. There are several reasons for using IT in CRM: to provide efficiencies, to create more customer value through improved customer knowledge and to improve the customer experience or to reduce cost. If a proposed IT investment in CRM cannot be justified on the benefits it brings it should be carefully re-examined.

A framework for project management

Projects are becoming increasingly widespread in every industry sector. This reflects not only an environment of greater complexity and rapid change but also the move throughout industry and government towards defined, goal-orientated, work activities.[13,14] In most projects these activities cross the functional boundaries of the organization. As a result there has been a greatly increased need for the cross-functional working discussed in the previous section on change management.

The reason for the upsurge in popularity of the cross-functional project team approach to management is that it provides the flexibility necessary for organizations to adapt amid constant change. Although project management is often thought of as comprising techniques aimed at the control of time and cost, it uses and enhances many of the common practices of general management including teamworking, cross-functional perspectives, process orientation and leadership. Today, project management has extended into sophisticated methods for the management and control of time, cost, resources, quality and performance.

Projects can be considered to be the vehicles for the delivery of one or more elements of a CRM or business strategy. The management of groups of projects is often known as either programme management or multi-project management. There is a framework or hierarchy of programmes, projects and activities, shown in Figure 7.11, that helps identify the different levels of project management activity.

Figure 7.11   Framework for project management

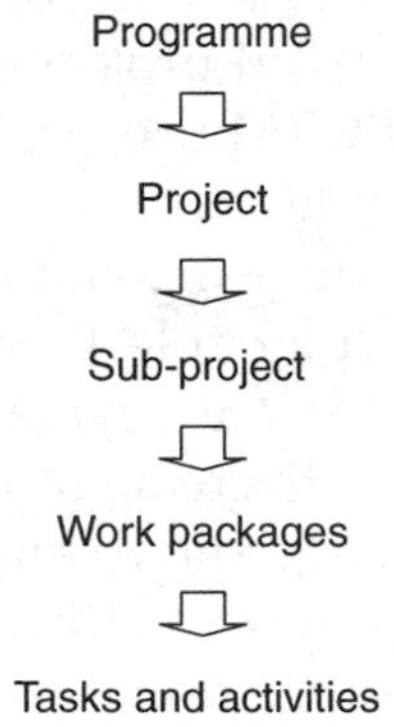

Programme

⌐⌐

Project

⌐⌐

Sub-project

⌐⌐

Work packages

⌐⌐

Tasks and activities

CRM 'projects' can fall within all of these levels depending on whether an enterprise-wide strategic initiative is involved or a much more tactically focused activity such as planning a particular campaign management activity.

The nature of projects

Projects are by their nature often unique. However, a very similar CRM project may have been done before but perhaps in a different department, division, company or industry sector. It is useful to look at the types of CRM projects that you have carried out and will undertake and categorize them, using an approach common in other forms of project management, into three major types: runners, repeaters and strangers.

Runners are projects that are commonplace in your business environment and have been undertaken successfully elsewhere (e.g. in another department) and hardly differ one from another in terms of technology. Projects of this type generally are of lower risk.

Repeaters are more complicated than runners. A similar project will have been done before (e.g. in another division of your company) and so its design and/or technology dimensions are known. The new project is much the same; however, it will require minor or moderate customization changes. Projects of this type generally are of moderate risk.

Strangers are new projects to the organization where the CRM technology solution is new to the organization. Such projects are quite common in CRM and by their nature are high risk. They are the most difficult to manage and if poorly managed can result in spectacular overruns in terms of time and/or cost.

This categorization, while simple, can help assign the correct level of resource to each individual project or sub-project.

A project involves a group of people working to complete a particular product or to achieve a specific task:

- by a specified date (time)
- within a specified budget (cost)
- meeting a specified standard of performance (quality).

These specifications of time, cost and quality are in a state of balance or equilibrium. Any increase or decrease in the level of any of them will affect the other elements. A model of these three elements is frequently drawn as a triangle that illustrates the trade-off between the three elements for a project with a defined scope. For example, if time needs to be decreased, to meet a particular customer need, then either cost or quality, or both will be affected. This is demonstrated in Figure 7.12 which shows two alternative trade-offs in terms of these three dimensions.

Figure 7.12 The project management equilibrium model

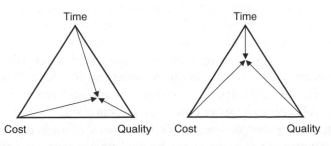

A further dimension also needs to be considered – the benefit to the organization. It is likely that there will be a series of trade-offs and values, cost and quality (or specification) that deliver different

CRM benefits to the organization. It is important to understand the relationship between project resources and the business benefits. We now examine an approach for considering this relationship.

Delivering business benefits

Large-scale CRM projects need to be managed so as to deliver benefits to the business, not just to deliver a CRM system on time and budget. A strategic project management tool has recently been developed which helps manage the delivery of business benefits. The Benefits Dependency Network (BDN) works backwards from the project's objectives to ensure that all necessary business changes are made, as well as CRM technology solutions implemented. The BDN approach has the following steps:[15–17]

1. *Define business drivers:* The drivers of the project are defined, based on the nature of the opportunity in relation to the strategy from the application portfolio. A driver is a view by top managers as to what is important for the business, such that the business needs to change in response to that driver, e.g. the need to achieve a greater return on shareholder funds.
2. *Determine investment objectives:* The investment objectives are a statement of how the project will contribute to achieving changes in relation to one or more of the drivers. Investment objectives may include increase in sales turnover, increase in market share, better targeting of most profitable customers, etc.
3. *Establish business benefits:* In order to achieve the investment objectives, some benefits will need to be delivered to the enterprise and/or its customers. These business benefits need to be explicitly identified and quantified. They may include increasing stockturn, better response from campaign management, improving customer service, etc.
4. *Identify business changes:* In order to achieve the benefits, it is necessary for the enterprise and its employees to work in different and more effective ways. These changes are identified at this stage in the BDN. Business changes may include online provision of sales and stock information to the field sales force, changes in channel structure, using the data warehouse to improve customer targeting, etc.
5. *Identify enabling changes:* These are other one-off changes that may also be needed before the technology can be implemented, for example to define new processes which are needed and to establish new skill requirements, e.g. refining customer segmentation, design of new customer service processes, introducing a new account management process.

6. *Determine CRM technology requirements and enablers:* It is only when this analysis of the objectives and benefits has been undertaken and the necessary changes to realize them have been identified, that the specific role that the CRM technology will play in the project's objectives can be defined in detail. These technology changes represent information systems and information technology (IS/IT) enablers that will lead to the realization of the business benefits. They include items such as extensions to the company's data repository, a new or improved web site, a sales force automation system, new mobile devices for field sales force, etc.

The Benefits Dependency Network represents a useful tool for identifying the business changes that are needed to make the new use of CRM technology effective. Managers wishing to use this tool may find it useful to examine worked examples from other industries. Such examples are documented in the research relating to the BDN and are listed in the references to this chapter.[18] A BDN framework can usually be agreed within two to three half-day workshops, however, detailed scoping of the CRM technology requirements may not be achieved within this timescale for more complex projects.

Key issues in CRM project management

In a study of twenty-three European companies, Stephan Henneberg of the University of Bath identified two CRM implementation approaches taken by organizations: a dominant 'hard' implementation of CRM (focusing on IT, analytics, centralization and campaign management) and a 'soft' implementation of CRM (focusing on decentralized customer experience management and customer relationships). Of the twenty-three companies examined, sixteen of them adopted the 'hard' approach, four adopted the 'soft' approach and three of them utilized a combination of approaches.[19] IT-based CRM project management will clearly be of greatest importance in 'hard' CRM implementations.

The 'hard' or analytical dimension typically emphasized integrated customer database with marketing data marts, a shared data model, marketing analysis and data-mining tools (such as propensity models for targeting and triggering activities), centralized CRM and campaign management functions, the integration of all touch-points/channels with feedback-loops to the centralized database, a standardization of customer interaction and service processes via treatment strategies. The main implementation activities here are software adaptation and integration, process redefinition, organizational integration, sales force automation and campaign management.[20]

Henneberg found that the 'soft' or customer experience dimension encompasses aspects of direct customer interaction management. It is more decentralized and focuses on customer interaction skills and strategies, a deep understanding of customer or customer segment relationship needs, the development of new customer-centric touchpoints and the ability to use the customer information to build relationships. The main implementation activities are skill advancement, process definition, organizational learning and the development of ways to capture customer information as part of the interaction routine.[21] This equates more to developing a customer-centric approach through change management as opposed to an IT-based approach.

Given the diversity of these different CRM implementation approaches, the key issues that will need to be addressed under the heading of CRM project management will vary greatly across different projects. However, three issues will be of importance to most organizations: determining if a CRM technology solution is likely to be of benefit; deciding if a pilot project should be undertaken; and planning for the CRM project's implementation. Considering these issues will also help the organization determine the relevant emphasis that needs to be placed on both project management and change management for its own CRM implementation.

Utilizing a CRM technology solution

Henneberg found that companies using the 'hard' CRM implementation approach often had only a vague strategic understanding of the CRM project in place before they defined the process and technical requirements. This suggests that standard IT processes may often be used to derive strategic CRM guidelines, a reversal of a best-practice approach where IT processes are developed from strategic and customer-based considerations.[20] The Strategic Framework for CRM outlined in this book emphasizes that strategic considerations should be addressed first – before the IT solutions. Tools such as the Benefits Dependency Network outlined above will then help identify the general CRM technology requirements in the context of business strategy and drivers.

Adopting a CRM solution

McKinsey & Company, drawing on research from AMR Research, point to the widespread adoption of CRM technology solutions. Two-thirds of all US telecom operators and half or more of all US financial services, pharmaceutical and transportation companies are either implementing or already operating such solutions. Across the USA and Europe, approximately 40 per cent of the companies in the high technology, aerospace, retailing and utilities sectors have invested in CRM systems.[22]

Most large organizations dealing with a substantial number of customers have adopted or will adopt one or more IT-based CRM solutions. Medium-sized and smaller organizations need to consider their existing and potential scale in relationship to the technology requirements. Management consultant Michael Gentle has written extensively on CRM project management. Drawing on a range of sources he outlines a number of organizational conditions that make a company an ideal candidate for adopting an IT-based CRM solution:

- Do you have a large number of people in sales and service in direct contact with customers, say more than 30?
- Are you in a highly collaborative environment, with customer interaction requiring input from multiple players within each function (sales and service)?
- Do you sell complex products that require a high degree of configuration and customization?
- Do you have a large number of customers, say more than 10 000?
- Is a typical customer relationship worth a lot to you from a profit standpoint, i.e. will it cost you to lose one?
- Can your customers interact with you across multiple channels?
- Do you have frequent contact with large groups of customers, or all customers, across multiple channels?
- Is there a need to customize what you are saying to each customer through these channels?[23]

Companies which respond 'yes' to most of these conditions should certainly consider adopting a CRM solution, if they have not already done so. For other companies, a consideration of the CRM strategy matrix (Figure 2.10 in Chapter 2) will help determine the relevance and timing of new CRM solution adoption. Having identified the need for adoption of a CRM technology solution, attention then needs to be turned to vendor selection, determining if a pilot project is required and detailed project planning.

Selecting a CRM vendor

The CRM software marketplace is extremely complex, with over 1000 products offered by a cluttered and dynamic community of more than 350 vendors worldwide.[24] Typically between 50 and 100 CRM vendors may be present at major CRM conferences. Faced with such a plethora of vendors, choosing the appropriate vendor or vendors can be daunting.

The starting point in understanding different vendors is to consider the broad categories of vendors within the CRM market and determine what types of categories are relevant to the company's needs. In Chapter 1 a classification of vendors for CRM applications and CRM service providers, based on a classification by Gartner, together with some illustrative examples of companies in each category, was presented. This listing is restated below.

The key segments for CRM applications include:

- Integrated CRM and ERP Suite (e.g. Intentia, Oracle PeopleSoft, SAP)
- CRM Suite (e.g. E.piphany, Siebel)
- CRM Framework (e.g. Chordiant)
- CRM Best of Breed (e.g. Avaya, NCR Teradata, Broadvision)
- Build it Yourself (e.g. IBM, Oracle, Sun).

The CRM service providers and consultants that offer implementation and support include:

- Corporate strategy (e.g. McKinsey, Bain)
- CRM strategy (e.g. Peppers & Rogers, Vectia, Detica, Sophron)
- Change management, organization design, training, HR, etc. (e.g. Accenture)
- Business transformation (e.g. IBM, PwC)
- Infrastructure build, systems integrators (e.g. Logica, Siemens, Unisys)
- Infrastructure outsourcing (e.g. EDS, CSC)
- Business insight, analytics, research, etc. (e.g. SAS, dunnhumby)
- Business process outsourcing (e.g. Acxiom).

The complexity of this vendor marketplace is compounded by a considerable ongoing consolidation within the CRM vendor marketplace, a constant stream of new entrants to the market, with some companies having a poor reputation for support and implementation and some established companies being very good at applications or implementation skills that they are generally not known for in the CRM marketplace.

It is beyond the scope of this book to review this huge list of CRM vendors. Such vendors are regularly reviewed by analyst firms such as Gartner, Forrester, Meta, DCI, Hewson, and AMR. Consultant Paul Greenberg provides an interesting historical perspective of some of the major players including Peoplesoft, Interact, Onyx, Siebel, Nortel, Microstrategy, Oracle, E.piphany and Kana.[25] However, this type of information in books can become outdated quickly given the rapid change and consolidation that is occurring within the CRM industry.

Subscribers to Gartner's services are able to obtain up to date and comprehensive overviews of many of the main CRM vendors. Such overviews provide vendor functionality ratings across a range of front-office applications including:

- field sales
- tele-sales
- E-commerce
- channel management
- PRM (partner relationship marketing) sales and marketing
- analytics – business intelligence
- analytics – predictive
- field service
- call centre management
- E-service, etc.

Further, Gartner evaluate all the major vendors in terms of ranking them on their CRM applications, their vertical industry expertise and their business stability. This includes ranking of each of these vendors on a matrix display based on their ability to execute specific CRM applications and the completeness of their CRM vision. A ranking of expertise in the following specific vertical markets is provided by them: retailing, banking/brokerage, automotive, pharmaceutical, insurance/healthcare, manufacturing and hi-tech and telecoms.

Customer management consultants Detica use six evaluation criteria for vendor selection. These criteria are functionality, technical complexity and integration, track record, implementation and timescales, risk and total cost of ownership. Figure 7.13 outlines a profile for two vendors based on these criteria.

This figure shows that the factors that contribute to whether the project succeeds are much broader than just functionality. Each of the factors

Figure 7.13   CRM vendors profiles on evaluation criteria

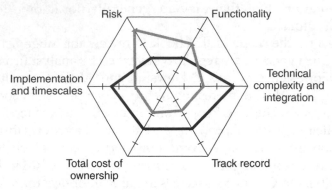

Source: Detica Limited

relevant to the CRM implementation concerned needs to be carefully evaluated. The risk dimension is one that often does not require sufficient attention. Gentle provides a comprehensive risk analysis questionnaire for CRM projects that enables managers to form a detailed view on the relative risk of the CRM project.[26] Where appropriate, the criteria should be weighted according to their relative importance.

We advocate developing your own criteria for CRM vendor selection. Checklists of criteria such as that provided above can be supplemented with issues and sub-issues relating to the particular circumstances of the company including its in-house capabilities and the nature of the CRM project. Such issues may include asking questions such as:

- Does the vendor have a well-integrated internal implementation or professional services team?
- What is the size of this group and how committed are they to existing projects?
- To what extent does it rely on third-party partners for implementation?
- Does it have significant relevant experience in your vertical market or one that is directly analogous?
- How forthcoming is the vendor with respect to introducing you to reference sites for similar projects?
- Can you get access to a range of users and managers from different functions within these sites?
- What is its on-time and on-budget performance with projects of similar size and complexity?

Finally, vendor stability is very important. In selecting vendors to help the business design and build the appropriate CRM architecture it also pays to take into account whether the vendor has a sufficiently strong and stable position in the market. An article in the *McKinsey Quarterly* quoted the example of one company that was developing a data warehouse and which had rejected a market-leading vendor in favour of one whose product was marginally faster. Unfortunately, within three years the latter vendor had fallen behind its more prominent competitors and its system had proven unreliable and costly to maintain. The company was then faced with high costs in moving to another supplier.[27]

Piloting CRM projects

Some organizations consider that a large-scale and very comprehensive approach to CRM improvement, covering many CRM initiatives more or less simultaneously, is necessary. Certainly, some companies need such a total, comprehensive and large-scale approach. However, we have found that more often an incremental and modular approach to CRM development or enhancement is appropriate. Such an approach involves a series of smaller individual CRM projects, undertaken in an appropriate sequence, each with clearly defined objectives and ROI outcomes. These projects will help determine whether the immediate emphasis needs to be placed on analytical CRM, operational CRM or collaborative CRM. The project might involve a specific task within a CRM process, such as upgrading a call centre operation or introducing an SFA procedure, or a complete CRM process, such as improving multi-channel integration. Further, many of these projects will best be initiated by means of a 'pilot' project.

There are various reasons for a pilot project to be considered. Pilots can be used to prove a CRM concept at a much lower cost, to trial an approach with high business or political risk, to avoid incurring large-scale licence fees before the application is proven, lack of existing or potential buy-in, and so on.

Buy-in is an important issue and it can be at many levels including individual, departmental, regional, national or international. We re-emphasize that the CEO and senior management should endorse and support any CRM project through their buy-in and active involvement. However, if support for a project does not currently exist, then those charged with CRM implementation may first wish to limit the programme to a pilot project for proof of concept and buy-in.

Interdepartmental conflict and disagreements, highlighted in the earlier section on change management, also are a frequent cause for lack of buy-in. It is easier to launch a pilot project when faced with organizational or cultural resistance to change than it is to 'hit the wall' head on. Without top-level support, innovators can only stretch the 'cultural elastic' so far and it may be counter-productive and politically misguided to attempt to challenge and overturn the company's system of beliefs and assumptions without piloting the project first. International CRM projects face particular problems that are amplified by geographic and cultural differences. For a review of critical success factors in international CRM projects, see Gentle.[28]

There are two types of CRM pilot: the 'conference-room' pilot and the 'operational' pilot or 'live' pilot. Siragher outlines the differences between them. The conference-room pilot takes place in a conference room, rather than in the working environment. It tests processes without the risk of any adverse impact on either customer relations or the reputation of the CRM solution within the business and paves the way for a more general pilot in the live environment. It can also be used for piloting CRM training concepts and it should replicate a complete period of use for the user – perhaps three months. This can be done in a fraction of the elapsed time and can provide extensive use of the solution in a short time-scale. Live pilots, by contrast, are typically more resource-intensive and require similar resources to when the project goes live. In a live pilot, the same hardware and ideally the same version of the software as planned for the roll out should be utilized. Siragher's work outlines the resources required for a pilot and an illustrative plan for a roadmap for a pilot CRM project including training. In practical terms, running pilot project training provides an opportunity to identify how easy or how difficult it will be for users to learn the solution and also to identify any issues relating to cultural change.[29]

Planning for CRM project implementation

The CRM project plan must be developed into specific actions that result in the project being implemented and the business objectives achieved. The CRM strategy framework outlines a set of clearly defined processes that should be addressed in the plan. The format of a CRM plan will vary considerably from one organization to another and it must be carefully crafted to meet the needs of the organization.

The CRM plan must be produced in a manner that stands the tests of completeness, consistency, ease of understanding and succinctness. Project plans are best communicated and managed if they are presented visually. Further, areas of potential risk should be considered. Here contingency planning has an important role to play. In practice, plans are not always developed in a linear manner. It should be recognized that the early stages of planning may be 'messy' and that planning is an interactive and iterative process. Further, as consultant Jill Dyche has observed, whatever its scope, planning a CRM programme is rarely as straightforward as it first seems.[30]

Establishing project priorities and their direction
In the planning phase of CRM projects it is necessary to develop an integrated plan covering projects, the project goals, metrics for measuring success and the project priorities and then develop a roadmap for implementing them. Determining priorities is especially important. Figure 7.14 shows the representation of seven component projects for a CRM programme for a large financial services organization.

This representation helped managers prioritize each project and create a uniform approach to the management of each project. In this company, projects were to be addressed as follows:

Figure 7.14 Business benefits/implementation matrix

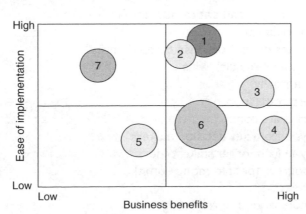

- a board member will oversee direction for each project
- each project will have an assigned project manager
- project managers will:
  - ○ suggest and assign task force members as appropriate to specific tasks (with senior management team agreement)
  - ○ propose a work plan, detailed action plans and timetable follow through with implementation
- a nominated director to be overall CRM programme coordinator.

Duration of projects varies considerably depending on their nature. A project involving setting up direct marketing activities can be completed within three months, while other projects such as sales force automation may take a number of years. Projects should be broken up into discrete steps with deliverables being defined at appropriate points in time. Experience suggests that with longer projects there is a high risk that the project may be discontinued if the project duration is more than three years or some tangible benefit to the business is not achieved within 18 months.

The CRM project plan
The activities in a CRM project plan will vary according to the timescale, the complexity and other issues such as whether a pilot has been undertaken. For a longer project lasting, say, three years, the typical activities involved in planning the project may include the following:

1st Year:

- Define project goal and critical success factors
- Develop a roadmap
- Discrete steps of no more than three months
  - ○ identify low risk, quick wins
- Sell plan internally
  - ○ find corporate sponsor
  - ○ get corporate commitment
  - ○ get buy-in from key decision makers
  - ○ get buy-in from other stakeholders
  - ○ get resources (people, money, time)
- Initiate project
  - ○ start monitoring and reporting

    ○ employee engagement
    ○ start preparation for roll-out
    ○ start delivery.

2nd Year:

- Review project goal and critical success factors, modify if necessary
- Review roadmap
    ○ continue with discrete steps of no more than three months
    ○ continue looking for low risk, quick wins
- Manage ongoing project
    ○ continue delivery
    ○ continue monitoring and reporting
- Continue internal marketing.

3rd Year:

- Further review of project goal and critical success factors, modify if necessary
- Further review roadmap
    ○ continue with discrete steps of no more than three months
    ○ continue looking for low risk, quick wins
- Manage ongoing project
    ○ continue delivery
    ○ continue monitoring and reporting
    ○ continue internal marketing
- Planning for project completion
    ○ politics
    ○ shareholders and stakeholders
    ○ business
    ○ customers
    ○ alliances.

As the CRM project plan is implemented two issues should be considered: creep in project scope and understanding the implications of scale. McKinsey & Co. point out that as a project grows in scope, the system's development can take on a life of its own, incorporating new features that do not support business objectives but add considerable complexity and cost. IT professionals have learnt that the bigger a project, the harder it is to integrate and the more likely it is to miss deadlines or be scrapped altogether.[31] The business objectives that the CRM system was intended to achieve must be kept under constant scrutiny and any efforts to increase the scope of the project must be evaluated very carefully.

As a project is planned it is critical that the implications of scale increase are understood. Point estimates of future demand are quite useless. Estimates should be based on three levels of potential future demand: optimistic, most likely and pessimistic. As the numbers of users and customers grow, the system must be robust enough to accept the changes in volume. Also, having sufficient capacity to provide high levels of customer satisfaction needs to be considered in the plan. The example from AT&T 's Internet service illustrates an approach where issues relating to capacity are taken into account in the project plan (see box).

We way over-invested in customer care to make sure that the phone gets answered in 30 seconds rather than in 30 minutes as it can when you call some Internet service providers.

We over-invested in modems and network capacity so that people don't get a busy signal when they call during a peak hour. If they're going to make this an important part of their lives, then they want it to be there.

We invested in redundancy so that we would have a highly reliable network. We have a lot of experience with scale, with growing very quickly.

We built a lot of navigation into the front end of the service because we want to help all of the new people to find their way around the Internet.

We announced that we would guarantee any transactions made with the AT&T Universal Card while they were using our services.

And, finally we offered a one-year free trial on the Internet with the first five hours of each month free.

Source: Tom Evslin, Vice President of AT&T WorldNet Services

The main features of CRM implementation can be summarized under three very broad headings: people, systems and processes. An organization cannot develop and operate appropriately customer-focused systems and processes without properly motivated and trained employees. Staffing resources need to be planned not only on the basis of most likely demand, but also potential peak demand. Ensuring the delivery of a superior customer experience during times of unexpectedly high demand requires the active engagement and commitment of all customer-facing staff and is a hallmark of a well-planned CRM implementation. The case study of Nationwide's adoption of a CRM solution provides an excellent example of the key issues that need to be addressed in CRM implementation including the importance of employee engagement.

Case 7.1 Nationwide fulfils its CRM vision with Unisys – Case study overview

Nationwide is one of the UK's leading financial services providers with more than 10 million members and over £85 billion in assets. They have over 12,000 employees, at call centres or in the branches throughout the UK, that require fast, accurate access to customer data. They needed a CRM solution so they could access customer data and update this data – in real time. The project needed to include consultancy, project management, testing, development, hardware and training to provide a flagship CRM system, which would in turn provide outstanding customer service for Nationwide's members.

Unisys, in collaboration with AIT, undertook this project. The CRM system they developed provides a single view of a member's profile and accounts so Nationwide employees can identify a customer's needs in a timely and accurate manner. In organizing for CRM implementation, considerable attention was placed on change management and employee engagement. A significant budget was set aside for training and change management so that Nationwide employees would be able to embrace their vision and the associated changes needed in process and behavior.

This CRM project has been highly successful and has resulted in increased sales, and profitablility, as well as the highest level of customer satisfaction ever. The reasons why this CRM project has succeeded included clear communication at every level throughout the organization, coupled with a high level of executive sponsorship. Nationwide has placed employee engagement at the heart of the business. Nationwide recognizes that delivering member value begins with happy, knowledgeable and committed employees. This has led to very low staff turnover and a waiting list of potential employees.

The full case study is at the end of this chapter (see p. 388)

Employee engagement

The last of the four elements element outlined at the start of this chapter is the engagement of employees to support the various initiatives that comprise the overall CRM programme. Employees have a crucial role to play within each of the CRM processes examined in this book and the change management and project management activities discussed in this chapter are highly dependent on engagement of employees for their success.

Increasingly, organizations are recognizing the significant value their employees contribute to the business, which extends well beyond the basic fulfilment of core duties. Employees are instrumental in implementing customer service policy, improving process efficiencies and nurturing consumer confidence and custom. Deservingly described as 'our greatest asset', an organization's people provide the prime mechanism for promoting customer satisfaction, improving productivity, assuring quality control and reducing costs. The importance of employee engagement is in the ascendant as companies focus more on creating an outstanding customer experience.

Employee engagement requires commitment from the company's personnel. However, across the world, research shows that employees have a general inability to commit. A landmark global study was conducted by Walker Information Global Network and the Hudson Institute. More than 9700 full and part-time employees representing business, non-profit and government organizations in 32 countries participated in the study.[32] The researchers found 34 per cent of employees are 'truly loyal', 8 per cent are 'accessible', 31 per cent are 'trapped' and 27 per cent are 'high risk'. Only slightly more than half feel a strong personal attachment to their employer and only six in ten employees believe their organization deserves their loyalty. This unwillingness to commit breeds an even weaker sense of loyalty.

'Truly loyal' employees are the most desirable employees as they feel a deep attachment to their organizations, want to be there and plan to stay for at least another two years. In turn, these truly loyal workers are prepared to go the extra mile to get the job done and often serve as role models for their peers. Accessible employees are satisfied with their employers, however, they may not stay with the organization. A much lower level of commitment is found among employees identified as trapped or high risk. Although trapped employees do not want to remain in the organization, they intend to stay because they do not have other options or may be unable or unwilling to make the effort to pursue other employment. An amazing 31 per cent of workers worldwide are 'trapped' – these workers are typically poorer performers, at least in part because they are not likely to go 'beyond the call of duty'. The 27 per cent of high risk employees do not want to stay, and plan to leave.

Among the most significant findings of this study is verification that an employee's job performance is directly tied to their level of commitment to the organization. Therefore, how all the company's human resources are engaged, but especially those who have any form of customer contact, is a key factor in determining CRM success. There is a wide body of research to support the claim that the surest way to enhance competitive performance is through recruiting and selecting the best employees, training and motivating them and providing effective leadership. This will maximize the likelihood of employees effectively engaging with both customers and their colleagues.

John McKean, a veteran CRM expert, has recently identified eight major areas the enterprise needs to focus on to achieve strong customer relationships, including:

- *Leading the human firm* – leading the human firm is about selecting, developing and fulfilling your employees so they can impact most effectively on the key needs of the customer.
- *Acknowledging customers* – understanding and acknowledging the customer's existence, importance, feelings and special requirements.
- *Treating customers with respect* – understanding how best to treat the customer and respecting factors such as their time, privacy, personal space and diversity.
- *Building trust* – customers should always be treated honesty and ethically. Responding rapidly to problems or queries helps develop trust.
- *Communicating humanly* – involves understanding and developing the skills to create the most effective communication between employee and customer.
- *Implementing the human touch consistently* – is concerned with making the customer feel that they are being treated by a caring fellow human being.
- *Understanding and applying the human touch as a process* – each human touch can be viewed as one of a series of steps to make up the total customer experience. Businesses should recognize the need to deliver a consistent experience regardless of the channel used by the customer.
- *Implementing technology to humanize* – CRM technology dehumanizes as much as it humanizes. Efforts must be made to create a similar level of outstanding customer experience to that of a personal experience with an employee.[33]

McKean's research supports the need to select, develop and empower employees to bring about their full engagement and their commitment to delivering an outstanding customer experience. We now address each of these issues.

Selecting employees

Employee engagement starts with the recruitment process – ensuring that the best employees are selected in the first place. The high cost of recruitment means that it is important for employers to find recruits with both the necessary skills and the willingness to be trained and retained by the company. Success rates can be greatly enhanced by providing potential employees with full and accurate information about job requirements and expectations and the work environment. Failure to do so can result in disillusioned employees, low employee retention rates and negative word of mouth as employees warn other potential recruits not to apply for positions within the company.[34]

Companies should exercise special care in selecting employees who not only demonstrate appropriate skills and experience, but whose values and motivations match those of the corporate ethos. More often than not technical or task-based aptitudes can be taught and developed once the person is in post. The individual's work ethic and psychological characteristics are likely to be less malleable. Companies should adopt an approach of 'recruit for attitude, train for skills'.

Techniques such as psychometric testing are becoming increasingly popular as a means of identifying the personality profile of people who are likely to be successful in delivering service quality and developing relationships with customers. Traditionally, such testing techniques were more likely to be used for management and graduate positions than for customer contact, or administrative or secretarial jobs. However, the high costs associated with employee turnover and the general trend towards greater job mobility have caused many organizations to hone their selection practices. Increasingly companies are using techniques such as psychometric testing and assessment centres for a wider range of employment positions. This underlines the importance that companies are now placing on the 'emotional content' of front-line roles.

Essential to understanding how employees add value is to recognize the different roles they play in the organization. Customer-facing employees can only function effectively with support from others in the company who, though they do not come into direct contact with the customer, nevertheless play a very important role and directly influence the service ultimately provided for customers. By viewing employees as a value-adding element, companies can direct the appropriate level of attention towards maximizing the impact of their activities and motivating and rewarding them to make the desired contribution.

Developing employees

Research has shown that employees who are unclear about the role they are supposed to perform become demotivated, which in turn can lead to customer dissatisfaction and defection. So new employees must be carefully prepared for the work ahead of them, as their early days in a company colour their attitudes towards it and perceptions. Those organizations lacking a strong service ethos may need to introduce a major change management programme aimed at all employees. Internal marketing programmes aimed at instilling customer consciousness and service orientation are increasingly being adopted by organizations.

The basic premise behind internal marketing involves getting employees to recognize the impact of their behaviour and attitudes on customers. This is especially important for employees who are as close – or closer – psychologically and physically to customers as they are to each other. Their skills and customer orientation are critical to the way the customer views the organization and, therefore, help determine their future loyalty.

Some of the best examples of employee engagement programmes come from the airline industry. Both Scandinavian Airline System (SAS) and British Airways reversed their fortunes during the 1980s. Faced with declining profits, increasing customer complaints, employee dissatisfaction and mounting competition, both airlines launched a series of programmes to refocus employees on customers. As such, employees were involved in the process of turning their company around through the development of increased awareness of the critical importance of the customer.

Employees were trained to develop new attitudes towards customers by emphasizing that the airline was in business to satisfy the needs of the customer. In turn, the company made employees feel wanted and cared for, building on the principle that those who are looked after will pass on this caring attitude. The success of this new direction for both airlines was manifested in greater customer and employee satisfaction and increased profits. But, such programmes have a limited life and now both airlines face a new challenge significantly to improve the motivation of their employees.

Some organizations such as Disney Corporation have been able to sustain this culture, at least in their American theme parks, over a much longer period of time (see box).

The Disney Corporation is a good example of a company with a strong employee engagement programme. Development of employees plays a major role in their success. Employees are rigorously trained to understand that their job is to satisfy customers. Employees are part of the 'cast' at Disney and must at all times ensure that all visitors ('guests') to their theme parks have a highly enjoyable experience. Dress codes, conduct rules and training are maintained in order that employees 'live the brand'.

Engaging and empowering employees

Employees need to be motivated to use their discretion in order to deliver a better quality service to customers. Engaging employees involves creating the right culture and climate for employees to operate in, hence the close linkage with change management. Employees need the knowledge that allows them to understand and contribute to organizational performance and the power to take decisions that influence organizational direction and performance. Au Bon Pain, a chain of bakery cafés on the east coast of the USA, illustrates this in practice (see box).

Au Bon Pain has focused on employee engagement as a means of creating increased employee value in its bakery café chain. Managers are empowered to make significant alterations to processes, procedures, store layout and other policies, in order to develop service quality and marketing activities designed to build stronger relationships with frequent customers. These changes led to a significant performance improvement. Staff turnover in one of the Boston stores dropped to 10 per cent per annum for entry-level jobs versus an industry norm of about 200 per cent. Absenteeism plummeted and sales soared as customers developed a relationship with counter staff. Productivity levels have increased despite the reduction in employee numbers. Under the Partner-Manager Programme at Au Bon Pain employees can earn double the industry-average wage. The type and quality of employees changed radically and word of mouth created a strong demand for jobs at all levels within the chain.

One of the barriers to employee engagement is middle managers feeling threatened when they have to delegate power and authority to subordinates. Equally, some staff are reluctant to take on such responsibility and believe that making decisions is a manager's responsibility. Engaged and empowered employees provide a faster and more flexible response to customers' needs. The benefits of employee engagement need to be balanced with potentially increased labour, recruitment and training costs. Hence the costs have to be seen as a long-term investment in CRM.

CRM training and development

CRM initiatives should usually include both employee training and executive development activities. Depending on their scope and scale these activities could be considered as part of change management or employee engagement. CRM training and development activity starts with a needs analysis. This will involve a thorough review to identify the requisite mix of knowledge, skills or attitudes that need to be developed for effective CRM to take place. It should be based on interviews with appropriate executives and employees within the firm and needs to be undertaken by someone with a good understanding of the organization and the particular training requirements of any CRM technology being adopted.

The focus of executive development will be on ensuring managers understand the full extent of the company's CRM initiative including its opportunities and potential problems. As noted earlier, research suggests that executives are often not fully aware of what they are implementing, or the costs and timing of the CRM programmes. We have found a number of instances where detailed employee training is in place but there is no supporting executive briefing or executive development.

Executive development activities programmes typically comprise a series of workshops or events involving managers drawn from all functions within the organization. These should precede employee training and should make management fully aware of the nature and objectives of the company's CRM initiatives. The objectives and scope of these programmes will vary considerably across different organizations, as shown by a selection of ones we have developed, shown in Figure 7.15.

Employee training may be focused on developing particular skills or on changing attitudes. A skills oriented approach may be appropriate

Figure 7.15   Examples of CRM executives development programmes

CRM Implementers Programme

Industry: Insurance

Objective: A senior executive programme of workshops to create a common understanding and vocabulary of CRM; to review findings of a CRM readiness audit and to determine key CRM actions to be implemented.

Scope: Top and senior management. A series of three two-day workshops involving a total of 50 executives.

CRM Promoters Programme

Industry: Postal services and logistics

Objective: A senior executive programme aimed at developing a full appreciation of the current and future role of CRM in a major postal administration. This executive group's role was proactively to promote CRM to its customers and internal staff.

Scope: One-day workshops for 150 top executives including business unit chief executives.

Customer Management Programme

Industry: Banking

Objective: A change management programme aimed at major improvement in external and internal customer service.

Scope: All employees in a major division of a North American bank. A series of one-day workshops for a target audience of 500 employees from board of directors to all managers, administrative and secretarial staff.

CRM Account Directors Programme

Industry: Telecommunications

Objective: A series of CRM workshops aimed at developing a common framework for CRM throughout the organization; sharing examples of customer successes and successful internal CRM applications; introduction and use of a new customer diagnostic tool.

Scope: A series of fifteen one-day workshops for account directors, senior sales staff and executives. Part of an integrated CRM initiative involving more specialized training, production of white papers, etc.

Customer and Strategy 'Focus' Programme

Industry: Telecommunications

Objective: A series of three-day workshops for top executives and one-day workshops for next level of management involving a detailed review of customer and business strategy.

Scope: A series of cascade programmes for 400 top managers. The first, 'Focus 100', aimed at 100 top executives reporting to divisional chief executives; The second, 'Focus 300', aimed at 300 managers reporting to these executives.

---

for introduction of a new call centre system. An approach emphasizing attitude change may be used to address issues such as improving customer service or building a customer-oriented culture. Where a CRM technology solution is adopted in the organization, the training should include sessions designed immediately to practice and apply the newly acquired knowledge.

Where implementation problems are being experienced they should be discussed frankly with employees, together with an explanation as to what is being done to address them. Lack of this awareness can cause CRM initiatives to falter or fail. For example, in a major sales force automation project in a large company the failure to communicate problems such as software synchronization and resulting resistance by the sales force to using the system, almost caused failure of the project.

In many instances a CRM employee training and executive development programme needs to be cascaded throughout the organization so that all levels of employees are informed and engaged. A large-scale CRM programme will typically have different component parts aimed at different levels within the organization. The case study on implementing CRM at Mercedes-Benz is a good example of an integrated CRM development programme that has a set of tailored developmental, experiential and executive development activities that cascade from the board of directors to all customer-facing employees.

Case 7.2 Mercedes-Benz: Implementing a CRM programme – Case study overview

Mercedes-Benz is one of the world's most successful premium car brands. In 2000 Daimler Chrysler UK (DCUK), distributors of the Mercedes-Benz marque in the UK, recognized they needed to revolutionize their dealer network to meet the new marketplace challenges. By 2004 they had re-organised their franchised network of 138 dealerships into 35 'market areas' (MAs) and introduced a new CRM programme. They developed a CRM programme to better integrate relationships between the new MAs, their customers and themselves.

The CRM project team recognised that the success of CMR would depend on a massive change in the mindset of people at every level within MAs and DCUK. A CRM training programme was devised with four individual modules, designed for various groups within the MAs and DCUK. This training was critical so employees understood their role in delivering CRM within the dealer network.

The initial results have been impressive. Pilot projects demonstrated improvements in both financial performance and customer satisfaction. Broadcasting these results to other MAs reinforced the business case for adopting CRM. Motivation for embracing the CRM concept has been achieved by showing the financial benefits to the MA.

The full case study is at the end of this chapter (see p. 391)

The CRM budget

Many CRM budgets are underfunded in terms of what is required for successful implementation. In this chapter we have examined four critical elements of a successful CRM programme that support the five key CRM processes examined in detail in the previous chapters – readiness assessment, change management, project management and employee engagement. Of these, the last three represent line items that may be seriously underfunded or totally neglected as line items in the budget. Only the readiness assessment represents an item that is generally modest in cost and which can be readily identified in terms of its cost.

If we examine the budget items that are typically associated with CRM when viewed from an IT perspective, the total is likely to be a very large amount. However, it may not be enough as costs associated with change management, project management and employee engagement may not have been taken into account. Lack of company experience about the real total costs of a major CRM initiative is the usual major reason for this.

In Chapter 6 we discussed the critical observation that most of the historical investment in CRM goes into data and technology, but these aspects represent only 25 per cent of the competency determinants for CRM success. It is the areas that involve people, organization, culture and change where the funding level may be neglected or not adequately provided for in the CRM budget. However, these areas are critical to the success of companies' CRM initiatives.

The IT department is frequently responsible for planning the CRM budget, as the most obvious and visible expenditure will be for the software licences, hardware, systems integration and consulting. However, as Gentle points out, the IT department is often less experienced with regard to CRM projects. As a result, they omit non-obvious costs in the budget and may make budgetary mistakes on both the hard and soft elements of CRM projects:

- seriously underestimating the number of data sources that need to be migrated over and the corresponding quality
- seriously underestimating how consulting costs can spiral out of control when there is no cross-functional agreement on business processes. This may result in a lot of additional work, as consultants and the business work to define things that the system integrator's methodology assumed were already known

- being unaware, or underestimating, certain business-related line items that are not present in other types of IT projects, which consequently fall through cracks. These include: user training on a far greater scale than what they are used to, resources for change management, to drive process change and ensure data quality; and resources for data operations, to manage the importing and exporting of data
- seeing the budget as a means to drive a project through to implementation only, after which time the project is assumed to be either self-sufficient or able to wait till the next budget cycle for subsequent funding.[35]

This provides a good argument for input from a cross-functional CRM team with representatives from marketing, human resources, procurement and finance, as well as IT, in the development of the CRM budget. A consideration of the full implications of change management, project management and employee engagement by these groups will help ensure a more accurate and balanced budget. Also, the benefit of a pilot will help identify budget costs more accurately.

For international projects, there is frequently the expectation that everything should be centrally funded. While this may be the case for software licences, consulting, implementation and IT costs, it is rarely so for in-country change management resources. With no central funding for the CRM project, countries may be unable or unwilling to provide the resources for this critical function.[36] As a result, the success of CRM initiatives in other countries may be under threat.

CRM budgets are difficult to determine and their preparation will benefit from early involvement with business-oriented internal finance staff and experienced CRM managers or consultants. Our experience in reviewing CRM budgets for large organizations points to several other problems in:

- significantly underestimating change management, training and employee engagement costs
- significantly overestimating licence costs and not understanding the discounts that could be achieved from vendors in a 'soft' market
- not understanding the items that could be capitalized as capital expenditure (capex) and the items that needed to be expensed as operating expenditure (opex)
- not understanding the internal financial approval system for large opex and capex expenditures by senior finance committees and the board

- using business case modelling that was superficial and based on point estimates (rather than looking at a range of estimates including pessimistic and optimistic scenarios)
- not properly considering the political issues associated with international business units and their agreement to sign up to potentially large local budget commitments
- key element of a CRM programme not being time and money 'boxed' to force the 80:20 rule of delivering quick wins
- not having some contingency funding sources available.

In summary, CRM budgets are frequently inaccurate, underfunded and poorly constructed. This is usually because of a lack of company experience in developing CRM budgets, a failure to consider non-IT related elements of CRM, not taking into account capex and opex considerations and not seeking independent expert advice in vendor assessment and licence negotiations. There is also a lack of published material on this topic.[37,38] Considerable efforts should therefore be directed at constructing thorough and well-argued budgets to implement the CRM project. Having progressed to the stage of developing a comprehensive and detailed plan for a strategic approach to a new CRM initiative, it would be highly disappointing to have the budget for it delayed or under-resourced because of reductions in budgeted items, or not approved.

Summary

The Strategic Framework for CRM developed in this book is a formal response to the confusion and frustration many companies are experiencing in their efforts to adopt CRM. Its purpose is to provide a comprehensive framework for the development of CRM strategy. The CRM Strategic Framework comprises five business processes: strategy formulation, value creation, information management, multi-channel integration and performance assessment. By breaking CRM down into its key cross-functional processes, it is possible to communicate the underlying principles of CRM strategy, demonstrate the interdependence of CRM activities and plan CRM activity on a strategic and well-integrated basis.

The framework positions CRM as a strategic set of activities that commence with a detailed review of an organization's strategy (the strategy development process) and conclude with an improvement in business results and increased shareholder value (the performance assessment process). It is based on the proposition that creation of value for the customer *and* for the company (the value creation process) is key to the success of relationships. CRM involves collecting and intelligently utilizing customer and other relevant data (the information management process) to build a superior customer experience at each touch-point where the customer and supplier interact (the multi-channel integration process).

The previous six chapters explain the development and logic of the strategic framework and review each of these five processes in detail. This chapter examines the topic of organizing for CRM implementation with reference to four elements that are critical to a successful CRM programme: CRM readiness assessment, CRM change management, CRM project management and employee engagement and addresses issues relating to the CRM budget. Implementing CRM represents a considerable challenge in most enterprises. Any successful CRM implementation should be preceded by the development of a clear, relevant and well-communicated CRM strategy. Organizations need to adopt a strategic definition of CRM that focuses on business issues rather than emphasizing IT issues.

This is especially important if the IT-based CRM failures of the past are to be avoided. The frequently quoted examples of CRM failure usually refer not to failure of CRM as a concept (unless very narrowly and inappropriately defined), but to the failure of a CRM technology project or CRM solution. In the late 1990s, when CRM was a novel approach, few people had experience of the new leading edge CRM solutions. As with pioneers in any area, managers who broke new ground with CRM solutions made mistakes. Today, as CRM develops, there is much less excuse for not taking a thorough, well planned approach to CRM strategy formulation and implementation and not learning from past experience.

We have now learnt a number of important lessons in implementing CRM. We have learned that short-term wins have more chance of securing enterprise-wide commitment than do drawn out CRM projects with over-ambitious goals. Moreover, a CRM strategy designed to deliver incremental returns provides the flexibility and scope for progressive improvement. We have also learned the benefits of benchmarking best practice in CRM. Among leading corporations around the world, benchmarking CRM has now become a more prevalent practice. Most of all, we have learned that an effectively implemented strategic approach to CRM is an important source of competitive advantage. In the past, many businesses have been able to prosper and still be poor at CRM. This has only been possible because other competitors in the industry have ranked even worse in terms of CRM effectiveness.

Successful CRM demands coordination and collaboration and, most of all, integration: integration of information and information systems to provide business intelligence; integration of channels to enable the development and delivery of a single unified view of the customer; integration of resources, functions and processes to ensure a productive, customer-oriented working environment and competitive organizational performance. CRM is admittedly a complex task, but by adopting a strategic approach, as outlined in this book, organizations should be able to realize the huge benefits of effective CRM and make progress on the journey towards achieving excellence in customer management.

Checklist for CRM leaders

CRM leaders need to review the following issues concerning *Organizing for CRM Implementation*

1. What is my organization's current level of CRM maturity?
   (a) pre-CRM planning
   (b) building a data repository
   (c) moderately developed CRM
   (d) well developed CRM
   (e) highly advanced CRM
2. Which of the following potential barriers to CRM success are likely to impact my organization?
   (a) lack of skills
   (b) inadequate investment
   (c) poor data quality and quantity
   (d) failure to understand the business benefits
   (e) functional boundaries
   (f) lack of leadership and top management involvement
   (g) inadequate measurement systems

3. What form of CRM audit is most appropriate for my organization?
   (a) an overview audit
   (b) a comprehensive audit (this audit follows in the Appendix)
4. Have we used the appropriate audit to identify key CRM priorities?
5. Have we considered the following CRM change management issues?
   (a) ensuring senior CRM sponsorship
   (b) establishing a CRM vision
   (c) developing a supportive culture for improved cross-functional working
6. Have we considered the following CRM project management issues?
   (a) developing a hierarchy of programmes, projects and activities
   (b) addressing trade-offs between time, quality and cost
   (c) building a project framework to deliver business benefits
   (d) determining if the adoption of a CRM technology solution is appropriate
   (e) having an informed understanding of the CRM marketplace and the role of different categories of vendor
   (f) if piloting of any planned CRM project is appropriate
   (g) developing a detailed plan for CRM project implementation, with an appropriate roadmap
7. Have we considered the key requirements for successful employee engagement?
   (a) selecting employees
   (b) developing employees
   (c) engaging and empowering employees
   (d) developing CRM training and development plans
8. Have we considered the full range of budget items and activities that need to be addressed in organizing for CRM and determined which represent capital expenditure (CAPEX) and operating expenditure (OPEX)?

Case 7.1   Nationwide fulfils its CRM vision with Unisys

The company

Nationwide is one of the UK's leading financial services providers, with more than 11 million members and over £108 billion in assets. Its origins lie in Northampton (1848) and within the cooperative movement in London (1883). Over a hundred mergers later – most notably with the merger between the Nationwide and the Anglia Building Societies in 1987 – it is now the UK's fourth largest mortgage lender and seventh largest retail banking, saving and lending organization by asset size. More significantly, it is the largest building society in the world.

Nationwide is a mutually owned organization; it belongs to its members and is run for their benefit. It is this mutual status that makes Nationwide different from traditional banks and it is committed to staying mutual. Its business strategy is very straightforward. It aims to offer a broad range of great value mortgages, savings and other financial products, while charging as little as possible for day-to-day services. Nationwide offers genuine long-term good value and gives members easy access to a wide range of products and services. Since 1996 it has delivered over £3.3 billion back to its members in better interest rates and lower charges.

Nationwide maintains an extensive branch network. This is complemented by services available by phone, post, Internet using a PC or MAC, WAP phones, PocketPC PDAs and TV Internet banking. Nationwide was the first to launch an Internet banking service in the UK, first to have an Internet banking service available through a TV and offered Europe's first PocketPC PDA mobile banking service.

The challenge

Nationwide has over 15 000 users, at call centres or in the branches throughout the UK, that require fast accurate access to customer data. They needed a CRM solution so it could access customer data and update this data – in real-time. The CRM system needed to handle over 2 million transactions per day, such as new data being recorded, updated, or employees interacting with the customer files. Any solution needed to be available and reliable to meet customers growing expectations in the competitive financial services space.

The project needed to include consultancy, project management, testing, development hardware, to provide a flagship CRM system for Nationwide, which would in turn provide outstanding customer service for Nationwide's members. Nationwide needed a strong partnership for such a large and highly complex CRM project, in a market where many other projects have failed.

Nationwide also recognized that, for successful CRM, project management needs to be supported by a change management programme that ensures employee engagement and commitment.

The solution

Unisys, the global IT services company in collaboration with AIT, was chosen to undertake this project because of its intimate understanding of Nationwide's business and in-depth experience in the financial services market. The project, involving on average a team of up to 60 people, began in June 2001 with the first 'go live' milestone in October 2002. A number of further releases have gone live since. Another major milestone was achieved when the system migrated to a Unisys ES7000 server for additional scalability.

AIT, a global provider of CRM software, delivered its product 'Portrait' in association with Unisys. The CRM system provides a single view of a member's profile and accounts so Nationwide employees can identify a customer's needs in a timely and accurate manner. The database also details previous conversations, which reduces time spent assisting the customer and ensures the customer feels more attention is being paid to their personal requirements.

The primary data source for the customer profiles is the Customer Information System (CIS), which Nationwide and Unisys had built previously. It contains details about all of Nationwide's 11 million customers, such as the product relationships held and all the contact address details. It is available 24 × 7 and is subject to an ongoing programme to maintain and improve the quality and completeness of the data, which are approaching complete accuracy. This is an invaluable asset without which Nationwide could not have contemplated building the CRM facility.

In organizing for this CRM initiative, attention was also placed on change management and employee engagement. A significant budget was set aside for training and change management so that Nationwide employees would be able to embrace its vision and the associated changes needed in process and behaviour. Nationwide ensured that the pace of change was driven by the organization and not the technology.

The results

This CRM project has been highly successful and has resulted in increased sales and profitability. There has been a wide range of benefits realized by using the CRM system. For example, Nationwide has reduced the number of mailings of leaflets it sends to members by one third, saving money and time. Statements and relevant customer leaflets can be issued together and this has enabled more targeted marketing. The building society is now 50 per cent more successful in encouraging members (via the direct mail) to use the Internet for their financial needs, be it banking, mortgage advice or insurance.

As Michael Humphreys, Programme Director for the CRM initiative at Nationwide, explains: 'This CRM project is aligned with Nationwide's values which include taking pride in what we do and in what we deliver to customers. Nationwide now has the highest level of customer satisfaction ever. The reasons why this CRM project has succeeded included clear communication at every level throughout the organization, coupled with a high level of executive sponsorship'.

Nationwide places great emphasis on collecting, analysing and acting on customer and employee feedback. On the customer side, Nationwide distributes 28 000 surveys every month. These are triggered by service interactions. With over 2 million transactions taking place each day across more than 600 branches and electronic channels, the response rate is nearly 28 per cent.[1] Their efforts have been recognized through a number of external industry awards. Nationwide won the Management Today/Unisys Service Excellence Award for the Financial Services sector in 2000 and, in 2002, won it again, as well as the Overall Winner Award. Nationwide was recognized for its strengths across all the dimensions assessed by the Award.

Nationwide is also an organization that puts employee engagement at the heart of the business. Nationwide recognizes that delivering member value begins with happy, knowledgeable and committed employees. This has lead to very low staff turnover and a waiting list of potential employees. The society also runs more than 20 incentive schemes, including employee of the month and year, and individual and team bonuses. These schemes distribute around £30 million per year to employees. It was recently ranked 18th in the *Sunday Times* 'Best Company to Work For' survey.

Nationwide has developed new and better ways to transform the way it interacts with its customers so that it delivers the right experience, but at the right cost. Employees can now easily gain visibility of members' profiles and their specific needs at a glance with their new CRM system, which means employees are more informed and their members have enhanced interactions with the society.

In the future, the CRM system and data will become more and more comprehensive. A more sophisticated data capture and analysis of customer profiles will enable the identification of significant events in the life cycle of the member, which will allow the building society to build models of customers' needs. Nationwide is also moving towards the 'seller-teller' model of the future, where customers can gain expert financial advice from whomever they speak to – whether in the branch or on the phone.

[1] Parts of this discussion draw on Clark, M. and Baker, S. *Business Success Through Service Excellence*, Oxford: Elsevier Butterworth-Heinemann, 2004.

Case 7.2 Mercedes-Benz: Implementing a CRM Programme

The Company

Mercedes-Benz is one of the world's most successful premium brands. Its technical perfection, innovative design features and numerous car legends have made the Mercedes star one the world's best known trademarks today.

The late 1990s and early 2000s saw major changes in the competitive structure of the European car market. After a long history of reigning over a sellers market, Mercedes-Benz experienced increased competition. Other premium brands such as BMW, Lexus and Jaguar were competing fiercely in the luxury car market where Mercedes was traditionally very strong. Also, many of these brands were expanding into new market segments. For example, the Mercedes 'A Class' focused on a new market segment that was more price sensitive than those in which the brand traditionally competed. Along with this increase in competition was a new threat – changes in legislation, known as 'Block Exemption'. These new EU laws changed the exclusivity of dealers to operate within the re-seller market, allowing freedom for companies to potentially sell or service any car that they might wish.

Historically, Mercedes-Benz was sold in the UK through a franchised network of some 138 dealerships. Each of these was autonomous, with the exception of three dealerships owned by the distributor DaimlerChrysler UK (DCUK). DaimlerChrysler had relatively little control over relationships between dealers and customers. Dealers managed their own relationships including customer research, data base management, acquisition and retention processes.

The Challenge

In the late 1990s, DCUK was faced with a challenge. Research suggested that some Mercedes-Benz customers were less than happy with the service they received. Although the technical quality of the product was highly regarded, customers complained that the service that they received was not of the same high standard. This translated into declining customer satisfaction and increased defection. DCUK recognised that the entire chain of relationships between manufacturer, dealers and customers needed a new approach.

Customers reported that there was an inconsistency between the communication that they received and the service that was delivered. Communication to the customer included both national product marketing along with some local marketing initiatives. Enquiries from the customer went directly to the dealerships and were handled through their internal processes. These were sometimes inadequate. So, for example, request for test drives may not have been followed-up by complacent salesmen, resulting in poor sales conversion rates. Research suggested that Mercedes-Benz customers received communication from DCUK and the dealerships that was not always coordinated. Such communication may not match customer needs at a particular point in time in their purchase cycle and may result in conflicting or duplicated messages.

A uniform problem across dealerships of most car marques in the UK was that, historically, each dealership operated its own database. The information in this database could be out of date, inaccurate and missing important information. One industry estimate was that only six per cent of prospects were captured in such databases. Critically, salespeople did not always appreciate that it was essential to record correct and complete customer information if effective contact was going to be sustained.

In the past, like most distributors, DCUK had focused primarily on the relationship with their dealer franchise network. In the future the company wanted to have a greater input into how the end customer relationship was managed. This entailed a new strategic approach to the distribution of cars.

The Solution

In 2000, DCUK decided to adopt a new distribution model for Mercedes-Benz passenger cars. They re-organized the market into thirty five new, larger geographical areas and invited a number of existing dealerships to enter into new retailer agreements. This entailed these dealerships taking over responsibility for the retail sales and service of Mercedes in specific geographic territories or 'market areas' (MAs). For most franchises, these new MAs included up to six dealer outlets and required a substantial additional investment in new premises and facilities. DCUK also decided to become much more heavily involved in retail operations through direct ownership of the MAs in London, Manchester and Birmingham. These three regions represented over one third of the retail passenger car sales volume in the UK. However, changes in the distribution was only the starting point for DCUK building improving relationships with customers.

Within DCUK, a project management team was established, drawn from managers in marketing and operations. The project management team set about identifying the key CRM processes and determining how each process would be implemented throughout the new retail structure. Every aspect of the customer relationship needed to be carefully examined, to ensure value was created at every opportunity: for the customer, the

MAs and DCUK. The first step was to benchmark Mercedes-Benz against other leading marques as well as best in class organizations. This research suggested that there were several areas where greater value could be delivered to the customer during both the sales process as well as during the ownership experience.

Under the new retail agreements entered into by the MAs, DCUK gained closer control of the valuable Mercedes-Benz brand, whilst providing greater support and guidance to the MAs on delivering the best experience to the customer. A new retail concept was devised, which required dealers to improve their showrooms and service areas. A new approach to the marketing structure within each MA was set out, which involved a centralized CRM and marketing team – one for each MA. Each team was given the responsibility of database management, customer support and regional marketing.

DCUK, working closely with one MA on a pilot programme, mapped out each of the critical customer processes. These included prospect management (enquiry through to sale); customer contact (communications throughout the period of customer ownership); and complaint management (acknowledging that complaints are an opportunity for improvement and also for forging deeper understanding with customers). Salespeople would continue to be the main contact with the customer during the sales process, but now they would have the backing of a dedicated CRM team to generate and qualify leads, ensure follow up during the sales process and maintain regular communication with customers during the customer ownership experience.

With the new, carefully set out CRM processes, every aspect of the customer relationship from prospect through ownership was set out along with a channel strategy for each stage. Instead of a salesman owning a customer, each relationship was carefully managed centrally through the new CRM marketing team set up within each MA. For example, the customer support team managed telephone enquiries and passed them to a salesperson. Follow-up was done by the customer support team, which ensured consistency of the customer contact and also accurate data gathering. Then, the customer support team continued building each customer relationship through a mix of mail, telephone, face to face and email – each contact carefully timed to fit with a typical ownership cycle.

Each communication channel was carefully integrated so that the customer received relevant messages by an appropriate channel at various critical points during the ownership cycle. So, for example, direct mail of a high quality magazine was sent to customers reinforcing the brand and improving the ownership experience. This was coupled with direct mail and follow up telephone calls for service bookings. The figure below outlines the process of integrating, the relationship between the customer, the retailer and DCUK.

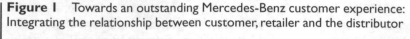

Figure I Towards an outstanding Mercedes-Benz customer experience: Integrating the relationship between customer, retailer and the distributor

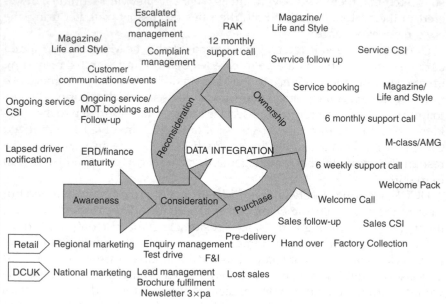

DCUK recognised that managing data was critical to the success of CRM at Mercedes-Benz. Central to the whole new approach was building a total picture of the customer. First, instead of multiple databases operated by each dealership and DCUK, a single database was set up. This was implemented across all MAs and DCUK. Using IT, every customer contact would now be recorded and acted upon using an organized approach. Second, the sales process was carefully set out to support data capture. Customer support and sales personnel were trained in how to accurately record important customer information, improving the quality of data. Salespeople were encouraged to obtain as much customer information as possible, whilst dedicated data capture agents were responsible for all data entry. Importantly, it was made clear to all staff and especially salespeople, the imperative of building a complete profile of a customer.

DCUK set targets for the MAs covering every aspect of the customer experience – including retail and after-sale. For example: prospect follow up target was increased to one hundred per cent; the number of prospects converted to test drive and subsequent sale was increased; and CSI (customer satisfaction index) on pre-delivery was improved.

At the outset of the CRM initiative, a business case was set out to win the support of dealers for CRM and to determine the benefits and returns that would be delivered to the customer, to each MA organization and to DCUK. It was critical that measures were put in place to prove that CRM delivered the anticipated results and justified the massive expenditure within the businesses. DCUK and the dealers agreed a range of measures and these were used in two ways. First, these monitored the success of all aspects of CRM including customer satisfaction, customer retention, sales performance, and profitability. Second, the measures would be used within the CRM margin, a critical portion of the reward structure for MAs ensuring that there was a total focus within the business on CRM processes.

One problem facing the CRM initiative was that the new dealer network included dealers at different stages along the road to CRM. Some MAs had undergone massive structural reorganization, including buying and selling of dealerships as well as many changes in staffing and roles. Other MAs had less experience with applying technology to understanding their customers. At the other end of the spectrum, some MAs had undergone little reorganization and were relatively sophisticated in their use of the customer data base to building customer relationships. An immediate task was to determine the state of readiness to adopt CRM within each MA, so that CRM processes could be implemented smoothly.

The CRM team recognized that processes alone would not deliver enhanced customer service; the success of CRM would depend on engaging the hearts and minds of both the leaders and employees throughout the distribution network. An examination of MAs pointed to the need for comprehensive training designed to educate employees at every level in CRM as well as to gain their commitment to it. The training programme was devised with four individual modules, designed for various groups within the MAs and DCUK.

CRM Best Practice Workshops: These workshops were designed specifically for the senior management teams within each MA, as well as Directors within DCUK with direct responsibility for the MAs. Each workshop aimed to build awareness of the benefits of CRM as well as educate how to implement successful CRM through case studies of best practice in CRM. The three day workshops entailed a mix of presentations and visits to companies where successful CRM was evident. The outcome would be a practical plan drawn up by each MA, that the senior management could use to help change the mindset within MAs and successfully implement the CRM strategy.

CRM Uncovered: This module was designed primarily for customer facing staff, both within the MAs and DCUK. The one day course aimed at building enthusiasm for CRM as well as creating understanding of the benefits of CRM for the MA, the customer and for themselves. The training programme was highly interactive so that participants could easily transfer the skills they learned to their work situation. Activities within the programme were designed to be fun and highly motivational, creating an excitement around CRM.

Systems and Processes: The CRM project team recognized that it was imperative that all staff within each MA as well as many within DCUK required comprehensive training on the new Kerridge CRM software. Training involved two steps. First was a basic training on the system, its benefits and capabilities. Second was specific training within the MA, to provide practical experience of operating the system.

Soft Skills: The fourth module of training involved specific soft skills training. An analysis of training needs would identify specific requirements and then groups of staff would attend appropriate courses. These skills related to building relationships with customers, including telephone skills, communication skills, customer complaint handling and customer service.

The Results

To win the hearts and minds of leaders and employees, it was critical that there would be some quick wins from CRM. These results could be broadcast through the dealer network to encourage others. One MA was chosen to test out processes and to confirm the benefits. Quickly the financial benefits to the MA were established as well as steady improvements in key measures of customer satisfaction and customer loyalty. Cross selling and up selling opportunities were used to advantage and the MA reported that relationships with customers were extended and deepened. The MA could justify the significant expenditure on CRM systems and processes by the impressive financial returns as well as improvements in critical customer measures.

For example, the additional volume of business generated by CRM activities was achieved in the following areas: services booked, extra work booked, sales leads, test drives, finance deals, and annual safety checks booked. Importantly, customers reported that they liked the new consistent approach in the way their relationship was handled.

Communicating these results to other MAs reinforced the business case for adopting CRM. Every opportunity was used by DCUK to share the experiences of dealers in implementing CRM. For example, the Best Practice training programme incorporated a session reporting progress on implementing CRM within the retail network. Individual dealers were invited to report their success with CRM as well as highlighting any problems and concerns.

Winning the CRM margin has become highly important for dealers and is ensuring that the CRM initiative stays at the forefront of people's minds. Staff are aware how their individual efforts contribute towards the success of CRM. For example, capturing complete and accurate information about customers is now a priority for all salespeople.

Despite widespread acceptance of the benefits of CRM, continual ongoing efforts need to be made to support attitudes to this new approach to the customer. Dealers have responded to this opportunity in different ways. For example, one dealer recognized the importance of nurturing a team spirit and so took all employees away to a five star hotel to say thank you for their efforts in CRM.

The initial results of the CRM implementation have been very encouraging. There is a great enthusiasm within both the MAs and DCUK for improving the customer experience and establishing closer relationships with customers. Already, two years into the programme, customers are reporting improvements in critical service quality measures. Importantly, there is now full recognition that the future of the Mercedes-Benz brand lies in a continuing journey of matching the highly acclaimed product with an outstanding customer experience.

Appendix

Comprehensive CRM audit – Part 1: The Strategy Development Process

Score each statement on a scale 0 to 5
Rating for our organization   (5 = applies fully; 0 = does not apply at all)
Importance to our organization (5 = very important; 0 = no importance)

	Rating for our organization	Importance to our organization

1.The Strategy Development Process

Business strategy
(including leadership and sponsorship)

1. Senior management in my organization have demonstrated strong leadership in introducing and supporting CRM initiatives
2. There is a strong and well-supported board level executive who is a committed sponsor of the organization's CRM initiatives
3. Senior management work together in a united manner and resolve cross-functional conflicts
4. My organization has a vision, mission, purpose, or statement of direction that clarifies its commitment to quality and customer focus and that is clearly understood by staff. My organization has a clear set of values that support the vision and these are shared by most of our staff
5. My organization develops and reviews strategic and annual business plans that incorporate an analysis of market trends, customer characteristics, industry evolution, the competitive landscape and technology impacts
6. My organization has a clear view on the value discipline on which it competes: customer intimacy, operational excellence or product leadership
7. The future impacts of electronic commerce and shifts in role of channels and intermediaries are considered on a regular basis by senior management
8. The overall strategic plan serves as the basis for the annual business plans of the organization and its functional departments

	Rating for our organization	*Importance to our organization*

9. Managers and supervisors understand their specific responsibilities in carrying out the actions in the strategic plan

10. My organization comprehensively reviews and improves its management systems at least annually to an international, industry-specific or internally developed standard

Customer strategy

11. My organization has a clear view on which customers it wishes to serve and which ones it does not wish to serve

12. My organization considers not only its immediate customers but also its customer's customer in making its marketing decisions

13. My organization has done a thorough and recent segmentation of its customer base

14. My organization has selected the appropriate level of segmentation of its customer base, i.e. macro-segments, micro-segments or one-to-one

15. We consider customer segments in terms of value preferences of benefits sought, in addition to more general customer characteristics

16. My organization customizes its product or service offer to different segments where appropriate

17. At least annually my organization seeks new customer opportunities beyond its existing offer to customers

18. Our business strategy and customer strategy are closely aligned

19. We have considered the appropriate degree of customer individualization given our position in the market and the nature of our competition

20. My organization has plans for future customer individualization and customer information requirements

Comprehensive CRM audit – Part 2: The Value Creation Process

Score each statement on a scale 0 to 5
Rating for our organization   (5 = applies fully; 0 = does not apply at all)
Importance to our organization (5 = very important; 0 = no importance)

	Rating for our organization	Importance to our organization

2. The Value Creation Process

The value the customer receives

1. The value the customer receives gets as much attention with senior management as the value they receive by way of revenue and profits
2. We have a clear view throughout the organization regarding the nature of the 'core' and 'augmented' offer made to our customers
3. At least annually we review whether further supplementary services should be added to our offer to increase the value received by our customers
4. Customer relationships and the impact of the brand are fully understood and managed within my organization
5. My organization recognizes the importance of maximizing the number of customer 'advocates' and taking action to minimize customer 'terrorists'
6. My organization has developed a written value proposition identifying the value offered to customers
7. Our value proposition is tailored to different customer segments
8. My organization assesses customer value and end-user customer satisfaction and quantifies overall satisfaction with specific attributes such as responsiveness, accuracy and timeliness
9. We set targets using comparative data drawn from high-performing organizations
10. We measure complaints and other key indicators of customer (end-user) dissatisfaction (e.g. returns, warranty claims), record these indicators by cause and act on them

	Rating for our organization	Importance to our organization

The value the organization receives

11. We utilize an appropriate level of segmentation based on satisfaction measures, sales, profits and other relevant historical information

12. My organization has identified how acquisition costs and annual profit earned per customer vary at the segment level. We have identified our most profitable customers and calculated our share of their wallet

13. We measure customer retention rates at the segment level and have quantified the profit impact of improvement in retention rates

14. The organization has identified profitable and non-profitable segments and adjusts the style and cost of campaigns, win-back strategies, customer service and support accordingly

15. We have identified the amounts we spend on both customer acquisition and customer retention at the aggregate and segment levels and have confirmed these are well-balanced

16. We have identified targets for customer retention improvement at the segment level and have developed plans to achieve them

17. The organization understands the value that each customer segment brings to the company in terms of their lifetime value

18. We have calculated the relative potential profit improvement from acquisition, cross-selling, upselling, retention and advocacy at the segment level and have plans to realize these profits

19. We use a comprehensive set of metrics to measure customer acquisition, retention, profitability and lifetime value at the segment level and these are reported to senior management at least quarterly

20. We regularly review competitive activity and quantify how this activity may impact on our customer value metrics; any significant changes are always communicated to senior management

Comprehensive CRM audit – Part 3:
The Multi-Channel Integration Process

Score each statement on a scale 0 to 5
Rating for our organization   (5 = applies fully; 0 = does not apply at all)
Importance to our organization (5 = very important; 0 = no importance)

	Rating for our organization	Importance to our organization
3. The Multi-Channel Integration Process: 'the customer contact zone'		
Channel options and strategies		
1. Our senior management have considered the future role of both existing and potential channel participants in our industry		
2. We have a clear view on the future impact of electronic channels in our industry		
3. Possible structural changes in our industry (disintermediation or reintermediation) have been fully considered		
4. We fully understand the advantages and disadvantages of the major channel categories (sales force, outlets, telephony, direct, e-commerce, mobile, etc.) when developing our channel strategies		
5. Our organization formally reviews the range of channel strategy options every year		
6. My organization understands the channels our customers wish to use at different stages of their relationship with us, e.g. pre-sales, sales and post-sales		
7. We know how customer channel preference varies at the segment level across different products or services sold by our company		
8. We utilize appropriate analytical tools such as market structure maps to identify the value and volume of goods and services passing through different channels for our company and for our competitors		
9. Changes in our customers' channel usage and preferences and general trends in channel usage are reviewed regularly		

	Rating for our organization	Importance to our organization

10. The organization has an agreed set of metrics for measuring channel performance

Customer experience and multi-channel integration

11. The organization has a strategy for integrated channel management
12. We monitor the customer experience within channel and across channels and compare our performance with that of our competitors
13. The organization has identified what constitutes an outstanding (or 'perfect') customer experience and strives to deliver it
14. The customer experiences consistency in 'look, touch and feel' across channels and this experience is in keeping with our brand image
15. The organization collects information on all relevant types of customer interactions (e.g. calls, faxes, mail, e-mail, web-based and EDI transactions) to ensure that customer requirements and targets are met
16. The economics of different channels are thoroughly understood
17. The organization is effective in adding new channels to complement existing channels
18. New channels are integrated with existing channels so that an individual is recognized as the customer regardless of the channels used
19. Customer-affecting applications, such as order handling, work across all our channels. Products purchased in one channel (e.g. the Internet) can be returned through other channels (e.g. a retail outlet)
20. We consider channel integration issues for our employees and partners as well as our customers

Comprehensive CRM audit – Part 4: The Information Management Process

Score each statement on a scale 0 to 5
Rating for our organization　(5 = applies fully; 0 = does not apply at all)
Importance to our organization (5 = very important; 0 = no importance)

	Rating for our organization	Importance to our organization

4. The Information Management Process

The data repository and CRM architecture

1. Where data on customers reside in different databases we know their location, accuracy and completeness
2. We have created a central data warehouse and have a single view of the customer. Information in the warehouse is accurate and complete
3. Our organization has an appropriate structure for its data repository (data warehouse, data marts, etc.) given our present and planned customer data requirements
4. Our data structure reflects our business and customer strategies in terms of segment granularity and personalization requirements
5. Our customer information links with the company's existing systems such as fulfilment, service and finance
6. We have an appropriate strategy for our IT systems including hardware and software. We have taken account of potential of developments such as web services, business process outsourcing and/or use of a business service provider and/or use of an application service provider
7. We effectively utilize general data mining tools for customer insight and task-specific analysis tools for market segmentation, customer profiling, profitability analysis, predictive modelling, etc.
8. We have identified and utilized appropriate front-office systems for CRM and considered integration issues with back-office systems
9. We realistically appraise and address significant systems integration, people, processes and training tasks associated with introduction of any new CRM system, e.g. sales force automation

	Rating for our organization	Importance to our organization

10. We fully investigate and budget for change management, project management and employee engagement issues associated with any proposed new CRM systems we plan to introduce

Information and customer knowledge management

1. My organization has introduced processes to provide relevant data and information for all appropriate staff
2. Our organization ensures the integrity of the data it collects in terms of relevancy, accuracy, currency and objectivity
3. We ensure security of all sensitive customer data (e.g. credit-card numbers and personal information)
4. We verify that all individuals who have access to sensitive and proprietary data understand the security requirements and protocols
5. My organization has implemented processes to prevent the unauthorized use or alteration of sensitive and proprietary data
6. We regularly consider opportunities to introduce new e-commerce applications to improve customer service or to reduce costs
7. There is an integrated plan agreed across all channels and functional departments for the collection and use of customer information
8. My customer information system allows information about individual customers to be recognized and used to produce summary information about the customer for use in customer applications and campaign management
9. My company uses customer analysis techniques to provide proactive customer information for cross-selling and upselling purposes
10. The company makes effective use of analytical techniques, such as predictive modelling, that use customer information to develop greater customer profitability and increased lifetime value

Comprehensive CRM Audit – Part 5:
The Performance Assessment Process

Score each statement on a scale 0 to 5
Rating for our organization   (5 = applies fully; 0 = does not apply at all)
Importance to our organization (5 = very important; 0 = no importance)

	Rating for our organization	Importance to our organization

5. The Performance Assessment Process

Shareholder results

1. Our top management recognize the importance of leadership in creating employee, customer and shareholder value

2. The key drivers of shareholder results – employee value, customer value, shareholder value and cost reduction – are fully understood

3. We place sufficient emphasis in our organization on employee value

4. We rank ourselves highly in terms of recruiting, selecting, developing and empowering our employees

5. We place sufficient emphasis in our organization on customer value

6. We rank ourselves highly in terms of delivering superior customer value opportunities in every attractive customer segment

7. We place sufficient emphasis in our organization on shareholder value

8. We rank ourselves highly in terms creating shareholder value compared with our major competitors

9. We take full advantage of all opportunities for cost reduction. Cost reduction strategies do not negatively impact customer satisfaction

10. We have developed, or are developing, a balanced scorecard or linkage model in our organization that addresses the relationship between employee satisfaction, customer satisfaction and business results

	Rating for our organization	*Importance to our organization*

Standards, metrics and key performance indicators

1. We have developed our own standards across all the areas of CRM that are important to us
2. We have adopted standards developed by others (e.g. CMAT or COPC standards) and used these to benchmark our performance against relevant external comparators
3. We have identified and put in place appropriate customer metrics
4. We have identified and put in place appropriate people and process metrics
5. We have identified and put in place appropriate strategic metrics
6. We have identified and put in place appropriate output and comparative metrics
7. A strategy map (or success map) has been developed that identifies the chain of 'cause and effect' logic that connects our company's strategy with the drivers that lead to commercial success
8. Our organization has identified the most important KPIs and these are reported to senior management on a regular basis
9. Frameworks such as the balanced scorecard are utilized to ensure there is a focus on all relevant areas of performance, not just financial ones
10. A CRM performance monitoring process is in place and attention has been given to making sure KPIs are communicated in a visually engaging manner to management and other relevant employees

References and notes

Chapter 1

1. Kotler, P. (1992). It's time for total marketing. *Business Week Advance Executive Brief*, 2.
2. Payne, A.F.T. (ed.) (1995). *Advances in Relationship Marketing*. London: Kogan Page.
3. Christopher, M.G., Payne, A.F.T. and Ballantyne, D.F. (2002). *Relationship Marketing: Creating Stakeholder Value*. Oxford: Butterworth-Heinemann.
4. Peppers, D. and Rogers, M. (1993). *The One-to-One Future; Building Relationships One Customer at a Time*. New York: Currency Doubleday.
5. Smith, K. (2001). Getting payback from CRM. Webcast on *CRMGuru.com*, November.
6. Stone, M. and Woodcock, N. (2001). Defining CRM and assessing its quality. In Foss, B. and Stone, M. (eds), *Successful Customer Relationship Marketing*. London: Kogan Page, pp. 3–20.
7. Khanna, Sunil (2001). Measuring the CRM ROI: show them benefits. Available at crm-forum.com. Accessed November '02.
8. Parvatiyar, A. and Sheth, J. (2001). Conceptual framework of customer relationship management. In Sheth, J., Parvatiyar, A. and Shainesh, G. (eds), *Customer Relationship Management – Emerging Concepts, Tools and Applications*. New Delhi: Tata McGraw-Hill, pp. 3–25.
9. Buttle, F.A. (2000). The CRM value chain. *Marketing Business*, February, pp. 52–55.
10. Gosney, J. and Boehm, T. (2000). *Customer Relationship Management Essentials*. Roseville, CA: Prima Publishing.

11. Peppers, D., Rogers, M. and Dorf, B. (1999). *The One to One Fieldbook*. New York: Currency Doubleday.
12. Hobby, J. (1999). Looking after the one who matters. *Accountancy Age*, 28 October, pp. 28–30.
13. Couldwell, C. (1999). Loyalty bonuses. *Marketing Week*, Feb 18.
14. Glazer, R. (1997). Strategy and structure in information-intensive markets: the relationship between marketing and IT. *Journal of Market Focused Management*, pp. 65–81.
15. Kutner, S. and Cripps, J. (1997). Managing the customer portfolio of healthcare enterprises. *The Healthcare Forum Journal* 4(5), pp. 52–54.
16. Payne, A.F.T. and Frow, P. (2005). A strategic framework for customer relationship management. *Journal of Marketing*, October.
17. ACNielsen MEAL. Based on qualitative research of 300 professionals in the CRM field between September 1999 and February 2000.
18. Datamonitor (2000). Market Expert Presentation.
19. Ryals, L. and Payne, A.F.T. (2001). Information empowered relationship marketing: leveraging customer information in financial services. *Journal of Strategic Marketing*, **9**, pp. 1–25.
20. Note that the term relationship marketing, while it is a familiar term among the marketing fraternity, may not the best descriptor for a general management audience regarding the management of relationships with all these stakeholders.
21. Sheth, J.N. and Parvatiyar, A. (2000). *The Handbook of Relationship Marketing*. Thousand Oaks, CA: Sage, p. 7.
22. Swift, R.S. (2001). *Accelerating Customer Relationships: Using CRM and Relationship Technologies*. Upper Saddle River, NJ: Prentice Hall.
23. Greenberg, P. (2001). *CRM at the Speed of Light*. Berkeley, CA: Osborne/McGraw-Hill.
24. Radcliffe, J. and Kirkby, J. (2002). CRM Vendors and Service Providers. Gartner Symposium ITXPO, Florence, April, 2002.
25. Payne and Frow, *op cit*.
26. Payne and Frow, *op cit*.

Chapter 2

1. Normann, R. and Ramirez, R. (1993). From value chain to value constellation: designing interactive strategy. *Harvard Business Review*, July–August, pp. 65–77.

2. Davidson H. (2002). *The Committed Enterprise*. Oxford: Butterworth-Heinemann. The following example and discussion on vision and values is based on his work.
3. *op cit.*
4. *op cit.*
5. *op cit.*
6. *op cit.*
7. Prahlad, C.K. (1999). Changes in the competitive battlefield. *Financial Times – Mastering Strategy*, Part 2, 4 October, pp. 2–4.
8. McDonald Wood, I. (2000). *The Bucks Start Here: How Great Digital Companies Create Lasting Value*. Oxford: Capstone.
9. Porter, M. (2002). Strategy and the Internet. *Harvard Business Review*, March, pp. 63–78.
10. Porter, M.E. (1980). *Competitive Strategy*. New York: Free Press.
11. Slater, S.F. and Olson, E.M. (2002). A fresh look at industry and market analysis. *Business Horizons*, January–February, pp. 15–22.
12. Christensen, C. and Overdorf, M. (2000). Meeting the challenge of disruptive change. *Harvard Business Review*, March–April, pp. 67–76.
13. Brandenburger, A.M. and Nalebuff, B.J. (1997). *Co-opetition: A Revolution Mindset That Combines Competition and Game Theory Strategy That's Changing the Game of Business*. New York: Doubleday.
14. Porter, M.E. (1985). *Competitive Advantage*. New York: Free Press.
15. Treacy, M. and Wiersema, F. (1995). *The Discipline of Market Leaders*. London: HarperCollins.
16. Abell, D.F. (1980). *Defining the Business*. Englewood Cliffs, NJ: Prentice Hall.
17. Rubin, M. (1997). Creating customer-oriented companies. *Prism*, Arthur D. Little, fourth quarter, pp. 5–28.
18. Peppers, D. and Rogers, M. (1993). *The One-to-One Future; Building Relationships One Customer at a Time*. New York: Currency Doubleday.
19. Godin, S. (1999). *Permission Marketing: Turning Strangers Into Friends, and Friends into Customers*. New York: Simon & Schuster.
20. Krishnamurthy, S. (2001). A comprehensive analysis of permission marketing. *Journal of Computer-Mediated Communication*, 6(2), January.
21. *op cit.*
22. Pine, B.J. (1992). *Mass Customization: The New Frontier in Business Competition*. Boston, MA: Harvard Business Press.

23. Pine, B.J., Peppers, D. and Rogers, M. (1995). Do you want to keep your customers forever? *Harvard Business Review*, March–April, pp. 103–114.
24. McDonald, M. and Dunbar, I. (1998). *Market Segmentation*. MacMillan, 2nd edn.
25. Payne, A.F.T. (2004). Customer Relationship Management: Choosing the Appropriate Strategy and Technology to Win and Retain Customers, draft working paper, Cranfield School of Management. The following discussion is based on this paper.

Chapter 3

1. This chapter draws on: Payne, A.F.T. and Frow, P. (2004). The Value Creation Process in Customer Relationship Management, draft working paper, Cranfield School of Management.
2. Levitt, T. (1983). *The Marketing Imagination*. New York: The Free Press, Chapter 4.
3. *op cit.*
4. Collins, B. (1995). Marketing for engineers. In Sampson, D. (ed.), *Management for Engineers*, Melbourne: Longman Cheshire.
5. Lovelock, C. (1995). Competing on service: technology and teamwork in supplementary services. *Planning Review*, July/August, pp. 32–39.
6. Davidow, H. (1986). *Marketing High Technology*. New York: The Free Press, p. 172.
7. Wayland, R.E. and Cole, P.M. (1997). *Customer Connections: New Strategies for Growth*. Boston: Harvard Business School Press.
8. Jones, T. and Sasser, W.E. (1995). Why satisfied customers defect. *Harvard Business Review*, November/December, pp. 88–99.
9. *op cit.*
10. Aaker, D.A. (1991). *Managing Brand Equity: Capitaltizing on the Value of a Brand Name*. New York: The Free Press.
11. Keller, K.L. (2002). *Strategic Brand Management: Building, Measuring, and Managing Brand Equity*, 2nd edn. New York: Prentice Hall, p. 9.
12. Gummesson, E. (1999). *Total Relationship Marketing*. Oxford: Butterworth-Heinemann, p. 92.
13. Lindstrom, M. and Andersen, T. (1999). *Brand Building on the Internet*. London: Kogan Page.

14. *op cit.*
15. Mazur, L. (2003). Brands are not doing justice to the web. *Marketing*, 23 October, p. 13.
16. Lindstrom and Andersen, *op cit.*
17. Bower, M. and Garda, R.A. (1985). The role of marketing in management. *McKinsey Quarterly*, Autumn, pp. 34–46.
18. Bower, M. and Garda, R.A. (1998). The role of marketing in management. In Buell, V.P. (ed.), *Handbook of Modern Marketing*, 2nd edn, New York: McGraw-Hill, pp. 1–3, 1–10.
19. Lanning, M. and Michaels, E. (1988). A business is a value delivery system. McKinsey Staff Paper.
20. Lanning, M. and Phillips, L. (1990). How market-focused are you? *Marketing*, October, pp. 7–11.
21. Lanning, M. and Phillips, L. (1991). Building market-focused organizations. Gemini Consulting White Paper.
22. *op cit.*
23. Kambil, A., Ginsberg, A. and Bloch, M. (1996). Re-inventing value propositions. NYU Centre for Research on Information Systems Working Paper IS-96-21, New York University.
24. *op cit.*
25. For example see: McDonald, M., *Marketing Plans: How to prepare them, how to use them*, 5th edn. Butterworth-Heinemann, 2002, pp. 203–217.
26. Lanning and Michaels, 1988, *op cit.*
27. For example, see: Aaker, D.A., Kumar, V. and Day, G.S. (1998). *Marketing Research*, 6th edn. New York: John Wiley & Sons.
28. *op cit.*
29. This section draws on: Christopher, M. (1997). *Marketing Logistics*. Oxford: Butterworth-Heinemann.
30. *op cit.*
31. Peppers, D. and Rogers, M. (1997). *Enterprise One-to-One*. London: Piatkus, pp. 102–105.
32. The discussion of this case is based on: Payne, A.F.T. and Frow, P. (1999). Developing a segmented service strategy: improving measurement in relationship marketing. *Journal of Marketing Management*, **15**, pp. 797–818; and Payne, A.F.T. and Frow, P. (1997). Relationship marketing: key issues for the utilities sector. *Journal of Marketing Management*, **13**, pp. 463–497.
33. Reichheld, F.F. and Sasser, W.E. Jr (1990). Zero defections: quality comes to services. *Harvard Business Review*, September–October, pp. 105–111.

34. *op cit.*
35. *op cit.*
36. For discussion see: Christopher, M.G., Payne, A.F.T. and Ballantyne, D. (2002). *Relationship Marketing: Creating Stakeholder Value*. Oxford: Butterworth-Heinemann, pp. 56–57.
37. Millennium Group (1998). *Creating Value with Technology: Consumer Lifestyles, Loyalty and Lifetime Value*, November, p. 94.
38. KPMG (1997). *The Hidden Advantage: A Research Report into Data Warehousing*. London: KPMG.
39. Storbacka, K. and Lehtinen, J.R. (2001). *Customer Relationship Management*. Singapore: McGraw-Hill.
40. Lowrie, R. (1997). Lifetime value: delivery in a financial services environment. *Journal of Financial Services Marketing*, **2**(3).
41. Peppers, D. and Rogers, M. (1993). *The One-to-One Future*. London: Piatkus, pp. 41–42.
42. Millennium Group (1998). *Creating Value with Technology: Consumer Lifestyles, Loyalty and Lifetime Value*, November, p. 114.
43. Blattberg, R.C., Getz, G. and Thomas, J.S. (2001). *Customer Equity*. Boston: Harvard Business School Press, Chapter 2.
44. Page, M., Pitt, L., Berthon, P. and Money, A. (1996). Analysing customer defections and their effects on corporate performance: the case of Indco. *Journal of Marketing Management*, **12**, pp. 617–627.
45. Payne, A.F.T., ACURA: A Framework for Value Creation, draft working paper, Cranfield School of Management, 2004. This section is based on this paper.

Chapter 4

1. Kotler, P. (1997). *Marketing Management: Analysing, Planning, Implementation and Control*. Prentice Hall, 1997, p. 45.
2. Johnson, B.A. (2000). Fault lines in CRM: new E-commerce business models and channel integration issues. In *Defying the Limits*, Andersen Consulting.
3. McDonald, M. and Dunbar, I. (1995). *Market Segmentation: How to do it, how to profit from it*. London: Macmillan Business.
4. McDonald, M. and Dunbar, I. (1998). *Market Segmentation: How to do it, how to profit from it*, 2nd edn. London: Macmillan Business.

5. This table, and sections of this chapter draw on: Payne, A.F.T. and Frow, P. (2004). *The Multi-channel Integration Process in CRM*, draft working paper, Cranfield School of Management.
6. Durlacher Research Limited (1999). *Mobile Commerce Report*. London.
7. CRM Group Limited (2001). *Mobile Relevance – Explore the Value of Wireless*. Helsinki.
8. Rosenbloom, B. (1999). *Marketing Channels: A Management View*, 6th edn. Orlando, FL: The Dryden Press.
9. McKinsey & Co. and Salomon Smith Barney Study (2002). Summary reported in press release on McKinsey website: www.mckinsey.com.
10. Christopher, M., Payne, A. and Ballantyne, D. (2002). *Relationship Marketing: Creating Stakeholder Value*. Oxford: Butterworth-Heinemann.
11. Storbacka, K. (2001). Customer relationships as assets: evaluating the impact of crm on your organisation's profitability and shareholder value. In *Profitable Customer Relationship Management Strategies*, ICBI Management Report, pp. 23–32.
12. Vandermerwe, S. (1996). *The Eleventh Commandment*. Chichester: John Wiley.
13. Jones, T. and Sasser, W.E. (1995). Why satisfied customers defect. *Harvard Business Review*, November/December, pp. 88–99.
14. Gummesson, E. (2002). Relationship marketing in the new economy. *Journal of Relationship Marketing*, **1**(1), pp. 37–57.
15. Wilson, H. and McDonald, M.(2001). Serving customers through multiple channels. In Rock, S. (ed.), *Unlocking Customer Value*. London: CBI Business Guide/Caspian Publishing, pp. 19–25.
16. *op cit.*
17. *op cit.*
18. Nash, T. (ed.) (2001). *Relationship Management*. London: Director's Publication Ltd.
19. McKinsey & Co. and Salomon Smith & Barney (2000). Amid E-tail Shakeout, New Study Highlights Viable E-tail Business Model, August 22, www.atmckinsey.com.
20. Gilmour, P. (2000). *The Experience Economy*. New York: The Free Press.
21. Storbacka, K. (2001). *RED – Relationship Experience Design*. Helsinki: CRM Group Ltd.
22. www.marketbridge.com
23. *op cit.*

Chapter 5

1. Peppers, D. and Rogers, M. (1993). *The One-to-One Future; Building Relationships One Customer at a Time.* New York: Currency Doubleday.
2. www.silicon.com/software/os/0,39024651,11002633,00.htm
3. Swift, R.S. (2001). *Accelerating Customer Relationships: Using CRM and Relationship Technologies.* Upper Saddler River, NJ: Prentice Hall.
4. Agosta, L. (1999). *The Essential Guide to Data Warehousing.* Englewood Cliffs, NJ: Prentice Hall.
5. Inmon, W.H., Welch, J.D. and Glassey, K.L. (1997). *Managing the Data Warehouse.* New York: John Wiley & Sons, Inc.
6. Kelly, S. (1997). *Data Warehousing the Route to Mass Customization.* Chichester: John Wiley & Sons.
7. Groth, R. (2000). *Data Mining: Building Competitive Advantage.* Englewood Cliffs, NJ: Prentice Hall.
8. Berry, M.J.A. and Linoff, G. (1997). *Data Mining Techniques, for Marketing, Sales, and Customer Support.* New York: John Wiley & Sons, Inc.
9. For a more detailed discussion see: McDonald, M. and Dunbar, I. (1998). *Market Segmentation*, 2nd edn. London: MacMillan; or Myers, J.H. (1996). *Segmentation and Positioning for Strategic Marketing Decisions.* New York: American Marketing Association.
10. *Information Week*, 29 February, 2000.
11. *Information Week*, 17 April, 2000.
12. This description is from: Appel, H. Chief Technology Officer and Sun Vision Council Member, Sun Microsystems.
13. Seybold, P.B. (2002). *An Executive's Guide to Web Services*, Patricia Seybold Group, May.
14. Dyche, J. (2002). *The CRM Handbook – A Business Guide To Customer Relationship Management.* Upper Saddle River, NJ: Addison-Wesley. This and the following reference provide a more detailed discussion and checklists.
15. Gentle, M. (2002). *The CRM Project Management Handbook.* London: Kogan Page.
16. See: Findlay, G. et al. (2002). Data protection. In Foss, B. and Stone, M. (eds), *CRM in Financial Services – A Practical Guide to Making Customer Relationship Management Work.* London: Kogan Page Limited.
17. *op cit.*

Chapter 6

1. Heskett, J.L., Sasser, W.E. Jr and Schlesinger, L.A. (1997). *The Service Profit Chain*. New York: The Free Press.
2. Reichheld, F.F. (1996). *The Loyalty Effect*. Boston, MA: Harvard Business School Press.
3. Bierbusse, P. and Siesfeld, T. (1997). Measures that matter. *Journal of Strategic Performance Management*, **1**(2), pp. 6–11.
4. McKean, J. (1999). *Information Masters – Secrets of the Customer Race*. New York: John Wiley.
5. Cornelius, I. and Davies, M. (1997). *Shareholder Value*. London: FT Financial Publishing.
6. *op cit.*
7. Myers, R. (1996). Metric wars, *CFO*, **12**(10), October, pp. 44–50.
8. McKean, *op cit.*, p. 31.
9. See: www.qci.co.uk
10. See: www.copc.com
11. Cutler, M. and Sterne, J. (2000). *E-Metrics: Business Metrics for the New Economy*. NetGenesis and Target Marketing.
12. Ambler T. (2002). *Marketing*, April 2002, p. 25.
13. Ambler, T. (2000). *Marketing and the Bottom Line*. London: Financial Times Prentice Hall.
14. *op cit.*
15. Kaplan, R.S. and Norton, D.P. (1996). *The Balanced Scorecard: Translating Strategy Into Action*. Boston: Harvard Business School Press.
16. Heskett, et al., *op cit.*
17. *op cit.*
18. See: www.cfigroup.com
19. Kaplan, R.S. and Norton, D.P. (2001). *The Strategy-Focused Organisation*. Boston: Harvard Business School Press, pp. 69–106.
20. Neely, A., Adams, C. and Kennerley, M. (2002). *The Performance Prism: The Scorecard for Stakeholder Relationship Management*. London: Financial Times Prentice Hall.
21. Rucci, A.J., Kirn, S.P. and Quinn, R.T. (1998). The employee-customer-profit chain at Sears. *Harvard Business Review*, January/February, pp. 83–97.
22. Neely, A. (2002). Measuring Business Performance, Cranfield University, April.
23. Neely et al., *op cit.*

24. Woodcock, N. (2000). Does how customers are managed impact on business performance? *Interactive Marketing*, **1**(4), pp. 375–389.
25. Ryals, L.J., Knox, S.D. and Maklan, S. (2000). *Customer Relationship Management: The Business Case for CRM*. London: Financial Times Prentice Hall: London, Management Research Report series.

Chapter 7

1. Payne, A.F.T. and Frow, P. (2005). Customer Relationship Management: from strategy to implementation, draft working paper, Cranfield School of Management. Sections of this chapter are drawn from this paper.
2. Ryals, L. and Payne, A.F.T. (2001). Information empowered relationship marketing: leveraging customer information in financial services. *Journal of Strategic Marketing*, **9**, pp. 1–25.
3. a.payne@cranfield.ac.uk
4. www.qci.co.uk
5. Waterman, R.H., Peters, T.J. and Phillips, J.R. (1980). Structure is not organisation. *Business Horizons*, June, pp. 14–16.
6. Child, P., Dennis, R.S., Gokey, T.C., McGuire, T., Sherman, M. and Singer, M. (1995). Can marketing regain the personal touch? *McKinsey Quarterly*, No. 3, pp. 112–125.
7. Rigby, D.K., Reichheld, F.F. and Schefter, P. (2002). Avoid the four perils of CRM. *Harvard Business Review*, February.
8. Davidson H. (2002). *The Committed Enterprise*. Oxford: Butterworth-Heinemann.
9. Siragher, N. (2001). *Carving Jelly: A Managers Reference to Implementing CRM*. High Wycombe, Bucks: Chiltern Publishing International Ltd.
10. Clark, M., McDonald, M. and Smith, B. (2002). *Achieving Excellence in Customer Relationship Management*, CRM Research Forum, Cranfield School of Management.
11. Johnson, G. (1992). Managing strategic change – strategy, culture and action. *Long Range Planning*, **25**(1), pp. 28–36.
12. Shipley, D. (1994). Achieving cross-functional co-ordination for marketing implementation. *Management Decision*, **32**(8), pp. 17–20.
13. Levene, R.J. (2001). *Project Management: Context and Processes*, Cranfield School of Management, September. For an excellent review of project management principles, see this and see fol-

lowing work. This section draws on Dr. Levene's work with his permission.

14. Levene, R.J. (1996). Project management. In *International Encyclopedia of Business & Management*. London: Thompson Learning, pp. 4162–4181.

15. Wilson, H., Daniel, E., McDonald, M., Ward, J. and Sutherland, F. (2000). *Profiting from eCRM*. London: Financial Times Prentice Hall.

16. McDonald, M. and Wilson H. (2002). *The New Marketing*. Oxford: Butterworth-Heinemann.

17. Ward, J.M. and Murray, P. (2000). *Benefits Management Best Practice Guidelines*. Bedford: Cranfield University School of Management.

18. *op cit.*

19. Henneberg, S.C.M. (2003). An Exploratory Analysis of CRM Implementation Models, 11th International Colloquium in Relationship Marketing, University of Gloucestershire, September, pp. 1–20.

20. *op cit.*

21. *op cit.*

22. Ebner, M., Hu, A., Levitt, D. and McCory, J. (2002). How to rescue CRM. *McKinsey Quarterly* (Special Edition: Technology), pp. 49–57.

23. Gentle, M. (2002). *The CRM Project Management Handbook*. London: Kogan Page.

24. Estimate by Ed Thompson, Vice President and Research Director, Gartner.

25. Greenberg, P. (2001). *CRM at the Speed of Light*. Berkely, CA: Osborne/McGraw-Hill.

26. Gentle, *op cit.*

27. Dempsey, J., Dvorak, R., Holen, E., Mark, D. and Meehan W. (1997). Escaping the IT abyss. *The McKinsey Quarterly*, No. 4, pp. 80–91.

28. Gentle, *op cit.*

29. Siragher, *op cit.*

30. Dyche, J. (2002). *The CRM Handbook*. Upper Saddle River, NJ: Addison-Wesley.

31. Ebner, et al., *op cit.*

32. Sweetman, K.J. (2001). Employee loyalty around the globe. *MIT Sloan Management Review*, Winter, p. 16. This is based on: Walker Information Global Network *Commitment in the Workplace: The 2000 Global Employee Relationship Benchmark Report, 2000*.

33. McKean, J., (2002). *Customers Are People: the Human Touch*. New York: John Wiley.
34. Clark, M. (1999). Managing Recruitment and Internal Markets: a Relationship Marketing Perspective, draft working paper, Cranfield School of Management.
35. Gentle, *op cit*.
36. *op cit*.
37. Siragher, *op cit*., Chapter 4.
38. Gentle, *op cit*., Chapter 7.

Note

The author wishes to acknowledge and thank Dr Andrew Dickson of BT and Jon Chidley, previously with BT and now with Opta Ltd, for their help with Figures 7.2 and 7.3 and for their input into the detailed audit.

CRM reading list: a comprehensive bibliography

Introduction

Customer relationship management (CRM) involves utilizing information technology (IT) to implement relationship marketing strategies. Relationship marketing is concerned with the management and improvement of organizations' relationships with their customers and other key stakeholders. Put succinctly CRM is 'information-enabled relationship marketing'. CRM should be viewed from a strategic perspective. CRM seeks to provide a strategic bridge between information technology and marketing strategies aimed at building long-term relationships with customers and enhanced profitability for the organization.

This list of books on CRM and related aspects follows the structure outlined in the *Handbook of CRM*. It is based on the CRM Strategy Framework outlined in this book. The framework presents CRM as a set of five strategic processes:

- Strategic development process
- Value creation process
- Multi-channel integration process
- Information management process
- Performance assessment process.

The list of books below includes ones that have been written specifically on CRM and a number that relate specifically to the five key processes. As many of these books address more than one of the categories above, they are listed once in what is considered their most relevant category.

This reading list is divided into the following categories:

(a) General books on CRM and relationship marketing:
1. customer relationship management
2. relationship marketing
3. general, including e-commerce
(b) CRM process 1: the strategy development process
1. business strategy
2. customer strategy
3. market segmentation and mass customization
(c) CRM process 2: the value creation process
1. the value customers and organizations receive
2. customer lifetime value
(d) CRM process 3: the multi-channel integration process
1. channel issues
2. direct marketing and permission marketing
3. key account management
4. integrated marketing and brand communication
5. customer experience management
(e) CRM process 4: the information management process
1. information management
2. data warehousing
3. data mining
(f) CRM process 5: the performance assessment process
1. shareholder value
2. the balanced scorecard
3. performance and satisfaction measurement.

(a) General books on CRM and relationship marketing

1. Customer relationship management

Anton, J. (1996). *Customer Relationship Management – Making Hard Decisions with Soft Numbers*. Prentice Hall.

Barnes, J. (2000). *Secrets of Customer Relationship Management.* McGraw-Hill.

Brown, S.A. (2000). *Customer Relationship Management.* John Wiley.

Buttle, F. (2004). *Customer Relationship Management: Concepts and Tools.* Elsevier.

Dyche, J. (2002). The CRM Handbook – *A Business Guide To Customer Relationship Management.* Addison-Wesley.

Foss, B. and Stone, M. (2001). *Successful Customer Relationship Marketing.* Kogan Page.

Foss, B. and Stone, M. (2002). *CRM in Financial Services – A Practical Guide to Making Customer Relationship Management Work.* Kogan Page.

Gamble, P.R., Stone, M. and Woodcock, N. (1999). *Up Close and Personal: Customer Relationship Marketing @ Work.* Kogan Page.

Gentle, M. (2002). *The CRM Project Management Handbook, Building Realistic Expectations and Managing Risk.* Kogan Page.

Gilmore, J. and Pine, B.J. (2000). *Markets of One.* Harvard Business Review Book.

Gosney, J. and Boehm, T. (2000). *Customer Relationship Management Essentials.* Prima Publishing.

Greenberg, P. (2001). *CRM at the Speed of Light.* Osborne/McGraw-Hill.

Hawkes, P. and Abram, J. (2003). *The Seven Myths of Customer Management: How to be Customer-Driven without being Customer Led.* John Wiley.

Institute of Directors, Oracle Corporation UK Ltd and Director Publications Ltd (1999). *Customer Relationship Management – How Directors Can Build Business Through Improved Customer Relations.* Kogan Page.

Jacobsen, P.O. (ed.) (1999). *The CRM Handbook From Group to Multiindividual.* PricewaterhouseCoopers.

Knox, S., Maklan S., Payne, A., Peppard J. and Ryals, L. (2003). *Customer Relationship Management Perspectives from the Marketplace.* Butterworth-Heinemann.

Lee, D. (2000). *The Customer Relationship Management Survival Guide.* HYM Press.

Little, E. and Marandi, E. (2003). *Relationship Marketing Management.* Thomson.

Newell, F. (2000). *Loyalty.com: Customer Relationship Management in the New Era of Internet Marketing.* McGraw-Hill.

Newell, F. (2003). *Why CRM Doesn't Work.* Kogan Page.

Nykamp, M. (2001). *The Customer Differential: The Complete Guide to Implementing Customer Relationship Management*. American Management Association.

Peppers, D., Rogers, M. and Dorf, B. (1999). *One to One Fieldbook*. Doubleday.

Peppers, D. and Rogers, M. (1997). *Enterprise One-to-One*. Bantam Doubleday Dell Publishing Group, Inc.

Peppers, D. and Rogers, M. (1993). *The One-to-One Future; Building Relationships One Customer at a Time*. Currency Doubleday.

Peppers, D. and Rogers, M. (2001). *One to One B2B: Customer Development Strategies for the Business-to-Business World*. Doubleday.

Roberts-Phelps, G. (2001). *Customer Relationsip Management*. Hawksmere.

Sheth, J., Parvatiyar, A. and Shainesh, G. (2001). *Customer Relationship Management – Emerging Concepts, Tools and Applications*. McGraw-Hill.

Siragher, N. (2001). *Carving Jelly: A Manager's Reference to Implementing CRM*. Chiltern Publishing International Ltd.

Storbacka, K. and Lehtinen, J. (2001). *Customer Relationship Management*. McGraw-Hill.

Swift, R.S. (2001). *Accelerating Customer Relationships: Using CRM and Relationship Technologies*. Prentice Hall.

Zikmund W.G., Mcleod, R. Jr and Gilbert, F.W. (2003). *Customer Relationship Management*. Wiley.

2. Relationship marketing

Christopher, M., Payne, A. and Ballantyne, D. (2002). *Relationship Marketing: Creating Stakeholder Value*. Butterworth-Heinemann.

Gummesson, E. (2002). *Total Relationship Marketing*, 2nd edn. Butterworth-Heinemann.

McKenna, R. (1991). *Relationship Marketing*. Addison-Wesley.

Payne, A., Christopher, M., Clark, M. and Peck, H. (1995). *Relationship Marketing for Competitive Advantage: Winning and Keeping Customers*. Butterworth-Heinemann.

Payne, A. (1995). *Advances in Relationship Marketing*. Kogan Page.

Peck, H., Payne, A., Christopher, M. and Clark, M. (1999). *Relationship Marketing: Strategy and Implementation*. Butterworth-Heinemann.

Sheth, J.N. and Parvatiyar, A. (2000). *The Handbook of Relationship Marketing*. Sage.

Vavra, T.G. (1992). *Aftermarketing: How to Keep Customers for Life Through Relationship Marketing*. Business One Irwin.

3. General, including e-commerce

Hallberg, G. (1995). *All Consumers Are Not Created Equal*. John Wiley & Sons, Inc.

Kalakota, R. and Robinson, M. (1999). *e-Business – Roadmap for Success*. Addison-Wesley.

Seybold, P.B. and Marshak, R.T. (1998). *Customers.com: How to Create a Profitable Business Strategy for the Internet*. Century Business.

Tapscott, D., Ticoll, D. and Lowy, A. (2000). *Digital Capital: Harnessing the Power of Business Webs*. Harvard Business School Press.

(b) CRM process I: the strategy development process

I. Business strategy

Campbell, A. and Luchs, K.S. (1997). *Core Competency-Based Strategy*. International Thomson Business Press.

Donovan, J.J. (1997). *The Second Industrial Revolution: Business Strategy and Internet Technology*. Prentice Hall PTR.

Hamel, G. (2000). *Leading the Revolution*. Harvard Business School Press.

Hamel, G. and Prahalad, C.K. (1994). *Competing for the Future*. Harvard Business School Press.

Treacy, M. and Wiersema, F. (1995). *The Discipline of Market Leaders*. Addison-Wesley.

2. Customer strategy

Blattberg, R., Getz, G. and Thomas J. (2001). *Customer Equity: Building and Managing Relationships as Valuable Assets*. Harvard Business School Publishing Corporation.

Jenkinson, A. (1995). *Valuing your Customers: From Quality Information to Quality Relationships through Database Marketing.* McGraw-Hill.

McDonald, M., Christopher, M., Knox, S. and Payne, A. (2000). *Creating a Company For Customers.* Financial Times Prentice Hall.

Rosen, E. (2000). *The Anatomy of Buzz – Creating Word-of-Mouth Marketing.* HarperCollins.

Wayland, R.E. and Cole, P.M. (1997). *Customer Connections.* Harvard Business School Press.

Wierema, F. (1997). *Customer Intimacy.* HarperCollins Publishers.

Woolf, B.P. (1996). *Customer Specific Marketing.* Teal Books.

3. Market segmentation and mass customization

Linneman, R.E. and Stanton, J.L. (1998). *Making Niche Marketing Work: How to Grow Bigger by Acting Smaller.* McGraw-Hill.

McDonald, M. and Dunbar, I. (1998). *Market Segmentation,* 2nd edn. MacMillan.

Myers, J.H. (1996). *Segmentation and Positioning for Strategic Marketing Decisions.* American Marketing Association.

Pine, B.J. II (1993). *Mass Customisation; The New Frontier in Business Competition.* Harvard Business School Press.

(c) CRM process 2: the value creation process

1. The value customers and organizations receive

Blattberg, R.C., Getz, G. and Thomas, J.S. (2001). *Customer Equity: Building and Managing Relationships as Valuable Assets.* Harvard Business School Press.

Gale, B.T. (1994). *Managing Customer Value.* The Free Press.

Knox, S. and Maklan, S. (1998). *Competing on Value.* Financial Times Pitman Publishing.

Lanning, M.J. (1998). *Delivering Profitable Value.* Perseus Publishing.

Normann, R. and Ramirez, R. (1994). *Designing Interactive Strategy: From Value Chain to Value Constellation.* John Wiley & Sons.

Woodruff, R.B. and Gardiel, S.F. (1996). *Know Your Customer, New Approaches to Understanding Customer Value and Satisfaction.* Blackwell Publishers.

2. Customer lifetime value

Reichheld, F.F. (1996). *The Loyalty Effect.* Harvard Business School Press.
Reichheld, F. (2001). *Loyalty Rules! How Today's Leaders Build Lasting Relationships.* Harvard Business School Press.
Rust, R.T., Zeithaml, V.A. and Lemon, K.N. (2000). *Driving Customer Equity: How Customer Life-Time Value is Reshaping Corporate Strategy.* The Free Press.

(d) CRM process 3: the multi-channel integration process

1. Channel issues

Friedman, L.G. and Furey, T.R. (1999). *The Channel Advantage: Going to Market with Multiple Sales Channels to Reach More Customers, Sell More Products, Make More Profit.* Butterworth-Heinemann.
Siebel, T.M. and House, P. (1999). *Cyber Rules: Strategies for Excelling at E-Business.* Currency Doubleday.
Siebel, T.M. and Malone, M.S. (1996). *Virtual Selling: going beyond the automated sales force to achieve total sales quality.* The Free Press.
Stern, L.W., EL-Ansary, A.I. and Coughlan, A.T. (1996). *Marketing Channels,* 5th edn. Prentice Hall.
Webb, G. (2001). *The M-Bomb: Riding the Multi-Channel Whirlwind.* Capstone Publishing.
Wheeler, S. and Hirsh, E. (1999). *Channel Champions: How Leading Companies Build New Strategies to Serve Customers.* Josey-Bass.

2. Direct marketing and permission marketing

Bird, D. (1993). *Commonsense Direct Marketing.* Kogan Page.
Godin, S. (1999). *Permission Marketing: Turning Strangers into Friends, and Friends into Customers.* Simon & Schuster.

3. Key account management

McDonald, M., Rogers, B. and Woodburn, D. (2000). *Key Customers: How to Manage Them Profitably*. Butterworth-Heinemann.
Storbacka, K., Sivula, P. and Kaario, K. (1999). *Create Value with Strategic Accounts*. Kauppakaari Oyj.

4. Integrated marketing and brand communication

Duncan, T. and Moriarty, S. (1997). *Driving Brand Value: Marketing to Manage Profitable Stakeholder Relationships*. McGraw-Hill.
Schultz, D.E. and Kitchen, P.J. (2000). *Communicating Globally – An Integrated Marketing Approach*. Macmillan Press.
Temporal, P. and Trott, M. (2001). *Romancing the Customer: Maximizing Brand Value Through Powerful Relationship Management*. John Wiley & Sons.

5. Customer experience management

Hochschild, A. (1983). *The Managed Heart: Commercialization of Human Feeling*. University of California Press.
McKean, J. (2003). *Customers are People: The Human Touch*. John Wiley.
Pine, B.J. and Gilmore, J. (1999). *The Experience Economy: Work is Theatre and Every Business a Stage*. Harvard Business School Press.

(e) CRM process 4: the information management process

1. Information management

Boar, B.H. (1994). *The Art of Strategic Planning for Information Technology*. Wiley.
McKean, J. (1999). *Information Masters – Secrets of the Customer Race*. John Wiley.

2. Data warehousing

Agosta, L. (1999). *The Essential Guide to Data Warehousing*. Prentice Hall.
Devlin, B. (1997). *Data Warehouse from Architecture to Implementation*. Addison-Wesley.
Inmon, W.H., Welch J.D. and Glassey, K.L. (1997). *Managing the Data Warehouse*. John Wiley & Sons, Inc.
Kelly, S. (1997). *Data Warehousing the Route to Mass Customization*. John Wiley & Sons.

3. Data mining

Berry, M.J.A. and Linoff, G. (1997). *Data Mining Techniques, for Marketing, Sales, and Customer Support*. John Wiley & Sons, Inc.
Groth, R. (2000). *Data Mining: Building Competitive Advantage*. Prentice Hall.

(f) CRM process 5: the performance assessment process

I. Shareholder value

Cleland, A.S. and Bruno, A.V. (1996). *The Market Value Process*. Jossey-Bass Publishers.
Cornelius, I. and Davies, M. *Shareholder Value*. FT Financial Publishing.
Heskett, J.L., Sasser, W.E. Jr and Schlesinger, L.A. (1997). *The Service Profit Chain*. The Free Press.
Slywotzky, A. J. (1996). *Value Migration*. Harvard Business School Press.
Stewart, G.B. III (1991). *The Quest for Value*. HarperCollins Inc.
Wilson, C.A. (1996). *Profitable Customers: How to Identify, Develop and Retain Them*. Kogan Page.

2. The balanced scorecard

Kaplan, R.S. and Norton, D.P. (1996). *The Balanced Scorecard*. Harvard Business School.

Kaplan, R.S. and Norton, D.P. (2001). *The Strategy Focused Organization*. Harvard Business School Press.

3. Performance and satisfaction measurement

Oliver, R.L. (1997). *Satisfaction: A Behavioural Perspective on the Consumer*. McGraw-Hill.

Shaw, R. and Mazur, L. (1997). *Marketing Accountability: Improving Business Performance*. FT Management Report, Financial Times Retail and Consumer Publishing.

Shultz, D. and Walters, (1997). *Measuring Brand Communication ROI*. ANA Inc.

The support of BT in producing this list is gratefully acknowledged.

Adrian Payne is Professor of Services & Relationship Marketing and Director, Centre for Customer Relationship Management at Cranfield University. He would welcome any comments on or suggestions for this reading list. Contact details: Professor Adrian Payne, Cranfield School of Management, Cranfield University, Cranfield, Bedford, MK43 0AL, UK. Tel: +44 1234 751122, Fax: +44 1234 751806, email: a.payne@cranfield.ac.uk

Index